FIELDING'S
BAHAMAS

The Buzz About Fielding...

Fielding Worldwide

"The new Fielding guidebook style mirrors the style of the company's new publisher: irreverent, urbane, adventuresome and in search of the unique travel experience."

—San Diego Union Tribune

"Individualistic, entertaining, comprehensive."

—Consumers Digest

"Guidebooks straight from the hip."

—Cincinnati Enquirer

"Guidebooks with attitude."

—Dallas Morning News

"Full of author's tips and asides, the books seem more personal and more credible than many similarly encyclopedic tomes."

—Los Angeles Times

"At Fielding Worldwide, adventurous might well be the order of the day."

—Des Moines Register

"Biting travel guides give readers a fresh look."

—Houston Chronicle

"For over 30 years Fielding guides have been the standard of modern travel books."

—Observer Times

"These guidebooks have attitude."

—Tampa Tribune

"Guidebooks not afraid to show honesty."

*—Deseret News,
Salt Lake City*

Fielding's Las Vegas Agenda

"A concise but detailed look at the capital of glitter and gambling."

—Atlanta Journal Constitution

Fielding's Los Angeles Agenda

"...contains much more than the standard travel guide. The lists of theatres, sports arenas and attractions are worth the book's price by itself."

—Baton Rouge Advocate

Fielding's New York Agenda

"Loaded with advice... puts the whole of the Big Apple in hand."

—Bon Appetit

Fielding's Guide to Worldwide Cruises

"...Lots of tips and inside information on each ship ... valuable beginner's information on the cruise life and choosing a cruise. Very detailed."

—Los Angeles Times

"... insightful, always independent, frequently witty and occasionally irreverent personal reviews..."

—Cruise and Vacation Views

" ... Whereas the term 'expert' is thrown about with abandon when it comes to travel writing, these two are the real deal. Harry and Shirley are cruise *experts.*'"

—Salt Lake City Tribune

"You can trust them [Fielding] to tell the truth. It's fun—and very informative."

*—New Orleans
Times-Picayune*

" ... If you have space for only one cruise guidebook in your library, it should be this one."

—Cruise Travel Magazine

Cruise Insider

"One of the best, most compact, yet interesting books about cruising today is the fact-filled *Cruise Insider.*"

*—John Clayton's Travel With a
Difference*

Fielding's The World's Most Dangerous Places

"Rarely does a travel guide turn out to be as irresistible as a John Grisham novel. But *The World's Most Dangerous Places*, a 1000-page tome for the truly adventurous traveler, manages to do just that."

*—Arkansas
Democrat-Gazette*

"A travel guide that could be a real lifesaver. Practical tips for those seeking the road less traveled."

—Time Magazine

"The greatest derring do of this year's memoirs."

—*Publishers Weekly*

"Reads like a first-run adventure movie."

—*Travel Books Worldwide*

"One of the oddest and most fascinating travel books to appear in a long time."

—*New York Times*

"...publishing terra incognito...a primer on how to get in and out of potentially lethal places."

—*U.S. News and World Report*

"Tired of the same old beach vacation?...this book may be just the antidote."

—*USA Today*

"Guide to hot spots will keep travelers glued to their armchairs."

—*The Vancouver Sun*

Fielding's Borneo

"One of a kind...a guide that reads like an adventure story."

—*San Diego Union*

Fielding's Budget Europe

"This is a guide to great times, great buys and discovery in 18 countries."

-*Monroe News-Star*

"...meticulous detail...incisive commentary."

—*Travel Europe*

Fielding's Caribbean

"If you have trouble deciding which regional guidebook to reach for, you can't go wrong with *Fielding's Caribbean*."

—*Washington Times*

"Opinionated, clearly written and probably the only guide that any visitor to the Caribbean really needs."

—*New York Times*

Fielding's Europe

"Synonymous with the dissemination of travel information for five decades."

—*Traveller's Bookcase*

"The definitive Europe... shame on you if you don't read it before you leave."

—*Travel Europe*

Fielding's Far East

"This well-respected guide is thoroughly updated and checked out."

—*The Reader Review*

Fielding's France

"Winner of the annual 'Award of Excellence' [with Michelin and Dorling Kindersley]."

—*FrancePresse*

Fielding's Freewheelin' USA

"...an informative, thorough and entertaining 400-page guide to the sometimes maligned world of recreational vehicle travel."

—*Travel Weekly*

"...very comprehensive... lots more fun than most guides of this sort..."

—*Los Angeles Times*

Fielding's Italy

"A good investment...contains excellent tips on driving, touring, cities, etc."

—*Travel Savvy*

Fielding's Mexico

"Among the very best."

—*Library Journal*

Fielding's Spain and Portugal

"Our best sources of information were fellow tour-goers and *Fielding's Spain and Portugal*."

—*New York Times*

Vacation Places Rated

"...can best be described as a thinking person's guide if used to its fullest."

—*Chicago Tribune*

"Tells how 13,500 veteran vacationers rate destinations for satisfaction and how well a destination delivers on what is promised."

—*USA Today*

Fielding's Vietnam

"Fielding has the answer to every conceivable question."

—*Destination Vietnam*

"An important book about an important country."

—*NPR Business Radio*

Fielding Titles

Fielding's Alaska Cruises and the Inside Passage
Fielding's Asia's Top Dive Sites
Fielding's Amazon
Fielding's Australia
Fielding's Bahamas
Fielding's Baja
Fielding's Bermuda
Fielding's Borneo
Fielding's Budget Europe
Fielding's Caribbean
Fielding's Caribbean Cruises
Fielding's Disney World and Orlando
Fielding's Diving Indonesia
Fielding's Eastern Caribbean
Fielding's England
Fielding's Europe
Fielding's European Cruises
Fielding's Far East
Fielding's France
Fielding's Freewheelin' USA
Fielding's Kenya
Fielding's Hawaii
Fielding's Italy
Fielding's Las Vegas Agenda
Fielding's London Agenda
Fielding's Los Angeles
Fielding's Malaysia and Singapore
Fielding's Mexico
Fielding's New Orleans Agenda
Fielding's New York Agenda
Fielding's New Zealand
Fielding's Paradors, Pousadas and Charming Villages
          of Spain and Portugal
Fielding's Paris Agenda
Fielding's Portugal
Fielding's Rome Agenda
Fielding's San Diego Agenda
Fielding's Southeast Asia
Fielding's Southern Vietnam on Two Wheels
Fielding's Spain
Fielding's Surfing Indonesia
Fielding's Sydney Agenda
Fielding's Thailand, Cambodia, Laos & Myanmar
Fielding's Vacation Places Rated
Fielding's Vietnam
Fielding's Western Caribbean
Fielding's The World's Most Dangerous Places
Fielding's Worldwide Cruises

FIELDING'S
BAHAMAS

By
Wink Dulles
and
Marael Johnson

Fielding Worldwide, Inc.
308 South Catalina Avenue
Redondo Beach, California 90277 U.S.A.

Fielding's Bahamas

Published by Fielding Worldwide, Inc.

Text Copyright ©1997 Fielding Worldwide, Inc.

Maps, Icons & Illustrations Copyright ©1997 Fielding Worldwide, Inc.

Photo Copyrights ©1997 to Individual Photographers

Some maps ©MAGELLAN Geographix, Santa Barbara, California, Telephone (800) 929-4MAP, www.magellangeo.com

FIELDING WORLDWIDE INC.

PUBLISHER AND CEO	**Robert Young Pelton**
GENERAL MANAGER	**John Guillebeaux**
MARKETING DIRECTOR	**Paul T. Snapp**
OPERATIONS DIRECTOR	**George Posanke**
ELEC. PUBLISHING DIRECTOR	**Larry E. Hart**
PUBLIC RELATIONS DIRECTOR	**Beverly Riess**
ACCOUNT SERVICES MANAGER	**Shawn Potter**
PROJECT MANAGER	**Chris Snyder**

EDITORS

Amanda Knoles   **Linda Charlton**

Reed Parsell

PRODUCTION

Martin Mancha   **Alfredo Mercado**

Ramses Reynoso   **Craig South**

COVER DESIGNED BY	**Digital Artists, Inc.**
COVER PHOTOGRAPHERS—Front	**Bahamas Tourist Board**
Back	**Ron Watts/Westlight**
INSIDE PHOTOS	**Bahamas Tourist Board, Wink Dulles**
M. JOHNSON'S PHOTO	**Kim Reierson**

Inquiries should be addressed to: Fielding Worldwide, Inc., 308 South Catalina Ave., Redondo Beach, California 90277 U.S.A., Telephone (310) 372-4474, Facsimile (310) 376-8064, 8:30 a.m.–5:30 p.m. Pacific Standard Time.

Website: http://www.fieldingtravel.com

e-mail: fielding@fieldingtravel.com

ISBN 1-56952-105-0

Printed in the United States of America

Letter from the Publisher

In 1946, Temple Fielding began the first of what would be a remarkable new series of well-written, highly personalized guidebooks for independent travelers. Temple's opinionated, witty and oft-imitated books have now guided travelers for almost a half-century. More important to some was Fielding's humorous and direct method of steering travelers away from the dull and the insipid. Today, Fielding Travel Guides are still written by experienced travelers for experienced travelers. Our authors carry on Fielding's reputation for creating travel experiences that deliver insight with a sense of discovery and style.

Wink Dulles and Marael Johnson personify the Fielding spirit with their passion for life and need to explore the world. Their coverage of the Bahamas will surprise you. In their candid and irreverent style, the authors capture the unique personality of the islands and the people of the Bahamas.

The concept of independent travel has never been bigger. Our policy of *brutal honesty* and a highly personal point of view has never changed; it just seems the travel world has caught up with us.

RYP

Robert Young Pelton
Publisher and CEO
Fielding Worldwide, Inc.

ACKNOWLEDGEMENTS

From Wink Dulles: Although we pull no punches in our analysis and ratings of the Bahamas' attractions, activities, dining and accommodations, no comprehensive guide could have been completed without the guidance and unbridled support of the Bahamas Ministry of Tourism. I would particularly like to thank Sr. Public Relations Executive Charity Armbrister. Also at the ministry, Danielle Knowles was especially valuable in initiating the authors to the budget accommodation scene in the Bahamas. Also warm thanks to all those who provided their unique insights to the islands. These include Randy Conliffe in Nassau, Sydney Cox and Peter Barratt in Freeport, "Jackie" Bootle of Marsh Harbour, Hideaways owner Peggy Thompson of Elbow Cay in the Abacos, Hilton Johnson and Abraham Johnson on Eleuthera, dive expert Jeff Fox on Harbour Island, Sandra Eneas of Atlantis Paradise Island and the tireless Abaco Tourism team of Wynsome and Kendy in Marsh Harbour. Also a special thanks to Martin Havill of Bluff House Club & Marina on Green Turtle Cay in the Abacos and particularly to Christopher J. Allison, the managing director of the Underwater Explorers Society (UN-EXSO) and the Dolphin Experience in Lucaya on Grand Bahama. On Andros my warm appreciation goes to Brian and Jennifer Hew for giving me the chance to explore their own little slice of paradise. Good luck with your villas.

In Redondo Beach, Calif., my warmest thanks to Fielding Worldwide Publisher Robert Young Pelton, who's had the guts to bring Fielding past the cutting edge of travel guides. Also to Fielding Director of Publishing John Guillebeaux, Editor Amanda Knoles, Public Relations Director Beverly Riess, Electronic Publishing Director Larry Hart, and Project Manager Chris Snyder.

ABOUT THE AUTHORS

Wink Dulles

Wink Dulles, 39, is Fielding's Southeast Asia correspondent and the author of *Fielding's Vietnam, Southern Vietnam On 2 Wheels* and *Fielding's Thailand, Cambodia, Laos & Myanmar*, as well as co-author of *Fielding's Southeast Asia, The Far East* and *The World's Most Dangerous Places*. He was formerly senior editor and Bangkok bureau chief for *Escape* magazine and Asia Editor for *UFM* magazine.

Dulles' articles on destinations around the globe have appeared in *National Geographic Traveler, Newsday,* a number of major daily newspapers and other national publications. His book, *Fielding's Vietnam,* was banned by the Vietnamese government for its candor.

Dulles brings the same irreverence and opinionated advice to *Fielding's Bahamas.* No stranger to the islands, the author first learned to scuba dive on Eleuthera in 1979 and has made numerous visits to the Bahamas since, to the glitzy resorts of Paradise Island and Freeport/Lucaya as well as the backwater cafes, remote surfing beaches and blue holes, inaccessible coves and lost-in-time mailboat ports of the Family Islands.

Marael Johnson

Marael Johnson is an award-winning freelance writer and poet who works and travels throughout the world. She's written guides to Australia, Louisiana and California for major travel publishers, and has contributed to dozens of other guidebooks.

Before and after taking up travel writing, the author designed and stitched clothing for rock stars, sold love beads outside American Express offices in Europe, worked as a barmaid in Spain, an artist's model everywhere and a set dresser. She has lived in paisley-painted communes in Santa Cruz, elegant Victorians in San Francisco, squats in London, handmade tents in Spain, chateaux in France, monasteries along the Pacific Ocean and currently resides in San Diego County. She has completely disproven her mother's theory that "you can't run away," as well as Thomas Wolfe's, who swore "you can never go home again." She does both—very successfully.

The author is an active member of the Society of American Travel Writers.

Fielding Rating Icons

The Fielding Rating Icons are highly personal and awarded to help the besieged traveler choose from among the dizzying array of activities, attractions, hotels, restaurants and sights. The awarding of an icon denotes unusual or exceptional qualities in the relevant category.

RATINGS: Fielding Award, Author Selection, Quality, Money Saver, Expensive, Inexpensive, Warning, Danger, Spacious, Cramped, Mild Disapproval

WHERE TO STAY: Simple, Luxurious, Cottage, Homey, Scenic, Business, Honeymoon, Chateau

CULTURAL: Museum/Art, Interesting Architecture, History, Book Reference, Artistically Important, Musically Interesting, Theatre, Crafts

INTERESTS: Singles, Romantic, Spectacular Cuisine, Wine Tasting, Shopping, Nightlife, Cafe Stops, Pro Sports

SIGHTS: Picturesque, Great Scenery, Market, Beaches/Resorts, Cultural, Fortress, Castles, Church

TRAVEL TIPS: Arrival/Departure, By Air, By Water, By Train, By Car, Bus/Local Transit, Calendar, Itinerary, Kids, Compass

ACTIVITIES: Relaxing, Workout, General Sports, Water Sports, Sailing, Swimming, Hiking, Walking, Cycling, Horseback Riding, Golf, Tennis, Scuba Diving, Snorkeling/Diving, Deep-sea Fishing, Freshwater Fishing

FOREWORD

Clapboard Houses on Bay Street, Harbour Island

My first taste of the Bahamas was in 1979, and it wasn't of the casinos and the bright lights of Nassau or Freeport. Instead, I journeyed to the Family Islands with my own family, who had the grand intention of discovering the Bahamas the Bahamians would call home, as well as getting a little R&R. But it wasn't to be. There were few places to stay other than resorts. In retrospect, after nearly 20 years and even more countries, I can safely say that I find no difference between a Club Med on Phuket in Thailand and one on Paradise Island in the Bahamas. But I'll get to that point in a moment.

My first stay in the Bahamas was at the Cape Eleuthera Yacht Club in southern Eleuthera. At the time, it was a beautiful resort for the Family Islands. Spacious, luxurious duplexes ringed an emerald, vodka-clear sea. There was a swimming pool, tennis courts, a state-of-the-art marina, a nine-hole golf course and even an airstrip. My brothers and I climbed coconut trees on the beach each afternoon as the sun began to set—not for the view but for the fodder of our evening rum libations.

I learned to scuba dive here, from a big, jovial Bahamian who went by the handle of Captain Mac. I was so enraptured with the dazzling stage shows and kaleidoscopes of the depths that I became a certified diver shortly after my arrival back in the States. Then there were the Bahamians themselves. Laid-back, disconnected with newspapers, the Cold War and Pizza Hut. My brother and I befriended a taxi driver who secretly drove us away from the resort to explore the island while the folks were playing golf. After all, the resort was "self-contained," and there was really no reason to leave the "property," so we were told. Of course, being teenagers, that explanation had become the biggest reason to indeed leave the "property."

This was my first trip out of the country, and it essentially inspired my career in travel writing, which has since taken me to some of the most remote reaches of the globe. In a fashion, that resort on the tip of Eleuthera was the root of my wanderlust. So when I returned 17 years later, I had every intention of returning to the resort at Cape Eleuthera.

"But there is nothing to see," cab driver Abraham Johnson told me. "It is gone." He was right. The Arab owners had pumped $34 million into the place and then had simply walked away from their investment. Weeds now sprout from the airstrip; it looks more like an old parking lot. The golf course has folded back up into the uterus of Mother Nature, the par going from 36 to 3600. The hollowed duplexes have become shelters for squatters. So much for "self-contained." It finally became a pimple the government decided to pop. It began selling off the duplexes for $200 apiece. But there was a catch—the land didn't come with them. So locals brought in pickup trucks and started disassembling the units brick by brick. Others simply made off with what they could cart away—furniture and floor tiles and the like.

Cape Eleuthera isn't alone. A slew of resorts in the south of the island have shut down in recent years: the Cotton Bay Club and a number in the Rock Sound and Governor's Harbour areas. Even the super-exclusive Windermere resort on Windermere Island shut its doors. The locals in Rock Sound these days cry in their Kaliks in nearly deserted seaside restaurants and lament odes to tourists long gone.

For most, the lure of the Bahamas is the resorts. Few visitors come here with the intention of exploring the islands and getting to know their people. Instead, the majority of the 3.5 million people who visit here each year never set foot off their hotel property, much less the island it's located on. And an even larger number visit the islands by cruise ship, which affords little opportunity to do anything truly Bahamian. And that brings me back to Phuket.

The Bahamas shouldn't be visited simply for the resorts, nor should the islands be entirely dependent on them. The Bahamas encompass 100,000 square miles of principally pristine land and underwater environments. The Bahamas is touted as the ultimate getaway. But it shouldn't be only something that you're trying to get away from that is the draw of these islands. Rather, the Bahamas also make for the perfect "get-to."

Beneath the neon surface of slot machines and umbrella drinks are a chain of islands just waiting to be explored and a culture rich in tradition, whose roots are marked in the most significant place and time in the history of the New World. These islands were the staging point for the "discovery" of America. They were the home of pirates such as Blackbeard and the sanctuary for explorers such as Columbus and Ponce de Leon. Here is where some of the first communities in the world were established by ex-slaves. The Bahamas helped make it possible for Americans to enjoy evening cocktails during the Prohibition.

So take a chance and do a little exploring of your own, even if you're staying at a resort—the delights of the Bahamas are not at all "self-contained." And you never know where a little wandering might take you. Isn't that travel?

And for the rest of you folks—who have no interest in Arawak Indians, Loyalist plantations or the Eleutherian Adventurers, nor any intention to travel farther than the swim-up bar—I have only this to say: party on! You've chosen a pretty good place to do it.

Wink Dulles

TABLE OF CONTENTS

LIST OF MAPS

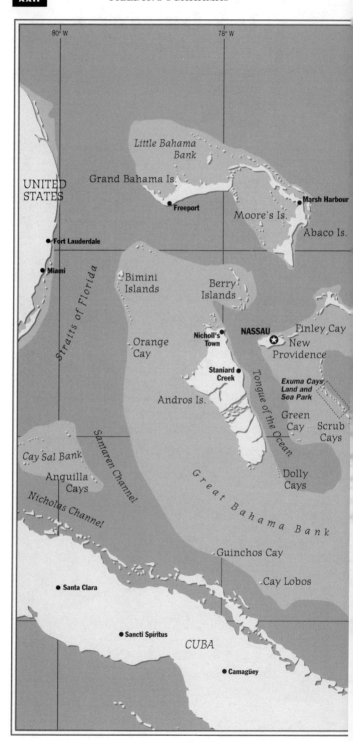

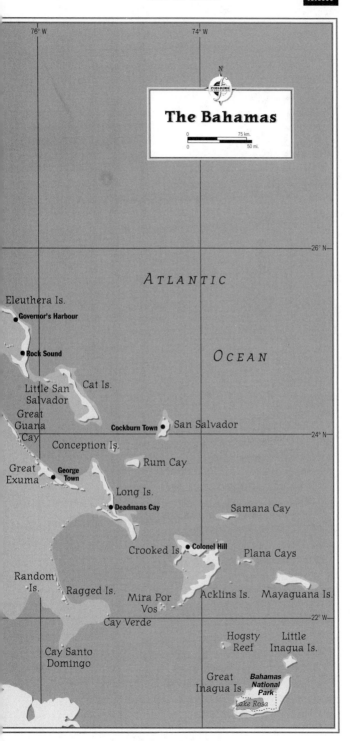

HEADED TO THE BAHAMAS

Jet skier skims the waters of The Bahamas

The Beacon

From the 17th century through the 19th century, the Bahamian economy was based on wrecking. When the Spanish arrived in The Bahamas in the late 15th century, they found little purpose for this chain of some 700 islands and 2050 islets—or cays (pronounced "keys")—starting in the Atlantic 75 miles off the coast of Palm Beach, Florida, and extending 760 miles southeast to Great Inagua, a mere 60 miles off the coast of Cuba. There wasn't any gold and nothing could be grown in the infertile limestone-based soil. Christopher Columbus and his successors found these subtropical islands inhabited by Lucayan Indians from South America. The Spanish promptly enslaved and exterminated many in the gold mines of Hispaniola (Haiti).

Subsequent visitors and inhabitants, including British "Puritans" and pirates the likes of Edward "Blackbeard" Teach and Anne Bonny, resorted to wrecking. Because the waters of The

Bahamas remained largely uncharted through the 19th century, they made fertile grounds for shipwrecks. And thousands of them between the 16th and 19th centuries kept most Bahamians alive, as they salvaged whatever could be pilfered from the foundered ships. This became such a lucrative profession that many wreckers simply weren't content to sit back and wait for the sounds of wooden hulls splintering against rocks and coral. Instead, these folks mounted false beacons to lure quite seaworthy ships into disaster on the reefs. And this was done quite intentionally, even with the blessing of their British colonial masters.

The Bahamas has always persevered off the misfortune of others, and it wouldn't be incorrect to say that the beacons of the 20th century are the casinos on Grand Bahama and New Providence, which bring millions into the Bahamas each year. The fantastic megaresorts of Cable Beach, Nassau, Paradise Island and Freeport/Lucaya, account for a good chunk of the other whopping sum The Bahamas receives from tourism each year.

To be fair, The Bahamas is not at all about false beacons. It is the number-one international mecca for scuba divers and sport fishermen. Its beaches, found in a 100,000 square mile tropical wonderland, are among the best anywhere on the globe. But, today, The Bahamas still relies on the misfortune of its visitors to make a buck—if that misfortune is defined by visitors spending a lot of money. The only difference between today and the days of the wreckers is that Bahamians do their best in these times to make you feel good about it. Even ecstatic. And, man, is this place expensive. Backpackers avoid this place like a job. But, boy, does the Bahamas succeed in sending a lot of happy campers home.

Build It and They Will Come

In 1956, American entrepreneur Wallace Groves had a vision of turning a huge landscape of pine trees and more pine trees into a huge international resort and industrial free zone/duty-free port. The result was Freeport and the beginning of the tourism boom in The Bahamas.

Today, visitors from all over the world flock to The Bahamas for its watersports, gambling and shopping—not to mention simply finding a deserted stretch of sand to hang out on for a week. Only two of the islands—New Providence and Grand Bahama—are fully developed. Here can be found the massive casinos and resorts. Every conceivable amenity can be found on these islands. There are lavish nightclubs and stage shows, yachts for rent and deepwater harbors that can handle more than a dozen cruise ships at once. And it's not unusual to see that many at one time during the high season between January and May. There are even ATMs that dispense U.S. currency.

Nassau's Bay Street is lined with swanky shops and designer boutiques. The cops, elegantly dressed in starched-and-pressed uniforms and pith helmets, all look like Rudyard Kipling at a piano recital. They patrol New Providence's tourist haunts twirling their nightsticks, looking a little silly and a little serious at the same time.

Reflecting the rapid urbanization of New Providence, teenagers swilling Kalik beer wrapped in brown paper bags converge on tourists in the alleys off of Bay Street looking to sell dope. They're harmless enough, but certainly not in the brochures at your cousin's travel agency in Poughkeepsie. And, yeah, folks on New Providence and Grand Bahama even shoot at each other occasionally. Come to these islands and you may think you're getting away from it all, but it's more like Pittsburgh with palm trees than anyone's likely to lead you to believe—or admit.

But most tourists on New Providence and Grand Bahama are whisked away to their self-contained resorts—like cruise ships, miniature cities where every need is fulfilled by pressing a button on the TV remote. Some of the resort guests and most of the cruise-ship passengers descend upon downtown Nassau in the daytime, which, with all the camcorders, begins to look like a convention of film students. Few venture "over the hill" of charming Nassau to Fox Hill, Over The Hill and other nearby towns that are home to New Providence's service and tourism industry employees. Here can be found the working-class shopping malls, old peeling churches, small restaurants designated by their hand-painted signs and mile-long traffic jams on the two-lane roads. Bleary-eyed Rastafarians lounge on the porches of dilapidated clapboard houses, while in downtown Nassau, old-guard white Bahamian business magnates muse about the decline of Bahamian architecture and the evils of Hollywood.

Driving to the airport on Thompson Boulevard from downtown, you pass on the left the Tourism College, a sprawling campus that's a testament to just how important tourism is to the livelihood of all Bahamians.

If Nassau has retained any of its former colonial charm, Freeport never achieved it in the first place. Freeport/Lucaya is the placebo of The Bahamas. Not the real thing. You may think you're in The Bahamas, but you're actually still in Florida.

Grand Bahama was developed in the 1950s and '60s and resembles Orlando and Daytona Beach more than any place Bahamian. The roads are new and wide—even the white lines aren't smudged. No one thinks of coming here for the island's historical attractions—there aren't any. You see and do here what you'd see and do on a three-hour skiff ride away: jet ski and swill brewskis against a backdrop of high-rises, pines and palmettos. Not that there's anything wrong with that, you see. The island's inhabitants are mostly transplants from the Family Islands drawn here by a better living catering to tourists. Sure they have their junkanoos and calypso here, but they're noticeably contrived, as is Lucaya's International Bazaar. Van Halen, Steely Dan and 7-Elevens would seem more indigenous.

But Grand Bahama has its casinos—at last check, Michael Eisner wasn't permitting any in Orlando. And the island is a mecca for watersports enthusiasts. Parasails fill the skies and banana boats and jetskis rip through the currents. At Kaptain Kenny's on the beach, muscular black beach boys in wetsuits dangling from the waist assist bikini-clad coeds in the art of jetskiing, and perhaps other pleasures. Lobster-red honeymooners and beer-bellied plumbers from Islip find sanctuary from the sun in the open-air bar and guzzle Kaliks while gyrating to the sounds of a live reggae band (which, appropriately, dishes out more American pop than reggae).

A stroll through the Lucaya marketplace to have your hair braided makes for a nice diversion if your partner is out on a shark or dolphin dive with the Underwater Explorer's Society, undoubtedly the best reason to come to Grand Bahama if you're a certified diver (even if you're not). Or you can hit the links at one of Grand Bahamas' four golf courses.

At night, you can have bangers and mash at The Pub, then catch a show at the Princess or the Lucayan, and polish the evening off with a nightcap at Kaptain Kenny's near the International Bazaar—or simply gamble the night away. More American than Bahamian, but a vacation or weekend escape nonetheless.

Don't Build It and They'll Still Come

Visitors searching for more solitude head for the Family Islands (formerly called the Out Islands), which are actually every island in the Bahamian chain with the exception of New Providence. Here, visitors find a far simpler way of life. There are few telephones and other reminders of the pressures back home. There are no fancy casinos, nightclubs and designer shops.

Most who come to the Out Islands do so for the isolation, and to find a modest, secluded place to relax. Of course, the Family Islands (there are perhaps 12 that are geared to host tourists) are also the destination of serious scuba divers and fishing enthusiasts. Here, one can see the old Bahamian clapboard cottages, pink sand beaches and life as it was a couple of centuries ago.

You can meet the weekly mailboat as it arrives at Andros Town from Nassau, when the sleepy little community perks up and the conversation is like the society page, as townsfolk greet their returning relatives and open their mail, turning the most innocuous news into a robust headline story for all who will listen—which is most.

You can escape to the romantic and private enclaves of the cays off the eastern shores of Great Abaco—with names such as Green Turtle Cay, Elbow Cay and Man-O-War Cay—whose inhabitants are the direct descendants of the islands' original Loyalist settlers, and where everyone seems to have the same last name.

You can roam the famous haunts of Ernest Hemingway on Bimini, where the bars he frequented will ensure you won't forget he drank there—even if *you* can't remember drinking there.

You can totally get lost in the Exumas, on Cat Island, Long Island and Mayaguana—and not be heard from again if it's your wish. The Berry Islands will also suit that purpose, but you'll be tempted to go out and catch some fish.

Spanish Wells is a good place to see how white Bahamians would live if the Abacos and Eleuthera had their way and remained colonies of England. And, speaking of race, there's nothing like the sight of 50,000 pink flamingos ascending from the ponds of Great Inagua, looking like a squadron of pistachio ice cream cones.

The Bahamas has something for everyone. For some, it's right out their back door. For others, it's a world away.

PEOPLE AND PLACES OF THE BAHAMAS

Bahamian policewoman

Who Are the Bahamians?

The first Bahamians were the original Lucayan Indians (or Arawaks), Amerindians who are believed to have migrated—or fled—north to The Bahamas from northeastern South America probably during the 10th century to put more distance between themselves and the marauding and cannibalistic Caribe tribes.

The Lucayans were a peaceful people who numbered about 40,000 at their peak and lived in relative harmony in The Bahamas for about 500 years, subsisting on the bounty of the sea as well as some primitive farming. The arrival of the Spanish in The Bahamas in the late 15th century spelled disaster for the Lucayans, who soon were enslaved by the conquistadors and put to work mining gold in Hispaniola, or present-day Haiti and the Dominican Republic. In a mere 25 years, the entire population of the Arawaks had been ravaged by disease, malnutrition and overwork. The Spanish had completed their unwitting genocide of the Lucayan people, and in The Bahamas it is not believed that a single descendent of the native Arawaks exists today—that's how thorough the extermination was.

The Spanish never settled The Bahamas, bypassing them entirely for the mineral riches of the Caribbean and Central and South America—so anyone of Spanish descent you meet in The Bahamas is a relatively recent arrival.

The first foreign settlers in The Bahamas were Caucasian religious pilgrims and Puritans fleeing the unrest of 17th-century Great Britain. The Eleutherian Adventurers settled Eleuthera in the 1640s, and that marked the first attempt to settle these uninhabited islands. Other pilgrims, shortly afterward, arrived on New Providence and built settlements on that island.

The first blacks to arrive in The Bahamas came as slaves with their masters during the last quarter of the 18th century. These "masters" were mainly white rich folks from America loyal to the British crown who were fleeing the newly independent United States of America and came to The Bahamas to start huge—ultimately unsuccessful—cotton plantations. The white descendants of the Loyalists can primarily be found in the Abacos, while descendants of the original Eleutherian Adventurers are found mainly on Eleuthera in Spanish Wells and Harbour Island.

By the time of the American Civil War in the mid-19th century, The Bahamas had become principally black, and by the mid-20th century, blacks constituted 80 percent of the population, a figure that stands today among the Bahamas' 300,000 people.

Long before, most had taken on the surnames of their masters, and on many islands you'll find that the majority of residents have the same last name. For instance, in the Exumas, it seems as if everyone has the last name of Rolle. Remarkably, folks seem to know who can get married to whom, and who can't.

Even though they composed a vast majority of Bahamians by the 20th century, blacks were not entitled to legally patronize restaurants, hotels and movie theaters until 1956. And the only hint of racial unrest before then occurred during World War II, when local New Providence blacks who had been hired at miserably low wages to work on an American and British air base in the west of the island decided to riot on Bay Street. It was at this time that antagonism toward the white establishment (the "Bay Street Boys") began to show. It was later personified more visibly by Prime Minister-to-be Lynden O. Pindling.

Regardless of the islands' kinetic racial schisms, the transition from white to black rule was amazingly peaceful, unlike similar transitions in Haiti and Jamaica. One reason was the blacks' loyalty to the British crown. The British (and British Americans) had given the islanders their language, their culture, their education and their legal system. Short of an all-out denouncement of the African heritage, blacks in The Bahamas did everything they could to become more British. Doing British things and behaving in a British way was a sign of social status. And it remained that way up until the 1950s and 1960s, when Bahamian blacks in general began to take more pride in their African ancestry.

Today, there is little racial tension in The Bahamas. Bahamians of all races simply want to be seen as Bahamian rather than white, black or mulatto. Blacks and whites coexist peacefully throughout the islands.

Christianity and Obeah

Like their former masters and the religious pilgrims who arrived in The Bahamas during the Puritan revolt of the mid-1600s, black Bahamians are deeply religious—meaning deeply Christian. On each of the islands, the church is the hub of most social events. Even the sparsest of backwater settlements has at least one church—and many two or three. Itinerant preachers make the rounds from island to island visiting the local churches.

But the most intriguing element of Bahamian religion is Obeah. Obeah is the Bahamian version of the Caribbean's voodoo. It is a mix of Haitian voodoo, Christianity, European superstitions, the Shango of Trinidad, the Santeria of both Brazil and Cuba, and the African Yoruban religion. It is a curious and unique blend of Christian and African beliefs, with more than a garnishing of black magic, which is actually playing a more significant role today in Bahamian spirituality than in the past, perhaps as black Bahamians focus more on their African heritage than European.

Obeah functions with "fixes" and "curses" and holds that *sperrids*, or spirits—ghosts of the dead—reside in the tips of silk cotton trees, which are found all through the islands. (Many African tribes worship cotton trees, believing they are occupied by spirits of the dead.) These *sperrids*, like their African counterparts, leave the trees to cruise around and create bad fortune for all who they encounter in their travels. Only a witch doctor, or Obeah master, can harness the power of the dead. Obeah practitioners regularly communicate with the sperrids through trances.

Obeah devotees can cast spells on one another (called "fixes"). They, along with conventional medical doctors, can also remove these fixes, as well as those cast by others. But what cannot be undone—or "cleared"—by others is a curse laid by an Obeah master. Only the person who performed the curse can clear it. In other words, if you've been cursed by an Obeah master and that person dies without having cleared it, you're up the creek. There are two forms of magic: black and white. White magic is considered less evil but more potent, and is even practiced to some extent by Christian priests in The Bahamas. Obeah is most prevalent in the Exumas, Andros and Cat Island.

Junkanoo

The Junkanoo festival, with its zenith the day after Christmas, is easily The Bahamas' most lavish and unabashed celebration. Although distinctly Bahamian in its roots, the celebration resembles Rio's Carnival and New Orleans' Mardi Gras, particularly with its ornate and outrageous costumes and street parades.

The Bahamian Junkanoo traces its beginnings to the colonial slave period, when there were only predefined days each year where the plantation owners permitted their slaves to drink alcohol and, essentially, have a good time. In those days, slaves created ornamented costumes from crepe paper stretched over wire, something like papier-mâché. Today, often costumes in the parades are sponsored by stores or companies, and can cost thousands of dollars. The whole thing has turned into the Bahamian version of the Rose Bowl parade, and retains little of the mystery and intrigue of its past, when slaves and others used the bulky, identity-concealing costumes as disguises for knifing enemies and rivals for romance in the crowd. Yet today's Junkanoo is still representative of the Bahamian life-goes-on attitude.

Goombay dancers participate in numerous festivals.

The Arts

Music

Jamaica has its reggae and Cuba its salsa and mamba; The Bahamas are known for distinctive **Goombay** and **Junkanoo** music.

Goombay (the Bantu word for "rhythm") music is the celebratory music of The Bahamas that ultimately spread to places such as Bermuda and the southern United States and evolved into Junkanoo music before the middle of this century. Goombay is characterized by outlandish and uninhibited dancing in wild costumes to the backdrop of the beating of goatskin drums, a practice that was considered barbaric by the colonial Britons but today encouraged—and even participated in—by the highest rungs of Bahamian society.

Goombay has its roots in the Egungun faction of West Africa's Yoruba tribe, although there are elements of Native American music and motifs of pure New World influence. The music seeks to capture the elements of the jungle and is accompanied by dancers in outrageous costumes of bright colors designed to resemble the colorful birds of the jungle. Both the musicians and the dancers are almost uniformly male, and routines, styles and songs are passed down through the generations. The music typically features a rolling, sustained rhythm with a simple melody in major key performed by a guitar, piano or wind instrument (the saxophone is the most popular). Included in the rhythm section might be congas, maracas, bongos, cow bells, whistles and rhythm sticks. Completely unlike the socially or politically tainted lyrics of reggae, the words to Goombay music often evoke images of simpler times, of boy-courting-girl, or a young boy's walk to the market, but with playful sexual undertones.

Junkanoo music is simply Goombay but on a more raucous scale.

Bahamian architecture

Architecture

The Bahamas are famous for their oft-mimicked, pastel-colored, clapboard-sided houses. The best examples in the islands can be found on Eleuthera at Spanish Wells and Harbour Island, and on Green Turtle Cay in the Abacos.

Looking much like their cousins in Cape Cod, Massachusetts, these houses didn't arrive in The Bahamas until the Loyalists appeared in the late 18th and early 19th centuries. The smaller Bahamian cottages are mounted on stilts, while the larger houses have foundations of coral or stone. For the best air flow possible, these houses were designed with large windows, shutters and tall ceilings.

Bahamian Cuisine

Although most visitors to the islands' posh resorts wouldn't know it, The Bahamas offers its own distinctive cuisine, and as you might guess, it's based on that which is caught from the sea. As well, most don't realize (due to the sandy, limestone nature of Bahamian soil) that The Bahamas grows much of its own produce, such as sweet potatoes, cucumbers, okra, cassava, corn and peppers.

But what islanders don't raise is cattle. Consequently, most meat—including beef and pork—is shipped into the islands frozen, leading to exorbitant prices on most meat dishes.

Seafood

Conch (pronounced "konk") is the mainstay of the Bahamian diet. This large mollusk is found in abundance throughout the islands and is prepared in numerous interesting ways. Both raw and cooked, conch meat is hard and rubbery, and therefore must be pounded—and often marinated—by the chef before cooking and serving. There are all kinds of ways to eat this creature. It can be steamed or curried, or creamed and eaten on toast. It can be eaten in soups or in salads. Conch chowder and conch fritters are the two most consumed variations of this giant snail, which is similar in both texture and taste with abalone.

Conch chowder is the popular soup made by adding conch with different ingredients, such as tomatoes, bacon, sweet peppers, potatoes, carrots, onions, thyme and bay leaf. There are as many variations of conch chowder as there are chefs.

Conch fritters are deep-fried batter balls made of conch, tomato paste, onions and sweet peppers.

Another popular variation of conch is what's called cracked conch. The conch meat is hammered and then dipped into a batter or breaded and sautéed.

If you want a complete conch meal, have conch salad for your next course. The conch is marinated in Old Sour sauce and then diced along with peppers and onions.

Grouper is the most popular fish consumed in The Bahamas. Like conch, it can be served in a variety of ways, most often steamed and served with rice under a bed of spicy Creole sauce. Also like conch, it is almost flavorless and therefore has to be garnished or sauced rather radically to get any taste out of it. Grouper can also be battered and sautéed, or used in a tasty soup that also includes lime juice, thyme, cooking sherry, celery, tomatoes and onions. One note of warning if you've caught or speared your own fish, however. I've known a few people who have caught a nasty intestinal disorder by eating some of the larger grouper caught off the Andros barrier reef.

Bonefishermen tend to eat most of their catch if it's less than trophy-sized. **Bonefish** is easy to prepare. It is sliced in half and then baked, after being seasoned with Old Sour sauce, pepper sauce and salt.

Bahamian **rock lobsters**, if prepared right, are excellent. Only the tail is eaten, and it can be served in any way you would use Maine lobster.

Baked crab is another Bahamian specialty. The meat is first taken from the shell and mixed with eggs, bread crumbs and seasonings before being placed back in the shell and baked.

Turtle is served with much less frequency than it used to be, as it's considered an endangered species, and Bahamians are becoming more hip to the environment. You will see, however, turtle soups and other turtle dishes in the backwaters of the Family Islands.

Meats and Vegetables

Beef and **pork** are imported from the United States, but chicken is raised locally in The Bahamas (although the American variety is more tender). The most popular chicken dish is called *souce* and made with sweet peppers, onions, lime juice, chicken and other ingredients and simmered in a big pot.

Meats are typically prepared in a continental fashion, and all your favorite stand-bys are readily available in The Bahamas. Given their druthers, Bahamian chefs will dress up the dishes with Bahamian touches, such as with coconut sauces, curries and fresh pineapple.

Johnnycake

Johnnycake is much like corn bread, the Bahamian version of—along with peas 'n rice—the food for the masses. This is a bread cooked in a pan made from sugar, flour, milk, butter, salt and baking powder.

Peas 'n Rice

This is another staple of the poor, and a simple combination of peas (black-eyed or pigeon), rice, salt pork and whatever else the cook wants to throw in, which is usually tomato, celery, carrots and onions.

Drinks

Water and Soft Drinks

Virtually throughout The Bahamas the water is potable, but, in all but the high-ticket resorts, usually tastes awful. This is because of the high salt content. Some of the better hotels double filter tap water, and this makes it quite acceptable. Bottled water is available at all the resorts and marinas as well as in most settlements. Popular American-bottled (or canned) soft drinks are found throughout the islands. You might want to try Pepsi's Junkanoo, canned in The Bahamas; it tastes like carbonated Hawaiian Punch.

Beer and Liquor

Kalik is the local Bahamian brew. It's quite smooth and light and tastes much like Jamaica's Red Stripe beer. Kalik Gold is labeled "Extra Strength" and, boy, is it. The alcohol content in this robust brew is a whopping eight percent. Imported beers are expensive.

Popular alcoholic beverages include rum and more **rum**. Some of the concoctions employing it are quite famous. The **Goombay Smash** is coconut rum and Triple Sec mixed with lemon juice, pineapple juice and perhaps a dash of grenadine. The **Bahama Mama** is concocted by mixing rum with orange juice, bitters, grenadine, creme de cassias and nutmeg. Another popular drink in the islands is the **Yellow Bird**, made with rum, creme de banana liqueur, orange juice, pineapple juice, Galliano and apricot brandy. The **planter's punch** is made in a variety of ways, usually with rum, sugar, lime juice and bitters.

Birds-Eye View

Fast Facts

The Bahamas are composed of some 700 islands and more than 2050 cays. Remarkably, only about 15 of them are developed to a level to handle tourism. Of the country's 300,000 people, 200,000 live on the islands of New Providence and Grand Bahama alone. In fact, 80 percent of the population is designated as living in an urban area. Nearly a third of all those employed work for the government. An equal number work in the tourist and service sector. Only 10 percent of the workers are businesspeople, with an equal number in the construction industry. Less than five percent of Bahamian workers are engaged in agriculture, and that's primarily growing fruit. Reflecting the times is the interesting statistic that 40 percent of the workforce is employed directly or indirectly in the tourist industry. Tourism accounts for a 50 percent of the country's income. On any given day there are 50 percent more tourists in The Bahamas than there are Bahamians! The Bahamas are the recipient of fully 15 percent of all the money spent by tourists in the Caribbean.

Blacks comprise more than 80 percent of the population, with Caucasians, Syrians and Chinese making up the remainder (the latter two constitute less than one percent of the population). The per capita income is hovering around $16,500. The literacy rate is a high 95 percent of the population. Life expectancy for women is 76 years and 70 years for men. More than half the population is Protestant (most of these being Baptist). The other half is equally split between Roman Catholics and Anglicans.

The Bahamas' islands and cays begin 70 miles off the Palm beaches in Florida and extend some 750 miles southward. The tropic of Cancer cuts through the archipelago at Long Island in the southern Bahamas, which technically means that some of the islands are subtropical and others tropical. But in reality, all of the islands enjoy a year-round balmy climate due to the warming factors of the Gulf Stream. Typical average temperatures in the chain only vary by about 10°F from summer to winter. Usual winter highs are about 78°F, with nighttime lows at about 70°F. In the summer, it heats up to the mid to upper 80s and drops to the mid 70s at night.

Queen's Staircase, Nassau

The Islands in a Nutshell

New Providence

Of the 3.5 million visitors The Bahamas receives each year, 2 million of them make a stop—for most, their only stop in the islands—on New Providence. New Providence, seven-by-21-miles long, is home to The Bahamas capital city of Nassau, a bustling (by Bahamian standards) but still cozy burg of 150,000 residents locked into colonial charm, garnished with a slight hint of its buccaneering past as a haven for pirates, rum runners and slave traders. This is the major watersports, shopping, dining and gambling center in The Bahamas.

Nassau: New Providence has three major tourist areas: Nassau (the capital of The Bahamas), Paradise Island and Cable Beach. Nassau is a superb natural anchorage and the traditional economic nerve center of The Bahamas that has turned over the centuries from a charming backwater into something of a concrete jungle. Nassau is preserved tradition wrapped in the ascending vines of modernity. The city, as well as Cable Beach and Paradise Island, is packed with tourists year-round; it's particularly like a theme park during the winter months. Bay Street, the route of the annual Junkanoo Parade, is the main tourist drag, and here can be found a full array of shops and restaurants. There is a unique combination of straw markets, art galleries and attractive, colonial-style government buildings found along the thoroughfare.

Cable Beach: Many visitors forgo Nassau altogether and head straight for Cable Beach, a few miles due west of the capital and ultimate mall of megaresorts. Every imaginable amenity and seaside leisure activity as well as gambling await visitors to Cable Beach. The oceanfront is stacked with hotels, so don't expect a lot of privacy along the vast stretches of clean, white sand.

Paradise Island: Paradise Island is a gambler's mecca. Three huge casinos, Atlantis Paradise Island Resort & Casino, the Paradise Island Casino and Paradise Club can be found under one roof, making the complex, which sprawls over perhaps three acres, one of the most outrageous and grandiose gambling venues in the world. Luxury condo high-rises flank the beaches. Sun worshippers head for Paradise Beach, a beautiful strip of sand on the island's western tip. This place is a corn-rowed Coney Island south without the rides or the pickpockets.

Grand Bahama

Only 60 miles off the shores of Palm Beach, Florida, and lacking both the colonial charm of New Providence and the laid-back ambience of the Family Islands, Grand Bahama is more like Miami with gambling. Gratefully, however, as The Bahamas fourth-largest island, there remain isolated pockets of pristine beaches and the quiet lifestyle found throughout the chain's other islands. Most visitors head for the two massive casinos in Freeport, Grand Bahama's largest city and the second largest city in the country behind Nassau. Some of the best shopping in The Bahamas is found on Grand Bahama, at the markets and bazaars found in Freeport and Lucaya. Fully a third of The Bahamas' 3.5 million annual visitors call on Freeport. About 3000 people a day are dropped off by the cruise ships. Freeport boasts nearly 3000 hotel rooms. There are four championship golf courses to choose from. A wall of hotels and resorts offer an array of watersports, golf, tennis and gambling.

The Abacos

These islands are a 130-mile-long string of cays with some 650 square miles of land and home to 10,000 people. The Abacos feature some of The Bahamas' best beaches, including Manjack Cay, Great Guana and Elbow Cay. The Abacos are also considered the sailing capital of The Bahamas. Abacos' widely known reputation as a haven for pirates and wreckers was well-founded from the 16th century through the mid-1800s. In the far north is found Walker's Cay, the northernmost island in The Bahamas, and Hole-in-the-Wall in the southwest. Wild boar still roam in the Abacos' dense pine forests. Marsh Harbour, is The Bahamas' third largest city. It has its share of tourist hotels and resorts, gift shops and boutiques, but is not nearly as built up as Grand Bahama and New Providence. The Abacos are The Bahamas' third-largest tourist destination. The marinas in the area are superb, making the Abacos a major deep sea fishing and boating mecca. The island's naturally protected waters and countless beautiful, isolated coves and inlets make the Abacos perhaps the most popular sailing destination in The Bahamas. The Abacos are also a major scuba-diving destination.

Andros

The largest of the Bahamian islands at 108 miles long and 40 miles wide at its widest point (2300 sq... miles). The best all-around diving in The Bahamas is found off Andros. Here is found the Andros barrier reef off the east coast of the island—the third-largest in the world—with all sorts of underwater attractions along its 140-mile length. Twelve-foot waters suddenly plunge to depths exceeding two miles at the Tongue of the Ocean. Dozens if not hundreds of drop-offs, coral gardens, blue holes, walls and wrecks await the adventurous. Blue holes are also a big attraction here; scientists describe Andros' oceanic and inland blue holes as the deepest and longest on the planet. Andros is also considered the "Bonefishing Capital of the World" by anglers from all over the globe. And Lowe Sound is the bonefishing capital of Andros. There is also good hunting on this largely unexplored island. Andros is also the home of the Bahamian batik industry; the bold and richly colorful designs and patterns are sold throughout the world.

Bimini

The Biminis (North Bimini and South Bimini) comprise a 26-mile-long chain, less then 50 miles east of Miami. The deep sea fishing here is considered by most as the best in the world, with giant game fish such as marlin, tuna, swordfish, dolphin, tarpon and grouper visiting the islands' waters at various times throughout the year. What few acres of land exist on North Bimini—the focal point of the islands—is bisected by a dusty "highway" flanked by bars and more bars. Ernest Hemingway spent some time here and worked on a couple of novels in Bimini: *Islands in the Stream* and *To Have And Have Not*. The writer made the bar at the Compleat Angler Hotel famous. The islands' principal town is slightly seedy but raucous Alice Town on North Bimini with a population of about 1600. Although there's an airport on South Bimini, there is very little development on the island, mainly a few private homes. Most who fly into Bimini do so by

Chalk's, whose seaplanes splash down in Porgy Bay at Alice Town. The island's capital wears different faces at different times of the day, transforming itself from a whitewashed ghost town during the day into a Barbary Coast by night.

The Berry Islands

The rarely visited Berry Islands are to the east of Bimini and about 150 miles east of Miami and 35 miles northwest of Nassau. They feature miles of deserted white sand. Many of the 30 islands that make up the group are privately owned. There are only about 600-700 people who call the Berry Islands home all year. The principal settlement is Bullock's Harbour on Great Harbour Cay, which is rather small at about eight miles long and two miles wide, but rambling compared to the other islands. Chub Cay, to the south of Great Harbour Cay, is considered one of the great deep-sea fishing and bonefishing venues in The Bahamas (many call its waters the best spot in the world). For divers, there are a number of nearby sites, including Mama Rhoda Rock and Chub Wall. Great Stirrup Cay has become a popular mini-stopover between Florida and Nassau, and cruise ship visitors can now expect all the trappings of tropical island cruise ship diversions, namely locals dressing up like Tahitians and performing limbo dances—which are about as Bahamian as ice sculptures. There is great birdwatching in the outer cays and there's a decent golf course on Great Harbour Cay.

Eleuthera

Besides being one of the best diving destinations in The Bahamas, Eleuthera is the site where the early Eleutherian Adventures made landfall and is thus considered the birthplace of The Bahamas. Eleuthera, called "Cigatoo" by the locals, starts about 70 miles east of Nassau and consists of some 200 square miles. It is bow-shaped, about 100 miles long and two miles wide. Perhaps 10,000 people call Eleuthera home these days. The island is beginning to rival the Abacos in the number of resorts. Eleuthera possesses arguably the best beaches in The Bahamas, one of the most incredible sights in the islands (that being the magnificent Glass Window) and one of the most thrilling dives in the world at the Current.

Harbour Island: Many frequent Bahamas visitors say that Harbour Island is the most beautiful of Bahamian islands. The entire eastern shore (the island is three miles long and about a half-mile wide) is adorned with a beautiful pink sand beach. Swimming is great year-round. The houses are pastel-colored clapboard structures, many of them among the oldest in The Bahamas; some have been magnificently restored. Hibiscus and bougainvillea fringe the white picket fences.

Spanish Wells: Spanish Wells is a small, quaint settlement named after the freshwater well the Spanish dug on the cay during the time of Ponce de Leon. The charm of present-day Spanish Wells are its people, most of them direct descendents of the original Eleutherian Adventurers. They live in simple, Cape Cod-style clapboard houses painted in pastel shades.

Governor's Harbour: About halfway down the 100-mile long island, this is the largest population center on Eleuthera after Rock Sound. There are a number of wonderful old homes in the area to explore, including an old Anglican church on Cupid's Cay and the 150-year-old Cupid's Cay bridge.

Rock Sound: Two-centuries-old Rock Sound is the biggest population center on Eleuthera and is a quiet fishing village that was one of the biggest pineapple producers and canners in the islands. There are some 200-year-old homes to check out here, as well as the magnificent Rock Sound Ocean Hole, a saltwater inland blue hole that links with the sea.

The Exumas

The Exumas start a mere 35 miles southeast of Nassau and extend in a straight line 90 miles south to Great Exuma, the chain's largest island and the site of the largest settlement, George Town. George Town is a tranquil island capital of 900 people and was once in the running for being named the capital of The Bahamas due to its superb natural harbor. The Tropic of Cancer slices directly through George Town. The majestic government administration building is modeled after Government House in Nassau. George Town is also the scene of the Annual Family Island Regatta, which attracts dozens of the most luxurious yachts found in the world. The Exumas are known for the great diving and fishing found off their shores (notably in the Exuma Cays National Land and Sea Park). Great Exuma has miles of pristine white sand beaches, as do Little Exuma and Stocking Island, a long, thin barrier island off the coast of George Town in Elizabeth Harbour. There is both superb bonefishing and deepsea fishing in the Exumas. Staniel Cay is famed for the clarity and hues of its waters, as well as some magnificent limestone formations, particularly Thunderball Grotto (named after the famous movie), poking from the calm sea off Staniel Cay.

Cat Island

Cat Island, 130 miles southeast of Nassau, is about as far off the beaten track as you can get and still have a decent resort to go home to at night. About 50 miles long and an average of two miles wide, this island is said to have been visited by Columbus, but no one's quite sure. About 2000 people live on Cat Island; one principal settlement is New Bight in the middle of the island. But most folks will be more familiar with Arthur's Town in the north, the hometown of actor Sidney Poitier. There is both splendid fishing and diving in the waters off Cat Island, but its most unusual attraction is perhaps the pint-sized Hermitage on Mt. Alvernia, an early 20th-century abbey hand-built by the island's most revered resident, Father Jerome Hawes. The island is densely forested and has superb beaches, some of them pinkish in color and all of them deserted. This is one of the sleepiest islands in The Bahamas; the only time it comes awake is for the annual three-day Cat Island Regatta.

Long Island

Long Island, about 70 miles long and 1.5 miles wide and located 150 miles southeast of Nassau, is home to one of the best dive resorts in

The Bahamas: the Stella Maris Resort Club, a Bahamian diving icon. About 3500 people call Long Island home, some of whom are employed by the Diamond Crystal Company, a large salt concern. Although most of the islanders live near the island's mid-point at Deadman's Cay, Stella Maris and the northern tip of Long Island are the destinations for tourists. The Stella Maris Club club also has its own airstrip, marina, shopping mall, bank and post office, making it perhaps the most self-contained resort complex in the Family Islands. Deadman's Cay itself remains pretty quiet for most of the year, picking up only with the annual Long Island Regatta in June. Then comes four days of sailboat races and other diversions.

San Salvador

San Salvador, covered with dozens of lakes and lying about 200 miles southeast of Nassau, makes the most believable claim to have been the first landfall of Christopher Columbus' first journey to the New World. Seventeenth-century pirate George Watling used San Salvador as a hit-and-run base. Although the island is 60 square miles, it has little land. There are numerous land-locked lakes; the largest of these, the Great Lake at 12 miles long, serves as the principal transportation link on the island. There's a Club Med here, as well as the popular Riding Rock Inn, which offer fishing and diving. One attraction here is the 165-foot-tall Dixon Hill Lighthouse near Graham's Harbour on the northern tip of the island. It was built in the mid-19th century and its kerosene beacon can be seen for up to 19 miles at sea. It is one of the few remaining hand-operated, kerosene lamps in The Bahamas.

Acklins and Crooked Islands

These two small islands located about 230 miles southeast of Nassau once served as shelters for pirates attacking ships in the vulnerable Crooked Island Passage. A mere 400 or so folks live on Acklins and Crooked Islands, making a meager subsistence on fishing and some scant farming. Some of the former Loyalist plantations can still be seen, although in ruins. There are a couple of good resorts on the islands offering diving and other watersports diversion. Crooked Island is ringed by some 45 miles of barrier reef, dropping from five to 50 feet, and then to more than 3600 feet in the Crooked Island Passage. The tarpon and bonefishing around the islands ranks with some of the best in The Bahamas.

Mayaguana

Small and virtually deserted, this island (110 sq. miles; pop. 500) in the far south of The Bahamas chain is the only backpackers' destination in the country. And even so, only a smattering ever show up. A good reason why most folks don't venture out here is because there isn't a gift shop at the airport, nor a liquor store at the marina, nor a marina. There's a missile tracking station here, and that's about it— besides privacy.

Ragged Island

There are actually a few people living on Ragged Island at a tiny outpost called Duncan Town, which can be reached by mailboat from Nassau. Off the west coast of Long Island, the Jumento Cays run 100 miles south to Ragged Island. There's a 3000-foot airstrip on the island, but no one uses it. And there are absolutely no tourist facilities.

Inagua

Great Inagua is The Bahamas' southernmost island. It's about 40 miles long and 23 miles wide and located 325 miles southeast of Nassau. There are two noteworthy attractions here on this rock of about 1200 people (other than the peace of mind that comes from getting away from it all). First, the island serves as the nesting grounds for more than 50,000 pink flamingos, as well as Bahamian parrots, Great Herons, spoonbills, cormorants, and more than a hundred or so other species of birds. The second attraction is the visually striking salt works at the Morton Salt Company. The beaches aren't so good here, and there are only marginal tourist facilities. Climb the Matthew Town lighthouse and see the mountain ridge silhouette of Cuba, a mere 50 miles away. Uninhabited Little Inagua, just to the north of Great Inagua, is about 40 square miles and sees an occasional fisherman or bird-watcher.

Attractions: Island by Island

Blackbeard's Tower, Nassau

New Providence

ATTRACTION	LOCATION
FORTS	
Fort Charlotte	*Off West Bay Street*
Fort Fincastle	*Bennett's Hill*
Fort Montagu	*East Bay Street*
GARDENS, PARKS & NATURE RESERVES	
Ardastra Gardens	*Near Fort Charlotte*
Royal Victoria Gardens	*Near Government House*
Versailles Gardens	*Paradise Island*
Botanical Gardens	*Near Fort Charlotte*
GOVERNMENT BUILDINGS	
Government House	*Blue Hill Road*
Public Library	*Shirley Street*
HISTORICAL SIGHTS	
Blackbeard's Tower	*Fox Hill Road*
Queen's Staircase	*Shirley Street*
Gregory Arch	*Near Government House*
Pompey Museum (Vendue House)	*Bay Street*
MUSEUMS & ANIMALS	
Sea Gardens	*East End of Nassau Harbor*
Coral Island	*Coral Island*
Hartley's Undersea Walk	*East Bay Street*
Junkanoo Expo	*Prince George Dock*
Nautilus Submarine	*Marina*
LOCAL SIGHTS	
Hair Braiding Pavilion	*Prince George Dock*
Water Tower	*Bennett's Hll*
Potters Cay	*Under Paradise Island Bridge*
Straw Market	*Market & Bay Streets*

Grand Bahama

ATTRACTION	LOCATION
SHOPPING & DINING PLAZAS	
International Bazaar	*Torii gate at West Sunrise Highway*
Port Lucaya Marketplace and Marina	*Lucaya*

Grand Bahama

ATTRACTION	LOCATION
LOCAL INDUSTRIES	
Straw Market	*Next to International Bazaar*
Perfume Factory	*Near International Bazaar*
Bahamas Arts and Crafts Market	*Near International Bazaar*
GARDENS, PARKS & NATURE RESERVES	
Rand Memorial Nature Center	*Settlers Way East*
Garden of the Groves	*Off Midshipman Road*
Lucayan National Park	*Eastern End*
Hydroflora Garden	*East Beach Drive*
MUSEUMS & ANIMALS	
Grand Bahama Museum	*Garden of the Groves*
The Dolphin Experience	*UNEXSO, Lucaya and Blue Lagoon Island, Nassau*

The Bahamas Family Islands

ATTRACTION	LOCATION
Abacos	
Manjack Cay	*North of Green Turtle Cay*
Albert Lowe Museum	*New Plymouth, Green Turtle Cay*
Memorial Sculpture Garden	*New Plymouth, Green Turtle Cay*
Hope Town Lighthouse	*Elbow Cay*
Wyannie Malone Museum and Garden	*Elbow Cay*
Tahiti Beach	*Elbow Cay*
Local Shipbuilding	*Man-O-War Cay*
Sea and Land Park Preserve	*Fowl Cay*
Tilloo and Pelican Cays	*South of Elbow Cay*
Art Colony at Little Harbour	*South of Marsh Harbour*
Acklins and Crooked Islands	
Bird Rock Lighthouse	*Crooked Island Passage*
Crooked Island Caves	*Crooked Island*
Marine Farm	*North End of Crooked Island*
Southwestern Beaches	*Crooked Island*
French Wells	*Crooked Island*

The Bahamas Family Islands

ATTRACTION	LOCATION
Andros	
Andros Barrier Reef	*Parallel to the East Coast of Andros*
Ocean and Inland Blue Holes	*Throughout the Island*
Morgan's Bluff	*North Andros*
Androsia Batik Works	*Fresh Creek*
Turnbull's Gut	*Off Small Hope Bay Lodge*
The Barge	*Small Hope Bay Lodge*
The Biminis	
Hemingway Memorabilia	*Compleat Angler Hotel,Alice Town*
Hall of Fame	*Anchors Aweigh Guest House, Alice Town*
The Sapona	*Between South Bimini and Cat Cay*
Cat Island	
The Hermitage	*Town of New Bight*
Deveaux Plantation	*Town of Port Howe*
Armbrister Plantation	*Near Port Howe*
Eleuthera	
Gregory Town Plantation	*Gregory Town*
Ocean Hole	*Tarpum Bay*
Preacher's Cave	*Bridge Point*
Glass Window	*Upper Bogue*
Hatchet Bay Plantation	*Hatchet Bay*
Hatchet Bay Cave	*Hatchet Bay*
Historic Churches	*Harbour Island*
The Exumas	
The Exuma Cays Land and Sea Park	*Northern Cays*
Stocking Island	*Exuma Sound,Off George Town*
St. Andrew's Church	*George Town*
The Hermitage	*Near George Town*
Thunderball Grotto	*Staniel Cay*
Rolle Town Tomb	*Rolle Town*
Williams Town Salt Marsh	*Williams Town*
Patience House	*Little Exuma*
Out Island Regatta	*George Town*

The Bahamas Family Islands

ATTRACTION	LOCATION
Inagua	
Inagua National Park	*Island interior*
Morton Bahamas Salt Company	*Near Matthew Town*
Long Island	
Dunmore's Cave	*Deadman's Cay*
Dunmore Plantation	*Deadman's Cay*
Father Jerome's Churches	*Clarence Town*
Spanish Church	*The Bight*
Conception Island	*Off Stella Maris*
Deadman's Cay Caves	*Deadman's Cay*
Adderley Plantation	*Cape Santa Maria*
Columbus Point	*North of Stella Maris*
San Salvador	
Observation Platform	*Near Riding Rock Inn*
San Salvador Museum	*Cockburn Town*
New World Museum	*North Victoria Hill*
Columbus Monuments	*Long Bay, Fernandez Bay, Crab Cay*
Grahams Harbour	*Northern San Salvador*
Father Schreiner's Grave	*Grahams Harbour area*
Fortune Hill Plantation	*Eastern San Salvador*
East Beach	*Northeast Cost*
Dixon Hill Lighthouse	*Dixon Hill*
Watling's Castle	*Sandy Point Estate*
Farquharson's Plantation	*Pigeon Creek*
Big Well	*Sandy Point Estate*
Dripping Rock	*Sandy Point*

PEOPLE AND PLACES OF
THE BAHAMAS

HISTORY OF THE BAHAMAS

Parliament Square, Downtown Nassau

Islands in the Stream

Early recorded history of the Bahamas is somewhat mired by two factors: first is that the Spanish essentially erased it after explorer Christopher Columbus first arrived on San Salvador on Oct. 12, 1492, and "discovered" the New World, and subsequently, along with his contemporaries, managed the genocide of the entire native Lucayan population.

Second is that reverence (do I venture to say adulation?) for the explorer among Bahamians is so great that the actions of the Spanish in decimating the peace-loving Lucayans are largely overlooked. (God knows the popular guidebooks to the Bahamas never refer to the Lucayan genocide more than fleetingly.) There aren't any Lucayans left in the world to keep the annals of their obliteration alive. Conflict and crimes against humanity simply don't jive with the laid-back, ear-to-ear smiles the Bahamas exudes both in its peoples and its tourist brochures. (Visi-

27

tors do not come to the Bahamas to remember; they come here to forget.) Tales of the enslavement of the Africans who were forcibly settled on the islands by greedy white landowners are an unpleasant memory juxtaposed with the current island paradise atmosphere.

The history of the Bahamas appears to be as whitewashed as the simple, crumbling-but-charming clapboard houses of its inhabitants—neatly rolled up into a 10-day cruise package and garnished with tales of pirates and rumrunners. It is a country of historic visits rather than of domestic societal, economic, political or scientific achievements—save, of course, for the transition to a black-led government in the 1960s and independence from Great Britain in 1973. There was, of course, the infamous visit by explorer Christopher Columbus to San Salvador in 1492, where he "discovered" the New World. There have been visits by both pirates and British royalty. It seems as if the Bahamas' history is simply composed of historic visits by history-makers making history somewhere else. Ernest Hemingway and Richard Nixon were frequent visitors. Everyone knows the day Winston Churchill set foot on the islands, as well as the days when Queen Elizabeth, Prince Charles, the Duke and Duchess of Windsor, and the Beatles came a-callin'. Islanders can also recall visits by Ian Fleming, Sean Connery and Douglas Fairbanks Jr., not to mention J.P Morgan, the Vanderbilts, the Astors and the Mellons, Howard Hughes, Zane Gray and Huntington Hartford. Today, the islands' indigenous history makers-to-be make a bee-line for Miami, New York and Boston for educations and decent careers before they can have any real impact at home. And most only return home once a year for their particular island's annual boating regatta—again, a history defined by visits.

In all fairness, this is not the Bahamians' fault, but rather the nature of the rocks they inherited from their white masters nearly 200 years ago. The only natural resources the conquering (or marauding) Spaniards found in the Bahamas in the late 15th century were the Lucayan people, which they promptly shipped off to the gold mines in Hispaniola. The soil wasn't any good for agriculture and there wasn't any gold. So, in their lust for riches (rather than in an actual drive for political possessions) they simply bypassed the Bahamas after vacuuming up its people.

This marked the first important visit to the Bahamas.

For more than a hundred years, the Bahamas lay in waste, unpopulated and infrequently visited by vagabond mariners such as Ponce de Leon in his quest for the Fountain of Youth. Finally, in the 1600s, religious pilgrims, not unlike those who landed at Plymouth Rock, called themselves the Eleutherian Adventurers and set out from Bermuda for a land they could call free. They wrecked off Eleuthera and started the first European settlements in the Bahamas.

This was the Bahamas' second-most-important visit.

In the late 18th century, British Loyalists from the newly formed United States did much the same thing, though for different reasons and, like the Spanish before them, left the islands after a relatively short stay. After fleeing from the former colonies with their boatloads of slaves, these wealthy white crown-kissers snatched up all the land on these uninhabited islands in the Atlantic and tried growing cotton. Plantations abounded during the late 18th and early 19th centuries, only to be deserted when it was finally discovered the nutrient-poor Bahamian soil just wouldn't support cash crops. But rather than bringing the slaves off the islands (emancipation occurred in 1834) with them in their retreat, the Loyalists left them there, the descendants of whom compose the vast crux of today's Bahamian population.

Today, most of the islands in the Bahamas long enough to land an airplane on have an airstrip. Also with the help of the Chris Craft century, the Bahamas now receives about 3.5 million tourists a year.

The Lucayans and the Spanish

During their peak, which was just before Christopher Columbus and the Spanish arrived, the Lucayan people numbered perhaps 40,000 across the Bahamas, most likely originating in northeastern South America and being driven north by the fierce, cannibalistic Caribe people. They had lived without conflict for at least 500 years in the Bahamas before the Spanish genocide.

The Lucayans were a peaceful society, existing on the sea and primitive agriculture, much the same as present-day Bahamians survive today. They wore little, if any, clothing, and customarily flattened the foreheads of their young and, particularly, women. This was done in the belief that flat heads were either signs of beauty or ugliness. It's more likely that the latter school of thought is correct. The Lucayans perhaps felt that by appearing ugly—or at least different from their enemies the Caribes—the Caribes would be less likely to rape the women or eat them all. They built long, wooden canoes and made perilous journeys to islands throughout the Bahamas. The Lucayans were skilled toolmakers and fashioned weapons for hunting, including bows-and-arrows and spears. But they were ill-trained and even less practiced in the art of war. Columbus found the Lucayans to be the most docile, loving people he had ever met and was astounded by their generosity.

But the Spaniards didn't reciprocate. Columbus landed on San Salvador to discover the New World on Oct. 12, 1492, and a mere 25 years later the Lucayan (or Arawak) Indians would be extinct.

The Spanish, thinking the Bahamas were barrier islands off the China coast, quickly departed San Salvador, and the rest of the Bahamas, for that matter. Gold had been discovered on Hispaniola (present-day Haiti and the Dominican Republic) and Cuba, and the native Taino tribespeople of Hispaniola, whom the Spanish had enslaved as miners, were dying off at alarming rates from disease, overwork and pestilence. The Lucayans, with their proximity to Hispaniola, made the perfect substitute. But the Lucayans, lacking the natural immunities to European diseases and toiling in the mines on a starvation diet, died as quickly as the Taino. In fact, many didn't even survive the boat trip to Hispaniola. A mere quarter-century after Columbus had arrived in the Bahamas, the Lucayan Indians were a dead race. In all, Columbus spent a total of 15 days in the Bahamas.

Tierra! Tierra!

The first European to set his eyes on the land of the New World was not Christopher Columbus but one of his sailors named Palos, who shouted the immortal words "Tierra! Tierra!" from the crow's nest of the Santa Maria during early morning hours of Oct. 12, 1492. The land he had spotted was more than likely named Guanahani (San Salvador Island by Columbus) in the southern Bahamas.

Columbus had four weeks earlier set out from Spain in three ships, the Santa Maria, the Nina and the Pinta, to discover the trade routes of the Far East. Known as Colon in Spain, Columbus had badly miscalculated how big the world was. After "discovering" the New World at San Salvador, he assumed China was just over the horizon, maybe a two-day sail from San Salvador. After trading gifts with the native Lucayans, Columbus quickly weighed anchor for "China" (actually Cuba) after hearing words from the Lucayans such as "Cubanacan" (meaning middle Cuba) which he mistook for "Kibble Khan."

He dispatched the Pinta to Cuba, to send men into the interior of the island to search for gold. Columbus himself wrecked the Santa Maria on a reef off Haiti, assumed command of the Nina, and left nearly 40 provisioned Santa Maria sailors stranded in what's the present-day Dominican Republic to wait for a rescue ship. (When Columbus returned in 1493, the sailors had all died.) The Nina and Pinta returned to Spain to accolades and parades. Not only did Columbus collect a 335,000 maravedi cash prize, but also the 10,000 maravedis offered to the first sailor to sight land. Palos dared not speak and, depressed, left Spain for Africa.

The Vagabonds and the Pirates

After Columbus' two voyages to the New World, Ponce de Leon, who was aboard Columbus' second journey, arrived in the Bahamas in 1513 in his search for the Fountain of Youth. There were few Lucayans left to enslave (the entire population was exterminated by 1520), although that wasn't on the explorer's agenda. Instead, he spent a brief time on the island of Bimini, thinking he had perhaps found his fountain in south Bimini. Discovering that he was still getting older, he moved on to St. Augustine in north Florida. Not finding what he was looking for there, he returned to the Bahamas. Again, the fountain eluded him.

Ft. Charlotte is a reminder of Nassau's colorful history.

Other Spanish adventurers stumbled upon the Bahamas and did their best to avoid them altogether; there was nothing of any value on the islands, and their barrier reefs were nothing but a pain in the rear. The Bahamas then remained entirely left alone; they weren't claimed by any nation. However, in 1629, Charles I claimed the islands for England. Although the claim was uncontested, England did little to settle the islands or administrate them, the opposite of what the British were doing in India at the time. Consequently they belonged to the Crown in name only. Even when France claimed several of the islands in 1633, England did nothing about it. And neither did France, for that matter.

The British didn't get serious about the Bahamas until 1648, when Bermuda and the Bahamas seemed a decent place to escape religious persecution. Charles I couldn't elude the ire of the Puritan revolt; he was beheaded in 1649. As the Puritan uprisings took more of a toll, many of the Puritans looked to the New World. Even in the early 1600s, religious factionalism was tearing at the seams of Bermuda.

In 1648, the first group of Puritans left Bermuda and didn't return. William Sayle's Eleutherian Adventurers landed on the island they would name Eleuthera in 1649 after their ship, the William, wrecked on a reef near the north of the island. After much hardship and internal conflicts, the group split into three, eventually settling Governor's Harbour, Spanish Wells and Har-

Fielding THE BAHAMAS

Pirates in Paradise

Piracy or privateering was a major industry in The Bahamas' early history. Blackbeard, Mary Read, and Anne Bonny were known for their cruel executions and malicious mischief. Pirates captured and looted ships, then used the islands as a place to hide out until Woodes Rogers became governor and drove them out.

Grand Bahama Island

Little Abaco Island

Treasure Cay

Freeport/Lucaya

FLORIDA

Bimini

New Providence

A stone tower five miles east of Fort Montagu was used as a lookout by Blackbeard.

Nassau

The Bahamas' Historical Society at Shirley St. and Elizabeth Ave. has a museum with prints and paintings depicting Blackbeard's adventures.

Nassau

New Providence Island

Andros Island

Andros Town

Andros

Morgan's Bluff is named for pirate Sir Henry Morgan who reportedly hid treasure that has yet to be found.

Blackbeard

Blackbeard or Edward Teach became a pirate in 1713. The 6 foot 4 inch man was an imposing figure who struck fear into the hearts of his victims and crew alike. Blackbeard with his ship, *Queen Anne's Revenge*, began a campaign of looting throughout the Bahamas and North America until 1718. Blackbeard was killed in battle during a fight with Captain Maynard of the Royal navy and his fleet.

Edward Teach

CUBA

Calico Jack, Anne Bonny, Mary Read

In early November of 1720, Calico Jack and his crew were celebrating a successful loot when they were apprehended by the British Navy. Reportedly the only two pirates that remained on deck to fight during the apprehension were Anne Bonny and Mary Read, disguised as men to fool the rest of the crew, including each other.

Great Abaco Island

Cat Island

Named after pirate Arthur Catt who used to meet at Port Howe with Henry Morgan and Blackbeard. Tales of buried treasure around Cat Island have become legend.

Mary Read

Eleuthera Island

San Salvador

Watling's Castle on the hill overlooking French Bay was reportedly the former home of pirate John Watling. Some say it's just the ruins of a Loyalist plantation.

Cat Island

Port Howe

San Salvador

BAHAMAS

Great Exuma Island

George Town

Rum Cay

Stella Maris

Long Island

Crooked Island

William Kidd

William Kidd was originally a privateer commissioned by the British to rid its shipping routes of pirates. Kidd turned into a privateer with no loyalties and began sacking British and French ships alike throughout the Bahamas, Atlantic, and even as far south as Madagascar.

William Kidd

Acklins Island

Great Inagua Island

bour Island. Through Sayle's heroic efforts to procure aid and food from abroad for the new islanders—he sailed a small shallop to Jamestown, Virginia, to seek aid—the settlers survived, although many returned to Bermuda. Food could simply not be grown in the Bahamas' thin topsoil and limestone and coral base.

But aid to the Puritans continued, mostly from the American colonies. The Adventurers traded island wood for food with the folks of Massachusetts. Although the experiment on Eleuthera ultimately failed (Sayles himself moved back to Bermuda), many of today's residents of these three small towns are direct descendents of the Eleutherian Adventurers.

Regardless of the harsh conditions found in the Bahamas for subsistence, other Britons followed the Adventurers. New Providence was founded in 1656 by a group with ties to Providence, Rhode Island. Many Eleutherian Adventurers resettled at Nassau.

Although Nassau was ostensibly founded for religious freedom reasons, the original settlers were hardly loving neighbors. To eke out a living, a high percentage of them turned to wrecking, or salvaging the cargo of ships having wrecked or foundered on the treacherous reefs. And many of these folks weren't content to wait for Mother Nature. They erected lights to fool seagoing vessels and trick them into running into the reefs. In fact, by the mid-1800s, it's guessed that three-quarters of all able-bodied men in the Bahamas had made careers of wrecking. And the Bahamas made a great place for this barbaric activity: they were largely uncharted, without lighthouses, and amidst unpredictable currents and winds and the trickiest reefs in the Atlantic. Thousands of ships went down in Bahamian waters during the 17th and 18th centuries, many of them coaxed by the false beacons of the wreckers.

Nassau (called Charles Town until 1695 and renamed in honor of King William III, the former William of Orange-Nassau) was more than a little unsavory from the beginning. Its 1100 residents by the end of the 17th century were unsavory types. There was little law on New Providence and even less human decency, making the island a perfect place for guys such as Edward "Blackbeard" Teach, Henry Morgan, Calico Jack Rackham and the notorious women pirates Anne Bonny and Mary Read (ruthless, cut-throat buccaneers who used to swing aboard their victims' vessels topless). Nassau, like much of the Caribbean, was in a state of anarchy and essentially governed by these pirates. They were known for showing no mercy with captured crews and preyed upon the treasure-laden Spanish galleons returning to Spain from Hispaniola and Central America—wholesale slaughters and executions were commonplace.

For more than 40 years up until 1718, pirate attacks against Spanish ships (even justified legally under British law that made okay to plunder ships belonging to the enemy) were relentless, and the Spanish responded by sacking Nassau four times in this period, causing the inhabitants to flee. But after each trashing of the city the ruffians would return.

In 1718, the British government finally decided to get serious about the Bahamas, and dispatched to Nassau its first governor, Woodes Rogers, himself a pirate, to clean up the island's act. And he did. One of his first acts was to hang eight pirates at what is now the site of the British Colonial Hotel when not enough pirates had taken him up on his offer of amnesty (Rogers needed the pirates to help him defend Nassau from the Spanish). And for the first time, in 1720, Nassau repulsed a Spanish attack. Nassauvians knew he was serious. In fact, Rogers was so effective that his pledge *Expulsis Piratis, Restituta Commercia* (Expel Piracy, Restore Commerce) became the motto of the nation until it was replaced in 1973 by Prime Minister Lynden O. Pindling with "Forward, Upward, Onward, Together."

The Loyalists

The Bahamas, through a succession of British governors, enjoyed relative stability until the American Revolution. In 1776, the fledgling Continental Navy conducted its first concerted attack, and it was on Nassau. It succeeded without even a shot being fired. The Americans' attack was directed at the British forces' arms and ammunition depot at Fort Nassau. They easily overran Fort Montague, but found that the British had removed its arms cache from Fort Nassau. The Americans hung out for a couple of weeks and drank rum with the locals before leaving. They attacked Nassau again in 1778 and raised the American flag over Ft. Nassau.

In 1782, the Spanish again attacked the capital and ruled it for a year until the 1783 Treaty of Versailles gave the Spanish Florida and the Bahamas back to the British. Back under British rule, the Bahamas became a logical choice for Loyalists fleeing the newly independent United States. They brought with them their thousands of slaves (the first African inhabitants of the Bahamas) and established huge cotton plantations. The Loyalists, however, mostly America's landed gentry and others of wealth, didn't get along with the then-native Bahamians. To make matters worse, the Bahamian soil wasn't suited for cotton growing. Land erosion and cotton bugs soon took their toll on the plantations, and most of the Loyalists went to the Caribbean or back to the United States, leaving their slaves on the islands. And emancipation in 1834 brought slavery to an end. The one mark the Loyalists did leave on the Bahamas was entirely changing the islands' ethnic composition.

The American Civil War Years

The next significant event for the Bahamas was the American Civil War between 1861 and 1865. The Bahamians witnessed a boom they wouldn't see for another 60 years. Somewhat ironically, the Bahamas, by now predominantly black, supported the South. But this was understandable in light of the people's great devotion to Britain, which also tacitly supported the rebels. American President Abraham Lincoln imposed a sea blockade of the southern states and while at first laughable, as the war stretched on, it became rather effective. But Bahamian boats had little trouble running the Yankee curtain, and the war made fortunes for more than a few folks. Cotton, guns and food supplies were easily run from Nassau to the southern states. Warehouses and other buildings were erected overnight in Nassau.

But with the end of the war came the end of the Bahamas' prosperity. Residents had to resort to the old standbys to eke out a living, namely by growing citrus fruit and wrecking. And wrecking, with the establishment of lighthouses and better charts of the waters, was soon becoming fossilized. Many started leaving the islands (and continued to do so up until the current tourist boom), becoming laborers in Florida.

Prohibition and the Growth of Tourism

But the money would start flowing again into the islands. In 1919, Prohibition was signed into law in the United States and Nassau, Bimini and Grand Bahama made lucrative bases for rumrunners. The docks in Nassau were piled high with crates of liquor from Europe bound for the Florida Keys, Miami and other continental destinations, such as New Jersey's "Rum Row." Smugglers were chased down by the U.S. Coast Guard; a number of boats were fired upon. But most smuggling ventures from the Bahamas were unwaveringly successful.

The Life of a Rumrunner

"The bootlegging of liquor from the Bahamas to the eastern seaboard from Florida to New York became an immensely profitable venture. The sale and export of liquor from the Bahamas was perfectly legal. Entry into the States was the illegal part and most transactions took place outside the three mile limit.

The Life of a Rumrunner

"To take advantage of the situation, the government of the Bahamas imposed an enormous tariff on all landed liquor and thus filled a public treasury that had for many years been quite dry. Quite a few Bahamians made fortunes, mostly Nassau merchants who were able to obtain exclusive agencies for top brands. Nassau became an immense warehouse for trans-shipment to Bimini and West End and then to the States. Small, fast powerboats would make two or three delivery runs a night to inlets on the east coast of Florida. These were mostly manned by Americans, but the longer hauls, such as to New York, were handled by Bahamians—like my father, and some Canadians as well.

"At this time, Dad was the captain of a three-masted vessel called the Alma R. He made several runs to New York where he would anchor outside the three mile limit and do business. Boats of every size and description would come and tie alongside the vessel and make their purchases. For fear of hijacking, nobody was allowed on board. The buyer would call out his needs and be given a price. A bucket was lowered and the full payment placed inside. Then the goods would be passed down. The bottles were packed in sixes, each covered with a straw sleeve and sewn up in a burlap sack. These could be easily passed or thrown down to customers in the small boats.

"After a few close calls from the U.S. Coast Guard, including an occasion when the Alma R dragged anchor into the three mile limit during a heavy blow, Dad decided to install a large diesel engine. On the second trip, the Alma R encountered gale force winds and rough seas prevented the small boats from making contact. The ship's New York agent provided a pilot and encouraged Dad to move inside to a protected bay that was well off the beaten track.

"Against his better judgment, Dad agreed. He moved in after dark and for several days there was brisk traffic—too much, perhaps. A message arrived from the agent saying the Coast Guard had been tipped off and Dad should leave at once.

"Unfortunately, the tide was low and before it was high enough to cross the bar and enter the safety of the three mile limit, the lookout announced the imminent arrival of the Coast Guard.

"They were trapped and knew it. Dad called a trusted crew member, a black man from Green Turtle Cay known as One-Eyed William Bowe. They packed all the proceeds from the expedition into a pillowcase and put it in with dirty laundry. Dad knew he would be arrested and imprisoned, but crewmen were usually released and given a reasonable amount of time to leave the country. His charge to William was to deliver the money intact to my mother.

"The Coast Guard boarded and, sure enough, Dad and the engineer were arrested. The rest of the crew, including William, were released and made their way to Miami then Nassau. One-Eyed William handed the money over to my mother without a cent missing.

"After a few days, the New York agent arranged to pay Dad's fines and he was released. The Alma R was sold at public auction and shortly thereafter was back on Rum Row again."

From "I Wanted Wings," by Leonard Maurice
Thompson, White Sound Press, 1995.

The money poured into Nassau. New hotels were built to handle the fledgling tourist arrivals. Mobsters and starlets consorted in Nassau; beautiful shops were opened. The Bahamas' first casino was opened.

Although the repeal of Prohibition in 1933 had an effect on the Bahamas similar to that at the end of the Civil War, the islands began noticing they had been discovered anew, this time by upper-crust socialites, financiers and industrialists, who began using the islands as their little getaways. Pan Am began daily flights to Nassau from Miami in 1929. An undersea cable had been laid from Jupiter, Florida, to New Providence—the Bahamas' first telephone line. The concept of escaping to balmy climes for a vacation had sunk in.

And few could take as much credit for the approaching tourist boom as Canadian gold magnate Harry Oakes. Oakes came to Nassau in the 1930s and soon left his mark. He built the country's first airport and the country's first golf course, the Cable Beach Golf Course. Oakes also built the Bahamas Country Club.

Sir Harry was mysteriously murdered in July 1943—there has yet to be a conviction—most likely by hired hit men of Miami's mob, irked by Harry's opposition to the opening casinos in the Bahamas. The story was the talk of the town both in Nassau and Miami. Oakes' son-in-law, Count Alfred de Marigny, who was known to dislike Harry, was tried for the murder but acquitted.

In 1939, the Duke and Duchess of Windsor arrived to govern the Bahamas. The Duke was formerly the king of England, but abdicated the throne to marry his American sweetheart, divorcee Wallis Warfield Simpson, in 1936. The two had spent most of their time flitting around Paris and the French Riviera until World War II and rumors (later strong evidence) that the Germans had plans to kidnap the two and use them as pawns to get the British to capitulate their war efforts. The plans were to place the two back on the British throne after the German defeat of Great Britain, where they would serve as puppet royalty. The plot alarmed Prime Minister Winston Churchill enough that he urged King George VI to send the couple as far away from the war as possible. When the duke approached the king about a role in the war effort against Germany, George VI sent the duke and his duchess packing for the Bahamas, about as far from the action as one could get. Many historians view the assignment as punishment for leaving the throne for a woman.

But if punishment was just for such an action, the Bahamians didn't know it. The duke was revered by the islanders who were tickled pink to be important enough to be ruled by the former king of England. They practicallyu deified him for being the great grandson of Queen Victoria, who had emancipated the slaves, and, spoke of him in romantic lore as the man who would not be king in order to be with his love.

The first brewings of racial discord came during war years. The Americans and British were building an air base on western New Providence and hired local black workers at so low a wage they set off as a mob to sack Bay Street, the center of white power in the islands. The gang members were called the Bay Street Boys. The mob was repulsed, but several people were killed in the uprising.

Lynden O. Pindling and the Birth of a Republic

Black unrest at the more than 300 years of white power in the Bahamas manifested itself in Lynden O. Pindling, a British-educated black lawyer who was elected to Parliament in 1956 as a member of the Progressive Liberal Party (PLP), the Bahamas' opposition party. He made no secret of his disdain for the Bay Street Boys and continually disrupted parliament sessions during his early years. During one such session in 1965, he tossed the speaker's mace through a window. Because the mace has to be present and within sight during all parliament sessions, the proceedings were suspended.

His continuing antagonism toward the Bay Street Boys and his ability to whip a crowd into a frenzy led to his peaceful assumption of power in 1967. The white flight fear was dispelled when it became apparent that foreign direct investment and tourism were high on Pindling's list of priorities.

As Britain's other colonial holdings had largely disappeared by the late 1960s, the Crown offered the Bahamas its independence. But through the early 1970s it seemed uncertain if the islands actually wanted it. Things overall had gone pretty well under British rule. Although Pindling's PLP cruised to re-election in 1972 and the Bahamas was granted independence on July 10, 1973, Bahamians voted to remain loyal to the queen by remaining in the Commonwealth of Nations. Pindling was even knighted by the queen in 1983.

The Bahamas, under Pindling, continued to grow throughout the '70s and '80s, basing its economy on tourism and banking. However, the continued allegations of corruption within government circles by lawyer Hubert Alexander Ingraham, the former chairman of the PLP, led to Pindling's downfall. On Aug. 19, 1992, Pindling was replaced as prime minister by Ingraham.

NUTS AND BOLTS

Bridge to Paradise Island

Entry and Departure Requirements

Travel Documents

To enter The Bahamas, you must have proof of citizenship and an onward-bound ticket, although rarely, if ever, is this asked to be shown by North Americans. A valid passport is preferred. However, a passport expired less than five years or a birth or baptismal certificate with photo I.D. is also accepted.

Citizens of Canada and the United Kingdom visiting for three weeks or less may enter upon showing a passport or the same items required for U.S. citizens. Citizens of Commonwealth countries do not need visas for entry.

All visitors must fill out and sign immigration cards. Vaccination certificates for smallpox and cholera are needed only for people coming from areas where such diseases still occur.

Ports of Entry

By air and sea, travelers can enter The Bahamas at the points of entry listed below. If coming in by private yacht, your designated points of entry are also listed below. If coming into The Bahamas by sea, boaters must go through immigration and customs at their first point of entry. The boat captain should fly a yellow quarantine flag when arriving at the port to let officials know they are checking in. A six-month cruising permit will be issued after the captain fills out Maritime Declaration of Health and Inward reports and provides officials with a list of all crew members and passengers, who will be required to have proof of citizenship. A passport, voter's identification card or birth certificate (an original, no photocopies) will do. Drivers licenses are not acceptable. After arriving at the first designated port of call, only the captain may go ashore until the boat and its passengers have cleared customs and immigration. The cruising permit should be kept in a safe place and must be presented to government officials when they request to see it.

Ports of Entry

THE ABACOS	*Grand Cay, Green Turtle Cay, Marsh Harbour, Sandy Point, Treasure Cay, Walker's Cay*
ANDROS	*Andros Town, Congo Town, Fresh Creek, Nicholl's Town, San Andros*
THE BERRY ISLANDS	*Chub Cay, Great Harbour Cay*
THE B!MINIS	*Alice Town, Big Game Fishing Club, Government Dock in South Bimini*
ELEUTHERA	*Governor's Harbour, Hatchet Bay, Harbour Island, Rock Sound*
THE EXUMAS	*George Town*
GRAND BAHAMA	*Freeport, Lucaya, Xanadu Marina, West End*
INAGUA	*Matthew Town*
LONG ISLAND	*Stella Maris*
NEW PROVIDENCE	*Nassau International Airport, Paradise Island, all marinas*
RAGGED ISLAND	*Duncan Town*
SAN SALVADOR	*Cockburn Town*

Departure Tax

Upon departure by air, travelers are required to pay a $15 tax from Nassau (on New Providence) or the Out Islands, and $18 from Freeport (on Grand Bahama Island).

Customs

Although no written declaration is required, baggage is subject to customs inspection. For dutiable items such as furniture, china and linens, a declaration is necessary. New items should be accompanied by sales slips. Any used household items are subject to assessment by the Customs Officer.

Each adult visitor is permitted 50 cigars or 200 cigarettes or one pound of tobacco and one quart of alcohol duty-free, in addition to personal effects.

Duty-Free Allowances

U.S. residents, including children, may take home duty-free purchases up to $600 in value if they have been out of the United States for more than 48 hours, and have not taken such an exemption within 30 days. The exemption includes up to two liters of alcohol per person over age 21, as long as one of the two liters is manufactured in The Bahamas or another CBI (Caribbean Basin Initiative) country. Families may pool their exemptions.

Canadians absent from their country for at least a week may take home up to $300 (Canadian) worth of duty-free merchandise, which must accompany the passenger.

Residents of the United Kingdom may take home duty-free purchases up to a value of £32.

Personal items such as jewelry, cameras and sports equipment may be brought in duty-free.

Pets

The Bahamian Ministry of Agriculture and Fisheries, with headquarters in Nassau, requires a permit for all animals entering the country. Written applications for permits should be submitted to the **Ministry of Agriculture and Fisheries**, *P.O. Box N-3208, Nassau,* ☎ *(809) 325-7502* or *325-7509.* Forms are available at The Bahamas Tourist Offices. Although most hotels exclude pets, several accept them when arrangements are made in advance and a permit has been obtained.

Drugs, Alcohol and Firearms

Possession of marijuana, cocaine or other such drugs is an extremely serious and punishable offense. If you indulge here or attempt to bring narcotics into the country, you are looking for trouble, especially since the government has been cracking down on drugs more than ever lately. The minimum drinking age is 21.

Under no circumstances may firearms be brought in without a Bahamian gun license.

Language

The language of The Bahamas is English, accented with West Indian, Scottish and Irish influences. Like Bermudians, Bahamians often substitute *w*'s for *v*'s. This is thought to date back to 18th-century English.

Dress

In The Bahamas, dress is generally casual although, in season, some hotels and restaurants request that men wear jackets and ties for evening meals. Off-season dress is more relaxed. At some of the larger hotels and posher resorts, long skirts or cocktail attire are preferred for women in the evening. In the Out Islands, dress is much more casual, except in one or two resorts. Beachwear is discouraged in the public rooms of hotels, and wearing short shorts in town is frowned upon for both men and women.

Business Hours

In Nassau, banks are open 9:30 a.m. to 3 p.m. Monday through Thursday, and on Fridays from 9:30 a.m. to 5 p.m. Note that international ATMs are located in strategic spots (such as casinos!). The ATMs dispense United

States currency and your bank account in the U.S. is debited. Stores are open 9 a.m. to 5 p.m. every day except Sundays and holidays.

Banks in Freeport are also open 9:30 a.m. to 3 p.m. Monday through Thursday and from 9:30 to 5 p.m. on Fridays. Most stores are open 9 a.m. to 6 p.m. except Sundays and holidays. Many shops in the International Bazaar and Port Lucaya stay open until 9 p.m. on Saturdays during the winter season. Some banks on the Out Islands are open only several days a week, with limited hours. Some are even only open one day a week for only a couple of hours. (If you have any banking needs while in The Bahamas, refer to the individual island chapters for bank listings, including opening and closing hours.) Many stores close for an hour or two for lunch.

Communications

On New Providence (including Paradise Island) and Grand Bahama, telephone and fax services are readily available. However, in the Family Islands phones and fax machines are few and far between. Many of the resorts in the Out Islands have only one phone, and that's at the front desk. Phones in the rooms are almost unheard of. Storms also play havoc with the phone system in the Family Islands. I don't know why but it's true. But rest assured that all the hotels have at least one phone if you must make contact with the outside world. Most communication in the Family Islands is by VHF radio. A few resorts provide VHF radios in the rooms. You should take care of all essential phone business before traveling to the Family Islands. Public phones, if working, are rare.

Author's Note

The area code for all of The Bahamas was 809. But keep in mind that, starting in January 1997, that the area code became 242.

Mail

Although more U.S. dollars seem to be in circulation in The Bahamas than Bahamian currency, postage stamps must be Bahamian. Postcards to the United States, Canada and the United Kingdom cost 40 cents, and letters cost 45 cents per half-ounce to the United States and Canada and 50 cents to Europe.

Accommodations

The large hotels and resorts have daily activities and many facilities such as shops, restaurants, large dining rooms, cycle rental stations and watersports equipment. Most also have nightly entertainment. When not located on a beach, many provide complimentary transportation. Most establishments that have few or no sports facilities will arrange sporting activities for their guests elsewhere. All large accommodations are fully air-conditioned. Smaller hotels and guest houses have fewer facilities and many are partially air-conditioned, if at all. Particularly in the Out Islands, many establishments rely on fans and trade winds. Some of the smaller guest houses are in former private homes and have shared baths. In the Out Islands, with power generators in wide use at hotels, visitors may sometimes find themselves without electricity for short periods of time. It is therefore a good idea to note the location of candles that are put in most guest rooms.

Hotels add an eight percent to 10 percent service charge/government tax to room rates. However, there is no sales tax in The Bahamas. They just invent other taxes. High season runs from about December through April. During the summer (or "Goombay") season, rates are about 20 to 30 percent lower.

In the **Accommodations Chart** at the back of this book, you'll find more information about the accommodations described in each island section as well as details about other establishments.

Renting Private Homes, Villas, Condos and Islands

Vacation Home Rentals, Worldwide *(235 Kensington Avenue, Norwood, NJ 07648,* ☎ *(800) 633-3284 or* ☎ *(201) 767-9393, FAX (201) 767-5510)* personally inspects all of the villas, condos and suites in its rental pool. This company has properties in Nassau, Freeport and the Out Islands. Following are some local real estate agencies that also handle private homes throughout The Bahamas:

- **Caribbean Management, Ltd.**, *P.O. Box N-1132, Nassau, The Bahamas;* ☎ *(809) 393-8618/9.*
- **Ingraham's Real Estate**, *Hospital Lane North, P.O. Box N-1062, Nassau, The Bahamas;* ☎ *(809) 325-2222/3433/8930.*
- **Jack Isaacs Real Estate Co., Ltd.**, *25 Cumberland Street, Nassau, The Bahamas;* ☎ *(809) 322-1069/325-6326.*
- **Grosham Property, Ltd.**, *P.O. Box N8189, Nassau, The Bahamas;* ☎ *(809) 322-7662.*

If you and some friends or relatives would like to have an island virtually all to yourselves—and if you can afford it—consider renting the luxurious villas on **Cistern Cay** *(☎ 809/326-7875)* in the peaceful Exuma Cays Land and Sea Park. The hefty $38,000 per week price tag covers three gourmet meals a day, liquor, a fishing guide, watersports equipment and more for up to 10 adults (and a couple of children).

Money Matters

Bahamian money is pegged to the U.S. dollar, with the same designations for bills and coins and exchanged at the same rate. Visitors are likely to receive change in mixed American and Bahamian dollars and coins. Traveler's checks are accepted throughout the islands and are cashable at banks and hotels. However, banks and some restaurants will add a service charge. Credit cards are widely accepted, but you may have to pay a service charge if you use American Express.

Most banks will cash verifiable personal checks. Nassau's American Express office for check cashing and cash advances is conveniently located downtown at the Playtours office, at the intersection of Shirley and Parliament streets. In Freeport, American Express is located in the Kipling Building, off Kipling Lane in Churchill Square. International ATMs can be found in various locations—including some hotels and casinos. But keep in mind that few to none are found in the Family Islands. If you lose your traveler's checks, contact:

American Express
   ☎ *(800) 221-7282*

Citicorp

☎ *(800) 645-6556, or collect* ☎ *(813) 623-1709*

Interpayment Services

☎ *(800) 221-2426, or collect* ☎ *(212) 858-8500*

These folks issue VIA traveler's checks.

Thomas Cook

☎ *(800) 223-7373, or collect (609) 987-7300*

MasterCard traveler's checks are issued by Thomas Cook.

CURRENCY CONVERSION CHART			
BAHAMIAN $	**U.S. $**	**U.K. £**	**CANADIAN $**
1	1	.63	1.29
2	2	1.26	2.58
3	3	1.89	3.87
4	4	2.52	5.16
5	5	3.15	6.45
6	6	3.78	7.74
7	7	4.41	9.03
8	8	5.04	10.32
9	9	5.67	11.61
10	10	6.30	12.90
15	15	9.45	19.35
25	25	15.75	32.25
50	50	31.50	64.50
75	75	47.25	96.75
100	100	63.00	129.00
125	125	78.75	161.25
150	150	94.50	193.50
175	175	110.25	225.75
200	200	126.00	258.00
225	225	141.75	290.25
250	250	157.50	322.50
300	300	189.00	387.00
350	350	220.50	451.50
400	400	252.00	516.00
450	450	283.50	580.50
500	500	315.00	645.00

NUTS AND BOLTS

Tipping

A 15 percent service charge is often automatically added to restaurant checks. Ask if you're not sure. Hotels also add an 8 percent to 10 percent service charge/government tax to their rates (so there is no need to leave a tip for the housekeeper). Taxi drivers usually receive 10 percent or 15 percent. Tour guides expect to be tipped a few dollars, depending on the cost of the excursion.

Taxis

Taxis are available in New Providence, Grand Bahama and most of the Out Islands. In Nassau and Freeport, as well as the Out Islands where there are no tour buses, drivers will serve as island guides. The rates, often negotiable, are about $16 an hour. Some Out Island roads are not in the best of repair. A bumpy ride with a friendly driver can be an adventure in itself.

In Nassau and Freeport, taxis, which are metered, wait for passengers at airports and hotels. If drivers don't turn on their meters, be sure to ask them to do so, even if they insist they know the fare. Otherwise, you're likely to be overcharged. From Nassau International Airport to a hotel on Cable Beach, two people should expect to pay about $10 and about $15 to Rawson Square; from the airport to Paradise Island, the ride will be about $20, including the $2 bridge toll. From Freeport's International Airport to the hotel districts, the fare will range from about $6 to $10. Taxis in the Out Islands are not metered and tend to be more expensive than in Nassau or Freeport. On most Out Islands, taxis (sometimes simply the cars or vans of local residents) meet planes. However, to be on the safe side, check with your accommodation about land transportation before arrival. Some Out Island resorts meet planes with their own vehicles. Ask how much you should expect to pay for a taxi from the airport to the hotel. Rides can vary anywhere from $10 to $50, so be prepared.

Rental Cars

Visitors with valid U.S. or Canadian driver's licenses can rent cars in The Bahamas. *Note that driving is on the left.* Daily rates range from about $70 to $80. You'll save renting by the week. Rental agencies in Nassau and Freeport are at airports, hotels and downtown locations. During high season, a reservation is suggested before leaving home. In addition to local companies, **Avis**, **Budget** and **Dollar Rent-A-Car** have offices at the Nassau airport. An Avis agency is in back of Nassau's British Colonial Beach Resort. You'll also find an Avis office in Freeport's International Bazaar. You can rent cars in the Out Islands (usually from taxi drivers), but many of the models are battle-scarred by years of use on bumpy roads. Be sure to check your car's condition before pulling off. You can import your own car for touring, duty-free, for up to six months. A deposit of up to 70 percent of the vehicle's value is required, but it is refunded if the car is shipped out within six months. The value is assessed by Customs upon arrival.

Motorbikes

Motorbikes are a popular mode of travel for tourists in The Bahamas. You'll see more tourists on motorbikes than Bahamians. At most hotels and resorts, you can rent mopeds on the premises or at nearby cycle shops if you are 16 or older. No driver's license is necessary. Wearing a helmet, which you are given with the moped, is required by law, although you'll see quite a few folks riding without them. Until you become accustomed to motorized bikes, it is best to practice riding in a low-traffic area. Renting a moped ranges from about $16 a day, $8 a half-day to about $30 a day, $18 a half-day, including insurance. You'll be asked to leave a deposit of about $30. Bicycles are about $15 a day. *Remember, Bahamians drive on the left.*

NUTS AND BOLTS

Buses

Visitors can take advantage of public transportation in getting around Nassau and Freeport. Bahamians will come to the rescue with directions if you seem uncertain. Nassau has buses and jitneys (minivans or small buses) you can pick up (about 75 cents) at bus stops, and they go to Cable Beach, downtown Nassau, public beaches and other points in the city. To go east, toward the Paradise Island bridge, pick up these public buses downtown at Frederick Street at the corner of Bay Street; to go west to Cable Beach, pick up buses and minivans in front of the British Colonial at Bay Street. Some hotels run complimentary buses to downtown Nassau and to the casino on Cable Beach. Buses on Grand Bahama (about $1) connect Freeport with Lucaya and all hotels with beaches, the International Bazaar and Port Lucaya. Vacationers traveling on package deals generally get prepaid vouchers for bus transportation between the airport and hotels.

Domestic Air Transportation

Bahamasair is the national carrier for The Bahamas and serves 19 destinations in the country, including airports on New Providence, Grand Bahama, Great Abaco, Andros, Eleuthera, Cat Island, Long Island, Great Exuma, Crooked Island, San Salvador and Inagua. Most of the aircraft are relatively modern DASH 8s, although there are a smattering of ancient Irish-made Shorts.

In typical Bahamian fashion, service is very, very slow. For domestic flights at all locations, show up at the airport at least an hour in advance. Clerks begin allowing standby passengers to board 30 minutes before the scheduled departure. On many flights between the islands there is no assigned seating, and even on flights with assigned seating, few people are seated where they should be.

Mailboats and Ferries

Ferries run between downtown Nassau and Paradise Island from Prince George Dock. These "water taxis" also operate in the Out Islands to various offshore cays.

Inter-island mail boats travel between Nassau and the Out Islands. The mail boats depart for the outer islands from Potter's Cay, next to the Paradise Island bridge, off East Bay Street in Nassau. Boats leave once a week, stopping at one or two islands, in a trip that takes almost a day and is usually made overnight.

Mail boats are an economical way of traveling, if only for the more adventurous visitor. Decks are crowded with local commuters, freight, varieties of cargo, produce and livestock. Schedules are constantly revised and there are often postponements. Passage cannot be arranged in advance. Bookings can only be made after arrival in The Bahamas.

Information on mail boats may be obtained at the Dock Master's office on Potter's Cay in Nassau ☎ *(809) 323-1064.*

Departing from Nassau's Shipyard on East Bay Street, Sealink now sails passengers to and from Marsh Harbour in the Abacos, Freeport on Grand Bahama, and Governor's Harbour in Eleuthera. You can even take your car aboard. While the ship travels at night between Nassau and Marsh Harbour, there are daytime cruises between Nassau and Freeport or Eleuthera. The cost is $30 each way for adults and $15 for children. Passengers are asked to wear rubber-soled shoes. (For further details, contact **Sealink**, ☎ *(809) 327-5444* in Nassau or ☎ *(305) 477-7667* in Miami).

Casinos

Gambling at the casinos of The Bahamas is legal for all visitors over the age of 21. Bahamian citizens, however, are not permitted to play. Two casinos are located in Nassau: one on Paradise Island, and the other on the mainland between Carnival's Crystal Palace and Radisson Cable Beach resort. Two more are found in Freeport, Grand Bahama—one between the Princess Tower Hotel and the International Bazaar, the other at the Lucayan Beach Resort and Casino. If you're a beginner and a little intimidated by the whole thing, see the "Gambling in The Bahamas" chapter for instructions on how to play the games offered in Bahamian casinos.

Time

Eastern Standard Time is in use throughout The Bahamas. Eastern Daylight Saving Time is used during the summer months coinciding with the United States. When it is noon in New York, it is noon in The Bahamas, year-round.

Electricity

American electrical appliances can be used in The Bahamas without adapters.

Insect Repellent

Don't forget to pack some. Many people find that fragrant Avon Skin So Soft, a bath oil, works very well as a bug repellent when smoothed on skin like lotion.

Medical Concerns

There are excellent medical services in The Bahamas. Hospital, public and private medical facilities, and personnel are available in Nassau and Freeport. There are also health centers and clinics in the Out Islands. In medical emergencies, patients are brought to Princess Margaret Hospital, a government-operated institution in downtown Nassau. The government also operates the 58-bed Rand Memorial Hospital in Freeport.

The water throughout The Bahamas is potable. However, on most Out Islands it is best to drink bottled or filtered water, if only because tap water can be quite salty.

Tar Alert

Unfortunately, tar from oil leaking from ships is hidden on some beaches in the Out Islands. Where this problem exists, hotels have "tar stations" or provide packets of "Tar Off" in rooms. You can also remove tar with Lestoil, vegetable oil, and Avon Skin So Soft (a bath oil that many have discovered works as a mosquito repellent as well).

Media

Nassau's two newspapers are the *Nassau Guardian*, published Monday through Saturday mornings, and the *Tribune*, an afternoon paper. Freeport's paper, the *Freeport News*, is published afternoons, Monday through Friday. *The New York Times*, the *London Times*, the *Daily Telegraph* and the *Wall Street Journal* are available at most of the larger hotels and newsstands, but sometimes a day late. The *Miami Herald* and the Ft. Lauderdale

Sun Sentinel can be found on New Providence, Grand Bahama and Bimini on the same day. American periodicals such as *Time*, *Newsweek* and *People* can be found at the newsstands on New Providence and Grand Bahama as well as at the large hotels and resorts. Radio Bahamas operates two radio stations in New Providence, ZNS1 and ZNS2, and ZNS3 in Grand Bahama. Its television station, TV-13 ZNS, operates out of New Providence.

Visitor Information

The address of **The Bahamas Ministry of Tourism** is *P.O. Box N-3701, Nassau, The Bahamas.* Contact the **Out Islands Promotion Board** at *1100 Lee Wagener Boulevard, Suite 206, Fort Lauderdale, FL 33315, ☎ (305) 359-8099 or (800) 688-4752,* or **The Grand Bahama Promotion Board**, *P.O. Box F650, Freeport, Grand Bahama.* Call ☎ *(800) 4-BAHAMAS* to reach The Bahamas Tourist Office closest to where you live. Listed on pages 49–51 are the locations and local phone numbers of the offices in the United States and Canada.

When to Go to The Bahamas

Although there is both a "low" and a "high" tourist season in The Bahamas, visitors are found throughout the islands year-round. Other than cooler weather, the high season—which runs from January–May—simply means everything is a lot more expensive than during the other months. The low season, June through January, makes for much better bargains as well as few crowds at the islands' attractions.

As most of the heavily touristed Bahamian islands are located above the Tropic of Cancer (which cuts through Long Island and Great Exuma), these islands can get rather cool during the winter months at night and in the early morning. However, overall, the winter weather in The Bahamas is quite springlike and even warm enough to swim in the sea. Daytime temperatures in the winter are typically in the 70s, with lows in the 60s and 50s. The average temperatures during the summer months are about 10 degrees higher.

During the summer months—particularly July and August—it can become quite sticky and uncomfortable, but it never seems to get as bad as south Florida. Besides, most visitors during the summer months spend most of their time either in the sea, on the sea, or in the resorts' swimming pools. And the summer months make The Bahamas the best time to visit for sailors and boaters, as the waters are at their calmest.

The hurricane season runs from June through November, and The Bahamas has recently been getting its share. In 1992, Hurricane Andrew decimated some of the islands, and in 1996, Hurricane Bertha took a toll on the easterly islands. But hurricanes shouldn't be a reason not considering a summer or fall trip to the islands. They strike The Bahamas infrequently, and there's always plenty of warning, as most of the storms have their origins off the coast of West Africa. For the latest on hurricane information, contact the nearest office of the National Weather Service (in the phone book it's under the U.S. Department of Commerce), turn on the Weather Channel on your television set, or telephone ☎ *(900) WEATHER* for the latest conditions in The Bahamas. The calls cost 95 cents per minute.

Summers in The Bahamas are not marred by a true "rainy season" and the incessant downpours that drench the tropics of the Northern Hemisphere during the summer months. The rainfall is greater in The Bahamas during the summer, but is primarily contained to passing showers and afternoon thunderstorms. Locals on New Providence will tell you that it doesn't rain at all in July. And for the most part, July is indeed a dry and sunny month.

Average Temperatures and Rainfall

Month	Average Temperature Fahrenheit/Centigrade		Average Rainfall Inches
January	70°	21°	1.9
February	70°	21°	1.6
March	72°	22°	1.4
April	75°	24°	1.9
May	77°	25°	4.8
June	80°	27°	9.2
July	81°	27°	6.1
August	82°	28°	6.3
September	81°	27°	7.5
October	78°	26°	8.3
November	74°	23°	2.3
December	71°	22°	1.5

AVERAGE HIGHS AND LOWS IN THE BAHAMAS (°F)

CITY	Jan.	Feb.	Mar.	Apr.	May	Jun.	Jul.	Aug.	Sep.	Oct.	Nov.	Dec.
NASSAU	77	78	80	82	85	87	89	89	88	85	82	79
(low)	62	63	64	66	70	73	75	75	74	72	68	64
FREEPORT	75	75	78	81	85	87	90	90	89	85	81	77
(low)	60	60	64	67	70	73	75	75	74	71	67	63
GREGORY TOWN	77	77	79	82	84	86	87	88	88	85	81	78
(low)	66	65	67	69	72	75	77	77	77	74	71	61

Holidays and Special Events

Junkanoo and Goombay are two festivals that may help you to determine when to visit The Bahamas. Junkanoo is a festival that occurs during the Christmas/New Year's season. Goombay is an annual series of special events to attract visitors during the summer season, when the weather is hotter and somewhat wetter. Other special events such as those for boaters, sports fishermen and divers will also help you decide when and where to go.

Month	Location	Event
Jan. 1	Nassau, Freeport and a few other islands	Junkanoo Parade*
2nd Wed. in Jan.	Nassau	Supreme Court Opening
Feb.	Nassau	Annual Miami-Nassau Boat Race
Feb.	Nassau	Annual Nassau Yacht Cup Race
Mar.	Nassau	International 5.5 Metre World Championships
Mar.	Nassau	Annual Bacardi Snipe Winter Championship
Mar.	George Town, Exuma	George Town Cruising Regatta
Apr.	Abaco	Annual Abaco Fishing Tournament
Apr.	George Town, Exumas	Family Island Regatta
1st Wed. in Apr.	Nassau	Supreme Court Opening
May	Walker's Cay Abaco	Annual Walker's Cay Billfish Tournament
May	Marsh Harbour, Abaco	Penny Turtle Billfish Tournament
June	Long Island	Long Island Sailing Regatta
June	Cat Cay	Cat Cay Billfish Tournament
June	Bimini	Bimini Big Game Blue Marlin Tournament
1st Fri. in June	Nassau & Freeport	Labour Day Parade
1st Wed. in July	Nassau	Supreme Court Opening
July	Abacos	Abaco Regatta
July 10	All Islands	Independence Day
July	Nassau	Pepsi-Cola Independence Open Golf Tournament
July	Nassau	Commonwealth Exhibition and Fair
July	Chub Cay Berry Islands	Chub Cay Blue Marlin Fishing Tournament
1st Mon. in Aug.	All Islands	Emancipation Day
Aug.	Bimini	Bimini Local Fishing Tournament
Aug.	Arthur's Town Cat Island	Cat Island Regatta

Month	Location	Event
Sept.	*Nassau*	Jazz Festival
2nd Tues. in Aug.	*Nassau*	Fox Hill Day Celebration
1st Wed. in Oct.	*Nassau*	Supreme Court Opening
Oct.	*Nassau*	Discovery Day Regatta
Oct.	*Nassau & San Salvador*	Discovery Day
Nov.	*Nassau*	Remembrance Day
Nov.	*Abaco*	Abaco Week Festival
Oct./Nov.	*George Town Exumas*	Annual Bahamas Bonefish Bonanza
Nov.	*Nassau*	Annual International Pro-Am Golf Championship
Dec. 26	*Nassau, Freeport, a few other islands.*	Boxing Day Junkanoo Parade*
Dec.	*Bimini*	Adam Clayton Powell, Jr. Memorial Fishing Tournament

*Visitors may join in the Junkanoo Parades by applying before December to The Bahamas Tourist Office.

Bahamas Tourist Offices

United States

Atlanta
> 2956 Clairmont Road, Suite 150
> Atlanta, GA 30345
> ☎ (404) 633-1793; FAX (404) 633-1575

Charlotte
> P.O. Box 221306
> Charlotte, NC 28222
> ☎ (704) 366-8850; FAX 366-8025

Chicago
> 8600 W. Bryn Mawr Avenue, Suite 820
> Chicago, IL 60631
> ☎ (312) 693-1500; FAX (312) 693-1114

Dallas
> World Trade Center, Suite 116
> 2050 Stemmons Freeway
> P.O. Box 581408
> Dallas, TX 75258-1408
> ☎ (214) 742-1886; FAX (214) 741-4118

Los Angeles
> 3450 Wilshire Boulevard, Suite 208
> Los Angeles, CA 90010
> ☎ (213) 385-0033; FAX (213) 383-3966

Miami
> 19495 Biscayne Boulevard, 8th Floor
> Aventura, FL 33180

☎ *(305) 442-4860; FAX (305) 448-0532*

New York

150 East 52nd Street
28th Floor North
New York, New York 10022
☎ *(212) 758-2777; FAX (212) 753-6531*

Philadelphia

Lafayette Bldg.
437 Chestnut Street, Suite 201
Philadelphia, PA 19106
☎ *(215) 925-0871; FAX (215) 925-0239*

San Francisco

44 Montgomery Center, Suite 500
San Francisco, CA 94104
☎ *(415) 398-5502; FAX (415) 397-6309*

Washington, D.C.

2220 Massachusetts Avenue NW
Washington, D.C. 20008
☎ *(202) 319-0004; FAX (202) 319-0012*

Canada

Montreal

1130 Sherbrooke Street West, Ste. 750
Montreal, Quebec H3A 2MB
☎ *(514) 845-1016; FAX (514) 448-5116*

Toronto

121 Bloor Street East, Ste. 101
Toronto, Ontario M4W 3M5
☎ *(416) 968-2999; FAX (416) 968-6711*

England

Surrey

9 Quarry Street
Guilford, Surrey GU1 3UY
☎ *(071) 629-5238; FAX (071) 491-9311*

France

Paris

7 Boulevard de la Madeleine
75001 Paris
☎ *(1) 42-61-61-30/42-61--60-20; FAX (1) 42-61-06-73*

Italy

Milan

Via Cusani, No. 7
20121 Milan
☎ *(2) 7202-3003/2526; FAX (2) 7202-3123*

Germany

Frankfurt

Moerfelder Landstrasse 45
D-60598 Frankfurt/Main
☎ *(069) 626-051; FAX (069) 627-311*

NUTS AND BOLTS

GETTING THERE

Bahamian taxi

By Air

A number of airlines fly to the Bahamas from the U.S.A., Canada, the Caribbean, Great Britain and Europe. At least 10 airlines now serve New Providence from North America and do so regularly. However, flights from the European continent stop in the United States first. Bahamasair is the national airline and has daily flights from Nassau to the Abacos, Andros, Eleuthera and Exuma. Flights to other Out Islands leave from Nassau several days a week. One of the problems with Bahamasair is that you can't fly from one of its Family Island destinations directly to another Family Island. One has to return to Nassau first, making a simple 200-mile trip in many instances an all-day affair. However, Bahamasair does fly from the U.S. mainland to Nassau and Freeport.

Some small airlines, in addition to those listed below, fly from Florida to Freeport, Abaco, Eleuthera, and Exuma. Round-trip fares between Florida and Nassau on the major airlines typically run $120-$150.

Although there are other points of entry (see Points of Entry in the "Nuts & Bolts" chapter), the busiest points are Nassau and Freeport. Approximate flight times are as follows:

Miami to Nassau
> *30-35 minutes*

Atlanta to Nassau
> *2 hours*

New York to Nassau
> *2-1/2 hours*

Philadelphia to Nassau
> *2-3/4 hours*

Charlotte to Nassau
> *2-1/4 hours*

In addition to Nassau and Freeport, a few major airlines provide a direct link between the United States and a few of the Family Islands. USAir flies to Eleuthera and Great Abaco from Fort Lauderdale. American Eagle flies to Great Abaco, Eleuthera and the Exumas from Miami. Chalk's International Airline flies to Bimini and Paradise Island with its amphibious aircraft from Fort Lauderdale's Jet Center Airport and Watson Island Airport in Miami. And Paradise Island Airlines flies from Miami, Fort Lauderdale and West Palm Beach to the airport on Paradise Island. The following are the airlines which offer service to the Bahamas:

USAir
> ☎ *(800) 428-4322*

American Airlines/American Eagle
> ☎ *(800) 433-7300*

Chalk's International Airline
> ☎ *(800) 4-CHALKS*

Paradise Island Airlines
> ☎ *(800) 432-8807, (305) 895-1223*

Bahamasair
> ☎ *(800) 222-4262*

Air Canada
> ☎ *(800) 776-3000*

Delta Airlines
> ☎ *(800) 221-1212*

Carnival Airlines
> ☎ *(800) 437-2110*

Airline	From	To
Air Jamaica	Jamaica	Nassau
American Eagle	Miami	Marsh Harbour, Treasure Cay, Great Exuma, Eleuthera
Bahamasair	Nassau	Freeport, All Out Islands (except Bimini, Berry Islands, Walker's Cay)
British Airways	London, Bermuda, Jamaica	Nassau, Freeport
Carnival Airlines	New York (JFK) Fort Lauderdale	Nassau
Club Med Charters	Miami	San Salvador
Island Express	Fort Lauderdale	Marsh Harbour, Treasure Cay, Great Exuma
Gulfstream Airlines	Miami, Fort Lauderdale	Marsh Harbour, Treasure Cay, Great Exuma
Major Air	Freeport	Bimini, Walker's Cay
Paradise Island Airlines	Miami, Fort Lauderdale, West Palm Beach	Paradise Island

Commuter, Charter and Hotel Air Services

A number of commuter airlines and charter services fly into the Bahamas from Florida. As well, some of the resorts on the Family Islands offer charter flights to the islands they're located on from Florida (see table). The best part about charter flights are the fares, which are typically 20 percent to 30 percent lower than those offered by the scheduled carriers. The drawback is the schedule, which is set in stone. There's little flexibility for the spontaneous or footloose traveler. You can't change your flight, and if you miss the plane you're SOL. No refunds, no credit—although you may be entitled to a partial refund should you cancel long enough in advance. Make sure you read then entire terms of your booking when you travel via a charter operator. As well, with charters, the required booking dates are often much further in advance than those required on the scheduled carriers—usually as much as 30-60 days before departure. Flights can also be cancelled up to 10 days before departure. So be warned. However, most charter flights are in conjunction with a land/hotel package, and fees are inclusive of other charges, such as accommodations and ground transportation. The following are a few of the reputable charter operators offering service to the Bahamas:

GETTING THERE

Travac
> ☎ *(800) TRAV-800, (212) 563-3303*

Nassau/ Paradise Island Express
> ☎ *(800) 722-4262*

CHARTER AIRLINES

	Phone Number	FAX Number
Air Link	☎ *(800) 882-LINK*	*(407) 283-1303*
Aerojet	☎ *(305) 772-5070*	
Cleareair	☎ *(809) 377-0341*	
Congo Air	☎ *(809) 327-5382*	*(809) 393-5802*
	(to or from Nassau only)	
Miami Air Charter	☎ *(305) 251-9649*	
Island Air Charters	☎ *(800) 444-9904*	
	☎ *(305) 763-8811*	

HOTEL CHARTERS

	Phone Number	FAX Number
Fernandez Bay Village, Cat Island	☎ *(800) 940-1905*	*(305) 792-7860*
	☎ *(305) 792-1905*	
Small Hope Bay Lodge, Andros	☎ *(800) 223-6961*	*(305) 359-8238*
	☎ *(305) 359-8240*	
Stella Maris Resort, Long Island	☎ *(800) 426-0466*	*(305) 359-8238*
	☎ *(305) 359-8236*	
Greenwood Inn, Cat Island	☎ *(809) 342-3053*	

By Cruise Ship

By cruise ship is one of the most popular ways of getting to the Bahamas. At least 10 cruise companies operating 20 ships make regular calls at Nassau and Freeport—as well as at small, privately owned Out Islands that some of the cruise lines utilize as their private playgrounds, such as Coco Cay, Gilligan's Island and Pleasure Isle.

Cruise ships are essentially self-contained resorts, and for some, there's neither reason nor motivation to leave the ship, even when it reaches a new port of call. All of the cruise ships that call on the Bahamas are jammed with amenities. Typically on board are a casino, one or more outdoor pools, fitness center, spa, beauty salon, showroom, library, youth and child programs, myriad bars and lounges, disco(s), Jacuzzis and a veritable shopping mall of shops and stores, to name but just a few. Some of the liners are so well-endowed that ports of call and destinations simply become anticlimactic.

Cruise ship shuttle, Grand Bahama

There are a number of factors that go into the selection of a cruise ship, and it pays heartily to research the vessels thoroughly before choosing a cruise. See "Fielding's CruiseFinder" on page 325 for ratings and details on the major cruise ships that call on the Bahamas.

SPORTS IN THE BAHAMAS

Sunfish on Cable Beach, Nassau

Sailing, Boating and Sportfishing

The Bahamas, at their closest point to the U.S. mainland, are a mere 55 miles off the coast of Miami, so it's no wonder they make a logical and beautiful boating playground for Florida's yachting set. Virtually all of the developed islands sponsor annual regattas, and many of the islands host more than one. In the Bahamas you can retrace the routes of everyone from Christopher Columbus and Blackbeard the Pirate to Ernest Hemingway and Richard Nixon.

Most yachts leaving from south Florida make Bimini the first stop on their Bahamas itinerary. The crossing is relatively easy but should be timed for periods of good weather to avoid the squalls of the deep Gulf Stream. And arriving in the Bahamas should be timed so that it's done in the daylight. None but expert mariners with heavy experience in Bahamian waters should attempt navigating the island's tricky and dangerous shoals and coral reef-laden flats and shallows at night. (It's well-known that Bahamian skippers themselves navigate by the color of the waters. The various hues of Bahamian waters allow the skippers to "read" the depth.).

Fast powerboats can make the crossing to Bimini in about three hours, while slower-moving trawlers and sailboats need perhaps seven or eight hours. Slower vessels should start their journeys during the wee hours of the morning or at about midnight to ensure reaching Bimini during daylight hours.

Regardless of the speed of your craft, if you're departing from south Florida you'll want to steer south of your intended port due to the 2- to 3-knot northward current of the Gulf Stream. If you're headed to Alice Town on North Bimini with a relatively quick boat, you'll want to set a course for 7–8 nautical miles south of Alice Town (if you plan on speeding over in three hours), and 2.5 miles farther south for every hour after that.

For those boaters reluctant to attempt a crossing on their own, the **Bahamas Ministry of Tourism** (☎ *[305] 932-0051)* and the **Bahamas Sports & Aviation Center** (☎ *[305] 932-0051, [800] 327-7678)* sponsor group crossings to both the Biminis and Freeport on Grand Bahama.

The Abacos

The Abacos are known as a yachting paradise and constitute the third-most-frequented destination in the Bahamas. They are also where most boaters make their first port call in the Bahamas if arriving from north of Palm Beach. Walker's Cay is the north-ernmost island in the Abacos (in all of the Bahamas, for that matter). The island has superb marina facilities, complete with at least 75 slips and all the amenities and supplies. Some yachtsmen opt for nearby Grand Cay, but the facilities and services are dismal in contrast, but adequate.

Heading south you'll come across groups of tiny cays. Uninhabited, they make for great snorkeling breaks and a sense that you're at the end of the world (though on weekends in the summer, you may not be alone). Great Sale Cay is where you might find other visitors taking advantage of the terrific natural harbor. Some of the other rocks rising, barely, from the sea are Little Sale Cay, the Double Breasted Cays, Barracuda Rocks and Miss Romer Cay, among others. Farther along are Carter Cay, Umbrella Cay, Moraine Cay, Guineaman Cay, Umbrella Cay and Pensacola and Allen's Cays. You will finally hit some civilization—and fuel—just south of Hawksbill Cay at Fox Town on Little Abaco. Or you can head on to Cooper's Town on Great Abaco for supplies, laundry, limited medical facilities, a telephone and the like.

Green Turtle Cay also has excellent facilities at the Green Turtle Club on the northern end of White Sound. The main settlement on Green Turtle Cay, New Plymouth, also has a broad range of services and supplies.

South of here on the Great Abaco "mainland" is Treasure Cay and the Treasure Cay Hotel Resort & Marina, a megaresort (by Family Island standards) with the amenities for boaters, including a full-service marina.

South of here and back off the mainland is Man-O-War Cay with its New England ambience. There's a 60-slip marina here with full services. On Elbow Cay, there is a 20-slip marina at Hope Town, a small settlement that offers an array of goods and services. There are restaurants and hotels here, as well.

Marsh Harbour, on Great Abaco, is the largest town in the Abacos and comes with a number of marinas. There are 60 slips at the Marsh Harbour Marina and 75 at the Conch Inn Marina in town. The Boat Harbour Marina has a whopping 150-slip, state-of-the-art operation.

The Biminis

The Biminis are where most folks head after putting out to sea for the Bahamas. Ernest Hemingway heard about this little place while living in Key West in 1934 and set out for the island aboard his boat, the *Pilar*, the following year. The rest is history—or what was rewritten of it.

Whereas the large cruise ships enroute to Nassau rely on the beacons of Great Stirrup Cay at the far north of the Berry Islands and Great Isaac Island at the top of the Great Bahama Bank for navigation, small craft skippers head for Nassau by cutting the bank from Gun and Cat Cays just south of Bimini to Chub Cay in the far south of the Berries.

Bimini plays host to a slew of annual fishing events, including the Hemingway Billfish Tournament, the party-time Native Fishing Tournament and the Bacardi Rum Billfish Tournament.

The Biminis are a magnet for anglers and boating enthusiasts worldwide and, as such, you can expect some world-class boating facilities and services. The Bimini Big Game Fishing Club is the most popular spot. It also serves as host for the island's biggest fishing tournaments. Facilities include a 100-slip, full-service marina with all the amenities. The next-most-popular yachters' hangout is Bimini's Blue Water Marina with its 32 modern slips. The Blue Water is the common host of the Hemingway tournament. Brown's Hotel & Marina has 22 modern slips and Weech's Dock has 15 slips. The best deep-sea fishing in the world can be found here as well as some of the best bonefishing in the Bahamas on the flats.

The Berry Islands

The Berry Islands offer boaters the clearest waters in the Bahamas, not to mention spectacular bonefishing and deep sea fishing. As many of the islands are privately owned, there are few boating facilities catering to the average Joe. There are essentially two, at each tip of the island chain.

In the north, there is an 80-slip marina at Great Harbour Cay. It's a full-service resort and marine facility that can accommodate vessels up to 150 feet long. Chub Cay, at the foot of the chain, also features a resort and 90-slip marina with all the amenities.

New Providence

The Tongue of the Ocean divides the Berry Islands from Nassau and some of the great deep-sea fishing in the world is found in this passage, which plunges to more than a mile deep.

Nassau Harbour is open at both ends, but be careful of which side you enter if you're headed for a marina east of the Paradise Island Bridge and you're on a sailboat taller than 70 feet. You'll have to come in from the east side. New Providence's full-service marinas include **Hurricane Hole Marina** (☎ *326-5441)* and **East Bay Yacht Basin** (☎ *326-3754)* west of the Paradise Island Bridge, and **Nassau Harbour Club, Nassau Yacht Haven** (☎ *393-8173)*, Brown's Boat Yard and Bayshore Marina on the Nassau side of the bridge. At the Nassau harbor's eastern entrance are the Royal Nassau Sailing Club and the Nassau Yacht Club. On the western end of New Providence is located a good marina at Lyford Cay.

Nassau has a deep harbor to accommodate the cruise ships; nearly a dozen can berth here at one time, and it's not uncommon to see half that many at any given daylight moment.

Grand Bahama

The four major marinas on Grand Bahama are the 77-slip Xanadu Marina and Beach Resort in Freeport, the 66-slip Running Mon Marina to the east, the 150-slip Lucayan Marina inside Bell Channel and the 50-slip Port Lucaya Marina at Port Lucaya. The Running Mon Marina is the base for the island's deep-sea fishing fleet. It's also one of the better places for chartering game fishing boats. Deep Water Cay Club has but a few slips on the eastern end of the island.

If you've got a powerboat, check out the man-made Grand Lucayan Waterway, which cuts through the island to the north side at Dover Sound.

The Exumas

Game fishermen flock to the Exuma Sound for deep-sea fishing and to the west coast for bonefishing the flats. Most recreational boaters head for the protected Exuma Cays Land and Sea Park (which stretches south from Wax Cay to Conch Cay). The park is more than 20 miles long (177 square miles) and is northwest of Staniel Cay. It makes for superb bird-watching, not to mention the magnificent sea gardens and coral reefs.

Cruising along the western rim of Exuma Sound is considered by most boaters the best in the Bahamas. On Leaf Cay can be found iguanas. Great beaches are found on the west side of Hawksbill Cay. The hutia, the only indigenous mammal in the Bahamas, can be found on Little Wax Cay. But don't try to catch one of these furry, bunny-sized creatures. They only come out at night—and it's illegal to do it, anyhow.

George Town transforms from a sleepy little backwater into the French Quarter of New Orleans each April when it hosts the Out Islands Regatta, perhaps the most popular yachting spectacle of the year in the Bahamas. The streets fill with revelers and Junkanoo parades, and everyone pretty much gets whipped on rum concoctions as contestants battle it out on the low seas in locally made wooden sailing vessels. The hotels are "packed" during this three-day festival, which also features arts & crafts exhibitions. There is also the Annual New Year's Day Cruising Regatta at the Staniel Cay Yacht Club in January and the two Bonefish Bonanza Tournaments held in October and November off George Town. Also at Staniel Cay is an annual bonefishing festival on July 10.

In George Town, facilities include **Club Peace & Plenty** (☎ *[809] 336-2552*) and **Exuma Fantasea** (☎ *[809] 336-3483*) for bonefishing, **Exuma Docking Services** (☎ *[809] 336-2578*) and **Sampson Cay Colony** (☎ *[809] 325-8864*). On Staniel Cay, facilities include the **Staniel Cay Yacht Club** *(☎ [809] 355-2024)* and **Happy People Marina** *(☎ [809] 355-2008)*.

Scuba Diving

Wall dive, Nassau

The Bahamas encompasses 700 islands and more than 2050 cays (pronounced "keys"), small islets that poke from the azure sea, that start 70 miles off the Palm Beaches in Florida and extend some 750 miles southward. The Tropic of Cancer cuts through the archipelago at Long Island in the southern Bahamas, which technically means that some of the islands are subtropical and others tropical. But in reality, all of the islands enjoy a year-round balmy climate due to the warming factors of the Gulf Stream. Typical average temperatures in the chain only vary by about 10°F from summer to winter. Usual winter highs are about 78°F, with nighttime lows at about 70°F. In the summer, it heats up to the mid to upper 80s and drops to the mid 70s at night.

Winter is considered high season in the Bahamas, but serious divers will be more attracted by the conditions found during the summer months. During the summer, the water temperatures rise to the mid-80s, making thermal suits unnecessary. The winds die down in the summer, as well, making for typically glass-smooth surface conditions that rarely exceed a light chop. These conditions help to enhance visibility, which improves to a remarkable 150-200 feet on most days during the low season. June through September bring the best visibility conditions. Although these crystal-clear conditions occur during the winter months, clear days are less frequent than during the winter. During the winter, divers will be more comfortable in a 2mm suit.

Bahamas Dive Operators and Live-Aboards

Bahamas Diving Association

> P.O. Box 21707
> Fort Lauderdale, FL 33335-1707
> ☎ (800) 866-DIVE; (305) 932-0051

Abaco

Brendal's Dive Shop

> ☎ (800) 780-9941

Dive Abaco

> P.O. Box 20555
> Marsh Harbour
> Abaco
> ☎ (800) 247-5338, (809) 367-2787
> FAX (809) 367-4004

Great Abaco Beach Undersea Adventures

> ☎ (800) 327-8150

Spanish Cay Diving

> ☎ (809) 365-0083

Spanish Cay Watersports

> P.O. Box 882
> Cooperstown, Abaco
> ☎ (809) 365-0083
> FAX (809) 365-0466

Walker's Cay Undersea Adventures

> U.S. Office
> P.O. Box 21766
> Fort Lauderdale, FL 33335-1766
> ☎ (800) 327-8150, (954) 462-3400
> FAX (954) 462-4100
> Bahamas ☎ (809) 352-5252
> Bahamas FAX (809) 352-3301

Andros

Small Hope Bay Lodge

> c/o P.O. Box N-1131
> Nassau
> ☎ (809) 368-2013/4
> FAX (809) 368-2015
> U.S. Office
> P.O. Box 21667

Fielding THE BAHAMAS

WRECK DIVES

The Bahamas has always had a large amount of sea traffic. Some ships didn't fare so well in the shallow water. Today the islands offer numerous wreck dive opportunities.

Grand
Island

● Miami Beach   N. Bimini

FLORIDA

S. Bimini ❶

❶ The Sopona, 20 feet

The Sopona was a 350-foot freighter broken in two pieces during a hurricane in 1926. The boat rests in only 20 feet of water, offering an excellent dive opportunity for snorkelers and divers alike. The wreck plays host to a variety of sea life.

❷ The Cienfuegos, 25 feet

This passenger liner, 292 feet in length, ran into a shallow coral reef in 1985. Thanks to a local seaman, the entire crew and passengers were ferried safely to shore. Off the north coast of Eleuthera, the wreck lies in 20 to 35 feet of water. The steam-powered engine and boilers (pictured) are still recognizable.

❸ Wreck on the Wall, 40 feet

The wreck is a confiscated, 40 foot drug-running trawler. The boat was purchased from the government and purposefully sunk to provide a good dive area. The boat lies on a coral wall that begins at a 40 foot depth and descends more than 1000 feet down.

CUBA

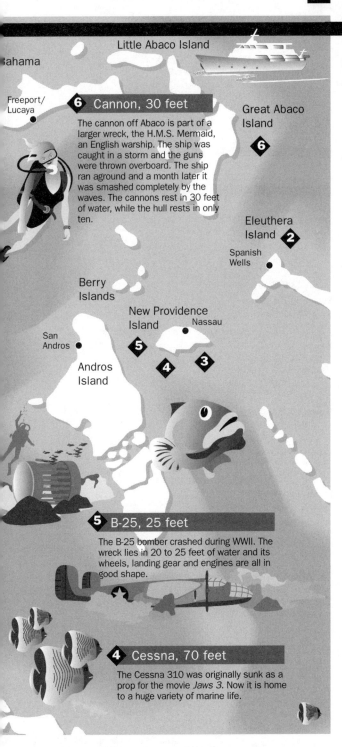

Little Abaco Island

ahama

Freeport/
Lucaya

6 Cannon, 30 feet

The cannon off Abaco is part of a
larger wreck, the H.M.S. Mermaid,
an English warship. The ship was
caught in a storm and the guns
were thrown overboard. The ship
ran aground and a month later it
was smashed completely by the
waves. The cannons rest in 30 feet
of water, while the hull rests in only
ten.

Great Abaco
Island

6

Eleuthera
Island **2**

Spanish
Wells

Berry
Islands

New Providence
Island   Nassau

San
Andros   **5**

Andros
Island   **4**   **3**

5 B-25, 25 feet

The B-25 bomber crashed during WWII. The
wreck lies in 20 to 25 feet of water and its
wheels, landing gear and engines are all in
good shape.

4 Cessna, 70 feet

The Cessna 310 was originally sunk as a
prop for the movie *Jaws 3*. Now it is home
to a huge variety of marine life.

Fort Lauderdale, FL 33335-1667
☎ *(800) 223-6961*

Andros Undersea Adventures

Andros Beach Hotel
Nicholl's Town, North Andros
☎ *(809) 329-2582*
or P.O. Box 21766
Fort Lauderdale, FL 33335
☎ *(305) 462-3400, (800) 327-8150*

Bimini

Bimini Undersea Adventures

P.O. Box 693515
Miami, FL 33269
☎ *(800) 348-4644, (305) 653-5572*
FAX (305) 652-9148

Cat Island

Cat Island Dive Center

Hotel Greenwood Inn
Port Howe, Cat Island
☎ *(809) 342-3053, (800) 661-3483*
FAX (809) 342-3053

Fernandez Bay Village

☎ *(800) 940-1905*

Eleuthera/Harbour Island

Romora Bay Club

P.O. Box EL27146
Harbour Island, Eleuthera
☎ *(809) 333-2323/5, (800) 327-8286*
FAX (809) 333-2500

Valentine's Dive Center

P.O. Box 1
Harbour Island, Eleuthera
☎ *(800) 383-6480, (809) 333-2309, (502) 897-6481*
FAX (502) 897-6486

Exumas

Exuma Fantasea

P.O. Box 29261
George Town, Exuma
☎ *(800)760-0700, (809) 336-3483*
FAX (809) 336-3483

Grand Bahama/Freeport

The Underwater Explorers Society (UNEXCO)

P.O. Box F-2433
Freeport, Grand Bahama
☎ *(800) 992-DIVE, (809) 373-1244*
FAX (809) 373-8956
U.S. Office
P.O. Box 22878
Fort Lauderdale, FL 33335-5608
☎ *(800) 992-DIVE, (954) 351-9889*
FAX (954) 351-9740

Xanadu Undersea Adventures

P.O. Box F-42846
Freeport, Grand Bahama

☎ *(800) 327-8150, (809) 352-5856*
FAX (809) 352-4731
U.S. Office
P.O. Box 21766
Fort Lauderdale, FL 33335
☎ *(800) 327-8150, (954) 462-3400*
FAX (954) 462-4100

Long Island

Stella Maris Resort

P.O. Box LI30105
Stella Maris, Long Island
☎ *(800) 426-0466, (809) 336-2106, (809) 338-2051*
FAX (809) 338-2052
U.S. Office
1100 Lee Wagener Blvd., Ste. 319
Fort Lauderdale, FL 33315
☎ *(800) 426-0466, (954) 359-8236*
FAX (954) 359-8238

New Providence/Nassau

Bahama Divers

P.O. Box 5004
Nassau
☎ *(800) 398- DIVE, (809) 393-6054, (809) 393-5644*
FAX (809) 393-6078
U.S. Office
P.O. Box 21584
Fort Lauderdale, FL 33335
☎ *(800) 398-DIVE, (954) 351-9740*

Custom Aquatics

☎ *(809) 362-1492*

Dive Dive Dive

P.O. Box N-8050
Nassau
(809) 362-1143, 362-1401
FAX (809) 362-1994
U.S. Office
1323 SE 17th Street, Ste. 519
Fort Lauderdale, FL 33316
☎ *(800) 368-3483*
FAX (954) 943-5002

Diver's Haven

P.O. Box N-1658
Nassau
☎ *(809) 393-0869, (800) 780-7640*
FAX (809) 393-3695

Nassau Scuba Centre

Coral Harbour
P.O. Box CB11863
Nassau
☎ *(800) 327-8150, (809) 362-1964*
FAX (809) 362-1198
U.S. Office
P.O. Box 21766
Fort Lauderdale, FL 33335
☎ *(800) 327-8150, (954) 462-3400*
FAX (954) 462-4100

Stuart Cove's Dive South Ocean

P.O. Box CB-11697
Nassau
☎ *(809) 362-5227, 362-4171*
FAX (809) 362-5227
U.S. Office
1405 SE 17th Street
Fort Lauderdale, FL 33316
☎ *(800) 879-9832, (954) 524-5755*
FAX (954) 524-5925

Sun Divers

P.O. Box N-10728
Nassau
☎ *(800) 298-4786, (809) 325-8927*

Sunskiff Divers

P.O. Box N-142
Nassau
☎ *(800) 331-5884, (809) 361-4075*
FAX (809) 362-1979

San Salvador

Riding Rock Inn

Cockburn Town
San Salvador
☎ *(809) 331-2631*
U.S. Office
1170 Lee Wagener Boulevard, Suite 103
Fort Lauderdale, FL 33315
☎ *(800) 272-1492, (954) 359-8353*
FAX (954) 359-8254

Live-Aboard Dive Boats

Blackbeard's Cruises

Sea Explorer, 65'
Morning Star, 65'
Pirate's Lady, 65'
P.O. Box 661091
Miami Springs, FL 33266-1091
☎ *(800) 327-9600, (305) 888-1226*
FAX (305) 384-4214

Bottom Time Adventures

Bottom Time II, 80'
P.O. Box 11919
Fort Lauderdale, FL 33339-1919
☎ *(800) 234-8464, (954) 921-7798, (954) 920-5578*
Also at:
Dream Too, 60'
P.O. Box 033271
Indiatlantic, FL 32903
(407) 723-9312

Nekton Diving Cruises

Nekton Pilot, 78'
520 SE 32nd Drive
Fort Lauderdale, FL 33316
☎ *(800) 899-6753, (954) 463-9324*
FAX (954) 463-8938

Out Island Oceanics

Sea Dragon, 65'

> 717 SW Coconut Drive
> Fort Lauderdale, FL 33315
> ☎ & FAX (954) 522-0161

Out Island Voyages
> P.O. Box N7775
> Nassau, Bahamas
> ☎ (800) 241-4591, (809) 394-0951
> FAX (809) 394-0948

Sea Dragon
> ☎ (305) 522-0161

Sea Fever Diving Cruises
> Sea Fever, 90'
> P.O. Box 39-8276
> Miami Beach, FL 33139-0276
> ☎ (800) 443-3837, (305) 531-DIVE
> FAX (305) 531-3127

The Dream Team
> ☎ (800) 741-5335

Bahamas Shark Dive Operators

Nassau/New Providence
Shark Wall/Arena

Dive Dive Dive
> ☎ (800) 368-3483

Nassau Scuba Centre
> ☎ (800) 327-8150

Stuart Cove's Dive South Ocean
> ☎ (800) 879-9832

Runway/Bahama Mama

Dive Dive Dive
> ☎ (800) 368-3483

Nassau Scuba Centre
> ☎ (800) 327-8150

Stuart Cove's Dive South Ocean
> ☎ (800) 879-9832

Shark Buoy

Stuart Cove's Dive South Ocean
> ☎ (800) 879-9832

Paradise Island
Lost Blue Hole

Bahama Divers
> ☎ (800) 398-DIVE

Diver's Haven
> ☎ (809) 393-0869

Nassau Scuba Centre
> ☎ (800) 327-8150

Grand Bahama/Freeport
Shark Junction

UNEXSO
> ☎ (800) 992-DIVE

Shark Alley

Xanadu Undersea Adventures
☎ *(800) 327-8150*

Abacos/Walker's Cay
Shark Rodeo

Walker's Cay Undersea Adventures
☎ *(800) 327-8150*

Ocean Cay
Shark Reef

Blackbeard's Cruises
☎ *(800) 327-9600*

Nekton Diving Cruises
☎ *(800) 899-6753*

Sea Fever Diving Cruises
☎ *(800) 443-3837*

San Salvador
Schooling Scalloped Hammerheads

Riding Rock Inn
☎ *(800) 272-1492*

Long Island
Shark Reef

Stella Maris Inn
☎ *(800) 426-0466*

Exuma Cays
Danger Reef

Blackbeard's Cruises
☎ *(800) 327-9600*

Bottom Time Adventures
☎ *(800) 234-8464*

Sea Dragon
☎ *(305) 522-0161*

Sea Fever Diving Cruises
☎ *(800) 443-3837*

Cay Sal Bank
Blue Shark Hole

Blackbeard's Cruises
☎ *(800) 327-9600*

Bottom Time Adventures
☎ *(800) 234-8464*

Nekton Diving Cruises
☎ *(800) 899-6753*

Sea Fever Diving Cruises
☎ *(800) 443-3837*

Where to Get Wet

Diving throughout the Bahamas offers an array of attractions, from man-made subaquatic wonders such as sunken ships to reefs teeming with tame underwater creatures. Each island offers its own delights, and some of the larger islands feature a diversity of environments. Described below are some of the highlights of the individual islands of the Bahamas.

The Abacos

The Abacos are great for wreck dives and blue holes.

The Abacos, with a population of about 7300 people, are located in the far northeast of the Bahama chain, and stretch some 130 miles, from Walker's Cay off the Palm Beach coast through the Little Bahamas Bank to Marsh Harbour, the country's third largest "city." In all, The Abacos cover nearly 650 square miles and feature major dive centers at Great Abaco, Spanish Cay, Green Turtle Cay and Walker's Cay. The Abacos make for a great getaway because most of its islets are quite small, and sparsely populated, allowing the subaquatic environments to remain pristine. Visibility can be particularly keen here as the boomerang-shaped sub-chain lies close to the Gulf Stream. This is also a great area for **wreck diving** and **blue holes**.

Certainly the best shark diving in The Abacos is found off Walker's Cay at an area known as **Shark Rodeo**. Here, Hammerheads, Bull, Nurse, Caribbean Reef and Blacktip sharks have taken a liking (most would call it a habit) to the frozen chum balls concocted by the local divemasters. Dozens (sometimes more than a hundred) of sharks feed frenziedly on the feast, exciting even divers who've "been there, done that." Off Walker's Cay can also be found **Pirate's Cathedral**, marvelous underwater caverns teeming with glass minnows, and **White Hole**, with its myriad coneys and groupers. **Spanish Cay** features a recently opened resort, giving divers access to numerous shallow reefs.

At **Green Turtle Cay**, not to be missed are the wrecks *Viceroy*, an early 20th-century steamship, and the *San Jacinto*, a Civil War gunboat that sank in 40 feet of water in 1865. The **Catacombs** are a spectacular set of ledges and caverns, while **The Pillars** and **Tarpon Reef** offer divers splendid views of feeding coral and schools of Tarpon.

However, most divers in The Abacos flock to **Marsh Harbour**, where the **Fowl Cay Land and Sea Preserve** is located. Because the preserve is protected, magnificent shallow reefs are the home to dozens of species of essentially tame sealife. Here it's possible kiss barracudas and bump-and-grind with a school of blue sharks while shooting your Nikon point-blank at a placid grouper tame enough to make Garfield look neurotic. Notable here are the **Towers**, a pair of coral towers that rise magnificently from 70 feet to only a few feet from the surface. Huge schools of silversides move like giant drapes in a breeze at **Maxi Cave Bay**, and at Maurice Bay can be seen an abundance of margate snapper, grouper, nurse sharks, turtles and even spotted eagle rays. And be sure to check out the Cathedral, a large cave at about 30 feet known for dazzling shafts of sunlight.

Andros

Although Andros is the largest island in the Bahamas, it's home to only 8000 people. The diving here is spectacular, primarily for the area's blue holes, reefs and shipwrecks. At 104 miles long and 40 miles wide, Andros offers an array of attractions, including a massive 120-mile-long barrier reef at the **Tongue of the Ocean** that plunges to depths greater than 6000 feet. Barracuda, grouper and giant sea turtles abound. Visibility is often 100 feet or more but occasionally drops to 40 feet. **Over the Wall** is a sheer drop from 80 feet.

On the north end of the island, perhaps the biggest attraction is the wreck of the 345-foot British tanker the *Potomac*, which sank in 1929. The *Barge* is also popular. It was sunk intentionally in 70 feet of water in the mid-1960s and makes for a superb artificial reef teeming with sealife.

Other attractions off Andros include the elkhorn corals and majestic sea fans of **The Garden** and black coral formations that compose the **Black Forest**.

Bimini

Bimini actually has two islands: North Bimini and South Bimini. Although just a sliver of sand (no more than about 70 yards at its widest point), the north is far more developed and home to **Alice Town**, the largest town on Bimini. Bimini's 1600 residents are almost entirely found on North Bimini.

Wrecks and superb visibility are two of Bimini's hallmarks. The **Bimini Barge** rests in about 90 feet of water. At 150 feet long, it makes for a large domicile to moray eels, giant groupers and horse-eye jacks. Two 18th-century anchors can be found close to the capsized *Bimini Trader*. The *Sapona* can be found at only 15 feet deep. In its holds can be found gray angelfish, grunts and squirrelfish.

Cat Island

Fifty-mile-long Cat Island, in the southern Bahamas, is remote and relatively inaccessible but has witnessed something of a surge in visitors in recent years as divers are starting to discover its underwater treasures and on-land lack of formalities. Here is found a get-away-from-it-all milieu that seems to mock Nassau's crumpet-and-tea set with its bare-bunned primitivism. Oh, yeah, there's also some pretty good diving, too—such as vertical cliffs, pristine corals and magnificent tunnels.

Shrouds of fish can be seen at **White Hole Reef**. Sharks abound at Tartar Bank, where a spur-and-groove coral plateau strides an 8000-foot-tall pinnacle. A giant wall starts at 80 feet at **Big Winding Bay**, featuring massive black coral trees, tube sponges and beautiful gorgonians. Swim-through tunnels can be found at **Tiger Shark Spot** and fields of acropora coral can be viewed only a few feet from the surface at **Elkhorn Gardens**.

Crooked Island

Known more for its bonefishing than its diving, Crooked Island nonetheless features more than 60 miles of wall diving, with such sites as **French Wells** (home to a giant Jewfish), **Black Coral Forest** (where the wall is covered with black coral) and **Haitian 44**, a series of six coral pinnacles that ascend about 30 feet from the bottom.

Eleuthera

Eight thousand people call Eleuthera home, making it the second-most-populated Out Island. The island is 100 miles long but only a couple of miles wide at its chunkiest. The three principal staging areas for discovering the island's surrounding depths are **Rock Sound** in the south, **Harbour Island** and **Spanish Wells** in the north.

Arguably the best dive off Eleuthera is at **Current Cut**, where you'll be blissfully swept away in the currents caused by the funneling tidal flows between two islands. The surge is so great, you'll be accompanied by a wave of tumbling fish, who are along for the ride, as well, as if they had queued in line for the adventure.

North of Spanish Wells is the site of a number of wrecks, the victims of the **Devil's Backbone**. The most intriguing is the *Train Wreck*, a Civil War-era barge that sank here carrying a steam locomotive.

Good news for those headed to Current Cut and Train Wreck is that most visiting divers to Eleuthera head to the reef off the eastern shore near Harbour Island. Groupers and jacks, as well a huge field of high coral ridges, can be found at the **Plateau**. **Grouper Hole** is the place to be on the first full moon of January, when mass amounts of groupers arrive here to spawn. If spotting grunts and barracudas is the order of the day, head to **The Arch**, a massive underwater grotto that slopes from 65 feet to more than 100 feet beneath the surface.

The Exumas

The Exumas have some 365 islands and cays that start about 35 miles southeast of New Providence and extend nearly 100 miles into the sea. The vast majority of the islands are uninhabited. Little Exuma and Great Exuma are the two population centers.

The Exumas consist of 365 islands and cays.

Beautiful, pristine diving can be found at **The Exuma Cays Land and Sea Park**. The underwater park covers 177 square miles and has been protected from fishing, coral collecting and trapping since 1958.

The two best dives in the Exumas are perhaps the **Coral Cut**, with its sensational mile-long underwater tidal ride, and the **Shark Encounter** off Danger Cay. Here can be found a slew of both nurse sharks and Caribbean reef sharks. Close to Great Exuma's George Town can be found a couple of nice ocean blue holes, **Crab Cay Crevasse**, which opens at 20 feet, and the spectacular **Angelfish Blue Hole**. It starts at 30 feet and dips to below 90 feet. It then becomes an extensive cave network. Also close by is **The Pagoda**. No, it's not an ancient Buddhist temple caught in the wrong oceanic stream, but is named after a cathedral-like grotto covered by multiple corals. Also accessible from George Town, are the spur and groove coral formations and the Pillar Coral colonies of **Dog and Puppy Reef**.

Also, near Highbourne Cay, check out the wreck of the *Edwin Williams*, a Bahamian naval vessel that was sunk intentionally in 55 feet of water. At **Blacktip Wall** are found blacktip sharks and large eagle rays lurking in the wall's spacious caves. **Hammerhead Gulch** is popular for its gray angelfish.

Long Island

Long Island, at 90 miles long and four miles wide, is similar to Eleuthera, but not as populated. In fact, virtually all who dive here do it through the Stella Maris megaresort which sits on 3000 acres and even has its own 4050-foot runway. The resort is best known for introducing the Bahamas' first shark dive in 1973. The best beaches are found in the north on and near **Cape Santa Maria**.

Of course, most divers here visit **Shark Reef**, where the shark dive was developed. Divemasters today continue the practice of feeding Caribbean reef sharks into a frenzy. At **Barracuda Reefs**, the groupers outnumber the barracudas, as they do at Grouper Valley. Stella Maris also offers day and overnight trips to **Conception Island**, which is known for its wrecks. One of the better dives off Long Island is the wreck of the *Comberbach*, a 125-foot freighter that stands upright at 100 feet deep.

San Salvador

If you're looking for shallow reefs, San Salvador will be a disappointment, as the island is the summit of a 13,000-foot underwater peak. But the visibility and wall diving are spectacular. Visibility is regularly at 200 feet. **French Bay** is the best place to head for clarity. **Telephone Pole** offers tame Nassau Groupers along a wall that begins in 35 feet of water. **Snapshot Reef** and **Macro Mania** are the only shallow reefs of note, and the *Frascate* makes for about the only wreck diving. The *Frascate* was a 280-foot steamship that sank in1902. At only 20 feet deep, it offers a lot of bottom time.

Off French Bay, good wall dives are at Sandy Point, Double Caves, Devil's Claw, Dr. John and La Crevice. Here you'll see groupers, barracudas, eagle rays, scalloped hammerheads and horse-eye jacks, as well as beautiful formations of black corals, antler, rope and azure vase sponges.

Grand Bahama

Conceived as home to a deepwater port by Wallace Groves, Grand Bahama is only 55 miles off Florida's Palm Beach coast. **Freeport** is the Bahamas second-largest city and makes for a great long-weekend base for local diving, although it would be tough to call Grand Bahama remote and isolated.

But because more than a million tourists get out to Grand Bahama, its dive spots have been well-charted and oft-visited. Local short trips from Freeport include stops at **Ben's Cave**, a beautiful cavern part of the Lucayan Caverns, and at **Gold Rock**, **Pygmy Caves**, **Silverpoint Reef** and **Blair House** for magnificent vistas of spur and groove coral beds. **Theo's Wreck** makes for the best wreck diving off Freeport and offers superb photo ops. The 230-foot freighter, resting on its port side and teeming with eagle rays, sea turtles, horse-eye jacks and morays, was intentionally sunk in 1982. Other popular underwater tourist attractions at Freeport include the **Dolphin Experience**, where Atlantic bottlenose dolphins have been trained to follow a boat in 45 feet of water from Sanctuary Bay to an offshore reef to the pleasure of accompanying divers, and **Shark Alley**, a very professional copycat of the Stella Maris shark feed show on Long Island. This one is run by UNEXSO, perhaps the best dive outfit in the Bahamas.

Away from the hustle-and-bustle and the camcorders is the West End of Grand Bahama, where live-aboards have ingress to the **Mount Olympus** wall dive, the spotted dolphins of **White Sand Ridge** and the **Sugar Wreck**.

New Providence

New Providence is home to the Bahamas' capital, Nassau, known equally for its banks—as in financial institutions—as for its banks of the ocean variety. While it's impossible to escape the tourist mob scene entirely, (fully 2 million swarm this small island annually) the fact that Nassau has been the long-running commercial hub of the islands means that a lot of ships have gone down off its shores—and a lot of wet sailors have been made shark bait. The wrecks are still around to behold, and the sharks have seemingly massed here, waiting for more. The best places to catch the shark shows are at **Shark Runway**, **Shark Wall** and **Shark Arena**. At these sites, divers are treated to a spectacle as the divemaster chums the water, attracting dozens of Caribbean reef sharks. Silky Sharks can be found in ample numbers at **Shark Buoy**.

For wrecks, the *Bahama Mama* is an icon, but take a number. Also popular are the ships sunk as dive attractions. The *Sea Viking* is a 95-foot, steel-hulled fishing vessel only recently sunk. There's also the 100-foot *Tears of Allah* and the 150-foot *Willaurie*. The **Graveyard** offers four wrecks of close proximity sunk intentionally. Some of the older wrecks, however, are barely discernible as ships. The *Mahoney* was a 212-foot steamship that sunk in 1929. Today, the wreck is pretty broken up.

The waters off New Providence have a little of something for every diver. Good wall dives can be had at the Tongue of the Ocean at such places as **Tunnel Wall** and **Razorback**. Shallow reefs are in abundance. A stunning one is **Goulding Cay**, with its Elkhorn Coral stretching nearly to the surface from 25 feet. **Southwest Reef** features magnificent staghorn, elkhorn, fire and star coral formations. **Pumpkin Patch** has an abundance of sealife.

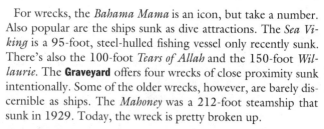

Insider Tip: Live-Aboards

The advantage of live-aboards over dive resorts is that you can hit a far greater number of dive sites and get in more dives during the course of the day. Live-aboards depart from Miami, Fort Lauderdale and West Palm Beach in Florida, and from Nassau and Freeport in the Bahamas. We provide a listing in this chapter.

Live-aboards offer the opportunity to take in a broad selection of dive attractions. Typical itineraries include wrecks such as the Hesperis and the Sugar Wreck along with blue hole, wall and shark dives at Cay Sal.

Snorkeling

Snorkelers at Bimini Beach

One needn't be a scuba diver to enjoy the underwater world of delights the Bahamas has to offer. The only requirements are mask, fins, snorkel and a sense of curiosity to open the doors of the gin-clear depths of Bahamian islands.

Virtually all of the resorts in the Bahamas offer snorkeling activities directly or indirectly. Or you can find your own private beach and simply head out on your own. Snorkeling doesn't require any formal training and is best enjoyed over shallow reefs. Dive operators usually offer snorkeling trips in addition or in conjunction with their daily dive excursions. And, obviously, the best snorkeling to be found in the Bahamas is usually where the best diving is to be found. That's the advantage of hooking up with a dive boat snorkeling trip.

For the Bahamas, the escorted snorkeling trips are a bargain. Divemasters, at least the good ones, possess a well of knowledge about the underwater environments you'll be visiting as well as their inhabitants. A snorkeling trip with these folks is as much an education as it is a glimpse into the brilliantly-hued world beneath. The half-day trips, running anywhere from $12 to $25, are well worth the expense, if for the ecological education alone.

There are, of course, superb snorkeling sites throughout the Bahamas, and it's difficult to rate the spots simply because there are so many of them. Your resort or hotel will be well-versed in the local sites, and even the smallest caravansaries on the out islands will invariable be able to supply snorkeling gear. A couple of personal recommendations for organized snorkeling trips in the Family Islands are:

Romora Bay Club Dive Shop

> *Box 146*
> *Harbour Island, Eleuthera*
> ☎ *(809) 333-2325, (305) 427-4830, (800) 327-8286*
> *FAX (809) 333-2500*

Instructor and divemaster Jeff Fox is an amiable and fun-loving American who's all business when it comes to diving and snorkeling, and one of the most ecologically knowledgeable underwater sports organizers in the Bahamas. He's been here 15 years, and his scuba and snorkeling trips show it. He'll explain exactly what you're seeing, why you're seeing it and its relationship with the overall environment. Plus, he's doing it in some of the best snorkeling and scuba diving waters in the Bahamas.

Underwater Explorers Society (UNEXSO)

> *Port Lucaya, opposite Lucayan Beach Casino*
> *Freeport/Lucaya, Grand Bahama*
> ☎ *(809) 373-1244, (800) 992-3483*

One of the class acts of the Bahamas, UNEXSO has been around nearly 30 years and is perhaps the biggest dive/snorkel operator in the islands. Known mainly for its dive facilities, it also runs superb snorkeling trips to a gorgeous shallow reef for $18 per person. Instructions cost $10 for 30 minutes. The facility has at least a dozen boats. UNEXSO also advises the island's other snorkel and dive operators on the best sites to be found around the island. Thoroughly recommended. There are also certainly other snorkeling trips offered on Grand Bahama, and you can pick up snorkeling gear just about anywhere. And there are also a number of glass-bottom boats for the more wary or less physically active.

Small Hope Bay Lodge

> *Fresh Creek/Andros Town*

Andros
☎ *(809) 368-2014, (800) 223-6961*
Another recommendation for this highly professional dive and snorkeling operation on Andros, which features snorkeling trips out to the world's third-longest barrier reef, just a short distance from the lodge. Regrettably, owner and Bahamas diving pioneer Dick Birch passed away during the summer of 1996. But as he would have said, the show must go on. And what a show it is. Visibility is almost always more than 100 feet and frequently gets up to 150-200 feet. Half-day snorkeling excursions to the reef cost $10.

In addition to the myriad sites for snorkeling found in the out islands, New Providence also has its share of fantastic snorkeling locations. And all the resorts on the island (as well as Paradise Island) offer snorkeling equipment and most a powerboat ride out to the sites, which include the Goulding Reef Cays, the Rose Island Reefs (for great views of underwater wrecks), Booby Rock Channel and Gambier Deep Reef. The best outfits on New Providence are:

Bahama Divers
P.O. Box 5004
Nassau
☎ *(800) 398- DIVE, (809) 393-6054, (809) 393-5644*
FAX (809) 393-6078
U.S. Office
P.O. Box 21584
Fort Lauderdale, FL 33335
☎ *(800) 398-DIVE, (954) 351-9740*
Half-day snorkeling trips to offshore reefs cost $20.

Stuart Cove's Dive South Ocean
P.O. Box CB-11697
Nassau
☎ *(809) 362-5227, 362-4171*
FAX (809) 362-5227
U.S. Office
1405 SE 17th Street
Fort Lauderdale, FL 33316
☎ *(800) 879-9832, (954) 524-5755*
FAX (954) 524-5925
Based in the southwest of New Providence, this is considered the best dive operation on the island by the locals, though its competition might dispute this. Regardless, excellent half-day snorkeling trips are offered for $25. The advantage of this firm is its south shore location; the best snorkeling sites off the island are only a few minutes away.

Of course, the other dive shops on the island offer snorkeling trips as well, with similar prices for half-day, boat-escorted trips. See the "Scuba Diving" section of this chapter for their names and addresses.

And for those who want to experience the wonders of the depths, but who just plain don't like to get their hair wet, there's an interesting experience offered in Nassau—where customers can walk on the ocean floor in a protective helmet. Contact:

Hartley's Undersea Walk

East Bay Street
☎ *(809) 393-8234*

Cruise along the ocean floor donning a special protective helmet. This is a 3.5-hour cruise aboard the Pied Piper from Nassau Harbour. You'll actually be submerged for about 20 minutes as you gaze at clouds of tropical fish and coral reef formations. No scuba diving certification is required and entire families can easily make the walk. Trips are run daily at 9:30 a.m. and 1:30 p.m. from Nassau Yacht Haven on East Bay Street. The cost is $40 per person in groups of five.

For the less-daring, there are glass-bottom boat and even submarine rides available on New Providence and Grand Bahama. This way you don't even have to dip a finger into the sea to experience sea gardens, coral reefs and the creatures that make these places at home. The best-known glass-bottom boat/submarine firms in the Bahamas are:

Atlantis Submarines

Charlotte Street, Prince George Dock
☎ *(809) 356-2837, 356-3842*

Three-hour submarine tours that explore marine life, coral reefs and shipwrecks. The cost $68 for adults and $34 for children. For better or worse, less than an hour is actually spent aboard the sub.

Mermaid Kitty

Port Lucaya Dock
☎ *(809) 373-5880*

This is a large glass-bottom boat that departs from the Lucayan Bay Hotel three times a day. The cost is $15 for adults and $8 for youngsters. The trip takes about 90 minutes.

GAMBLING IN THE BAHAMAS

Princess Casino, Freeport

For some, one of the principal attractions of The Bahamas is gambling. Low- and high-rollers alike can take advantage of the casinos located on New Providence, Paradise Island and Grand Bahama.

The Bahamas offers four modern and large casinos. In Cable Beach, near Nassau, is the Crystal Palace Resort & Casino. On nearby Paradise Island can be found the $125 million mega-resort Atlantis Paradise Island Resort & Casino. Grand Bahama also boasts two ultra-modern casinos: The Princess Casino at the Bahamas Princess Resort & Casino and the Lucayan Beach Casino at the Lucayan Beach Resort. Although they're all similar and offer the same games, it's fair to say that the two casinos on and off New Providence are quite a bit larger than their Freeport counterparts. Here are the casinos in a nutshell:

Crystal Palace Resort & Casino

West Bay Street, Cable Beach
☎ *(809) 327-6459*

You name it and it can be found here at this joint venture between Carnival Cruise Lines and the Continental Companies of Miami. This place out-Vegases Vegas with its 35,000 square feet, 750 slot machines, 51 blackjack tables, nine roulette wheels, seven craps tables, a baccarat table and a big six. The coloring of the place is out of "Miami Vice" and the lighting superb. Giant football-shaped bar. The Casino Lounge offers live entertainment. The only difference between here and Vegas is that this place actually closes every day— from 4–10 a.m. It's packed both at closing and at opening. Dress is casual and you have to be at least 21.

Atlantis Paradise Island Casino

Atlantis Paradise Island Resort & Casino
Casino Drive, Paradise Island
☎ *(809) 363-3000*
Hey, man, this is it—the center of nightlife on Paradise Island. Even if you don't gamble, you've got to take a cruise through this place. Thirty thousand square feet, 60 blackjack tables, 12 craps tables, 10 roulette wheels, three for baccarat and one for big six. Oh, yeah— there's about a thousand slot machines, and you can feed these 24 hours a day. Take a stroll through Bird Cage Walk with its tons of restaurants, shops, bars and cabarets and you'll think you're on a massive space station light years from Earth. The tables close from 4–10 a.m. daily but are open every minute otherwise. Dress is casual and you've got to be 21 to play.

Lucayan Beach Casino

Lucayan Beach Resort, Royal Palm Way
Lucaya
☎ *(809) 373-7777, (800) 772-1227 in the U.S.*
Freeport/Lucaya's two casinos are about the same size; this one is the draw in Lucaya. More than 550 super slot machines and an equal number of other game tables. Large gambling hall at 20,000 square feet. Beginners can take free lessons at 11 a.m. and 7 p.m. Happy hour from 4 to 7 p.m. Casino open daily 9 a.m.–3 p.m.

Princess Casino

Bahamas Princess Resort
The Mall at W. Sunrise Highway
Freeport
☎ *(809) 352-7811, (800) 422-7466 in the U.S.*
A huge, Moorish-domed building, this is one of nicest casinos in The Bahamas, if not the entire Caribbean. Twenty thousand square feet with 450 slot machines, 40 blackjack tables, eight roulette wheels, eight dice tables and two money wheels. Elevated bar for a great view of the action. Vegas-style stage shows. Gourmet restaurant. Open daily 9 a.m.–4 a.m.

The games offered at Bahamian casinos are super slots, craps, blackjack, roulette, baccarat, big six and Caribbean stud poker.

Bahamian casinos tend to be a little lower key than their counterparts in Las Vegas and Atlantic City, and there are comparatively more opportunities for low-rollers at the Bahamian venues. More $5 and $15 tables can be found, and these are usually the tables that are the most crowded, particularly on weekend nights when the cruise ships are in town. On a Saturday night at the Atlantis, players may have to spend quite a few minutes finding an open chair at the low-roll tables, while the $150 tables are virtually deserted.

Bahamian casinos are also more user-friendly than those found in the States. In Vegas and Atlantic city, there is typically little interaction between players and dealers. At Bahamian casinos, on the other hand, croupiers and dealers are more likely to help beginning players and give them advice on how to better their odds. It takes some of the intimidation away and some of the bite out of losing 20 or 50 bucks.

As noted in the above casino descriptions, lessons in the games are given by the casinos. If you want to be taught how to lose money, these are friendly sessions that usually last about 90 minutes, or until you are out of questions. And you should ask as many as come to mind. Most folks leave these classes ready to make a killing; few do. Although you shouldn't, as a beginner, entirely rely on the following before tossing the dice, it does provide an introduction to games of The Bahamas. But remember, this is a very simplistic overview. If you want intense training in the games (particularly blackjack, which is one of the only games requiring talent, experience and skill), contact the **Gambler's Book Club** (☎ *[702] 382-7555*) for catalogs on instructional books, videos and software.

A Crash Course in Gambling

The Slot Machines

This is by far the easiest way to lose money known to man short of cheating on your income taxes. It's also the most popular way.

The game is quite simple: simply insert a coin and pull on the arm. Three windows of rolling figures will spin before your eyes. If the figures meet the right configurations, you win, and coins will spill out into a vessel at the base of the machine.

Slots are generally set up for 5 cents, 25 cents, $1 and up to $25 per pull. You can play one coin or several of them to increase the odds. The casinos usually offer slot machine tournaments. There is a buy-in for each tournament, which are run along various themes such as Halloween, etc., which usually starts at $199. Tournaments are also offered as part of packages that may include airfare and accommodations.

Baccarat

Baccarat is a game that uses eight full decks of cards. All cards, except 10s and face cards (which have no value), count as face value. The object of the game is to obtain a total closest to nine. Two 2-card hands are dealt between the player and the banker (who is in fact not the house but another player). The banker is the player dealing the cards. Whoever is closest to nine wins. Any hand over nine is subtracted by 10. So an eight and a seven would total five; a 10 and a three would total three. Bets are made on either player.

Baccarat in Bahamian casinos is usually played in two versions: regular and mini. The difference between the two is based on how the bets are placed. Mini baccarat is played at a much faster pace and is generally preferred by most players.

Big Six

This is one of the simplest casino games for trying your luck. This is also called the Wheel of Fortune and involves a wheel spinning with a pointer, that you bet will stop on the numbers you've wagered on. You can bet on more than one number, and the payout odds are determined by how often a given number appears on the wheel.

Blackjack

Blackjack is the most popular table game played at Bahamian casinos and is considered the only casino game that requires talent and skill to win. Blackjack is about the only game that can be played professionally. It is also the game where the house faces the greatest odds.

Basically, players in blackjack (also called "21") are pitted against the dealer. Two cards are dealt face up to each player. The dealer, on the other hand, is dealt one face-up and the other face-down. Number cards are worth their face value, while picture cards are worth 10. The object of the game is to get as close to 21 without going over, which is an automatic "bust." Players can ask for "hits" if they feel they can add to their hand without going over 21. The key is in guessing what the dealer's "hole" card is. If your "stand" is closer to 21 than the dealer's hand, you win.

Caribbean Stud Poker

Caribbean Stud Poker, offered in the Atlantis and in other forms elsewhere, is a five-card poker game with a maximum payoff of $5000. First you place an ante and are dealt five cards. After examining your cards, you place a bet. If your cards beat the dealer's hand you receive even money plus a bonus.

Craps

Anyone around a craps table can play this popular game (where can be seen the most hard-core gambling junkies) by simply placing chips on the various, numbered blocks and betting on the "shooter." The shooter then rolls the dice. If he or she comes up with a seven or 11, it's an automatic win—called a "natural." If a two, three or 12 comes up on the first roll, it's an automatic loss—or "craps." If anything else comes up it's called a "point," and the shooter must equal that number again before rolling a seven.

You can bet for or against the shooter, and the shooter can even bet against himself, but all bets are actually against the house.

Roulette

Roulette is the old spinning wheel game where you place bets on where the ball is going to end up. The perfectly balanced wheel has 38 numbers and there are 11 different betting options. Betting straight up means putting your money on a single digit. Or you can bet on red or black, or on an odd or even number. But there are further complicated configurations of betting on roulette. There are American-style "Double Zero" tables and French-style "Single Zero" tables.

In roulette, you can place an inside bet or outside bet. An inside bet is on a specific number, and pays back 36 to one. An outside bet is made on the ball ending up on either black or red or on an even or odd number; this pays even money, as does a bet on 1–18 or 19–36. Also an outside bet is wagering on the trio of 34, 35 and 36, or on the first 12, second 12 and third 12 boxes—which pay two-to-one.

NEW PROVIDENCE

St. Anne's Church in Fox Hill, New Providence

Of the 3.5 million visitors the Bahamas receives each year, fully 2 million of them make a stop—for most, their only stop in the islands—on New Providence. New Providence, seven-by-21-miles long, is home to the capital city of Nassau, a bustling (by Bahamian standards) but still cozy burg of 150,000 residents locked into colonial charm, garnished with a slight hint of its buccaneering past as a haven for pirates, rumrunners and slave traders.

Today, beneath its more staid image, is buccaneering of a different sort—behind Windsor knots and Waterman pens. Nassau is home to no fewer than 400 banks, an offshore, tax-free pit stop for the fruits of covert wheeling-and-dealing and laundered dollars, francs, pounds, marks, pesos, yen, baht and rials. Chalk's flights from Miami to Nassau are half-filled with tourists and half with their bankers. In no other environment will you see so many grown men and women handcuffed to their carry-on luggage, with their heads stowed beneath the seat in front of them

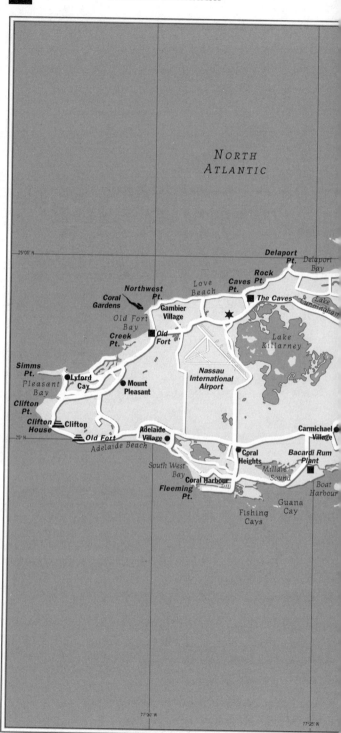

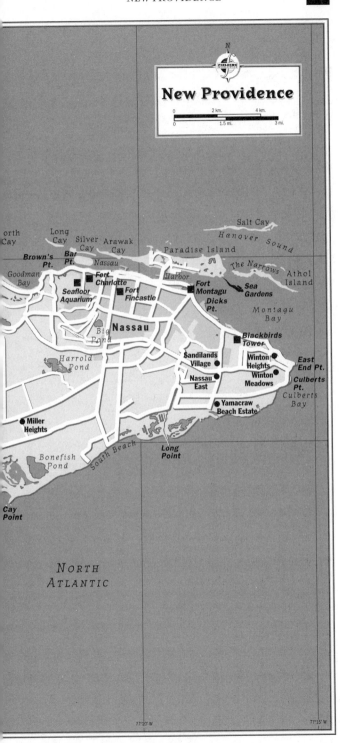

for takeoff and landing. All with the right to remain silent, and exercising it.

But New Providence is far more than a Casablanca for the '90s. In fact, there's little intrigue here, and even the cops—in their pressed red-striped trousers, pith helmets and starched white dress jackets—look better-suited for serving tea than directing traffic, which is about the most perilous duty they face.

New Providence is home to about 60 percent of all Bahamians and is a very conservative place indeed. Sculpted gardens buffer the quaint colonial-style houses and buildings. Judges still don those silly British wigs and look like Bob Marley after a peroxide job. Motorists drive on the left hand side of the road, despite most of their cars coming from America, with the steering on the left. This is what makes the job hard for the cops, as drivers have a much better view of window-shopping, halter-topped, cruise-ship beauties than they do of traffic. And speaking of cruise ships, more than 20 of them regularly pay a call at Prince George Wharf, dropping off more than 1 million passengers annually to swamp the gift shops on Bay Street and the market at Potter's Cay Dock.

Yet Nassau isn't New Providence's only destination. In fact, for many, it isn't a destination at all. Paradise Island, with its grand resorts and casinos, is making a real tug at Nassau for the island's tourist dollars. And Cable Beach has become something of a Cancun with its resort-lined crescent-shaped beach, and something of a tropical Atlantic City with its casinos, particularly the Crystal Palace and Casino.

Few people venture beyond the mainstays of New Providence: Nassau, Cable Beach and Paradise Island, which is good news for those who want to get a little more intimate with the true Bahamas, especially for those with limited time on their hands. The People-to-People Program allows visitors to New Providence the chance to stay with Bahamian families and experience an island culture separate from the glitz and bustle of the usual tourist haunts. You may be invited on family gatherings, to picnics and other social events, as well as participate in the day-to-day activities of the islanders. Contact one of the Bahamas Tourism Centres, or make arrangements through the People-to-People Program at ☎ *(809) 328-7810.*

Or simply find a way of cruising the island yourself. Just over the hill on the other side of Nassau is a small town named—you guessed it—Over the Hill. Except for a couple of supermarkets and copycat wannabe-chic shops (and the dreaded traffic), here you've been instantly transformed from a tourist mecca to a funky enclave of Bahamian life—and a little bit of that Third-World Bahamas creeps into the picture. Though barely a mile from the estates of Iranian sheiks and the cloisters of the rich,

Over the Hill and nearby Fox Hill offer the few visitors who get here a taste of the real Bahamas.

Nassau

Nassau is a superb natural anchorage and the traditional economic nerve center of the Bahamas that has turned over the centuries from a charming backwater into something of a concrete jungle. Cement is replacing the ramshackle wooden shops and the traffic can be as heinous as rush hour in Detroit. Yet you won't find any left-hand-turn lanes, medians and wide shoulders, as the traditional colonial buildings hug the narrow streets as if they still expect nothing more imposing than the occasional horse-drawn carriage to trot on by. And that is the spirit of the capital city: preserved tradition wrapped in the ascending vines of modernity.

If ever there was a tourist village, Nassau is it. Upscale shops line Bay Street like the one-arm bandits found in the Atlantis. Locals hang out in the shade of the awnings and people-watch. Others cruise the thin alleys around the Straw Market checking faces and trying to peddle dope. But it's not as seedy as you might expect—you won't be approached unless your appearance and age suggest you possibly might be amenable to such a transaction. And those who appear like this are usually with the DEA.

Nassau was once known as Charlestown but was later renamed in honor of the Prince of Orange-Nassau, who would become William III of England. In the 17th century, Nassau was a base for British and other pirates who preyed upon Spanish and French ships. This, of course, didn't sit well with the Spanish and French, who periodically invaded the island, sometimes allied, as they did in 1703. Most of the inhabitants fled, and the city was a shantytown until Briton Woodes Rogers arrived in 1718 as the first royal governor of the Bahamas.

During the mid-1700s, the town expanded; in the 1740s, Fort Montague was built. But after 1780, Nassau again lapsed into disrepair, not to really recover until the building boom of the 1860s, when the city became a supply link and blockade headquarters during the American Civil War. The population of Nassau more than doubled during the 1860s, and started to witness a flow of Out Islanders drifting into the city in search of work and to find riches.

The next boon for Nassau came during the Prohibition between 1919 and 1933, when the city became the center for bootlegging and rumrunning. Stack upon stack of smuggled cases and barrels of liquor waited on the quai of Nassau awaiting shipment to the States.

It wasn't until the 1950s that tourism replaced these other dubious means to riches as the Bahamas' principal industry. Today,

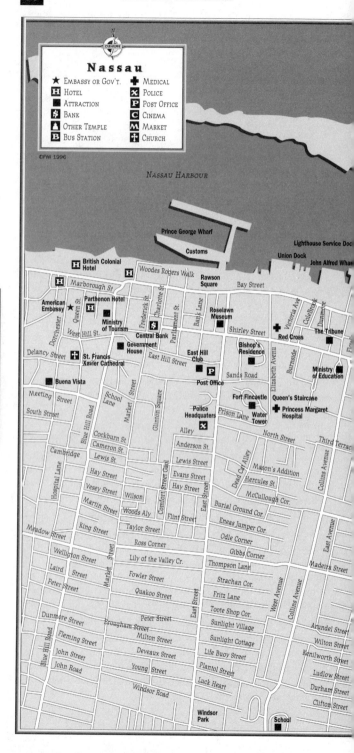

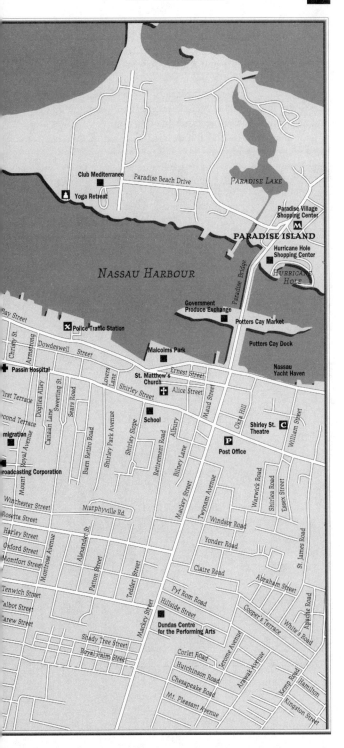

Club Mediterranee

Yoga Retreat

Paradise Beach Drive

PARADISE LAKE

Paradise Village
Shopping Center

PARADISE ISLAND

Hurricane Hole
Shopping Center

*HURRICANE
HOLE*

NASSAU HARBOUR

Government
Produce Exchange

Potters Cay Market

Police Traffic Station

Potters Cay Dock

Bay Street

Malcolms Park

Nassau
Yacht Haven

Christy St.

Armstrong

Dowdeswell Street

Ernest Street

Passin Hospital

Lovers Lane

St. Matthew's
Church

Alice Street

Maud Street

Oka Hill

First Terrace

Doglea Alley

Sweeting St.

Sears Road

Shirley Street

Shirley St.
Theatre

William Street

Second Terrace

Canaan Lane

Shirley Park Avenue

Shirley Slope

School

Albury

Immigration

Buen Retiro Road

Retirement Road

Post Office

Warwick Road

Shirlea Road

Essex Street

Broadcasting Corporation

Mount Royal Avenue

Bilney Lane

Mackey Street

Twynam Avenue

Winchester Street

Murphyville Rd.

Windsor Road

St. James Road

Rosetta Street

Yonder Road

Harley Street

Montrose Avenue

Alexander St.

Claire Road

Abraham Street

Oxford Street

Patton Street

Apache Road

Montfort Street

Cooper's Terrace

White's Road

Tenwich Street

Tedder Street

Pyf Rom Road

Talbot Street

Hillside Street

Jerome Avenue

Carew Street

Mackey Street

Dundas Centre
for the Performing Arts

Arawak Avenue

Kemp Road

Hamilton

Shady Tree Street

Corlet Road

Royal Palm Street

Hutchinson Road

Chesapeake Road

Mt. Pleasant Avenue

Kingston Street

Nassau is packed with tourists year-round; it's particularly like a theme park during the winter months. Bay Street, the route of the annual Junkanoo Parade, is the main tourist drag, and here can be found a full array of shops and restaurants. There is a unique combination of straw markets, art galleries and attractive, colonial-style government buildings found along the thoroughfare. If you're thinking about coming to Nassau for secluded beaches, forget it. On the other hand, if resort living and tropical, colonial ambiance with a dash of Vegas is more your pace, Nassau's your place.

Junkanoo Expo, Nassau

NEW PROVIDENCE

What to See and Do in Nassau

Prince George Wharf

If you've got nothing else to do and haven't already arrived by ship, take a stroll along this dock, the busiest area of Nassau. This is where all the cruise ships dock, not to mention all the private pleasure craft, fishing vessels, tug boats and charter boats. Shops and restaurants abound and vendors hawk their wares in this colorful and bustling environment. You'll notice the statue of Little Harbour in Abaco that was chiseled by Randolph W. Johnston in honor of Bahamian women.

Junkanoo Expo

On the wharf in the old customs warehouse. ☎ *(809) 356-2731. Admission: $1 adults; 50¢ children. Open daily 10 a.m.–4 p.m.*

If you can't actually experience the twice-yearly (Dec. 26 and Jan. 1) Junkanoo festivities and parades, this pavilion is the next best thing as it houses all sorts of bright costumes and colorful floats used in the parades.

Rawson Square

Between Prince George Wharf and the government buildings across Bay Street

If you're a cruise ship passenger, this is the first sight of Nassau you'll get after disembarking and plying your way through the crowds at Prince George Dock. This is the start of the walking tour of old Nassau. Horse-drawn carriages (surreys) pick up passengers here for tours of the city. A 30-minute tour costs about $5 a head. And the place is packed. You'll be competing with hotel guests in town as well as cruise ship passengers for both the surreys and taxis. Walking in the area is equally as crowded, making a hot day even hotter. Close by is where the ferries depart for Paradise Island and Coral World Marine Park. This is packaged tourism to the max.

Woodes Rogers Walk

Along the waterfront

This is a delightful albeit sometimes crowded stroll where the Straw Market is found across from the cruise ships. Some of the best food in the city is sold by the locals, who cook it in and peddle it from the trunks of their cars. Local delicacies and fruit are sold from carts. Delicious if you don't mind the crowds.

Parliament Square is The Bahamas' government center.

NEW PROVIDENCE

Parliament Square

Bay Street across from Rawson Square. For opening ceremonies informa-
tion, ☎ *(809) 322-7500.*

This attractive complex of pink, colonnaded government buildings is
the Bahamas' center of government. These buildings were designed
after the southern colonial architecture found at New Bern, the early
capital of North Carolina, and were constructed in the early 1800s by
Loyalists from North Carolina. Worth seeing are the Supreme Court,
the House of Assembly, the office of the Colonial Secretary, the Central Police Station and the prison-turned-athenaeum Public Library
building. In Parliament Square, you'll see a statue of young Queen
Victoria that was erected on May 24, 1905. The two-house parliament is divided into the 16-member Senate, called the Upper House,
and the 43-seat House of Assembly, or the Lower House. The Minis-
terial cabinet is run by the prime minister. Similar to Britain's Houses
of Parliament in almost every way, the opening ceremonies—held
four times a year in the first weeks of January, April, July and October—even feature white wigs. You might also want to spend some
time at the Garden of Remembrance, a monument honoring the war
dead.

St. Matthew's Anglican Church

East Bay and Dowdeswell roads

This is a beautiful, palm-studded setting for a large stone church that
is one of the oldest in the Bahamas. The Eastern Cemetery is an
above-ground cemetery in front of the church.

Where to Stay in Nassau

Graycliff $125–$285 ★★★★

P.O. Box N-10246, West Hill Street, Nassau
☎ *(800) 423-4095 U.S., (809) 322-2796; FAX (809) 326-6110*
Single: $125–$175; Double: $215–$285

More than 200 years ago Graycliff was home to Graysmith—Captain
John Howard Graysmith, a notorious (and wealthy) pirate who built
his mansion right in the thick of Old Nassau, just across the street
from the present Government House. Functioning on-again, off-
again as a hotel since the mid-1800s, Graycliff's walls and bedsprings
have been privy to an eclectic array of rich and famous guests including, Aristotle Onassis, Sir Winston Churchill, the Duke and Duchess
of Windsor, Perry Como, Paul Newman and the Beatles. Italian
entrepreneur Enrico Garzaroli has poured his Italian style and lire into
the mansion, assuring that Graycliff is the place to stay for the genteel
set. Nine guest rooms and five suites are individually decorated with
high-end antiques. A swimming pool and gourmet restaurant share
the space. Service is superb. Amenities: swimming pool, room service,
concierge, massage, sauna, health club, Continental breakfast. Credit
cards: AE, DC, MC, V.

Coral World Villas $215–$250 ★★★

P.O. Box N-7797, Silver Cay, Nassau
☎ *(800) 328-8814 U.S., (809) 328-1036; FAX (809) 323-3202*
Single: $215–$250; Double: $215–$250

Approximately half-way between central Nassau and Cable Beach, the
private island of Silver Cay is the setting for this idyllic resort complex.

Individual villas feature private swimming pools, bare-all sunbathing enclosures, ocean views, king-size beds, equipped kitchens, marble baths (with sea views from the oval tub), and island decor. The place is ideally suited for couples who—for the time being—only have eyes for each other, though kids-in-tow can be stashed away on the pull-out sofa bed. A private beach, snorkeling trail and nearby marine park and underwater observatory (free admission for guests) are other highlights. Amenities: private swimming pools, private beach, restaurant, room service, laundry, room service, free daytime transportation to nearby attractions, Continental breakfast. Credit cards: AE, DC, MC, V.

Best Western British Colonial
Beach Resort $100–$195   ★ ★ ★

P.O. Box N-7148, 1 Bay Street, Nassau
☎ *(800) 528-1234 US., (809) 322-3301; FAX (809) 322-2286*
Single: $100–$195; Double: $100–$195

This huge, vintage-1920s pink monument is a prominent landmark on Nassau's bay front. With 325 rooms on eight tropical acres, this resort is big enough to accommodate large groups and their large group-y proclivities—a restaurant, cafe, and crowded bar, local entertainment, tropical drink extravaganzas, a full range of watersports, three lighted championship tennis courts, an Olympic-size swimming pool and a private beach. The rooms are hit or miss—if you're picky, shell out the extra bucks for an ocean view. Amenities: swimming pool, tennis courts, private beach, restaurant, cafe, lounge, room service, Continental breakfast. Credit cards: AE, DC, MC, V.

El Greco Hotel $60–$90   ★ ★

P.O. Box N-4187, W. Bay Street, Nassau
☎ *(809) 325-1121; FAX (809) 325-1124*
Single: $60–$80; Double: $70–$90

Situated in the Bahamas, owned by Greeks, features an Italian restaurant, and has Spanish styling. The two-story, 25-room El Greco is a study in homey-cozy. Europeans love the place (it's so pension-y). Nicely furnished rooms with Spanish decor and tiled baths surround a small courtyard with vines, hedges and a swimming pool. The hotel is just a few minutes from the center of town, and just across the street from a public beach. Amenities: swimming pool, restaurant. Credit cards: AE, DC, MC, V.

The Little Orchard $60–$90   ★ ★

P.O. Box N-1514, Village Road, Nassau
☎ *(809) 393-1297; FAX (809) 394-3526*
Single: $60–$90; Double: $60–$90

Individual cottages cluster around the swimming pool and garden at this small complex in a quiet Nassau neighborhood, near Montagu Beach. Cottages have fully equipped kitchens, plus there's an adjacent restaurant and a nearby supermarket. Daily maid service is provided at this good-value choice for those who would rather be near than in the center of town. TVs, phones, and minibars are thrown into the deal. Amenities: swimming pool, kitchens Credit cards: AE, DC, MC, V.

Nassau Harbor Club $60–$75   ★

P.O. Box SS-5755, Nassau
☎ *(809) 393-0771; FAX (809 393-5393*
Single: $60–$75; Double: $60–$75

If you crave noise, crowds, and late-night munchies, this 50-room 1960s-era establishment was made for you. Join the salts or locals at the bar, snack in the restaurant until dawn, strike up a chat whenever with whomever you please, or just sit and listen to traffic zip by on the way into town. The rooms are unmemorable but feature air conditioning, tropical decor, tile floors and balconies with harbor or pool views. Beware spring break when the student throngs make this their home away from. Amenities: swimming pool, two restaurants, bar. Credit cards: AE, DC, MC, V.

Budget Nassau

Nassau's hotels where traveling Bahamians stay also make great places for budget travelers from the rest of the world. These places make the Bahamas accessible to more than just monied honeymooners and people with last names like architectural styles and geological periods.

Park Manor Guest House $37–$67

P.O. Box N4164
45 Market Street, North
(East of Government House and south of Gregory Arch)
Nassau, New Providence
☎ *(809) 325-3554, 356-5471; FAX (809) 356-5471*
Rooms: $37; efficiency apartments: $42; deluxe efficiency apartments: $57; studio apartments: $50; deluxe studio apartments: $67; Cottage: $45
A few steps away from the hustle and bustle of Nassau, and all its historic sites, this is a plain-Jane hotel with excellent amenities for the prices. Bahamians and tourists alike take advantage of these rates and all the good stuff that comes with them: in-room refrigerators, microwave ovens, 2- or 4-burner stoves, satellite TVs, telephones, air conditioning, ceiling fans, laundry facilities, swimming pool and a picnic table in the shade. That's a lot for the price. There's no beach, but a couple are within walking distance. Credit cards: AE, V, MC.

The Buena Vista $55–$90

P.O. Box N564
Delancy Street
Nassau
☎ *(809) 322-2811/2, 322-4039; FAX (809) 322-5881*
Single: $55–$80; Double: $65–$90
This elegant, early 19th-century building is known as one of Nassau's best and most popular restaurants, but few visitors realize that upstairs are five beautifully decorated and spacious bedrooms and suites. And they can be had at more than reasonable prices. The Victorian-styled rooms are all air-conditioned and have cable TV with 45 channels. There are even fireplaces in some of the rooms—although they're rarely necessary. The ceilings reach for the sky. Telephones are in the rooms as well as clock radios. The beaches and downtown Nassau are only a five-minute walk away. This is one of Nassau's best-kept secrets for the budget-conscious. You'll know that when you go downstairs to eat, which will cost you nearly as much as the room. Credit cards: All major credit cards.

Pick-A-Dilly $57.50–$68.30

P.O. Box N4138
18 Parliament Street
Nassau, New Providence

☎ *(809) 322-2836; FAX (809) 326-7196*
Single: $57.50; Double: $68.30

This is a downtown establishment also more known as a popular restaurant/bar than a caravansary. But an inn it is indeed, although you'd think it would be more comfortable than it is. The rooms are small, almost miniature, with some decorated as if for children rather than adults. And the room amenities are sparse. But there is something of a European inn atmosphere here, and you can't beat the downtown location and the ambience of the downstairs restaurant and bar. For my money, it's still a bit overpriced, even by Nassau standards.

Dillet's Guesthouse **$50** ★★

Dunmore Avenue & Strachan Street, Chippingham
P.O. Box N204
Nassau, New Providence
☎ *(809) 325-1133, 327-7743; FAX (809) 325-7183*
Single: $50; Double: $50

This is the most charming bed & breakfast on New Providence and perhaps in all the Bahamas. Old Nassau is not just written all over the place, it is the place. In fact, this is the only true guesthouse in the islands. This is a beautiful home built in the 1920s and enveloped by an acre of stately royal palms and lush tropical gardens. Guests stay in airy, air-conditioned and spacious suites on the second floor, many with a private sitting room and kitchenette. Home-cooked meals at the family-run guesthouse are served in the dining room. There's a beautifully decorated living room with a fireplace. Here is where the guesthouse's sole telephone can be found. At no other establishment in the Bahamas will you feel so much at home, rather than at a hotel. Even the kitchen feels like home—and it's just as accessible. This is the legitimate Bahamian experience—a number of writers and artists come for the solitude and the peace of mind that seems to waft through the guesthouse like a gentle trade breeze. Your hosts, Iris Dillet-Knowles and Danielle Knowles, are renowned for their hospitality and unpretentiousness. And, for the price, there's no better bargain in the islands for this kind of ambience. The beach and all of Nassau's attractions are within easy walking distance. But if you'd rather pedal, rental bicycles are available. When there's enough interest, the Knowles will bring guests to Poppy Bay, their cozy beachfront guesthouse property in Adelaide, for picnics, swimming and sunning. A definite Fielding's choice. Credit cards: V, MC.

Other New Providence Budget Considerations

The following is a list of other small hotels in Nassau and on Paradise Island that usually don't make it into the brochures of travel agents. These hotels are popular with budget-minded European and Bahamian tourists. For the most part, the rooms run for under $70. Call or fax for details and reservations.

Aliceanna's Guest House

P.O. Box N220
Bay Street
Nassau, New Providence
☎ *(809) 325-4974; FAX 326-2378*
6 rooms.

Club Crystal Resort

P.O. Box N9329
Ferguson Street (off Taylor Street)
Nassau Village, New Providence
☎ *(809) 393-0746, 393-4442; FAX (809) 394-0943*
20 rooms

Curry's Motel

Boyd Road
P.O. Box SS6725
Nassau, New Providence
☎ *(809) 323-4020; FAX (809) 326-2226*
5 rooms.

The Diplomat Inn

P.O. Box N4
Delancy Street
Nassau, New Providence
☎ *(809) 325-2688; FAX (809) 323-7151*
7 rooms.

Glowell Motel/Villas

P.O. Box SS6066
St. Alban's Drive
Nassau, New Providence
☎ *(809) 322-8622*
9 rooms.

Makeba Beach Hotel

P.O. Box N785
Holiday Drive (South Beach)
Nassau, New Providence
☎ *(809) 361-4596*
16 rooms.

Mignon Guest House

P.O. Box N786
12 Market Street (North)
Nassau, New Providence
☎ *(809) 322-4771*
6 rooms.

Mondingo Inn

P.O. Box N9669
Alexander Boulevard, Nassau Village
Nassau, New Providence
☎ *(809) 393-0333; FAX (809) 393-0783*
8 rooms.

Morris Guest House

P.O. Box CB13953
Davis Street, Oakes Field
Nassau, New Providence
☎ *(809) 325-0195; FAX (809) 323-3506*
7 rooms.

Olive's Guest House

P.O. Box GT2130
Blue Hill Road
Nassau, New Providence
☎ *(809) 356-0268*
14 rooms.

Parliament Hotel

P.O. Box N4138

128 Parliament Street
Nassau, New Providence
☎ *(809) 322-2836; FAX (809) 326-7196*
10 rooms.

The Parthenon Hotel

P.O. Box N4930
17 West Street, North
Nassau, New Providence
☎ *(809) 322-2643/5; FAX (809) 322-2644*
18 rooms.

Sir Charles Hotel

P.O. Box GT2448
East Street & Malcom Road
Nassau, New Providence
☎ *(809) 322-5641; FAX (809) 361-5887*
20 rooms.

Smith's Motel

P.O. Box N51
East Street, South
Nassau, New Providence
☎ *(809) 323-6873*
20 rooms.

The Corner Motel, Restaurant & Bar

P.O. Box N1118
Carmichael Road & Faith Avenue
Nassau, New Providence
☎ *(809) 361-7445/6; FAX 361-7448*
25 rooms.

Sun Fun Resorts

P.O. Box FH14569
West Bay Street
Nassau, New Providence
☎ *(809) 327-8827; FAX (809) 327-8802*
20 rooms.

Arawak Inn

P.O. Box N3222
West Bay Street
Nassau, New Providence
☎ *(809) 322-2638; FAX (809) 328-4014*
6 rooms.

Villas in Paradise

P.O. Box SS6379
Paradise Island
Nassau, New Providence
☎ *(809) 363-2998; FAX (809) 363-2998*
25 rooms.

Chaplin House

P.O. Box SS6034
Western end of Paradise Island
Nassau, New Providence
☎ *(809) 363-2918; FAX 363-2918*
7 rooms.

The Pink House

P.O. Box N1968
Paradise Island
Nassau, New Providence

☎ *(809) 363-3363; FAX (809) 393-1786*
4 rooms.

Paradise Harbour Club & Marina

P.O. Box SS5804
Paradise Island Drive
☎ *(809) 363-2992; FAX (809) 363-2840*
16 apartments and suites.

Club Des Iles

P.O. Box N4432
23 Delancy Street
Nassau, New Providence
☎ *(809) 356-5636*
2 rooms.

Sunshine Paradise Suites

P.O. Box SS5206
Nassau, New Providence
☎ *(809) 363-3955; FAX (809) 363-3840*
16 apartments and suites.

Coral Island

P.O. Box N7797
Nassau, New Providence
☎ *(809) 328-1036; FAX (809) 323-3202*
22 villas.

J.R.'s Country House

P.O. Box N3216
Sugar Hill Road
Nassau, New Providence
☎ *(809) 324-2912*
13 rooms.

Southwestern New Providence

South Ocean Beach and Golf Resort ★★★

P.O. Box N-8191, Nassau
☎ *(800) 228-9898 U.S., (809) 362-4391; FAX (809) 362-4728*
Single: $135–$205; Double: $135–$205

On the southwestern shore of New Providence, about a 40-minute drive from Nassau, this plantation-style resort should appeal to people desiring seclusion along with their beach and golf experience. Some of the facilities at this 180-acre, country-club-like property include a dreamy beach, challenging 18-hole golf course, four tennis courts (two lighted), two freshwater swimming pools, scuba diving and a whole agenda of other watersports. Guests can sign on for free tennis and golf clinics. Indoor action centers around the restaurants, bars, and nightclub with nightly dancing and live entertainment. Accommodations are well-decorated though lacking in light, and feature private oceanfront balconies or patios. Amenities: two freshwater swimming pools, two restaurants, three bars, nightclub, snack bar, 18-hole golf course, four tennis courts, dive shop, travel services. Credit cards: AE, DC, MC, V.

Coral Harbour Beach House and Villa $65–$75

P.O. Box N9750
Nassau, New Providence
☎ *(809) 361-6514; FAX (809) 361-6514, 363-2210*
Suites: $65–$75

This establishment touts itself as an Out Island experience in Nassau. The villas are located far from Nassau in the southwestern portion of the island, which is itself more like the Family Islands than Nassau. But Coral Harbour is nicely tucked away from the hustle and bustle of Nassau on its own stretch of sand south of the international airport. The villas are less than luxurious, more like spartan (but tastefully furnished) apartments. But they're large and comfortable—and right next to the sea. Each features a kitchen, satellite color TV and air conditioning. The sofas can be pulled out into king-sized beds. Scuba diving and horseback riding are only a couple of minutes away. Seaside living at these prices may not be available anywhere else in the Bahamas. Credit cards: MC, V

Love Beach/Compass Point

Compass Point $100–$300   ★ ★ ★ ★

West Bay Street, Gambia, Love Beach, New Providence
☎ *(809) 327-7309; FAX (809) 327-3299*
Single: $100–$300; Double: $100–$300

Music lovers will be interested to learn that this hotel hidden away on the northwest shore is owned by Jamaican-born Christopher Blackwell (Bob Marley promoter) and sits next to Compass Point recording studios. This place, with its myriad color scheme, looks quite strange from the air, but enhances the lively atmosphere that makes Compass Point such a delight. Accommodations are in private bungalows with high ceilings, open beams and some kitchenettes. The only problem with the bungalows seems to be their extremely close proximity to each other and the paper-thin walls, which might discourage sober honeymoon couples from consummating their union. There are also a couple of two-story villas. The atmosphere is on the trendy side of casual, while the musical trend is decidedly Caribbean. The hotel restaurant serves delectable Bahamian cuisine. Amenities: swimming pool, tennis court, restaurant, bar. Credit cards: AE, DC, MC, V.

Where to Eat in Nassau

Graycliff   ★ ★ ★ ★ ★

West Hill Street at Cumberland Road, Nassau
☎ *(809) 322-2796*
Continental cuisine
Lunch: Mon.–Fri., noon–3 p.m., entrees $16–$22
Dinner: daily, 7–10 p.m., entrees $30–$90

This former mansion home of pirate John Howard Graysmith is now the setting for dishes he never would have fathomed. The Graycliff has built its esteemed reputation around such concoctions as gourmet terrines, foie gras with thinly sliced truffles, and wondrous grilled and spit-roasted meats and fowl. Which wine to choose? A hard decision, with about 175,000 bottles in the cellar. And, après dinner, take your pick of about 90 types of Cuban cigars. The ambiance is exquisite and elegant with seven dining areas, expensive antiques, soft piano sounds, and impeccable service. Jacket required at dinner. Reservations recommended. Credit cards: AE, DC, MC, V.

Buena Vista   ★ ★ ★ ★ ★

Delancy and Meeting streets, Nassau
☎ *(809) 322-2811*
Continental cuisine
Dinner: daily, 7–10 p.m., entrees $25–$40
Closed mid-April through Christmas

Well-heeled locals and visitors have been flocking to this early-1800s hilltop colonial mansion, one block west of Government House, since the 1940s. Situated in a sprawling home, amid five tropically landscaped acres, diners—served by tuxed-out waiters, serenaded by smooth-handed pianists—are seated in the main dining room, in the smaller Victorian Room, or in the sky-lighted Garden Patio Room. Continental cuisine, Bahamian seafood, daily pastas and specials, plus Mrs. Hauck's Orange Pancakes—a Buena Vista signature dish since 1946—are complemented by chic settings of crystal, china and silver. Reservations recommended. Credit cards: AE, DC, MC, V.

Sun And...   ★ ★ ★ ★ ★

Lake View Road, off Shirley Street, Nassau
☎ *(809) 393-1205*
French/Continental cuisine
Dinner: Tues.–Sun., 6:30–9:45 p.m., entrees $28–$38
Closed August through September

If you're allowed only one big splurge it should be at this spot. Sun And... has been wowing big names such as Queen Elizabeth, Sir Winston Churchill, Diana Ross (make that Miss Ross) and Sean Connery for more than a century. Housed inside a former private home—replete with drawbridge, courtyard and gorgeous tropical garden—the restaurant is famed for its to-die-for French and Continental gourmet cuisine (including daily seafood specials), sensuous sauces, artistic presentations and impeccable service. Sit inside the dining room, or out on the cozy patio. Don't leave without ordering one of the famous soufflés (and don't have your cholesterol checked for at least a month!). Jackets and ties requested. Reservations recommended. Credit cards: AE, DC, MC, V.

East Villa Restaurant   ★ ★ ★

East Bay Street (one-half mile east of the Paradise Island Bridge), Nassau
☎ *(809) 393-3377*
Chinese/Continental cuisine
Lunch: Mon.–Fri., Noon–3 p.m., Sun. 12:30–3 p.m.
Dinner: Mon.–Sat. 6 p.m.–midnight, Sun. 6–10 p.m.

Opened in 1991, the East Villa is a bright spot to let's-try-something-new diners who rave over the Chinese Continental offerings. The broiled New York strip steak is a must for carnivores and the lamb chops are so tender they might have come off Mary's little lamb. Mandarin and Szechwan specialties can be ordered mild to hot. The atmosphere is pure Chinese-romance—dim lights, bubbling aquarium, chic decor. "Proper dress required" probably means men should wear jackets at dinner. Reservations recommended. Credit cards: AE, MC, V.

Europe ★★★

West Bay Street, in the Ocean Spray Hotel, Nassau
☎ *(809) 322-8032*
German/Continental cuisine
Breakfast: Mon.–Fri., 8 a.m.–noon
Lunch: Mon.–Fri., Noon–5 p.m., entrees $6–$14
Dinner: Mon.–Sat., 5–10 p.m., entrees $11–$25

Located opposite the Western Esplanade, this informal establishment offers German cuisine (with plenty of German clientele doing the essen)—make that hearty German cuisine—along with fondues, escargots and Bahamian rock lobster. Wash it all down with draft beer from Europe, or a selection of beer and wine from around the world. Credit cards: AE, MC, V.

Coconuts ★★★

East Bay Street, Nassau
☎ *(809) 325-2148*
International cuisine
Dinner: daily 5:30-10:30 p.m., entrees $16–$30

Near the harbor's edge, two dining rooms (one with garden view, the other looking over the harbor) serve hungry patrons delectable portions of well-prepared seafood (including several lobster dishes), fresh grouper, shrimp, scallops and a bevy of beef, chicken, veal and lamb dishes. Head upstairs to Le Shack for drinks and dancing to live bands. Credit cards: AE, MC, V.

Cappuccino Cafe and Specialty Shop ★★

Mackey Street, in the Royal Palm Mall, Nassau
☎ *(809) 394-6332*
Deli
Breakfast and lunch: Mon.–Sat., 10:30 a.m.–6:30 p.m.

The locals head here for cappuccino, salads, deli sandwiches, gourmet concoctions, patés and such. Eat on the premises, at one of the indoor or outdoor tables, or have your food packed up for a picnic lunch (picnic baskets are also available). Toss in a Cuban cigar or two. Cappuccino happy hour is on from 3–6 p.m., while alcohol is poured 4–6 p.m. Credit cards: AE, MC, V.

Green Shutters Restaurant and Pub ★★

48 Parliament Street, Nassau
☎ *(809) 35-5702*
English/Bahamian cuisine
Lunch: daily, 11 a.m.–5 p.m., entrees $8–$10
Dinner: daily, 6–11 p.m., entrees $12–$24

Fill up on traditional English fare in this two-centuries-old former Bahamian home. You'll be transported back to Merry Olde England as you suck down fish and chips, shepherd's pie, bangers and mash, roast dinners, prime rib and Yorkshire pudding. Wash it all down with draft British beer, shipped over from the U.K. Live music is also on tap most nights, and major sporting events are picked up via two satellite dishes. Credit cards: AE, MC, V.

Gaylord's Authentic Indian Restaurant ★★★

Dowdeswell Street, off Bay Street, Nassau
☎ *(809) 356-3004*

NEW PROVIDENCE

Indian cuisine
Lunch: daily Noon–3 p.m.
Dinner: daily 6:30–11 p.m.

The Gaylord's restaurant chain has infiltrated the Caribbean with this newest location, inside a 125-year-old Bahamian mansion. All your favorite Indian treats are on the menu, including Tandoori, Punjabi, Nepalese and Mughali specialties. Afternoon tea is served 3-5:30 p.m., and a spice shop sells everything you need to put together your own Indian dishes. No jeans, shorts, or beach attire are allowed. Reservations recommended. Credit cards: AE, MC, V.

Double Dragon Chinese Restaurant

Mackey Street, Bridge Plaza Commons (at the foot of the Paradise Island Bridge), Nassau
☎ *(809) 393-5718*
Chinese cuisine
Lunch: Mon.–Fri., Noon–5 p.m.
Dinner: Mon.–Sat., 5-11 p.m., Sun. 5–10 p.m.

Good Szechwan, Hunan, Mandarin and Cantonese meals that won't make wonton of your wallet. Eat in the informal dining room, or fill some little white containers and head to your favorite hideaway. With a minimum $20 purchase, the restaurant will deliver free, at night, in the downtown area. The full bar serves beer, wine and cocktails. Credit cards: AE, MC, V.

House of Wong

Marlborough Street, opposite British Colonial tennis courts, Nassau
☎ *(809) 326-0045*
Chinese cuisine
Lunch: daily, 11:30 a.m.–3 p.m., entrees $6–$12
Dinner: daily 6–11 p.m., entrees $8–$22

Peter Wong and family—formerly of the fabled Mai Tai Peking House—have set up shop at this site in downtown Nassau, and are still famous for their Cantonese, Szechwan and Polynesian dishes. Regulars seem to favor moo shu pork, kung pao chicken, deviled Bahamian lobster, wonton soup, and shrimp toast. Stop by the bar for a killer concoction such as Island Zombie, Lover's Paradise, Bahama Scorpion or Volcanic Flame, and you probably won't even remember—or care—what you eat. Credit cards: AE, MC, V.

Montagu Gardens ★★★

East Bay Street, next to Waterloo, one mile east of the Paradise Island Bridge, Nassau
☎ *(809) 394-6347*
Lunch: Mon.–Sat., 11:30 a.m.–3 p.m.
Dinner: Mon.–Sat. 6–11 p.m.

Situated on Lake Waterloo, this old Bahamian home has been converted into a restaurant noteworthy for its blackened and flame-grilled seafood, beef, chicken and lamb. Specialty of the house is filet mignon smothered with mushrooms, though lighter eaters can order salads, soups or pasta dishes. Credit cards: AE, MC, V.

Passin' Jacks Restaurant

East Bay Street, top floor of Nassau Harbour Club, one-half mile east of the Paradise Island Bridge, Nassau
☎ *(809) 394-3245*
Bahamian/American cuisine
Breakfast: daily 7–10:30 a.m.

Lunch: daily Noon–3 p.m.
Dinner: daily 6–10 p.m., entrees $10–$16
The semicircular shape, wraparound verandah, and position at the top of Nassau Harbour Club assure that fantastic views will accompany everything from American burgers and salads to Bahamian cracked conch and peas 'n' rice. Locals like the casual atmosphere and good-value prices. Credit cards: AE, MC, V.

Pick-A-Dilly at The Parliament Inn ★ ★

18 Parliament Street, near Bay Street, Nassau
☎ *(809) 322-2836*
Bahamian/American cuisine
Lunch: Mon.–Sat. 11 a.m.–3 p.m., entrees $6–$15
Dinner: Mon.–Sat. 5–10 p.m., entrees $8–$18
Situated in the garden of The Parliament Inn bed-and-breakfast, the Pick-A-Dilly offers a festive ambiance as well as tasty snacks and meals. Bahamian seafood, pastas, puddings and daily market specials are all popular. Late afternoons find the outdoor bar abuzz with buzzed locals sipping daiquiris, gin and coconut water, and the enticing-sounding drink known as a "Schizo." Credit cards: AE, MC, V.

Silk Cotton Club ★ ★ ★

Market Street, off Bay Street, Nassau
☎ *(809) 356-0955*
Dinner: Tues.–Sat. 6:30–10 p.m.
Primarily known for its terrific live jazz entertainment, this snazzy club offers health-conscious gourmet fare.. Try the chef's specials (coconut soup, conch chowder, calypso chicken, Silk Cotton grouper), as well as pastas, salads, desserts and coffee drinks. Credit cards: AE, MC, V.

Tamarind Hill ★ ★ ★

Village Road, near Shirley Street, Nassau
☎ *(809) 393-1306*
Caribbean cuisine
Lunch: daily 11 a.m.–3 p.m., entrees $6–$10
Dinner: daily 5–10:30 p.m., entrees $10–$24
The tamarind tree in the front yard of this 1960s-was-good-to-it home in a residential area, draws locals to its colorful, vibrant atmosphere with indoor/outdoor dining, and its excellent and inexpensive Caribbean fare. Among the entrees are chicken in mango glaze and Bahamian seafood platters, though homemade soups, pastas, burgers and gourmet pizza are also popular. There's live entertainment on the weekends. Reservations recommended. Credit cards: AE, MC, V.

The Poop Deck ★ ★ ★

East Bay Street, Nassau
☎ *(809) 393-8175*
Bahamian cuisine
Lunch: daily 11 a.m.–5 p.m., entrees $8–$16
Dinner: daily 5–10:30 p.m., entrees $9–$30
Nassau residents love this been-in-business-25-years waterfront eatery, with its nautical decor, friendly ambiance and deck overlooking the harbor and Paradise Island bridge. Bahamian seafood specialties are fresh and well-prepared—try the conch chowder, grouper fingers, grilled Bahamian whole lobster. Order a bottle from the well-stocked wine cellar. Credit cards: AE, MC, V.

NEW PROVIDENCE

Sugar Reef Harbourside Bar and Grille ★★

Deveaux Street, off Bay Street, Nassau
☎ *(809) 356-3065*
Bahamian/Caribbean cuisine
Lunch: daily 11 a.m.–3 p.m.
Dinner: daily 6–10:30 p.m.

This casual bar and grill, set along the harbor, features glass mosaic and broken tile decor—a perfect setting for the casual fare and flair. Munch on Bahamian or Caribbean dishes, or choose seafood, pasta, salad, burger or sandwich. The Sugar Reef's claim to fame is its "killer" appetizers. Espresso, cappuccino and a daiquiri gazebo bar are some of the drink possibilities. Credit cards: AE, MC, V.

Bahamian Kitchen ★★

Trinity Place, off Bay Street, Nassau
☎ *(809) 325-0702*
Lunch: Mon.–Sat. 11:30 a.m.–5 p.m., Sun. 1–5 p.m., entrees $6–$16
Dinner: Mon.–Sat., 5–10 p.m., Sun. 5–8 p.m., entrees $10–$25
A good, straightforward venue for "real" Bahamian cooking. Specialties include okra soup, pan-fried turtle steak, conch salad, Bahamian-style lobster, corned beef and grits—all accompanied by johnnycake. Take-out service is available for picnickers. Credit cards: AE, D, MC, V.

Tony Roma's ★★★

West Bay Street, opposite Saunders Beach, Nassau
☎ *(809) 325-2020*
Lunch: daily Noon–5 p.m.
Dinner: daily 5–11 p.m.
Ribs, ribs and more ribs—barbecued in Tony's special (and addicting) sauce. The location, about midway between Nassau and Cable Beach, affords verandah views of the beach—not that you'll be looking at anything other that rib you're chomping on. Lunch and dinner menus are pretty much the same, only the portions vary. Other favorites are barbecued chicken and beef, London broil and juicy burgers and sandwiches. Salads are available, but why even come here if you just want some rabbit food? Credit cards: AE, MC, V.

Nightlife in Nassau

There was once a time when there wasn't a heck of a lot to do in Nassau or on New Providence after dark. And it wasn't that long ago. Today, it's a different story. Most of the hotels have their own nightclubs or discos, and the burgeoning number of clubs is testament to the new tourist cry that "I can't just sit around on the beach all day!"

Most of the real "action," if that's what you dare call it, takes place in Cable Beach and Paradise Island rather than in Nassau itself.

Clubs/Bars/Discos

Bahamen's Culture Club

Nassau and W. Bay Streets (behind the Dolphin Hotel), Nassau
☎ *(809) 356-6266*
Nassau's singles scene is here. Moondoggers from Long Island (New York, that is) in their City Streets and Bugle Boy best (with no socks) and a limited selection of Euro jetsetters strut their stuff on a checkerboard dance floor to a live band 9 p.m.–3 a.m. Wed.–Sun. nights.

Club Waterloo

East Bay Street, Nassau

☎ *(809) 394-0163*
Same crowd as the Culture Club, but you can dance later here—until
4 a.m.—to the house band every night of the week except Sundays.
The band takes the night off on Mondays.

Cudabay

East Bay Street (lower floor of the Harbour Club), Nassau
☎ *(809) 393-0771*
Sort of like a sports bar, Bahamas-style. Big-screen TVs and dart-
boards. Popular with boozers in the daytime and karaokeheads and
disco soft-cores in the evening. Drinks are about $3.50, but no cover.

Le Shack

East Bay Street, Nassau
☎ *(809) 325-2148*
Harbor-front bar offering a mix of live reggae, calypso, soca and
medium rock. Attracts both a young and older crowd, especially when
the calypso is heating up. A lot of the crowd is simply the curious spill-
over from the next-door Le Shack Bar & Grill dinner scene, including
couples and their kids. A nice pit stop but not the focus of a night on
the town.

Shopping in Nassau

Nassau isn't exactly a shopper's paradise unless, of course, you're loaded.
But bargains are to be found, especially on imported items such as watches,
crystal, cameras and designer clothing. Nassau is the center for shopping on
New Providence and the majority of shops are found on Bay Street between
the British Colonial Hotel and Rawson Square as well as a number of side
streets off Bay Street. Don't expect to do any bargaining in the shops, although negotiating is key at the Strawmarket Plaza on Bay Street.

Import duties were abolished in 1992 on 11 categories of luxury items,
including the items mentioned above, as well as leather goods, fine linens,
jewelry, china and perfume. Antiques have always been duty-exempt. While
this has brought many prices down, in many instances it has simply brought
them down to U.S. levels. Americans who have been away from the country
for 48 hours and have not had a similar exemption in the past 30 days can
bring back to the States $600 worth of merchandise duty-free—as well as
two liters of wine.

Most shops are open Monday-Saturday from 9 a.m.–5 p.m., although
the straw market and some sundry shops are open Sundays. Many stores
close at noon on Thursdays; others close at noon on Fridays.

Arts, Crafts and Antiques

Marlborough Antiques

Corner of Marlborough and Queen streets
☎ *(809) 328-0502*
Displays works of Bahamian artists Brent Malone and Maxwell Taylor. Antique engravings, antique books, antique maps and other
unusual relics from the past. There is a great collection of photography of the Old Bahamas. Also old table settings and English silver.
Antique china and Victorian and Edwardian furniture.

Balmain Antiques

Bay Street (near Charlotte Street in Mason's Bldg.), Nassau
☎ *(809) 323-7421*

There is an atlas here that dates 435 years if it hasn't been snatched yet. Also antique 19th-century maps, engravings and old bottles, as well as work by Bahamian artists.

Charlotte's Gallery

Charlotte Street, Nassau
☎ *(809) 322-6310*
Oil paintings and other original pieces of art from Bahamian artists.

The Green Lizard

Bay Street (near the El Greco Hotel), Nassau
☎ *(809) 356-3439*
A hammock heaven for those who just can't get enough of them. There is work here from both local and foreign craftsmen, including chimes and other items.

The Kennedy Gallery

Parliament Street, Nassau
☎ *(809) 325-7832*
Known mostly for its frames, this shop also offers art and sculptures by local artists.

Pyfroms

Bay Street, Nassau
☎ *(809) 322-2603*
Unusual musical items and crafts, including steel drums.

China, Silver and Crystal

Bernard's China & Gifts

Bay Street and 5th Terrace, Centreville
☎ *(809) 322-2841*
Excellent selection of crystal and china from Royal Worcester, Royal Copenhagen, Wedgwood, Baccarat, Royal Crown Derby, Crown Staffordshire, Lalique, Coalport and Royal Doulton.

Little Switzerland

Bay Street, Nassau
☎ *(809) 322-8324*
Silver, pottery, jewelry, Waterford crystal, leather, cameras, designer cosmetics, perfumes and other items all top brand. Great selection of Swiss watches and figurines from Lladro and Royal Doulton.

Marlborough Antiques

Corner of Marlborough and Queen streets
☎ *(809) 328-0502*
Displays works of Bahamian artists Brent Malone and Maxwell Taylor. Antique engravings, antique books, antique maps and other unusual relics from the past. There is a great collection of photography of the Old Bahamas. Also old table settings and English silver. Antique china and Victorian and Edwardian furniture.

The Scottish Shop

Charlotte Street, Nassau
☎ *(809) 322-4720*
Stoneware and bone china from Highland and St. Andrew.

Treasure Traders

Bay Street, Nassau
☎ *(809) 322-8521*

The best selection of crystal and china in the islands. Royal Copenhagen, Wedgwood, Baccarat, Waterford, Royal Crown Derby, Crown Staffordshire, Lalique, Coalport and Royal Doulton.

Fashion

Alexis

Rosetta and Montgomery streets, Nassau
☎ *(809) 328-7464*
Women's shoes from Bandolino, Evan Picone, Timothy Hitsman and others.

Barry's Unlimited

Bay Street, Nassau
☎ *(809) 322-3118*
Perhaps Nassau's most formal store with English cashmere and an array of woolen items. Sportswear and Irish linen handkerchiefs. Chinese Guayabera shirts and crochet blouses, cufflinks and studs.

The Bay

Bay Street, Nassau
☎ *(809) 356-3918*
Designer clothing for men and women.

Bonneville Bones

Bay Street, Nassau
☎ *(809) 328-0804*
Expensive jeans and sportswear; Perry Ellis suits.

Brass & Leather Shop

12 Charlotte Street, Nassau
☎ *(809) 322-3806*
Designer leather handbags, belts, briefcases, wallets, etc.

Cole's of Nassau

Parliament Street, Nassau
☎ *(809) 322-8393*
Designer fashions for women, including formal wear, swimwear and lingerie.

Fendi

Bay Street, Nassau
☎ *(809) 322-6300*
High-end Italian shoes and handbags.

The Girls from Brazil

Bay Street, Nassau
☎ *(809) 323-5966*
Swimwear for women.

Gucci

Bay Street (Saffrey Sq., corner of Bank Lane), Nassau
☎ *(809) 325-0561*
Evening and casual wear, shoes, scarves and ties for men and women. Luggage, leather handbags, briefcases, wallets and much, much more.

Leather Masters

Parliament Street, Nassau
☎ *(809) 322-7597*
Leather bags, wallets, luggage and accessories by Lancel of Paris, "i Santi" of Italy, Ted Lapidus, Etienne Aigner, Lanvin and others. Designer clothing, watches, pens and sunglasses.

Mademoiselle Ltd.

Bay Street at Frederick Street, Nassau
☎ *(809) 322-1530*
Women's clothing and accessories, including swimwear, batik, sarongs and jeans. Androsia fashions; soap, unguents and other ingredients for herbal massages. Branches in many of the better hotels.

The Nassau Shop

284 Bay Street, Nassau
☎ *(809) 322-8405*
The oldest and largest department store in Nassau. Piaget watches and Hermes perfume are here, as well as Pringle and Ballantyne cashmeres, Shetland pullovers and cardigans.

National Hand Prints (Bahamas Hand Prints)

Mackey Street, Nassau
☎ *(809) 393-1974*
Silk-screen prints on Bahamian fabrics, including shirts and dresses, towels, aprons, tablecloths—you name it.

Jewelry

Coin of the Realm

Charlotte Street, Nassau
☎ *(809) 322-4862*
Bahamian coins set in jewelry.

Crown Jewelers

Bay Street, Nassau
☎ *(809) 322-8651*
Specializes in watches.

John Bull

Bay Street and Frederick Street
☎ *(809) 322-3328, 322-4252*
Great selection of jewelry, cameras, watches, cosmetics and perfumes. Jewelry from Nina Ricci, Yves Saint Laurent and others.

Little Switzerland

Bay Street, Nassau
☎ *(809) 322-8324*
Silver, pottery, jewelry, Waterford crystal, leather, cameras, designer cosmetics, perfumes and other items all top brand. Great selection of Swiss watches and figurines from Lladro and Royal Doulton.

The Nassau Shop

284 Bay Street, Nassau
☎ *(809) 322-8405*
The oldest and largest department store in Nassau. Piaget watches and Hermes perfume are here. Huge selection of jewelry.

The Treasure Box

Bay Street, Nassau
☎ *(809) 322-1662*
Jewelry made from seashells and coral.

Coins and Stamps

Bahamas Post Office Philatelic Bureau

At the GPO, E. Hill and Parliament streets
☎ *(809) 322-3344*

Here's a tip: Snatch up the four different "Discovery" stamps, which should become collector's items by the end of the decade. The place for Bahamas stamps.

Clocks

Tick-Tock

Bay Street, Nassau
☎ *(809) 325-7136*
Wooden clocks from Germany's Black Forest.

Cosmetics and Perfumes

The Beauty Spot

Bay and Frederick streets
☎ *(809) 322-5930*
Duty-free cosmetics at the largest cosmetics store in the Bahamas. All the big names are here.

Body Shop

Victoria Street, Nassau
☎ *(809) 326-7068*
Full range of perfumes and cosmetics.

Cameo

W. Bay Street (across from the Straw Market), Nassau
☎ *(809) 322-1449*
Skin treatment products and unguents. Exclusive distributor of the La Prairie line of skin products. Hard-to-find French and Italian brands.

City Pharmacy

Bay Street, Nassau
☎ *(809) 322-2061*
Wide range of perfumes and cosmetics.

John Bull

Bay Street and Frederick Street
☎ *(809) 322-3328, 322-4252*
Great selection of jewelry, cosmetics and perfumes. Jewelry from Nina Ricci, Yves Saint Laurent and others. Perfumes from Estee Lauder, Chanel and others.

Little Switzerland

Bay Street, Nassau
☎ *(809) 322-8324*
Designer cosmetics, perfumes and other items all top brand. Great selection of Swiss watches and figurines from Lladro and Royal Doulton. Perfumes from Passion, Giorgio Beverly and others.

Perfume Bar

Bay Street, Nassau
☎ *(809) 322-3785*
Exclusive retailer of Sublime, Clarin and Boucheron.

The Perfume Shop

Corner of Bay & Frederick streets, Nassau
☎ *(809) 322-2375*
Famous- brand scents for both men and women.

Linens

Linen & Lace

Bay Street, Nassau
☎ *(809) 322-4266*

All sorts of lace and linen products.

The Linen Shop

Savoy Bldg., Bay Street, Nassau
☎ *(809) 322-4266*

Women's blouses, tableware, scarves, bed linen and Irish handkerchiefs. The embroidery here is quite exquisite.

Tobacco

Pipe of Peace

Bay Street, Nassau
☎ *(809) 325-2022*

This is the place in town for Cuban cigars. But smoke as many as you can, because it's illegal to bring them back to the States. Also fine Jamaican and Honduran cigars as well as an extensive pipe tobacco selection.

Books and Maps

Balmain Antiques

Bay Street (near Charlotte Street in Mason's Bldg.), Nassau
☎ *(809) 323-7421*

Antique 19th-century maps, engravings and old bottles, as well as work by Bahamian artists.

Island Merchants Limited

Bay Street, Nassau
☎ *(809) 322-1011*

Bookstore with a decent selection of novels, travel guides and international magazines. It's best for its Bahamian titles.

Music

Cody's Music & Video Centre

E. Bay Street, Nassau
☎ *(809) 325-8834*

Great selection of Caribbean and Goombay and Junkanoo music, as well as calypso, reggae and soca. CDs, tapes and videos are sold here.

Cable Beach (and Saunders Beach)

Many visitors forgo Nassau altogether and head straight for Cable Beach, a few miles due west of the capital and ultimate mall of megaresorts. Cable Beach got its name from the telegraph cable that was laid here from Jupiter Beach in Florida in 1892. Every imaginable amenity and seaside leisure activity await visitors to Cable Beach, not to mention the sole reason a good many arrive here for: gambling.

Cable Beach may start to resemble Mexico's Cancun in a few years—and its endless canyon walls of resorts—if the developers have their way. A new Sandals opened here to compete with the other resorts. And West Bay Street (or Dual Carriage Way, as it's called here), in many stretches along Cable Beach, has been widened to four lanes—not a good sign. But for now, the thoroughfare—for the most part—still meanders through canyon walls of casuarina trees rather than stucco. It's one of the most scenic drives on the island, and the resorts, particularly the Radisson,

pierce the sky more like Oz than the midtown Manhattan sky-
line. And you can expect to find pockets of privacy along the vast
stretches of clean, white sand. And if you don't mind being so
close to the road (West Bay Street/Dual Carriage Way), there
are a number of stretches of open sand, occupied by the occasional Bahamian family. Rent a scooter and select your spot.

What to See and Do in Cable Beach

Watersports

Cable Beach, mainly through its slew of hotels, offers the watersports
enthusiast every conceivable activity, from banana boating, jet skiing,
waterskiing, sailing and parasailing to snorkeling, scuba diving, windsurfing and deep-sea fishing. There are a number of private vendors,
although for "safety reasons" the hotels recommend that their guests
use their own services. I suspect it's for more than safety reasons. See
"Sports on New Providence."

Gambling

High rollers head straight for the Crystal Palace Resort & Casino in
Cable Beach (see "Nightlife in Cable Beach").

Where to Stay in Cable Beach

Nassau Marriott Resort and
Crystal Palace Casino $175–$325   ★ ★ ★ ★

P.O. Box N-8306, West Bay Street, Cable Beach, Nassau
☎ *(800) 453-5301, (809) 327-6200; FAX (809) 327-5227*
Single: $175–$325; Double: $175–$325

This former Carnival-holding-turned-Marriott is pink as your plastic
flamingos and glitzy as your Liberace-impersonator leisure suit. Five
high-rise towers, with high-tech inspirations and aspirations, shelter a
conglomeration of accommodations, shopping arcades, restaurants,
bars, a disco, casino and a cabaret theater. Predictably, there's heaps
to do—beach activities, watersports, tennis, golf, a health club, aerobics classes, and a swimming pool with a 100-foot water slide. This is
not the place to come for peace and quiet, though even the most
sober and somber visitors will be knocked out by the lighting. Accommodations number 736, and are modern and certainly more soothing
than the public areas. Amenities: swimming pool, Jacuzzis, health
club, 18 tennis courts, 18-hole golf course, sauna, exercise machines,
aerobics, 13 restaurants, six lounges, disco, cabaret theater, shopping
arcade. Credit cards: AE, DC, MC, V.

Forte Nassau Beach Hotel $150–$240   ★ ★ ★

P.O. Box N-7756, Cable Beach, Nassau
☎ *(800) 225-5843 U.S., (809) 327-7711; FAX (809) 327-7615*
Single: $150–$240; Double: $150–$240

This vintage 1940s property, renovated in the 1990s, is a good choice
for those who prefer a less-frenetic environment for their island stay.
Understated decor, lovely landscaping and a white-sand beach blend
nicely with the full schedule of activities that include watersports, tennis (with clinics) and an excellent children's program. The 411 guest
rooms sport dark woods and elegant touches and balconies, many
with sea views. Theme restaurants can get a bit cutesy. Amenities:

swimming pool, exercise room, six restaurants, four bars, six tennis courts, minibars. Credit cards: AE, DC, MC, V.

Sandals Royal Bahamian Resort　　　$1400–$1950　　　★★★

P.O. Box N-10422, W. Bay Street, Cable Beach, Nassau
☎ *(800) 726-3257, (809) 327-5400; FAX (809) 327-1894*
Single: $1400–$1950 per person, per week

The former French-ified Le Meridien Royal Bahamian Hotel has been taken over by the couples-couples-everywhere Sandals chain. One all-inclusive price will buy you and the companion of your choice one week's worth of accommodations, meals and all the activities you can handle. Everything's included—taxes, gratuities—even the booze (and not just beer and wine, like over at Club Med). Amenities: swimming pool, health club, tennis courts, water sports, saunas, Jacuzzis, free shuttle to the casino. Credit cards: AE, DC, MC, V.

Radisson Cable Beach Casino and Golf Resort　　　$145–$200　　　★★★

P.O. Box N-4814, Cable Beach, Nassau
☎ *(800) 327-6000 U.S., (809) 327-6000; FAX (809) 327-6987*
Single: $145–$200; Double: $145–$200

Linked to the Crystal Palace Casino via a shopping arcade, this curvaceous nine-story, 700-room Radisson features plenty of bustle and traffic. All of the customary activities are offered, including free scuba- and dance classes, a comprehensive children's program, and special deals at the Marriott's health club and the Cable Beach Golf Club. Accommodations are decorated with lively furnishings and prints, and many feature beachfront balconies. Bars, lounges, and public areas are rife with frivolity and various entertainments.

Amenities: swimming pool, 18 tennis courts, room service, five restaurants and bars, beauty salon, concierge, shops.

Credit cards: AE, DC, MC, V.

Days Inn Casuarinas　　　$70–$140　　　★★

P.O. Box N-4016, Cable Beach, Nassau
☎ *(800) 327-3012, (809) 327-7921; FAX (809) 327-8152*
Single: $70–$140; Double: $70–$140

Built by enterprising local, Nettie Symonette, this 86-unit hotel is a complex of seven brown and white buildings, nestled in and among the casuarina trees. This family-run operation is a favorite among visitors who prefer to be treated like a welcome guest rather than an ugly tourist. The homey atmosphere is infectious, from the cozy accommodations to the two notable restaurants. Save your appetite for the all-you-can-eat Bahamian buffet, spread out every Friday night. Room prices are based mainly on location—those closer to the beach cost more, though none are that far away, and some have kitchens. Amenities: two swimming pools, a tennis court, two restaurants, two bars, lounge. Credit cards: AE, DC, MC, V.

Orange Hill Beach Inn　　　$70–$100　　　★★

P.O. Box N-8583, W. Bay Street, Nassau
☎ *(809) 327-7157*
Single: $70–$85; Double: $85–$100

Situated a few miles west of the Cable Beach frenzy, this low-key, 32-room, family-run operation grabs a good share of budgeting honeymooners. Not even married? The inn will plan your entire Bahama-style ceremony, including legalese. The owners are fantastic, friendly folks who will pour your drinks and nip a little themselves, giving Orange Hill a next-door-neighbor-type ambience. The extreme hospitality also distracts from the physical layout of the place, which is something of a cross between a Catholic girls' school campus and an old Motel 6. Rooms are smallish and peaceful and devoid of phones. Some have kitchenettes, and all have balconies or patios with pool- or sea views. The on-site restaurant turns out superb home-cooked meals for breakfast and dinner, while scuba diving is one of the more popular outdoor activities. Call it the house specialty. Amenities: swimming pool, restaurant, bar, kayak rentals. Credit cards: AE, MC, V.

Where to Eat in Cable Beach

Androsia Steak and Seafood Restaurant

Cable Beach Shoppers Haven, near Crystal Palace Casino, Cable Beach
☎ *(809) 327-7805*
Steak/seafood
Dinner: daily 6–10 p.m., entrees $18–$27

Named after the island of Andros, this intimate restaurant, situated in a small shopping area, serves delectable fresh seafood including, Bahamian grouper, flounder, red snapper and lobster thermidor. The pepper steak *au Paris* (the house specialty) is prepared from an actual recipe handed down from Les Halles in Paris. Specialty coffees (known as "adventurous" coffees) are a good follow up to your meal. Reservations recommended. Credit cards: AE, DC, MC, V.

Cafe Johnny Canoe

West Bay Street, in the Forte Nassau Beach Hotel, Cable Beach
☎ *(809) 327-3373*
Bahamian/American cuisine
Breakfast: daily 7:30–11 a.m., $5–$8
Lunch: daily 11 a.m.–5 p.m.
Dinner: daily 5–11 p.m., entrees $7–$24

This casual, colorful restaurant is especially popular with families who can assuage everyone's hunger pangs with a menu that features everything from steaks and burgers to blackened fish and barbecued ribs. Both indoor and outdoor dining is available, a calypso band is usually on hand Thursday through Sunday nights, and the atmosphere is joyful and relaxed. Credit cards: AE, MC, V.

The Round House ★★★

West Bay Street, in Casuarinas of Cable Beach, Cable Beach
☎ *(809) 327-7921*
Bahamian/American cuisine
Lunch: Wed.–Mon. Noon–3 p.m., entrees $9–$18
Dinner: Wed.–Mon. 6–10:30 p.m., entrees $13–$21

This very private, very intimate restaurant is housed in an old mansion, run by the illustrious Nettie Symonette, the Bahamas' very legendary proprietress. Nettie's menu includes many of her renowned favorites—Spanish Wells grouper, Abaco lobster, Eleuthera chicken, Andros conch and other fresh catches. Drinks and desserts are generous and addicting. Business people have the use of an adjoining suite for pre-dinner drinks and schmoozing. Credit cards: AE, DC, MC, V.

Rock 'n' Roll Cafe

Frilsham House, two blocks east of Crystal Palace Casino, Cable Beach

☎ *(809) 327-7639*
Bahamian/American cuisine
Lunch: daily noon–5 p.m., entrees $8–$14
Dinner: daily 5–11 p.m., entrees $10–$24

Rock 'n' rollers will swoon with nostalgia over the memorabilia, artifacts, and music, and anyone who's ever patronized a Hard Rock Cafe may mistake this place for a branch location. The eclectic menu includes pleasers such as appetizers, finger foods, stuffed potato skins, thick sandwiches, and platters of seafood and chicken. Both indoor and outdoor seating are available. Open until 2 a.m. nightly. You can pulse with live bands Thursdays through Saturdays, or opt for karaoke music on Tuesdays and Sundays. Credit cards: AE, MC, V.

Riviera Restaurant   ★★★★

West Bay Street, Riviera Tower, in the Radisson Cable Beach Hotel, Cable Beach
☎ *(809) 327-6000*
Seafood cuisine
Dinner: Mon., Wed.–Sat. 6–10:30 p.m., entrees $21–$40

The Radisson's signature restaurant, situated above the lobby with Cape Cod-ish decor and sea views, is renowned for its meticulously prepared seafood cuisine. Lobster, salmon, tuna, shrimp and crab cakes are all the menu, as are marvelous desserts and specialty coffees. Jackets and ties required. Reservations required. Credit cards: AE, MC, V.

Japanese Steak House   ★★★

West Bay Street, Cable Beach
☎ *(809) 327-7781*
Japanese cuisine
Dinner: daily 4–11:30 p.m.

Just opened in 1996, this establishment thrills Japanese-food lovers with its Kobe steak, New York strip steak, lobster, conch, shrimp and vegetable dishes. Food is prepared before your eyes by knife-wielding chefs at Hibachi tables. Saki, Kirin and plum wine are in stock, and early bird specials are excellent bargains. Credit cards: AE, DC, MC, V.

Dicky Mo's Deck   ★★

West Bay Street, Cable Beach
☎ *(809) 327-7854*
Seafood/American cuisine
Breakfast: daily 7–11 a.m.
Lunch: daily noon–4 p.m.
Dinner: daily 5–10:30 p.m.

Located downstairs from the Japanese Steak House, Dicky Mo's is another new entry to the Cable Beach dining scene. Menu offerings include hearty breakfasts, and a varied lunch and dinner menu. Topping the list is garlic crabs and shrimps, plus there's a wide range of wines, beers and tropical cocktails. Credit cards: AE, MC, V.

Nightlife in Cable Beach

Casinos

Crystal Palace Resort & Casino

West Bay Street, Cable Beach
☎ *(809) 327-6459*

You name it and it can be found here at this joint venture between Carnival Cruise Lines and the Continental Companies of Miami. This place out-Vegases Vegas with its 35,000 square feet, 750 slot machines, 51 blackjack tables, nine roulette wheels, seven craps tables, a baccarat table and a big six. The coloring of the place is out of "Miami Vice" and the lighting superb. Giant football-shaped bar. The Casino Lounge offers live entertainment. The only difference between here and Vegas is that this place actually closes every day— from 4–10 a.m. It's packed both at closing and at opening. Dress is casual and you have to be at least 21. You also have to be a tourist because, while they let a lot of people in here, they don't allow locals. The locals wouldn't come, anyhow.

Clubs/Bars/Discos

Banana Boat Bar

Forte Nassau Beach Hotel
Cable Beach
☎ *(809) 327-7711*
Typical beach hotel lobby bar with the standard innocuous Bahamian music played by a live band. But it is one of the more relaxing bars in Cable Beach. Drinks start at $3.75 but are half-price during happy hour from 5 to 7 p.m. Open until midnight.

Fanta-Z

Crystal Palace Resort & Casino
West Bay Street, Cable Beach
☎ *(809) 327-6200*
Part of the casino, the light show is pretty nifty here. Great view of the sea. But this place is pricey, with a $15 cover and drinks that start at $4. No shorts and no jeans. Open Thurs. and Sun. 9 p.m.–2 a.m. and Fri.–Sat. 9 p.m.–4 a.m.

Rock & Roll Cafe

Forte Nassau Beach Hotel
Cable Beach
☎ *(809) 327-7711*
Modeled after the Hard Rock Cafes found the world over, this isn't much different. Expensive munchies and beer ($4) set to a rock motif. The older set might get a little miffed, but staid by rockers' standards. No cover.

The Zoo

West Bay Street
Saunders Beach
☎ *(809) 322-7195*
This is the place to go on New Providence if daylight simply hurts your eyes. Behemoth-like complex with five bars on two floors. Go into any bar and you'll think you're in a different establishment entirely. They all are patterned after different motifs (i.e., "Jungle," "Gilligan's Island," "Sports Bar," etc.). Most of the action is found on the lower level dance floor. Also a "VIP" bar and restaurant. Sports nuts will be in heaven with the large-screen TVs with all kinds of games being shown. Stiff covers at $20 Sun.–Thurs. and a whopping $40 Sat. and Sun.

Stage Shows

Palace Theater

Crystal Palace Resort & Casino
West Bay Street, Cable Beach
☎ *(809) 327-6200*

Vegas shows transplanted to the Bahamas. The most spectacular stage performances in the islands. 800-seat theater. Lavish productions and stunning visuals. Not to be missed if staying at Cable Beach (or anywhere on New Providence for that matter). Open Tues.-Sun. Showtimes Tues.-Sat are at 7:30, 9:30 and 11:30 p.m. Dinner (if desired) is at 6 p.m. No dinner on Sun. and Thurs.; one show at 9 p.m. On Wed. and Fri., dinner's at 7, followed by two shows at 9 and 11 p.m. Reservations are recommended.

Paradise Island

Atlantis, Paradise Island

Not too long ago, four-mile-long Paradise Island had a less than auspicious name, Hog Island (after the fact that it served as little but a hog farm for Nassau during the centuries before it became a magnet of the rich and famous), until it was renamed by millionaire Huntington Hartford after he bought the property in 1960.

Today, Paradise Island, which sits but 600 feet off the north shore of Nassau, resembles little of its former self. Gone are the hogs and in are the high-rise condos and hotels for the snow birds who need a little sleep between sessions at the craps tables. The island, rich in tropical flora, is a gambler's mecca. Three huge complexes, Atlantis Paradise Island Resort & Casino, the Paradise Island Casino and Paradise Club can be found under one roof, making the complex, which sprawls over perhaps 12 acres, one of the most outrageous and grandiose gambling venues in the world.

Both cruise-shippers and Nassau hotel guests swarm Hartford Beach in back of the Atlantis, Paradise Island Resort & Casino, a decent strip of sand—when you can see it—a short walk from the Paradise Island Bridge. This place is a corn-rowed Coney Island south without the rides or the pickpockets. The place is packed, in season and off. Take my advice and hoof it a quarter-mile east

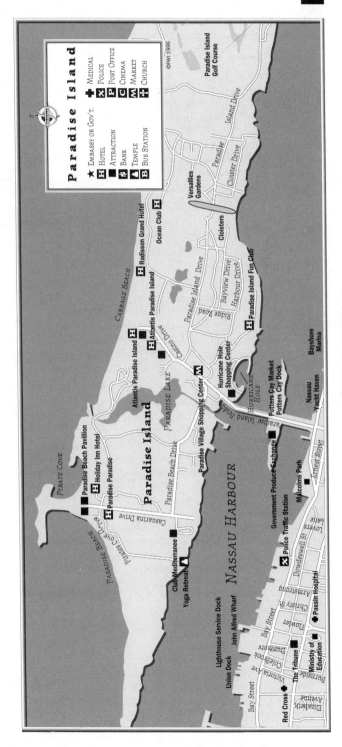

up the sand to where the crowd thins out and the beach is wider. You'll just have to walk awhile to get to the nearest bar.

What to See and Do on Paradise Island

Blue Lagoon Island

Off the eastern end of Paradise Island

Easily accessible by boats that run regularly back and forth from Nassau Harbour, Blue Lagoon features seven beaches, all snowy white. A desert isle escape in Nassau's back yard. It's used by the cruise ship companies for theme parties, and called a different island by each. One calls it Fantasy Island, another Gilligan's Island. Just a little silly, but that's what holidays are all about. Right?

Gambling

Paradise Island is a gambling Oz. The yellow brick road crosses the Paradise Island Bridge to the massive Atlantis Paradise Island Resort & Casino-Paradise Island Casino-Paradise Club complex, a virtual shopping mall of roll-of-the-dice vice.

The Beaches

Paradise Beach, of course, on the western tip of the small island, was the island's best reason for coming here before the roulette wheels came spinning into town (and still is if you're not a gambler). Cabbage Beach, though not as popular as Paradise Island Beach and Hartford Beach, is frequented by locals and much less crowded. It's a fine stretch of powdery white sand, as is the eastern end of Hartford Beach and Snorkeler's Cove Beach.

The Resorts

Anywhere else, it would be silly to list resorts as attractions. Not so in the Bahamas. Even if staying somewhere and you don't gamble, no trip to Paradise Island is complete without a stroll through the thoroughly posh Atlantis Paradise Island Resort & Casino with its Vegas-style stage shows, shopping malls, scores of restaurants and shops and, of course, the massive casino. The resort was originally named the Britannia Beach Hotel, and Howard Hughes once rented out the entire top floor of the place. Tourists who are not even staying here—hordes of them—come to tour the "grounds" of the complex, which are more like "undergrounds," with tunnels flanked by huge seawater tanks teeming with marine life, including bizarre-looking saw sharks, hammerheads, nurse sharks, giant jewfish, spiny lobsters, porcupine fish and giant rays. Divers regularly plunge into the tanks—which, remarkably, are man-made extensions of the sea (although the fish can't get out)—to feed the creatures. The tunnels are a veritable sub-aquatic zoo.

The Cloisters

At the Versailles Gardens

Media mogul William Randolph Hearst shipped the remnants of a 14th-century French stone monastery to the United States during the 1920s and Huntington Hartford brought the structure to Paradise Island in the 1960s. There's an interesting sculpture at the center of the "ruins" by American sculptor Dick Reid called "Silence." It's quite appropriate.

Cloisters, Paradise Island

Versailles Gardens

At the Ocean Club
☎ *(809) 363-2501*

In these beautiful, lush gardens can be found fountains and statues of various historical figures, including Franklin D. Roosevelt, Hercules and Napoleon. A great change of pace and a place to chill out. This is also a favorite spot for weddings.

Potter's Cay

Underneath the Paradise Island Bridge

A bustling dockside seafood market where fishermen peddle their catch to both locals and area restaurants. Conch is the big draw here, and both raw and various prepared versions can be had.

Where to Stay on Paradise Island

Atlantis Paradise Island
Resort and Casino $110–$280   ★ ★ ★ ★

P.O. Box N-4777, Paradise Island
☎ *(800) 231-3000 U.S., (809) 363-3000; FAX (809) 363-3957*
Single: $110–$280; Double: $110–$280

After a multimillion-dollar refurbishment, this world-unto-itself property re-opened for business in early 1995. The self-contained resort is what would happen if Las Vegas popped out of Waterworld. There is water, water everywhere—swimming water, viewing water, saltwater, fresh water, underwater and purely decorative water. The casino is one of the few dry spots—30,000 square feet of every conceivable gambling activity, including nearly hundreds of round-the-clock slots. Don't know how to play? Sign up for one of the free daily classes. Need more of a Vegas fix? Take in the full-on Vegas-in-the-Bahamas revue. Accommodations at this 1150-room property are inside one of two towers or in the more private Villas. All the rooms are comfy and feature water-view balconies and personal refrigerators. Other on-the-spot action includes five swimming pools, nine tennis courts, championship par-72 golf, health club, dance club, water sports, jogging paths, discos, nightlife, 12 restaurants and as many bars, and a wear-the-little-darlings-out children's program. Travel services and car rentals are also on hand. Amenities: casino, five swimming pools, 12 restaurants, 12 bars, health club, dance club, nine tennis courts, jogging path, beauty salon, travel services, car rental, children's program, room service, concierge desk. Credit cards: AE, DC, MC, V.

Club Land'Or   **$155–$235**   ★ ★

P.O. Box SS-6429, Paradise Drive, Paradise Island
☎ *(800) 446-3850 U.S., (809) 363-2400; FAX (809) 363-3403*
Single: $155–$235; Double: $155–$235

Three levels of one-bedroom time-share units cater to those who are more into "doing for themselves." Accommodations include fully equipped kitchenettes, separate bedroom and living rooms, and garden- or water-view balconies or patios. The property has its own lounge, restaurant, swimming pool and organized activities, but you'll have to drive to get to the beach or casino. Amenities: swimming pool, restaurant, two bars, minibars.

Club Mediterranee   ★ ★ ★

P.O. Box N-7137, Casuarina Drive, Paradise Island
☎ *(800) 258-2633 U.S., (809) 363-2640; FAX (809) 365-3496*
Single: $800–$1500 per person, weekly

Flying under the Club Med banner, this 21-acre property features standard Club Med-isms—everything is included in the price except the booze (although wine and beer at lunch and dinner are thrown into the deal). You'll have free reign to join exercise classes, take golf lessons, participate in all the water sports (including wind surfing), hang out on three miles of beach, and stuff your face three times a day. Tennis is a major feature here with 20 Har-Tru courts and intensive tennis clinics, to boot. The 312 guest rooms are basic, but comfortable (no one stays inside their rooms for long here, anyway). Unlike many Club Meds this one attracts as many couples (including honeymooners and parents running away from their kids) as it does on-the-make singles. Amenities: swimming pool, 20 tennis courts, golf, fitness center, aerobics classes, three restaurants, three bars, disco. Credit cards: AE, MC, V.

Ocean Club   **$200–$575**   ★ ★ ★ ★ ★

P.O. Box N-4777, Ocean Club Drive, Paradise Island
☎ *(800) 321-3000 U.S., (809) 363-3000; FAX (809) 363-2424*
Single: $200–$575; Double: $200–$575

This former private club—once owned by zillionaire Huntington Hartford—is, without doubt, the most chic resort on Paradise Island. You won't find any of the glitz (or water) of the Atlantis, just plenty of elegance, pampering and hobnobbing with other sophisticates. The setting is a knockout—fabulous terraced gardens, a stunning adjacent beach, statuary, reflecting pools and country-club-like grounds. Accommodations renovated in 1994—number 67 (plus several suites and villas) and are large and luxuriously decorated, with high ceilings, private verandahs, marble baths and high-end amenities. The gourmet restaurant and nine tennis courts (with full-time pro) are extra bonuses. Amenities: swimming pool, nine tennis courts, croquet, two restaurants, three bars, concierge, complimentary shuttle to golf course and casino. Credit cards: AE, DC, MC, V.

Pirate's Cove Holiday Inn
SunSpree Resort   **$85–$155**   ★ ★ ★

P.O. Box SS-6214, Casuarina Drive, Paradise Island

☎ *(800) 234-6835 U.S., (809) 363-2100; FAX (809) 363-2206*
Single: $85–$155; Double: $85–$155

If a 566-room high-rise (the Bahamas' tallest, at 17 stories) on a private beach is your idea of a home-away-from-home, this place might be your best bet. The prices are decent, the activities options are extensive, and the cherry accommodations will put you in the get-up-and-go mood. This is an especially popular choice for families. Kids can knock themselves out in the special supervised day camp or over in the video arcade and game room. Other action takes place at the water-sports center (check out the parasailing), or on the tennis and volleyball courts, or swimming pool area—with its 90-foot-long replica of the Bonnie Anne pirate ship. Amenities: swimming pool, beach, exercise room, two tennis courts, travel services, car rental, three restaurants, two bars, two Jacuzzis, water-sports center. Credit cards: AE, DC, MC, V.

Radisson Grand Resort $130–$225 ★★★

P.O. Box SS 6307, Casino Drive, Paradise Island
☎ *(800) 325-3535 U.S., (809) 363-2011; FAX (809) 363-3193*
Single: $130–$225; Double: $130–$225

The 360-room Radisson is a mere 14 stories high, compared to the towering 17 at Pirate's Cove Holiday Inn. Still, it fronts a good stretch of beach, is next door to the casino and is appropriately posh. Accommodations are deluxe and afford exquisite water views from small, private balconies. There are plenty of water activities—including water-skiing and parasailing—as well as three restaurants and bars, a lounge, nightclub, swimming pool, and four tennis courts. Amenities: swimming pool, four tennis courts, three restaurants, three bars, lounge, nightclub, water-sports, room service, travel services. Credit cards: AE, DC, MC, V.

Bay View Village $120–$420 ★★★

P.O. Box SS-6308, Harbour Road, Paradise Island
☎ *(800) 321-3000 U.S., (809) 363-2555; FAX (809) 363-2370*
Single suite: $120–$165; One bedroom penthouse suite: $170–$230;
Townhouse: $195–$270; Villa: $205–$290; Villa deluxe: $220–$320;
Six-person villa: $295–$420

Condo-lovers or those traveling with a group will appreciate these units positioned near the harbor and beach. All accommodations come with private patios or balconies, fully equipped kitchens and daily maid service, with a mini-market, bar and snack bar on the premises. If you can't live without a telephone, stay elsewhere or bring the old cell phone along. The villas are large and airy; they could be your home! Super comfortable with huge kitchens. They also have large living rooms and a dining area. Although not on the water, Bay View makes for a great base. Everything is within walking distance. Facilities include three swimming pools, a tennis court and bicycle rental. Larger groups might want to sprint for the larger townhouses, villas or penthouse apartments. Amenities: three swimming pools, tennis court, TVs. Credit cards: AE, MC, V.

Comfort Suites Paradise Island $125–$205 ★★★

P.O. Box SS-6202, 1 Paradise Island Drive, Paradise Island
☎ *(800) 228-5150 U.S., (809) 363-3680; FAX (809) 363-2588*
Single: $125–$205; Double: $125–$205

Opened in 1991, this all-suite low-rise, across from the Atlantis Resort, is particularly favored by honeymooners who enjoy the relative peace and quiet but still get to use the myriad facilities at the bustling resort. A swimming pool with swim-up bar and an adjacent restaurant are on site. Accommodations offer tropical decor, a separate living area, in-room safes, minibars, hair dryers and kitchens, plus continental breakfast is included. Amenities: swimming pool, bar, bicycle rentals, tour desk. Credit cards: AE, DC, MC, V.

Paradise Paradise Beach Resort $90–$140 ★★

P.O. Box N-4777, Casuarina Drive, Paradise Island
☎ *(800) 321-3000, (809) 363-3000; FAX (809) 363-2540*
Single: $90–$140; Double: $90–$140

When the name has a twins attached to it, you know it has to be a cutesy place that caters to those funner-than-fun young singles. The rooms are teenager-simple (and worn), while the list of activities is fairly lengthy. Positioned on a good beach, watersports are the focus, though aerobics and casino-shuttling are also on the list. A casual restaurant is on the premises. Amenities: swimming pool, restaurant, bar. Credit cards: AE, DC, MC, V.

Where to Eat on Paradise Island

Cafe Martinique ★★★★★

Casino Drive, in Atlantis Paradise Island Resort and Casino, Paradise Island
☎ *(809)363-3000*
French/Continental cuisine
Dinner: daily 7–11 p.m., entrees $32–$44
Sunday brunch 11:30 a.m.–2:30 p.m., $30

Even James Bond (in the film, *Thunderball*) dined at this fancy schmancy restaurant with its *fin de siècle* decor and ambiance. Don't come here if you're in a hurry, as this dining experience should be savored slowly and carefully, along with the food and drink. Don't be surprised if you're offered the dessert menu first—the famous soufflés need plenty of time for preparation, and they are worth every second (the Grand Marnier soufflé is especially sublime). Most of the classic French and continental dishes are superb and exquisitely prepared and presented. The Sunday brunch is an orgy for one. As might be expected, the wine cellar is up to the task of accompanying every morsel. Jackets required. Reservations required. Credit cards: AE, DC, MC, V.

Courtyard Terrace ★★★★

Ocean Club Drive, in the Ocean Club, Paradise Island
☎ *(809) 363-2501*
Continental/Bahamian cuisine
Dinner: daily 7–9 p.m., entrees $24–$37

This wonderful, sophisticated atmosphere—former mansion, Edenesque garden, bubbling fountain, colonial verandahs, soft Calypso sounds, Wedgwood settings—appeals to an upscale clientele. Menu choices include dishes such as chateaubriand, Nassau grouper, roast rack of lamb and grilled duck's breast. Jackets required. Reservations required. Credit cards: AE, DC, MC, V.

Mama Loo's ★★★

Casino Drive, in the Coral Towers, Atlantis Paradise Island Resort and Casino, Paradise Island

☎ *(809) 363-3000*
Chinese/Caribbean cuisine
Dinner: Tues.–Sun. 6:30–11 p.m., entrees $18–$30
The ambiance in this intimate dinner-only restaurant is British-gone-troppo-at-the-turn-of-the-century—decor such as potted palms, wicker wingback chairs, ceiling fans, torchlight chandeliers. Choose from Cantonese, Szechwan, Caribbean or Polynesian menu selections—mild, curried or spicy flavors. Wash it all down with a strong exotic drink or weak ordinary tea. Credit cards: AE, DC, MC, V.

Villa d'Este

Casino Drive, in the Coral Towers, Atlantis Paradise Island Resort and Casino, Paradise Island
☎ *(809) 363-3000*
Italian cuisine
Dinner: Thurs.–Tues. 6:30–11 p.m.
This namesake to the snob-nobbing hotel on Italy's Lake Como features stylish decor, Italian murals and dim lighting to go along with luscious Italian cuisine. Best bets are the fettuccine Alfredo and veal parmigiana, and don't even think of passing on the pastry selections. Classical guitar music is featured most nights. Credit cards: AE, DC, MC, V.

Rotisserie

Casino Drive, in the Radisson Grand Resort, Paradise Island
☎ *(809) 363-2011*
Steak/grilled meats
Dinner: daily 6:30–10 p.m., entrees $21–$32
This hotel's fine dining restaurant features a romantic setting with ocean view in which to chomp on perfectly prepared thick steaks, prime ribs, grilled meats or—for the non-carnivores—fresh seafood. Diners can watch through glass as they master chefs prepare their selections. Fine wines and fussy desserts are also offered. Reservations recommended. Credit cards: AE, DC, MC, V.

Blue Lagoon Seafood Restaurant

Club Land'or, Paradise Beach Drive, Paradise Island
☎ *(809) 363-2400*
Seafood/International cuisine
Breakfast: Mon.–Sat. 7:30–11 a.m., $4–$8
Dinner: daily 5-10 p.m., entrees $16–$30
Come for a casual Bahamian breakfast, or save your appetite for well-prepared dinners—served by candlelight—that include lobster thermidor, stuffed grouper, grilled chicken and pasta dishes. The lounge provides live entertainment most nights, and dress is casual. Credit cards: AE, MC, V.

Columbus Tavern   ★ ★ ★

Paradise Island Drive, Paradise Harbour Club and Marina, Paradise Island
☎ *(809) 363-2534*
Daily 7 a.m.–midnight
Catch a good view of the boating scene on Nassau Harbour as you feast on lobster thermidor, beef Wellington, desert crepes and other dishes in this nautical-decor tavern. Finish off your meal with a cup of the special Bahamian coffee. Reservations recommended. Credit cards: AE, MC, V.

Swank's Cafe   ★ ★

Paradise Island Shopping Center, Paradise Island
☎ *(809) 363-2765*
Breakfast: daily 7:30–11 a.m., $5–$9
Lunch and dinner: daily 11 a.m.–11 p.m.

Sick of all the chic restaurants, delicate sauces and Bahamian specialties? Head to this casual cafe, as the locals do, and feast on 15 or so
varieties of pizza, or a plain breakfast. No frills, good deal. Credit cards:
AE, MC, V.

Nightlife on Paradise Island

Casinos

Atlantis Paradise Island Casino

Atlantis Paradise Island Resort & Casino
Casino Drive, Paradise Island
☎ *(809) 363-3000*

Hey, man, this is it—the center of nightlife on Paradise Island. Even
if you don't gamble, you've got to take a cruise through this place.
Thirty thousand square feet, 60 blackjack tables, 12 craps tables, 10
roulette wheels, three for baccarat and one for big six. Oh, yeah—
there's about a thousand slot machines, and you can feed these 24
hours a day. Take a stroll through Bird Cage Walk with its tons of restaurants, shops, bars and cabarets and you'll think you're on a massive
space station light years from Earth. The tables close from 4–10 a.m.
daily, but are open every minute between. Dress is casual and you've
got to be 21 to play.

Stage Shows

Cabaret Theatre (Le Cabaret)

Atlantis Paradise Island Resort & Casino
Casino Drive, Paradise Island
☎ *(809) 363-3000*

Here can be seen a $2 million production that gives anything in Vegas
a run for its money. Vaudeville at its campiest—magicians, skaters,
showgirls, acrobats, circus performers, clowns, comedians, jugglers,
you name it, all perform on five different sets, including an ice skating
rink. The dinner show starts at 7 or 8 and at 5:30 on Saturdays and
costs $48. Cocktail shows run at 7:15 and 9 p.m. on Saturdays; they
cost $30 and include two drinks. There are no shows Sundays.

Bars/Clubs/Discos

Club Pastiche

Atlantis, Paradise Island Resort & Casino
Casino Drive, Paradise Island
☎ *(809) 363-3000*

Packed disco with an amazing light show. Drinks are about $4. An
international cast of jetsetters, models and playboys. If you wanna get
lucky, bring a lot of money, honey.

Coral Towers pool bar

Atlantis, Paradise Island Resort & Casino
Casino Drive, Paradise Island
☎ *(809) 363-3000*

Swim-up bar that seems effective for singles trolling for mates. More
than a few weekend romances have been spawned astride the bar's
submerged perches.

Gallery Bar

Beach Towers
Atlantis, Paradise Island Resort & Casino
Casino Drive, Paradise Island
☎ *(809) 363-3000*

English-style club atmosphere and a relaxing place to take a daytime break from shopping or gaming in the complex.

Le Paon

Radisson Grand Resort
Paradise Island
☎ *(809) 363-2011*

Another popular disco that mixes in calypso and old pop from the 1970s into the repertoire.

Mama Loo's

Atlantis, Paradise Island Resort & Casino
Casino Drive, Paradise Island
☎ *(809) 363-3000*

If you've come to the Bahamas for those silly umbrella cocktails served in pineapple and coconut shells, you'll find tacky Polynesian nirvana alive and well at Mama Loo's, next to the casino's arcade.

Oasis Lounge

Club Land'Or
Paradise Island
☎ *(809) 363-2400*

Beautiful lakeside setting. If you're looking to cool down some, this isn't a bad place. A lot more quiet than the other choices. Calypso at night.

Sports Bar

Atlantis, Paradise Island Resort & Casino
Casino Drive, Paradise Island
☎ *(809) 363-3000*

Huge bar that takes up the entire floor of the casino. For those betting on the Dolphins.

Comedy Clubs

Joker's Wild

Atlantis, Paradise Island Resort & Casino
Casino Drive, Paradise Island
☎ *(809) 363-3000*

Local and imported funny men (and ladies) clown around here in nightly 90-minute shows beginning at 9:30. Three comedians perform per show. Closed Mondays. Expensive drinks at $5.

Sports on New Providence

Scuba Diving/Underwater Activities

The best places to catch the shark shows are at Shark Runway, Shark Wall and Shark Arena. At these sites, divers are treated to a spectacle as the divemaster chums the water, attracting dozens of Caribbean Reef Sharks. Silky Sharks can be found in ample numbers at Shark Buoy.

For wrecks, the Bahama Mama is an icon, but take a number. Also popular are the ships sunk as dive attractions. The *Sea Viking* is a 95-foot steel-hulled fishing vessel only recently sunk. There's also the 100-foot *Tears of*

NEW PROVIDENCE

Allah and the 150-foot *Willaurie*. The **Graveyard** offers four wrecks of close proximity sunk intentionally. Some of the older wrecks, however, are barely discernible as ships. The *Mahoney* was a 212-foot steamship that sunk in 1929. Today, the wreck is pretty broken up.

The waters off New Providence have a little of something for every diver. Good wall dives can be had at the Tongue of the Ocean at such places as Tunnel Wall and Razorback. Shallow reefs are in abundance. A stunning one is Goulding Cay, with its Elkhorn Coral stretching nearly to the surface from 25 feet. Southwest Reef features magnificent Staghorn, Elkhorn, Fire and Star Coral formations. Pumpkin Patch has an abundance of sealife.

Bahama Divers

> *P.O. Box 5004*
> *Nassau*
> ☎ *(800) 398- DIVE, (809) 393-6054, (809) 393-5644; FAX (809) 393-6078*
> *U.S. Office*
> *P.O. Box 21584*
> *Fort Lauderdale, FL 33335*
> ☎ *(800) 398-DIVE, (954) 351-9740*
> Full-service dive center offering rentals and twice-daily, three-hour dive trips to wrecks, coral reefs, drop-offs and blue holes. Beginner instruction. Half-day trip for beginners with instruction costs $60 at last check. Certified divers can join half-day trips for $35 to offshore reefs, $60 to offshore reefs at deeper depths, blue holes and drop-offs. Ages 8 and older. Reservations required. Free transportation to and from hotels.

Custom Aquatics

> ☎ *(809) 362-1492*
> Full-service dive center offering rentals, instruction and trips.

Dive Dive Dive

> *P.O. Box N-8050*
> *Nassau*
> ☎ *(809) 362-1143, 362-1401; FAX (809) 362-1994*
> *U.S. Office*
> *1323 SE 17th Street, Ste. 519*
> *Fort Lauderdale, FL 33316*
> ☎ *(800) 368-3483; FAX (954) 943-5002*
> Full-service PADI dive center offering rentals, instruction and trips. The scuba lessons are free at the Radisson Cable Beach pool. Dives to caves reefs and shark sites.

Diver's Haven

> *P.O. Box N-1658*
> *Nassau*
> ☎ *(809) 393-0869, (800) 780-7640; FAX (809) 393-3695*
> Full-service dive center offering rentals, instruction and trips.

Hartley's Undersea Walk

> *East Bay Street*
> ☎ *(809) 393-8234*
> Cruise along the ocean floor donning a special protective helmet. This is a 3.5-hour cruise aboard the Pied Piper from Nassau Harbour. You'll actually be submerged for about 20 minutes as you gaze at clouds of tropical fish and coral reef formations. No scuba diving certification is required and entire families can easily make the walk. Trips

are run daily at 9:30 a.m. and 1:30 p.m. from Nassau Yacht Haven on East Bay Street. The cost is $40 per person in groups of five.

Nassau Scuba Centre

Coral Harbour
P.O. Box CB11863
Nassau
☎ *(800) 327-8150, (809) 362-1964; FAX (809) 362-1198*
U.S. Office
P.O. Box 21766
Fort Lauderdale, FL 33335
☎ *(800) 327-8150, (954) 462-3400; FAX (954) 462-4100*
Full-service PADI dive center offering rentals, instruction and trips. Dives to caves reefs, and shark sites.

Stuart Cove's Dive South Ocean

P.O. Box CB-11697
Nassau
South Ocean Beach & Golf Resort
☎ *(809) 362-5227, 362-4171; FAX (809) 362-5227*
U.S. Office
1405 SE 17th Street
Ft. Lauderdale, FL 33316
☎ *(800) 879-9832, (954) 524-5755; FAX (954) 524-5925*
Full-service dive center offering rentals, instruction and trips. Dives to caves, reefs, shark sites and wrecks off the island's south coast. Two dives a day to reefs at 9:30 a.m. and 1:30 p.m. Longer trips to Eleuthera, Exuma Cays and Andros (Tongue of the Ocean) are available. The advantage with this firm is that dive sites are only a few minutes from shore. Beginner's program costs $99. Morning dives for certified divers cost $65. Certification course costs $350. Known for their shark dives at Shark Arena and Shark Buoy.

Sun Divers

P.O. Box N-10728
Nassau
☎ *(800) 298-4786, (809) 325-8927*
Full-service dive center offering rentals, instruction, snorkeling gear and trips. Dives to caves, drop-offs and shallow and deep reefs. Trips leave at 9 a.m. and 1 p.m.

Sunskiff Divers

P.O. Box N-142
Nassau
☎ *(800) 331-5884, (809) 361-4075; FAX (809) 362-1979*
Full-service dive center offering rentals, instruction and trips.

Banana Boating

Banana boating is simply holding on to a large rubber banana being towed by a motorboat. Great for kids; not particularly thrilling for anyone else.

Funsea

Crystal Palace Resort & Casino
West Bay Street, Cable Beach
☎ *(809) 327-6200*

Sea & Ski Ocean Sports

Radisson Grand Resort, Cable Beach
☎ *(809) 363-3370*

NEW PROVIDENCE

Sea Sports
Forte Nassau Beach Hotel, Cable Beach
☎ *(809) 327-6058*

Bowling

Village Lanes
Village Road
☎ *(809) 393-2427*
Alley with 20 lanes. Prices range from $2.75 per game (9:30 a.m.–5 p.m.) to $3 (after 5 p.m.). After 10 p.m. they drop to $2.50. Shoe rentals are $1.

Deep-Sea Fishing

The Bahamas are a deep-sea fisherman's paradise, especially west of Nassau where the Tongue of the Ocean is located. Many consider the best ocean fishing in the world. In all, more than 20 fishing tournaments are held in the Bahamas each year. The best time of the year for serious anglers is between May and September, when blue marlin, barracuda, wahoo, grouper, black-fin tuna and bonito are their feistiest and most numerous. Charters typically cost $300 per half day for a party of 2–6 and twice that for a full day.

Brown's Charters
☎ *(809) 324-1215*

Charter Boat Association
☎ *(809) 363-2335, 393-3739 (after 6 p.m.)*
With more than a dozen boats, this is the biggest firm on New Providence. Half- and full-day rentals.

Nassau Yacht Haven
☎ *(809) 393-8173*
Full- and half-day charters of either a 42-foot boat or a 35-foot boat.

Fitness Clubs

Atlantis, Paradise Island Fitness Center
☎ *(809) 363-3000*
Exercise bikes and treadmills, sauna. Free.

Gold's Gym
☎ *(809) 394-6975*
Daily fees available ($8–$12). NordicTrack, free weights, tanning booths, juice bar, nursery.

Le Meridien Royal Bahamian Hotel
Cable Beach
☎ *(809) 327-6400*

Open to the public for a pricey $20 a day (free for guests), this is a state-of-the-art facility and one the best in the Bahamas, with free weights, universal exercise machines, aerobics, aqua aerobics, steam room, spa, sauna, whirlpool, facials and massages. Make reservations for facials ($25 for 30 minutes), massages ($60 for 50 minutes) and mud baths ($25 for 30 minutes). Open daily 8 a.m.–7:30 p.m.

Palace Spa
Crystal Palace Resort & Casino
West Bay Street, Cable Beach
☎ *(809) 327-6200*
On par with the gym at Le Meridien. Free weights, Stairmaster, steam room, sauna, whirlpool. Non-guests pay $15 a day while guests pay

$10 a day. Open Mon.–Fri. 6 a.m.–9 p.m. and Sat.-Sun. 7 a.m.–9 p.m.

Total Fitness Center

Centreville
☎ *(809) 323-8105*
Free weights, rowing machines.

Windermere

East Bay Street, Nassau
☎ *(809) 393-8788*
Free weights, aerobics, sauna. The charge is $7 a day.

Golf

Cable Beach Golf Club

Box N 4914
W. Bay Street
☎ *(809) 327-6000, (800) 333-3333*
Owned and managed by the Radisson Cable Beach Hotel in association with Arnold Palmer Golf Management Co., this par-72, 18-hole course (7040 yards) is the best in the Bahamas. Greens fees: guests, $50; non-guests, $60. Nine holes are available at $25 for guests and $30 for non-guests. Electric cart is required, which is $40 for 18 holes and $25 for nine holes. Club rentals are $20. Make reservations in advance.

Coral Harbour Golf Club

☎ *(809) 326-1144*
18 holes. Make reservations in advance.

Paradise Island Golf Club

Box N 4777
☎ *(809) 363-3925, (800) 321-3000*
This 6419-yard, par-72 course was designed by Dick Wilson. Challenging, but not as long nor as good as Cable Beach of South Ocean. Greens fees: May–Nov, $45 for 18 holes and $22.50 for nine holes. Dec.–Apr., $50 for 18 holes and $25 for nine holes. Carts cost $46 for 18 holes and $23 for nine holes. Clubs rent at $20. Make reservations in advance.

South Ocean Beach & Golf Resort

Box N 8191
☎ *(809) 362-4391*
Nearly as magnificent as the Radisson course, this is New Providence's newest. Located in the secluded southern portion of the island, this 18-hole, par-72 course stretches out 6707 yards and features rolling hills (in the Bahamas!) and ravines. Greens fees: $55 for guests and $70 for non-guests for 18 holes (includes cart fees). Clubs can be rented for $15. Make reservations in advance.

Horseback Riding

Happy Trails Stables

Coral Harbour
☎ *(809) 362-1280*
Two miles from the international airport. Horseback rides fetch $45 per person. There's free transportation from your hotel. Nobody more than 200 lbs. permitted. Make reservations. The ride lasts only about 90 minutes but the scenic trail takes you to the beach.

Parasailing

Atlantis, Paradise Island

☎ *(809) 363-3000*

$30 for six minutes.

Radisson Grand Resort

Paradise Island

☎ *(809) 363-3500*

$30 for eight minutes.

Sea & Ski Ocean Sports

Radisson Grand Resort

Paradise Island

☎ *(809) 363-3370*

$30 for seven minutes; $45 for 10 minutes.

Sea Sport Ltd.

Forte Nassau Beach Hotel

☎ *(809) 327-6058*

$30 for six minutes.

Sailing

New Providence's full service marinas include **Hurricane Hole Marina** (☎ *326-5441*) and **East Bay Yacht Basin** (☎ *326-3754*) west of the Paradise Island Bridge and **Nassau Harbour Club**, **Nassau Yacht Haven** (☎ *393-8173*), Brown's Boat Yard and Bayshore Marina on the Nassau side of the bridge. At the Nassau harbor's eastern entrance are the Royal Nassau Sailing Club and the Nassau Yacht Club. On the western end of New Providence is located a good marina at Lyford Cay. The best places for rentals are:

Funsea

Crystal Palace Resort & Casino

Cable Beach

☎ *(809) 327-6200*

Lessons, rentals. Hobie Cats rent for $37 an hour and Sunfish for $22 an hour.

Le Meridien Royal Bahamian Hotel

Cable Beach

☎ *(809) 327-6400*

Small sailboats rent for $30 an hour.

Sea & Ski

Paradise Island

☎ *(809) 363-3370*

Hobie Cats rent for $35 an hour and Sunfish for $20 an hour.

Sea Sports

Forte Nassau Beach Resort

West Bay Street, Cable Beach

☎ *(809) 327-6058*

Hobie Cats can be rented for $40 for the first hour and $30 for each additional hour. Sunfish can be rented for $30 for the first hour and $20 for each additional hour. Kayaks can be had at the inflated rental fee of $10 per half-hour; paddleboats go for $15 per 1/2 hour.

Tennis/Squash

Most of the large hotels have tennis courts. In the sports complex across from the Nassau Marriott also has squash and racquetball courts. Squash and racquetball can as well be played at the British Colonial Beach Resort.

Atlantis, Paradise Island

☎ *(809) 363-3000, ext. 6118*
12 courts; $5 per hour. Non-guests welcome.

Best Western British Colonial Beach Resort

☎ *(809) 322-3301*
Three hard courts, lights. $5 for unlimited use per court. If the courts are crowded and others are waiting (they rarely seem to be), it's courteous to play only an hour. Non-guests welcome.

Forte Nassau Beach Hotel

Cable Beach
☎ *(809) 327-7711*
Six Flexipave courts. $5 per person for unlimited use. If others are waiting, it's expected that you'll play only an hour. Non-guests welcome.

Le Meridien Royal Bahamian Hotel

☎ *(809) 327-6400, ext. 22*
Two Flexipave courts; lights. Court charge is $12 per hour. Non-guests welcome.

Nassau Squash and Racquet Club

Independence Drive
☎ *(809) 323-1854, 322-3882*
Three squash courts at $7 per hour.

Pirates Cove Holiday Inn

Paradise Island
☎ *(809) 326-2100*
Four asphalt courts. $3 per hour per court. It gets very hot out there on this surface. Non-guests welcome.

Radisson Grand Resort

Paradise Island
☎ *(809) 363-3500*
Four asphalt courts; lights. $3 per hour per court. Racquet rentals at $3. Non-guests welcome.

The Village Club

☎ *(809) 393-1760*
Three squash courts at $8 per hour. $1.50 charge for racquet rentals.

Water-Skiing

Crystal Palace Resort & Casino

☎ *(809) 327-6200*
$27 for three miles. If you fall three times, well, three strikes and you're out of the water.

Sea Sports

Forte Nassau Beach Hotel
Cable Beach
☎ *(809) 327-6058*
$25 for 15 minutes.

Sea & Ski Ocean Sports

Radisson Grand Resort

NEW PROVIDENCE

Paradise Island
☎ *(809) 363-3370*
$25 for 3.5 miles.

Windsurfing

Le Meridien Royal Bahamian Hotel
☎ *(809) 327-6400*
$12 an hour for windsurfer rentals; $30 for lessons.

Sea & Ski Ocean Sports

Radisson Grand Resort
Paradise Island
☎ *(809) 363-3370*
Windsurfer rentals at $20 an hour.

Sea Sports

Forte Nassau Beach Hotel
Cable Beach
☎ *(809) 327-6058*

Boards for $25 an hour for the first hour and $15 for each additional hour. Guests can windsurf for free. Lessons for $35 for half-hour.

Beaches of New Providence

Most of those staying in Nassau head straight for Paradise Beach, a beautiful but often-crowded stretch of sand on the western tip of Paradise Island. But bring some money to tan here. The admission is $3 per person ($1 for children under 12) and you'll have to shell out another $10 in deposit for the return of the towels. The beach is reached from Nassau by taking the boat from Prince George Wharf. That also costs $3 per person round trip. Instead, if you want to walk across the Paradise Island Bridge, even that costs 25 cents a head. If you've got a family, it can add up.

In Nassau itself is found the Western Esplanade, which stretches west from the British Colonial Hotel on Bay Street. There are plenty of facilities, including restaurants, souvenir and food kiosks and changing facilities/rest rooms. The beach is often quite crowded.

Still west, past the bridge to Coral World, is Saunders Beach across from Fort Charlotte. This is where most of the locals flock to on the weekends and there are fewer tourists.

Cable Beach is a long, crescent-shaped stretch of sand flanked by a wall of hotels. If you're not staying at one of the caravansaries, there are plenty of local vendors who will steer you toward the myriad watersports activities offered here.

Caves Beach is farther west still, on the north shore some seven miles from Nassau. The crescent-shaped beach is small and intimate, and usually doesn't see the same crowds as its sisters to the east. It's found near Rock Point, just before the turnoff on Blake Road that leads to the airport.

Just east of Northwest Point is Love Beach, across from Sea Gardens. Technically a private beach for residents, there seems little hostility on the part of the locals when the uninvited show up.

On the south shore are found South Beach, at the base of Blue Hill Road, and Adelaide Beach, at the end of Adelaide Village. These are two nice lengths of beach that see only a fraction of the tourists found on the beaches on the north shore.

Directory

Insider Tip

Bahamas addresses rarely, if ever, indicate the street number. And in some of the more remote areas, streets are not even marked or named. When going somewhere, get thorough instructions and a drawn map if possible.

Transportation

Nassau

By air, the gateway to New Providence is modest, no-frills **Nassau International Airport**, ☎ *(809) 377-7281*, which is located by Lake Killarney about eight miles west of Nassau. Paradise Island also has a private airport, which is used mostly by charter and private aircraft, but is also a base for Paradise Island Airlines (see below). Flying times are as follows: 35 minutes from Miami, 2.5 hours from New York, 2.75 hours from Philadelphia, 2 hours from Atlanta, 2.25 hours from Charlotte. At least 10 airlines now serve New Providence from North America and do so regularly. That's where the convenience stops, at least if you're on a budget. There are no buses into town from the airport and, unless you're being met by your hotel or have other arrangements, you'll have to take a taxi, which costs about $19 into Nassau, $23 to Paradise Island (including the $2 bridge toll fare) and $15 to Cable Beach. And be prepared to pay the driver an additional 15-percent tip. It's expected, and most drivers will ask for it. Thought you should know. There is a $15 departure tax at the airport.

By sea, cruise ships and other sea vessels enter New Providence at Nassau's Prince George Wharf. More than 300 liners cruise the Caribbean and most of them call on Nassau. To accommodate the convoys, Nassau has built berths for as many as 11 cruise liners at one time! When the berths are full, as they often are during the high season, Nassau is literally jammed with tourists, seriously compromising the means of vendors, services and shops to facilitate the mob of visitors. Some of the bigger cruise lines calling on Nassau are Carnival Cruise Lines, Dolphin/Majesty Cruise Lines, Norwegian Cruise Line, Premier Cruise Lines and Royal Caribbean Cruise Line. If you come in via a chartered or private craft, vessels have to check in with customs at Nassau. If it is your first stop in the Bahamas, you'll receive a cruising clearance permit, which must be turned in at the point of departure.

If you can get in by land, immediately report the activity to the U.S. Army Corps of Engineers and the *Guinness Book of World Records*.

Paradise Island

Paradise Island is reachable by air from Palm Beach, Fort Lauderdale and Miami. The carriers that make the runs are Chalk's International Airline (from Miami) and Paradise Island Airlines (from Miami, Fort Lauderdale and Palm Beach). Planes land at the relatively new **Para-**

dise Island International Airport (☎ *[809] 363-2845*). If you're headed to a resort on Paradise Island it makes sense to fly directly there to avoid the pricy taxi ride from Nassau International Airport. As well, the customs procedure at Paradise Island takes less time. Remember that taxis from Nassau International Airport to Paradise Island cost about $23 plus an additional $2 to cross the bridge.

There's little reason to rent a car if you plan to spend most of your time on Paradise Island, as most of the attractions are within walking distance. If you need to go a little farther, a taxi will be fine. Or you can take the Casino Express for $1, a bus that runs around Paradise Island virtually all day and night, making stops at all destinations on the island as well as the casinos. If you're a guest at one of the resorts of the Atlantis Paradise Island Resort & Casino, there is a daily shuttle service that runs into Nassau's Rawson Square, departing from Paradise Towers. Tickets are issued at the bell captain's stand.

There is also a ferry service to Nassau from Paradise Island departing from the Cafe Martinique on Casino Drive for Nassau's Bay Street. The trip costs $2 round trip with boats leaving every 30 minutes, from 9:30 a.m.–4 p.m. Of course, the easiest way is to just walk across the Paradise Island Bridge, which will set you back 25 cents. If you want to get to Prince George Wharf, water taxis shuttle between Paradise Island and the wharf every 20 minutes for a round-trip fare of $3.

If you arrive directly into Paradise Island keep in mind there is no tourist office on the island, though it's unlikely you'll need one; the hotels themselves are excellent sources of tourist information.

Airline Offices

Air Canada
☎ *(800) 776-3000*
Twice-a-week nonstops from Montreal and Toronto.

American Airlines and American Eagle
☎ *(800) 433-7300*
AA flies to Nassau nonstop from New York City and Miami, with at least a dozen daily departures from Miami (sometimes as many as 16).

Bahamasair
☎ *(800) 222-4262)*
The national carrier; flies from six to 10 times a day from Miami, and from 5 to 7 times a day from Fort Lauderdale.

Carnival Airlines
☎ *(800) 222-7466*
Flies daily from Fort Lauderdale and twice a week from Baltimore, Cleveland, Philadelphia and Pittsburgh. Also flies to Fort Lauderdale twice a week from Los Angeles with connections to Nassau.

Chalk's International Airline
☎ *(800) 4-CHALKS*
Says it's the world's oldest airline of continuous service. Operates seaplanes from Miami's Watson Island Airport and the Jet Center Airport in Fort Lauderdale to Paradise Island.

Delta Airlines and Comair
☎ *(800) 221-1212*

Daily nonstops from New York's LaGuardia Airport, Orlando and
Fort Lauderdale. Twice-a-day nonstops aboard Comair from Orlando
and Fort Lauderdale.

Nassau-Paradise Island Express

☎ *(800) 722-4262*
Daily nonstops from Newark, NJ.

Paradise Island Airlines

☎ *(305) 359-8043, (305) 895-1223, (800) 432-8807*
Daily flights from West Palm Beach, Fort Lauderdale and Miami to
Paradise Island.

USAir

☎ *(800) 622-1015*
Daily flights from Atlanta, Baltimore, Charlotte, Memphis and Philadelphia, as well as from Fort Lauderdale and Tampa in Florida.

Local Transportation

By Car

Car rentals are readily available but are generally quite a bit more
expensive than in the States. The rare find is a car under $50 a day.
Expect to pay anywhere between $60–$100 a day and $280–$550 a
week. And gasoline is a little outrageous at close to $3 a gallon (at
press time). But there an abundance of rental firms on New Providence. Check out the CDW requirements before choosing a company. Some policies cover the entire damage cost, while others require
a $1000 deductible. Also, remember to drive on the left hand side of
the road. **Avis Rent A Car** (☎ *[800] 331-2112*) has branches at Nassau International Airport (☎ *[809] 377-7121*), at the docks on West
Bay Street (☎ *[809] 322-2889*), the British Colonial Hotel
(☎ *[809] 326-6380*) and the Pirates Cove Holiday Inn on Paradise
Island (☎ *[809] 363-2061*). **Budget** (☎ *[800] 472-3325*) is at the
airport (☎ *[809] 377-7405*) and at the Chalk's Airline Terminal on
Paradise Island (☎ *[809] 363-3095*). **Hertz** (☎ *[800] 654-3001*) is
located downtown (☎ *[809] 327-6866*). **Dollar** is located at the airport (☎ *[809] 377-7301*), on Marlborough Street near Cumberland
Street (☎ *[809] 325-3716*) and at the Radisson Cable Beach
(☎ *[809] 377-6220*). **National** (☎ *[800] 328-4567* or *[809] 377-
7405*) has offices at the airport and at Carnival's Crystal Palace Hotel.
You can also try the local rental firms **Teglo** (☎ *[809] 362-4361*) and
McCartney (☎ *[809] 328-0486*). There is no tax on car rentals and
you have to be at least 25 years of age with a major credit card and a
valid license. You may be able to get away with a cash deposit in lieu
of a credit card (what's the flight risk?), but it will be hefty. Call ahead.
And don't expect speedy service anywhere.

By Taxi

Working meters are required by law in the Bahamas, as are, it seems,
exorbitant prices. The first quarter-mile costs $2, and 30 cents for
each additional 1/4 mile. Throw in another two bucks for each additional passenger. You can also hire taxis by the hour for sightseeing
and other purposes. The prices range from $23–$25 an hour. Currently, there are three radio-dispatched services on New Providence.
The oldest is **Bahamas Transport** (☎ *[809] 323-5111/2*). Or try the

Taxi Cab Union, ☎ *(809) 323-4555* or **Li'l Murph & Sons** at ☎ *(809) 325-3725*. Taxi stands on Paradise Island are served by **Paradise Taxi Co.** *(☎ [809] 363-3211)*. At Cable Beach, there is a stand at the **Forte Nassau Beach Hotel** *(☎ [809] 327-7865)*.

By Water Taxi

Water taxis run between Prince George Wharf and Paradise Island daily at 20-minute intervals from 8:30 a.m.–6 p.m. The round-trip cost is $3. There is also water taxi service between Rawson Square and Paradise Island, with departures every 30 minutes from 9:30 a.m.–4:15 p.m. The cost is $2 each way.

By Jitney

Volkswagen and Japanese minibuses here are called jitneys, which operate around the island and stop at the hotels from 6:30 a.m.–8:30 p.m. They also stop at the beaches, shopping areas and residential areas. The cost per ride is between 75 cents–$1. Regrettably, they're not allowed to operate at the airport. In downtown Nassau, most can be found on Frederick Street between Woodes Rogers Walk and Bay Street. Many of the upscale hotels offer their own free jitney service.

By Moped

Outrageously expensive at $25 a half-day and $40 a full-day, motor scooters (or mopeds) are a favored way of getting around New Providence. They're available at most of the hotels or through **Ursa Investment** at Prince George Wharf *(☎ [809] 326-8329)*. You must wear a helmet, which is included in the price.

By Surrey

These are the horse-drawn carriages that ply Nassau's streets. The horses look silly with their straw hats, but I suppose they're more comfortable. They cost about $5 for a 25-minute ride, but you can try negotiating. Most can be found at Rawson Square, just off Bay Street. They're available usually from about 9 a.m.–4:30 p.m., seven days a week, but the horses are sometimes rested between 1–3 p.m. from May–Oct. and 1–2 p.m. Nov.–Apr.

Emergencies

Ambulance

☎ *(809) 322-2221/2861*

Princess Margaret Hospital

Sands Road
☎ *(809) 322-2861*.
Government run, 455 beds. The best in the Bahamas.

Doctors Hospital

1 Collins Avenue at Shirley Street
☎ *(809) 322-8411*.
Privately run, 72 beds.

American Express

Shirley Street
☎ *(809) 322-2931*

Police/Fire

☎ *919*

Drugs Action Service

☎ *(809) 322-2308*.

Will provide emergency prescriptions.

Post Office

Nassau General Post Office

East Hill Street on the top of Parliament Street
☎ *(809) 322-3344*

Open Mon.–Fri., 9 a.m.–5 p.m. and Sat. 9 a.m.–1 p.m. Postcards to the U.S. cost 40 cents, as well as to Canada. Letters less than half-ounce cost 45 cents, and 45 cents for each additional half-ounce to the U.S. and Canada; 50 cents to the UK.

Telephone and FAX Services

All the major hotels have IDD and fax services. Overseas calls and faxes can also be sent from the main post office or at:

Bahamas Telecommunications Corp.

John F. Kennedy Drive, on the seafront road leading to Cable Beach
☎ *(809) 323-4911*

Banks and Moneychangers

There are hundreds of banks in the Bahamas, most of them centered in Nassau. You'll have little problem finding one. Banks are open on New Providence Mon.–Thurs. 9:30 a.m.–3 p.m. and on Fri. 9:30 a.m.–5 p.m. The biggest banks here are **Citibank, Barclays Bank, Chase Manhattan Bank, Royal Bank of Canada, Canadian Imperial Bank of Commerce, Bank of the Bahamas** and dozens of others. Those with U.S. dollars need not change money, as the Bahamian dollar is on par with the American dollar. The currencies are interchangeable. Those with other currencies, including the British pound, must change their money at the banks. Hotels offer the poorest exchange rates.

Libraries

Nassau Public Library & Museum

Bank Lane, Nassau
☎ *(809) 322-4907*

Open Mon.–Thurs. 10 a.m.–8 p.m., Fri. 10 a.m.–5 p.m. and Sat. 10 a.m.–4 p.m. No admission. Housed in the old Nassau Gaol.

Newspapers and Magazines

The three Bahamian newspapers available in Nassau are the *Nassau Guardian*, the *Tribune* and the *Freeport News*. American papers most widely circulated are the *Miami Herald*, the *New York Times*, *USA Today* and the *Wall Street Journal*; also available are the *Daily Telegraph* and the *Times* of London. Don't expect to find the same day's paper, with the exception of the *Miami Herald*. American periodicals are readily available, including *Time*, *Newsweek*, *People*, etc.

Maps

Maps are available at the tourist offices as well as in most hotels.

Tourist Offices

Ministry of Tourism

Nassau International Airport ☎ *(809) 377-6833*
Rawson Square ☎ *(809) 326-9781/9772*
Prince George Wharf ☎ *(809) 325-9155*

Embassies

U.S. Embassy Consular Section

Mosmar Bldg.
Box N 8197
Queen Street, Nassau
☎ *(809) 322-1181*

Canadian Consulate

Out Island Traders Bldg.
East Bay Street, Nassau
☎ *(809) 393-2123*

British High Commission

Bitco Bldg.
East & Shirley Streets, Nassau
☎ *(809) 325-7471*

Religious Services
Anglican

St. Matthew's

Shirley Street and Church Lane, Nassau
☎ *(809) 325-2191*

Christ Church Cathedral

King and George Streets, Nassau
☎ *(809) 322-4186*

Baptist

Zion

East & Shirley Streets, Nassau
☎ *(809) 325-3556*

Catholic

Sacred Heart Church

East Shirley Street, Nassau
☎ *(809) 326-6274*

St. Francis Xavier's Cathedral

West & West Hill streets, Nassau
☎ *(809) 323-3802*

Methodist

Ebenezer

East Shirley Street, Nassau
☎ *(809) 393-2936*

Trinity

Frederick Street, Nassau
☎ *(809) 325-2552*

Presbyterian

St. Andrew's Kirk

Princes Street, Nassau
☎ *(809) 322-4085*

Lutheran

Lutheran Church of Nassau

John F. Kennedy Drive, Nassau
☎ *(809) 323-4107*

Photography

John Bull

Bay Street, Nassau
☎ *(809) 322-3328*

Cameras, accessories and film. Open Mon. and Thurs. 9 a.m.–5 p.m.; Tues., Wed. and Fri. 9 a.m.–5:30 p.m.; Sat. 8:30 a.m.–5:30 p.m.

Tour Operators

Bowtie

Box N 8246
Nassau
☎ (809) 325-8849

Happy Tours

Box N 1077
Nassau
☎ (809) 323-5818

Majestic Tours

Box N 1401
Cumberland
☎ (809) 322-2606

One of the best operators on New Providence with offices in many of the major hotels, Majestic offers a 2-hour city and country tour leaving at 2:30 p.m. for $18 per person. The extended tour costs $25 a head and also leaves at 2:30 p.m. Combination tours leave Tues., Wed. and Thurs. at 10 a.m. for $33 per person. Half price on all tours for children. There are also nightclub tours Mon.–Fri. for $55 per person including dinner, $24 without.

Playtours

Box N 7762
Nassau
☎ (809) 322-2931

Richard Moss Tours

Box N 4442
Nassau
☎ (809) 393-2753

Walking Tours

Ministry of Tourism Guided Walking Tours

☎ (809) 326-9772, 326-9781

Organized by the Ministry of Tourism, these welcoming tours cost $2 per person and leave from the Tourist Information Booth at Rawson Square at 10 a.m. and 2 p.m. every day except Sunday. The tours are 45 minutes long and cover all of downtown Nassau's sights. No reservations needed.

Underwater Tours

Atlantis Submarines

Charlotte Street, Prince George Dock
☎ (809) 356-2837, 356-3842

Three-hour submarine tours that explore marine life, coral reefs and shipwrecks. The cost is $68 for adults and $34 for children. For better or worse, less than an hour is actually spent aboard the sub.

Hartley's Undersea Walk

East Bay Street
☎ (809) 393-8234

Cruise along the ocean floor donning a special protective helmet. This is a 3.5-hour cruise aboard the *Pied Piper* from Nassau Harbour. You'll actually be submerged for about 20 minutes as you gaze at clouds of tropical fish and coral reef formations. No scuba diving certification is required and entire families can easily make the walk. Trips are run daily at 9:30 a.m. and 1:30 p.m. from Nassau Yacht Haven on East Bay Street. The cost is $40 per person in groups of five.

Helicopter Tours

Island Ranger Helitours, Ltd.

☎ *(809) 363-1040*

Helicopter tours are run from the old Chalk's seaplane airport on Paradise Island. The views of the surrounding reefs are spectacular, as well as those of Nassau. Flights cost anywhere from $10–$50 depending on the length.

Boat Tours

Calypso Cruises

☎ *(809) 363-3577, 363-3578*

Daytime sails and moonlight cruises to Blue Lagoon Island. Daytime cruise includes snorkeling and lunch. Lunch is served at the island's elevated party pavilion, which is often packed with cruise ship guests getting into their incessant limbo contests. Usually there is live music at the pavilion. Call for reservations.

Flying Cloud

Paradise Island, West Dock
☎ *(809) 363-2208*

Cruises on a 57-foot catamaran for 50 people on day trips, 30 for dinner. The dinner cruise is $50 per person and half-price for children. A half-day charter costs $30 person. The sunset cruise costs $25. Daily except Thursday and Sunday. Transport to and from hotels is provided. Five-hour trips on Sunday leave at 10 a.m. and cost $45. Half-day trips leave at 9:30 a.m. and 2 p.m. Call for reservations.

Island Fantasy Ltd.

☎ *(809) 393-3621, 323-1988*

Snorkeling cruises aboard a fishing boat, but a nice fishing boat at that. Included are a buffet lunch, cocktails and a stop at an uninhabited island. Scuba trips are also offered. Call for reservations.

Majestic Tours Ltd.

Hillside Manor
☎ *(809) 322-2606*

Two huge catamarans, the *Yellow Bird* (which carries 250 passengers) and the *Tropic Bird* (170 passengers) embark on three-hour cruises from Prince George Wharf. Tour includes a stop at Paradise Island's Cabbage Beach. For both boats, the cost is $15 a person; half price for children under 12. Make reservations.

Nassau Cruises Ltd.

Paradise Island Bridge
☎ *(809) 363-3577*

These are basically a couple of party boats that head off to an uninhabited cay for six hours of baking under the sun and slammin' down a few brewskis. A buffet lunch is included in the $35 price. There is also a three-hour half-day trip at $20 per person and a once-a-week dinner cruise for $35 per person. Call to make reservations.

Robinson Crusoe Shipwreck Cruises

☎ *(809) 322-2606*

There are three decks on this 85-foot catamaran, which, with a backdrop of live calypso music, sails to an uninhabited island for snorkeling and exploring. Included is lunch, wine and the use of snorkeling gear. There are also dinner-dance cruises twice a week. Call for details.

Sea Island Adventure
☎ *(809) 325-3910, 328-2581*
Snorkeling cruises to an uninhabited island. Included are lunch and drinks. Call for details and reservations.

Topsail Yacht Charters
British Colonial Hotel Dock
☎ *(809) 393-0820*
The company has a fleet of three ketches: the 54-foot *Riding High*, the 41-foot *Wind Dance* and the 36-foot *Liberty Call*. Different types of cruising possibilities are offered here, from all-day snorkeling trips to sundowner cocktail cruises. Half-day snorkeling trips cost $35. A full day costs $150 per head. The cocktail cruises cost $35 per person and special 3-hour private dinner cruises run $350 per person. Call for reservations or private charter.

Where to Eat in Southwestern New Providence

Traveller's Rest ★★★
West Bay Street, near Gambier
☎ *(809) 327-7633*
Bahamian/seafood cuisine
Lunch: daily noon–4 p.m., entrees $7–$17
Dinner: daily 5–10:30 p.m., entrees $12–$19
Closed last two weeks of September
You might happen upon Mick Jagger or some other celeb at this oceanfront spot about one mile from The Caves and nine miles west of central Nassau. Nonetheless, the atmosphere is casual and low-key with seating either outside on a terrace or portico, or inside the cozy tavern-style building. Local dishes are the featured cuisine—conch, crawfish and grouper are all on the menu, though this place is also known as "home" of the internationally famous banana and strawberry daiquiris. Guava cake is another can't-pass-it-up specialty. Credit cards: AE, MC, V.

Where to Eat in Love Beach

The Restaurant at Compass Point ★★★★
West Bay Street, Gambia, Love Beach
☎ *(809) 327-7309*
Bahamian cuisine
Lunch: daily 11:30 a.m.–3 p.m., entrees $7–$16
Dinner: daily 7:30–11 p.m., entrees $17–$29
Formerly a 1960s private home (we're not impressed), this seafront establishment is part and parcel of the Compass Point Hotel, just a dreadlock away from the famous Compass Point recording studio (we are impressed!). The Bahamian meals are creatively prepared and artistically presented, consisting of all the favorites—grouper, conch, rack of lamb, etc.—done up in innovative, foodie-heaven, ways. Desserts, appetizers, and accompaniments are all equally delectable. Credit cards: AE, DC, MC, V.

NEW PROVIDENCE

GRAND BAHAMA

International Bazaar, Freeport, Grand Bahama

Lacking both the colonial charm of New Providence and the laid-back ambience of the Family Islands, Grand Bahama is more like Miami with gambling, cut off from the mainland as if it were the victim of a recent hurricane while a convention of shoe salesmen was stuck in town. There's more apple pie here than steak and kidney pie, more Brooklyn than Bahamas. How could it be any other way being only about 60 miles off the shores of Palm Beach? Gratefully, however, as the Bahamas' fourth-largest island, there remain isolated pockets of pristine beaches and the quiet lifestyle found throughout the chain's other islands.

Most, though, never discover the island's hidden tranquility but instead head for the two massive casinos in Freeport, Grand Bahama's largest city and the second-largest city in the country behind Nassau. Fully a third of the Bahamas' 3.5 million annual visitors call on Freeport. Few venture anywhere else in the islands. About 3000 people a day are dumped off by the cruise ships plying the gambler's shuttle route between South Florida and Freeport. Freeport boasts nearly 3000 hotel rooms these days, and more are in the works. The harbor has been dredged

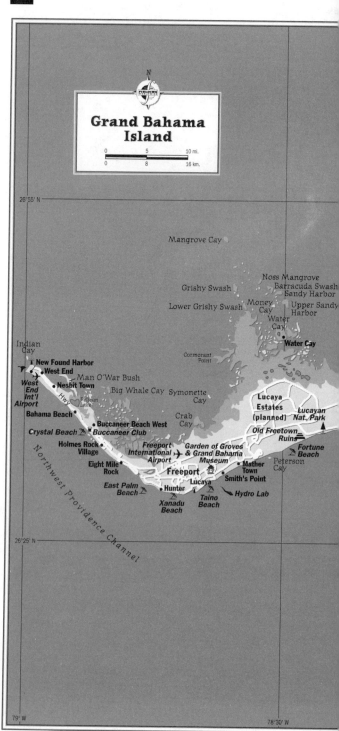

Atlantic Ocean

Little Abaco Island

Little Cave Cay

Cross Cays

Big Jerry Cay

Halls Point

Northside Riding Point

August Cay

Rocky Creek

McLean's Town

Jackson's Cay

Bonefish Cay

U.S. Air Force Base

High Rock Village

Queen's

Hwy

Pelican Point

Big Harbour Cay

Little Harbour Cay

Well Cay

Riding Pt.

Freetown

Sweeting's Cay

Lightbourn's Cay

Gainum's Cay

Big Cross Cay

Jacob Cay

Michael's Cay

Long Cay

East End Point

Red Shank Cay

Big Bersus Cay

75° W

to allow more cruise ships to dock. There are now four championship golf courses to choose from.

But it wasn't always this way. In fact, even 40 years ago, Grand Bahama was a little more than a flat rock poking from an emerald sea. In the 1920s, Grand Bahama, to a lesser extent than Nassau, was a major embarkation point for liquor being smuggled into Prohibition Florida. In the 1950s, entrepreneurial visionary and ex-Virginian Wallace Groves decided that more money could be had by turning Grand Bahama into a giant tax-free port than by chopping down pine trees, which is how he'd been making his living on the island. In 1955, he was instrumental in getting the Hawksbill Creek Agreement signed, setting in motion the creation and massive development of Freeport and neighboring Lucaya. Soon came a port, along with roads, a power plant and other infrastructure, along with, of course, an airport.

The two cities developed simultaneously and are now virtually indistinguishable from each other—a wall of hotels and resorts offering an array of watersports, golf, tennis and gambling.

Grand Bahama looks little like its sister Bahamian islands to the south, save for its lack of elevation. Its flora (and much else) resembles central Florida far more than the southern Bahamas, with towering pines trees growing amidst palmetto thickets at their bases. The road system also has a distinctly U.S. touch, with well-marked, four-lane roads meandering between the resorts. Save for the cars driving on the left and side of the road, one may as well be in Orlando.

But it is the Bahamians that make Grand Bahama Bahamian. Although most here seem to be from the other Family Islands farther to the south, they bring to Grand Bahama their warmth and good nature, their ubiquitous conch dishes and, of course, their junkanoo culture.

What to See and Do in Freeport/ Lucaya

Dolphin Experience, Grand Bahama

The Dolphin Experience   ★ ★ ★

At the UNEXSO dock across from the Lucayan Beach Resort & Casino;
☎ *(809) 373-1250, 373-1244 or 800/992-DIVE*

Originally from Mexico, these special dolphins are part of a unique probe started in 1987 into the mysteries of dolphin behavior and the potential of their relationships with humans. The dolphins in this experiment are not constrained in pools or by barriers in the sea. Instead they're entirely free to roam the seven seas if they so choose. But, amazingly, they don't. Instead, they remain close to their human mentors, which gives you the opportunity to scuba dive with the creatures in the open sea if you're certified, or to caress and play with them near the surface if you're not. The underwater photo ops for divers are incredible and numerous. The cost is $25 if you're not a certified diver (you'll be permitted to dangle your feet in the water and interact with the dolphins from aboard a special dock in Sanctuary Bay or to step into waist-deep water on submerged docks for an encounter session) and $100 for those who are certified and wish to scuba dive among the mammals. Despite the tourist trappings of the experience, I highly recommend the trip for divers and landlubbers alike. UNEXSO is a class act and one of the most professional aquatic organizations probing the depths and its creatures. In the open water, you'll never get the opportunity to mingle with dolphins in such a fashion, unless you're doing something illegal. For diving with the dolphins, make reservations 2–3 months in advance, and at least two weeks for the non-diving Dolphin Experience.

Garden of the Groves, Grand Bahama

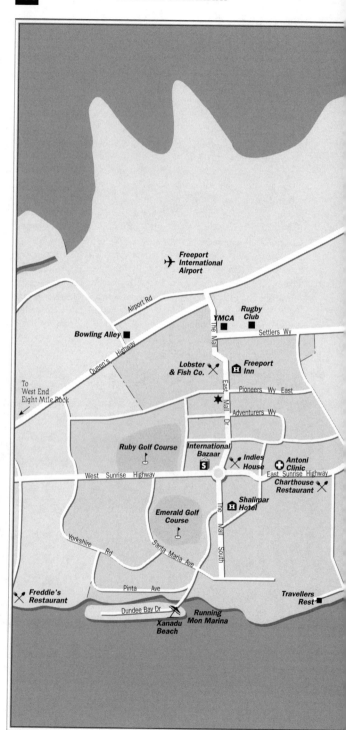

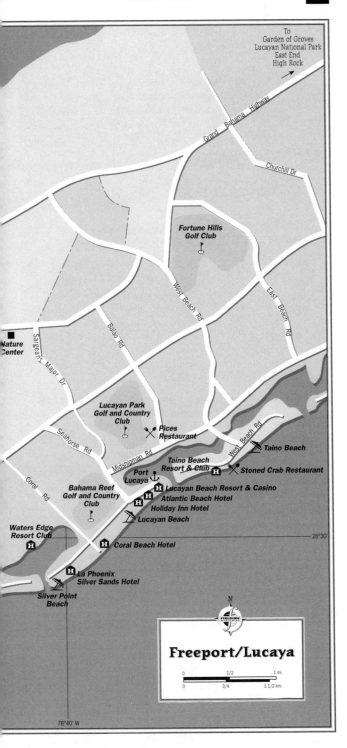

To
Garden of Groves
Lucayan National Park
East End
High Rock

Grand Bahama Highway

Churchill Dr

Fortune Hills
Golf Club

West Beach Rd

East Beach Rd

■
Nature
Center

Sargeant Major Dr

Balao Rd

Lucayan Park
Golf and Country
Club

Pices
Restaurant

West Beach Rd

Taino Beach

SeaHorse Rd

Midshipman Rd

Taino Beach
Resort & Club

Stoned Crab Restaurant

Port
Lucaya

Coral Rd

Bahama Reef
Golf and Country
Club

Lucayan Beach Resort & Casino

Atlantic Beach Hotel

Holiday Inn Hotel

Lucayan Beach

Waters Edge
Resort Club

26°30'

Coral Beach Hotel

La Phoenix
Silver Sands Hotel

Silver Point
Beach

N

FIELDING

Freeport/Lucaya

0   1/2   1 mi.

0   3/4   1 1/2 km.

GRAND BAHAMA

78°40' W

Garden of the Groves ★★

Off Midshipman Road, about eight miles east of downtown. ☎ *(809) 352-4045.*

Open weekdays 9 a.m.–4 p.m.; 10 a.m. – 4 p.m. weekends and holidays. Admission: $5.

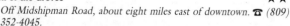

Popular as a place to get married, this scenic and relaxing 12-acre garden is named for Freeport's founder, Wallace Groves, and features perhaps 5000 rare varieties of flowers, trees, ferns and shrubs. There are also small man-made waterfalls and hanging gardens here, as well as artificial streams and ponds. The newlyweds have their photos taken in the gardens after being married in the grotto, trying to stay away from the signs which identify the plants and trees. This is a good stop if you've got a couple of hours to kill between rumrunners and jetskiing. A casual stroll of the garden takes about 20 minutes, 30-40 if you stop to smell the roses. Refreshments and snacks are available at the cafe.

Hawksbill Creek

Just east of the harbor

A nice break from the hustle and bustle of Freeport, this area gives you a glimpse of the real Bahamas, with its fish markets and small villages, many of which are a century or more old. Small settlements dot the area, with quaint names such as William's Town, Smith's Point and Copperstown. You may want to check out Eight Mile Rock and even farther west, the old Star Hotel, said to be the oldest hotel on Grand Bahama. It's not really a functioning hotel any longer, but there's a great restaurant and bar here for either kicking back or dancing to calypso music.

INSIDER TIP

Some of Grand Bahama's best attractions are also some of its most quiet–the relaxing restaurants and bars found toward the west of the island. Near Holmes Rock, check out the unostentatious **Buccaneer Club**, *with it's great American and continental cuisine served seaside.* ☎ *(809) 349-3794.*

Hydroflora Gardens ★★

East Beach Drive east from the bazaar along East Sunrise Highway. Open Monday to Sat. 9:30 a.m. to 5:30 p.m. Admission: $2. ☎ *(809) 352-6052.*

If you're a botany nut, this is a must stop. Classical music sets the mood as you're given a tour of these beautiful grounds for demonstrations of hydroponics, the growing of plants in water. Visitors may be given a complimentary hibiscus, mango or guava, and then discover how conch shells are formed, or how the grapefruit got its name. There's a museum here. The gardens are a 10-minute bus ride from Port Lucaya Marketplace or a 20-minute walk from the International Bazaar.

Bus Tours

Buses take visitors on tours of Freeport/Lucaya and the nearby environs, including area beaches, celebrity homes, nature reserves and parks, and the West End. Many of the tours take a break for lunch. One tour can be taken aboard a red, double-decker bus that was shipped over here from London. The price runs from $10–$15 per person. Make reservations and get information from your hotel's tour desk.

Lucayan National Park ★ ★

Eastern end, 20 miles past Lucaya. Contact the Rand Memorial Nature Center at ☎ (809) 352-5438.
Free admission.

More than a mile of footpaths and elevated walkways meander through gumbo limbo trees and wild tamarind at this 40-acre park bursting with ming trees, cedar, mahogany, coca plums and sea-grapes. Gold Rock Creek flows through the park and its mangrove swamps to the ocean where it meets beautiful, secluded Gold Rock Beach. There is an observation tower in the park and an underwater cave system believed to be among the most extensive in the world at more than seven miles long with 36,000 passages in the network. Two of the openings, made visible after part of the earth collapsed, are accessible by stairways and ramps, including Ben's Cave, which is reached via spiral steps. Burial Mound Cave is where the bones and flattened skulls of early Lucayan Indians were found. The Lucayans flattened the skulls of their young to make themselves less attractive as meals for the vicious Carib people, who once hunted the peaceful Lucayans down and munched on them for dinner. Sheltered pools near the caves contain a number of rare marine species. A tour of the park takes about 30 minutes. If you wish to dive the caves, contact UNEXSO at ☎ *(809) 373-1244*. For details on tours, contact the Rand Memorial Nature Center at ☎ *(809) 352-5438*.

International Bazaar ★ ★

Entrance through Torii gate on West Sunrise Highway at Mall Drive, next *to the Princess Tower Hotel and Casino.*
Open daily (except Sundays) until midnight. No admission charge.

Built in 1967, designed by Hollywood special-effects wizard Charles Perrin and originally conceived as a pacifier for wives while their husbands hit the craps tables or golfed, this is a grand complex of perhaps 100 designer shops, boutiques and restaurants with goods available from two dozen countries. Superb deals (sometimes 50 percent off U.S. prices) can be had here on Thai silks, gems and silver from South America, French cosmetics, perfumes and British china. A day here and your friends back home will think you traveled around the world. Restaurants abound along the narrow alleys. Keep in mind that this place is swamped with tourists. Craftsmen and artisans display their wares at the Bahamas **Arts & Crafts Market**.

Perfume Factory ★

Near International Bazaar.
Box F 770
☎ (809) 352-9391

Have you ever had dreams of creating the perfect scent or perfume? Here's where you can have a stab at it. That's right; Fragrance of The Bahamas is located here (the creators of the Bahamas best-known fragrances using local flowers) and you can tour the mixology lab and concoct your own fragrance, choosing from ginger, jasmine, gardenia and cinnamon among the 140 different choices. Then, for about $20, it will be bottled and tagged with the name of your choice. We've seen everything from "Edna," bottled by a grandmother from Tamarac, to "Exhaustacy," blended by a couple of biker chicks from New Jersey.

Port Lucaya Marketplace and Marina   ★★

On the waterfront near the UNEXSO dock, across from the Atlantik Beach Hotel.

If you're not yet thoroughly shopped out or not yet broke, head over to Port Lucaya. This huge complex has 12 pastel shingle-roofed buildings that appear somewhat colonial, somewhat Bahamian traditional, but are home to 75 modern shops, bars and restaurants. Shops sell watches, jewelry, clothes, perfumes, leather goods, old coins and resortwear, not to mention the crafts of local artisans, who do their magic on the premises. Wood stalls sell tropical fruit drinks and cocktails. To enhance the traditional colonial ambience created here, functioning red British telephone booths dot the complex's walkways, and a bandstand sits close to the channel. The two-story arcade provides great views (especially at sunset) of the magnificent yachts and sailboats in the marina, some of which are available for short trips and excursions.

It was Count Basie, the legendary jazz pianist and band leader who lived on Grand Bahama until his death, who first had the idea for this plaza and promenade. So it's not surprising that the centerpiece of the complex is Count Basie Square. Here is where a vine-covered gazebo-type bandstand is the stage for steel drum and calypso bands, as well as gospel singers, who toot their pipes for the entertainment of both shoppers and passersby. And it's all free. Many of the shops and restaurants are open late.

Rand Memorial Nature Centre   ★★

Settlers Way East.

Open Monday through Friday and Sunday. Guided tours at 10:30 a.m., 2 p.m., and 3 p.m. and on Sunday, 2 and 3 p.m. Admission: $3–$5 for adults; $2–$3 for children 5–12.

This magnificent 100-acre park has more than 600 species of birds and plants. On the guided tour of the park (named for and financed by James H. Rand, a former president of Remington-Rand) you'll encounter more than 200 species of birds and some 400 varieties of plants, 140 of them indigenous. Pink flamingos grace the tropical-setting pool. There are native boa constrictors, orchids and raccoons. The tour is also a course in local crafts and customs, where you'll discover how bubble gum is "grown" and the source of Bahamian "straw." Here is also located the intriguing Lucayan Village Exhibit, a 1995 recreation of an early Lucayan village. Not to be missed.

Straw Market   ★

Next to the International Bazaar.

Open daily.

The Bahamian straw markets are some of the few places in the islands where you can actually bargain for goods, and here is no exception. Freeport/Lucaya's Straw Market carries a wide variety of hats and handbags, mats and baskets. There are also fine wood carvings from pine and mahogany, as well as jewelry made from conch shells and the usual selection of touristy T-shirts and ball caps.

Underwater Explorer's Society (UNEXSO)

Adjoining Port Lucaya
☎ *(809) 373-1244, (800) 992-3483*

For scuba divers this is a must stop. More than 12,000 divers a year use their services to explore surrounding Treasure Reef ($2 million worth of Spanish treasure was discovered here in the 1960s) and other subaquatic environs. This is a large, full-service dive facility that organizes trips and rents and sells equipment. It is a magnet for the area's divers and visiting enthusiasts, and a great place to pick up location tips from both the staff and visitors alike. A single lesson and dive can be had for $79 if you're not certified. The meek (or budget conscious) can settle for snorkeling for about $15. (See "Diving The Bahamas.") These folks also have one of the two recompression chambers found in the Bahamas. A top-shelf organization, perhaps the best in the Bahamas.

Where to Stay in Freeport/Lucaya

Freeport

Bahamas Princess Resort and Casino $115–$205 ★ ★ ★ ★

P.O. Box F-2623, the Mall at W. Sunrise Highway, Freeport, Grand Bahama
☎ *(800) 223-1818 U.S., (809) 352-6721 (Princess Country Club), (809) 352-9661 (Princess Tower); FAX (809) 352-4485*
Single: $115–$205; Double: $115–$205

This huge 2500-acre complex holds title as the largest resort in the area with a full plethora of resort-isms at hand. Take your pick between the Princess Country Club and the Princess Tower. The 563-room country club offers two- and three-story accommodations, attractive to families and the more casual visitors, while the 10-story tower provides more sophisticated ambience. The two provide heaps of dining and drinking options, tennis courts, two 18-hole par-72 golf courses, saunas, Jacuzzis, playgrounds, a beach club, an exercise room, a theater and dance club, and a wide range of water sports. Still bored? Try your luck at the 20,000-square-foot casino, one of the islands' largest. Amenities: nine restaurants, six bars, exercise room, saunas, Jacuzzis, two golf courses, nine tennis courts, jogging paths, room service, concierge, beauty salon, travel services. Credit cards: AE, DC, MC, V.

Xanadu Marina and Beach Resort $95–$145 ★ ★ ★

P.O. Box F-2438, Sunken Treasure Drive, Freeport, Grand Bahama
☎ *(800) 772-1227 U.S., (809) 352-6782; FAX (809) 352-5799*
Single: $95–$145; Double: $95–$145

Formerly the digs of reclusive billionaire Howard Hughes (you can eyeball his book collection in the small library), this "Pink Palace" offers plenty of pink-ness, a superb French restaurant and tropical-motif rooms. Nearby golf and watersports can be arranged, and the sandy beach is just a short stroll away. Amenities: swimming pool, dock, three tennis courts, three restaurants, three bars, room service. Credit cards: AE, DC, MC, V.

Running Man Marina and Resort $85–$105 ★ ★ ★

P.O. Box F-2663, 208 Kelly Court, Freeport, Grand Bahama
☎ *(809) 352-6834; FAX (809) 352-6835*
Single: $85–$105; Double: $85–$105

The 1990s-built, 32-room hotel was built around the vintage 1960s 66-slip marina. The marina has always been the big draw here, though the accommodations are attractive enough—albeit a tad on the simple side. A restaurant and dive shop are on the premises, and traditional music plays nightly on the marina-view dining deck. Amenities: swimming pool, restaurant, bar, dive shop, meeting room, travel services, marina. Credit cards: AE, DC, MC, V.

Castaways Resort $75–$105   ★★

P.O. Box F-2629, Freeport, Grand Bahama
☎ *(809) 352-6682; FAX (809) 352-5087*
Single: $75–$105; Double: $75–$105

This lower-priced resort is a good option for anyone wanting to be in the thick of Freeport action, while keeping tabs on the old wallet. Practically within breathing distance of the Bahamas Princess Casino and the International Bazaar, this two-building, 130-room hotel offers simple motel-type accommodations in cheerful surroundings. Nightly entertainment in the nightclub, plus a disco, will keep you tapping your toes. Amenities: swimming pool, restaurant, bar, nightclub, free transportation to the beach.

Lucaya

Atlantik Beach Clarion $110–$180   ★★★

P.O. Box F-531, Royal Palm Way, Lucaya, Grand Bahama
☎ *(800) 622-6770 U.S., (809) 373-1444; FAX (809) 373-7481*
Single: $110–$155; Double: $110–$180

This 16-story property is Lucaya's one and only high-rise, and it also harbors the island's only windsurfing school. Aside from the comprehensive watersports facility, guests have access to a large pool and private beach as well as tennis and golf. Nicely furnished rooms feature ocean or harbor views. This is a popular spot for European visitors (notice the action around the old espresso bar). A full American breakfast is included in the room rates. Amenities: two restaurants, espresso bar, shopping arcade, two bars, 18-hole golf, tennis, water sports facility, windsurfing school, deep-sea fishing, room service, beauty salon. Credit cards: AC, DC, MC, V.

Lucayan Beach Resort and Casino $150–$200   ★★★

P.O. Box F-336, Royal Palm Way, Lucaya, Grand Bahama
☎ *(800) 772-1227 U.S., (809) 373-7777; FAX (809) 373-6916*
Single: $150–$200; Double: $150–$200

When you spot a red and white lighthouse tower, you'll know you've arrived at this popular low-rise resort. Notable for its glistening stretch of beach, the complex also features a large pool area, four lighted tennis courts, children's activities, five restaurants and bars, and one of the island's two casinos. Guest rooms, housed in two wings, are luxurious and all offer sea, bay or canal views. If you get bored with the beach or gambling, sign up for the free Bahamian dance lessons or tilt your pelvis to the limbo beat. Amenities: five restaurants, five bars, swimming pool, casino, four lighted tennis courts, beauty salon, room service, children's program, cabaret. Credit cards: AE, MC, V.

Radisson Lucaya Beach Resort   ★★★

P.O. Box F-2496, Royal Palm Way, Lucaya, Grand Bahama
☎ *(800) 333-3333 U.S., (809) 373-1333; FAX (809) 373-8662*

The once-glorious beach, ravaged in 1992 by Bad Guest Hurricane Andrew, is little by little making a comeback. Other than that, this four-story sprawl remains intact and freshly renovated. Families love this place for the wide range of let's-do-things-together activities such as treasure hunts, sand-castle construction, etc. Shoppers can get their fix from various outlets around the lobby. Some 500 guest rooms—all renovated and recarpeted in 1995—are decked out in local decor and most have ocean-view balconies. Amenities: two restaurants, two bars, snack bar, swimming pool, dance club, room service, tennis courts, children's playground, sailing and deep-sea fishing charters. Credit cards: AE, DC, MC, V.

Silver Sands Sea Hotel   **$105–$115**   ★★

P.O. Box F-2385, Royal Palm Way, Lucaya, Grand Bahama
☎ *(809) 373-5700; FAX (809) 373-1039*
Single: $105–$115; Double: $105–$115

Situated seven miles east of Freeport International Airport, this unobtrusive (and somewhat outwardly unimpressive) complex features spacious studio and one-bedroom apartments with dining areas, fully equipped kitchens and private balconies. Two tennis courts are available, as is the beautiful nearby beach (try to overlook the cesspool you must walk past). Amenities: Swimming pool, snack bar, two tennis courts, meeting room. Credit cards: AE, MC, V.

Port Lucaya Resort and Yacht Club   **$95–$135**   ★★

P.O. Box F-2452, Lucaya, Grand Bahama
☎ *(800) 582-2921 U.S., (809) 373-6618; FAX (809) 373-6652*
Single: $95–$135; Double: $95–$135

Opened in 1993, this resort located adjacent to the Port Lucaya marketplace offers 160 guest rooms as well as a private 50-slip marina. Accommodations are situated within 10 pastel buildings surrounding an Olympic-sized swimming pool and features tropical decor, tile floors, rattan furnishings, and pool, garden or marina views. Guests get special deals on marina activities. Amenities: Swimming pool, Jacuzzi, restaurant, two bars, dock. Credit cards: AE, MC, V.

Southeastern Grand Bahama

Club Fortuna   **$125–$420**   ★★★

P.O. Box F-2398, 1 Doubloon Road, Freeport, Grand Bahama
☎ *(809) 373-4000; FAX (809) 373-5555*
Single: $125–$295; Double: $215–$420

Think of this place as sort of an Italian-style Club Med. Only opened in 1993, located some six miles east of the Freeport International Airport, Club Fortuna is run as an all-inclusive resort—one price gets you a good-looking room (many with ocean views), all buffet-style Italian meals, nightly entertainment, use of a private beach, and numerous activities, including windsurfing, sailing, weight training, tennis, aerobics- and Italian-language classes. Though it's catching on in the American market, you're still more apt to run into European guests, particularly Italians. Could be a lot of fun. Amenities: Restaurant, bars, disco, nightly entertainment, tennis, aerobics classes, nearby golf, exercise room, children's playground, beauty salon. Credit cards: AE, DC, MC, V.

Where to Eat in Freeport/Lucaya

Crown Room ★★★★

The Mall at West Sunrise Highway, in the Bahamas Princess Casino, Freeport
☎ *(809) 352-7811*
French/Continental cuisine
Dinner: Tues.–Sat. 6:30 p.m.–midnight, entrees $23–$38

Sheltered from the casino madness, this flatteringly lighted, art-deco-ish dining room, is conveniently located for those who need an elegant respite from their cool game. Treat yourself to richly prepared escargot, lobster casino, rack of lamb, filet mignon, and other gastronomic mainstays. The dessert cart is tempting as a winning hand. Jacket required. Reservations required. Credit cards: AE, DC, MC, V.

Ruby Swiss ★★★

West Sunrise Highway, at West Atlantic Avenue, Freeport
Adjacent to the Bahamas Princess Tower, Bahamas Princess Resort
☎ *(809) 352-8507*
Continental cuisine
Lunch: daily 11 a.m.–4 p.m., entrees $5–$15
Dinner: daily 6–10:30 p.m., entrees $14–$30

Partly elegant, partly festive, Ruby Swiss has been wowing locals and visitors since it opened in 1986. Guests eat in the spacious dining room, ordering from a long list of Continental favorites with many seafood and beef dishes. House specialties include steak Diane, filet Stroganoff, and—for dessert—Viennese strudel. Lunch and late-night snack menus lean towards salads, burgers, club sandwiches and omelets. The wine list is extensive, featuring labels from more than a dozen countries. Reservations required for dinner. Credit cards: AE, DC, MC, V.

Escoffier Grill Room ★★★

Sunken Treasure Drive, in the Xanadu Beach Resort, Freeport
☎ *(809) 352-6782*
Bahamian/seafood cuisine
Dinner: daily 6–10:30 p.m., entrees $14–$42

Housed inside the Xanadu Beach Resort, Escoffier takes up the same space that once was billionaire Howard Hughes' private dining room. The cozy-enough-for-a-billionaire, wood-paneled room accommodates fewer than 20 tables at which patrons feast on Bahamian-style seafood and other specialties such as smoked salmon and chateaubriand. Jacket required. Reservations required. Credit cards: AE, DC, MC, V.

Rib Room ★★★

The Mall at West Sunrise Highway, in the Bahamas Princess Country Club, Freeport
☎ *(809) 352-6721*
Seafood/steak cuisine
Dinner: Thurs.–Mon. 6–11 p.m., entrees $21–$32

How about some British hunting lodge decor during your Bahamian odyssey? This gourmet room with its tartan carpets, red leather chairs and other lodge-isms will satisfy your fancy while stuffing your belly with steak Diana, rack of lamb, prime rib of beef (with, of course, Yorkshire pudding) and such. The wine list is admirable. Jackets required. Reservations required. Credit cards: AE, DC, MC, V.

Guanahani's

The Mall at West Sunrise Highway, in the Bahamas Princess Country Club, Freeport
☎ *(809) 352-6721*
Seafood/barbecue cuisine
Dinner: Sun.–Thurs. 5:30–10:30 p.m., entrees $15–$26
Three lovely dining areas, separated by archways, are adorned with high ceilings, rattan chairs, brass chandeliers, plenty of wood (paneling, ceilings, tables), and other tropical touches. Hickory-smoked ribs are the featured specialty, but you'll do well with any of the barbecued meats or seafood. Come before 6:30 for the early-bird specials. Reservations recommended. Credit cards: AE, DC, MC, V.

Morgan's Bluff

The Mall at West Sunrise Highway, in the Bahamas Princess Tower, Bahamas Princess Resort, Freeport
☎ *(809) 352-6721*
Seafood cuisine
Dinner: Thurs.–Sat. 6–9 p.m., entrees $16–$28
This casual seafood house is a favorite with families who dine on a large selection of fresh island catches and specialties (including grouper, conch and lobster tail) while sitting amid kitschy nautical decor and artifacts. Reservations recommended. Credit cards: AE, DC, MC, V.

La Trattoria

The Mall at West Sunrise Highway, in the Bahamas Princess Tower, Bahamas Princess Resort, Freeport
☎ *(809) 352-9661*
Italian cuisine
Dinner: daily 5:30–10:30 p.m., entrees $15–$25
A variety of pastas, pizzas and other staples of Italian fare are on the menu at this informal dining spot. Early-bird dinners, served before 6:30 p.m., are a particularly good value, with a prix-fixe three-course meal going for under $15. Reservations recommended. Credit cards: AE, DC, MC, V.

Pier 1

Freeport Harbour, Freeport
☎ *(809) 352-6674*
Bahamian/seafood cuisine
Lunch: Mon.–Sat. 11 a.m.–4 p.m., entrees $5–$22
Dinner: daily 4–10 p.m., Sun. 3–10 p.m., entrees $16–$40
Watch the cruise-ship scene from this lively restaurant perched on stilts and accessed via a drawbridge. No surprise that the interior is done up in nautical theme. Diners (often cruise-ship passengers doing their "Bahamian thing"), enthusiastically sample baby shark (the house specialty), oysters, clam chowder, grouper, flounder and—yes, the occasional prime rib. Reservations recommended for dinner. Credit cards: AE, MC, V.

Geneva's

The Mall at West Sunrise Highway, Kipling Lane, Freeport
☎ *(809) 352-5085*
Bahamian cuisine
Breakfast: daily 7 a.m.–noon
Lunch: daily noon–5 p.m.
Dinner: daily 5–11 p.m., entrees $7–$16

Family-owned and operated. Local dishes such as grouper and conch, served in unpretentious surroundings, at good prices. The rum-spiked Bahama Mama is a house favorite. Credit cards: No credit cards.

Pub on the Mall ★★★

Ranfurly Circus, Sunrise Highway, Freeport
☎ *(809) 352-5110*
International cuisine
Lunch: daily 11:30 a.m.–4 p.m.
Dinner: Mon.–Sat. 5:30–11 p.m.

Pick and choose from three theme-type restaurants in the same building, across from the International Bazaar. The British pub-like **Prince of Wales Lounge** does up fish-and-chips, Shepherd's pie, roasts, and authentic English ale. The **Baron's Hall Grill Room** is a little fancier in its medieval-type ambiance and offers a range of meals including seafood, prime rib, and certified Angus beef. Head for the fancier-yet **Silvano's** for Italian specialties made for large appetites. Reservations recommended. Credit cards: AE, MC, V

International Bazaar

Becky's Restaurant and Lounge ★★

International Bazaar, Freeport
☎ *(809) 352-8717*
Bahamian/American cuisine
Breakfast: daily 7 a.m.–10 p.m., $4–$6
Lunch: daily noon–5 p.m., entrees $3–$11
Dinner: daily 5–10 p.m., entrees $7–$16

Duck into this pink-and-white eatery, at the gate to International Bazaar, for authentic and inexpensive Bahamian meals and American mainstays. A lively crowd congregates here, particularly in the afternoon, to chat, people-watch and fortify themselves for the shops or casino. Credit cards: No credit cards.

Cafe Michel ★★

International Bazaar, Freeport
☎ *(809) 352-2191*
Bahamian/American cuisine
Breakfast: Mon.–Sat. 8 a.m.–noon
Lunch: Mon.–Sat. noon–4 p.m., entrees $5–$9
Dinner: Mon.–Sat. 5–10 p.m., entrees $11–$22

This no-frills bistro offers informal meals amid the frenzy of the bazaar. Coffees are excellent and the outdoor, umbrella-sheltered tables are perfect for watching the passing action. Credit cards: AE, MC, V.

Japanese Steak House ★★★

International Bazaar, Freeport
☎ *(809) 352-9521*
Japanese cuisine
Dinner: daily 5–10:30 p.m., entrees $10–$24

Japan meets the tropics in this popular dining spot featuring Asian decor, conventional or on-the-floor seating, and dramatic displays of chefs roaring away at the table-top hibachi. Most hibachi meals come with soup, salad, rice and veggies—a good deal, especially during the early bird special. Popular choices include Kobe, New York, sukiyaki, and teppanyaki steaks; chicken and seafood are also available. Credit cards: AE, MC, V.

China Palace ★★★

International Bazaar, Freeport
☎ *(809) 352-7661*
Chinese cuisine
Lunch: Sun.–Fri.
Dinner: Sun.–Fri.

Chinese dragons and symbols will greet you as you ascend the stairs to this convivial dining room noted for well-prepared Cantonese and Szechwan dishes. Try to make it for the 4-6 p.m. happy hour when the focus is on potent tropical drinks with scary-sounding names. Credit cards: AE, MC, V.

Bavarian Beer Garden ★

International Bazaar, Freeport
☎ *(809) 352-5050*
German cuisine
Lunch and dinner: 10:30 a.m.–9 p.m., entrees $4–$12

Could you really visit the Bahamas without stopping in at a German beer garden? This spot is definitely not fancy but you'll enter into Teutonic bliss with various wursts, imported beers and recorded oompah tunes. Gemuchlekeit, here you come! Credit cards: No credit cards.

Lucaya

Don Luigi's ★★★

Royal Palm Way, in the Radisson Lucaya Beach Resort, Lucaya
☎ *(809) 373-1333*
Italian/International
Dinner: Tues.–Sun. 5–10 p.m., entrees $18–$29

The name is somewhat of a misnomer—only part of the menu lists Italian dishes, the remainder is a mix of international fare, including a smattering of Bahamian cuisine. Some of the choices include fettuccine Alfredo, Bahamian grouper, rack of lamb, and veal marsala. The ambiance is romantic, on the cozy side, with candlelight, fresh flowers, and floral decor. Jacket required. Reservations recommended. Credit cards: AE, MC, V.

Luciano's ★★★★

Port Lucaya Marketplace, Port Lucaya
☎ *(809) 373-9100*
Italian/French cuisine
Dinner: daily 5:30–11 p.m., entrees $16–$26

Don't be put off by this establishment's location upstairs from a Pizza Hut. Once inside, you'll be transported to a genteel dining room with sophisticated decor, flattering lighting, water views, and exquisitely prepared Italian and French cuisine. Specialty of the house is veal Luciano (named for owner Luciano Guindani) with a crown of lobster, shrimp and a delectable sauce. Steak Diane is another top choice, and fresh seafood is almost always on the menu. Reservations required. Credit cards: AE, MC, V.

Monte Carlo ★★★★

Royal Palm Way, in the Lucayan Beach Resort and Casino, Lucaya
☎ *(809) 373-7777*
Continental cuisine
Dinner: daily 6 p.m.–midnight (closed Tues. in summer), entrees $20–$40

Continental cuisine with a hint of French is offered in this sophisticated, posh and upscale restaurant housed within the Lucayan Beach

GRAND BAHAMA

Resort and Casino. The ambiance reeks of understated elegance and highbrow service. Rack of lamb and chateaubriand are two noteworthy specialties of the house, with Bahamian-style lobster tail and other lobster preparations close runners up. Reservations recommended. Credit cards: AE, MC, V.

Stoned Crab ★★★

Taino Beach, Lucaya
☎ *(809) 373-1442*
Seafood cuisine
Dinner: daily 5–10:30 p.m., entrees $18–$40

Excellent seafood, served in large portions, has made this spot a favorite with locals who steer the more likable visitors to its doors. Situated along dreamy Taino Beach, diners can eat their lobsters, stone crabs and other seafood meals either on the patio or indoors beneath a 14-story pyramid roof. The house-label burgundy is commendable, and the Stoned Crab cocktail is a knockout. Reservations required. Credit cards: AE, MC, V.

Britannia Pub ★★

King's Road, on Bell Channel, Lucaya
☎ *(809) 373-5919*
Bahamian/English/Greek cuisine
Dinner: daily 4 p.m.–4 a.m., entrees $5–$15

This relic of the late 1960s—done up in mock-Tudor style— is a fun, friendly, British-style pub, just perfect for throwing darts, watching sports on TV, guzzling draft English beer and such. Aside from traditional English pub fare, the menu includes Bahamian seafood, and—thanks to one of the Greek owners—unexpected treats such as moussaka and shish kebab. Credit cards: AE, DC, MC, V.

Fatman's Nephew ★★★

Port Lucaya Marketplace, Port Lucaya
☎ *(809) 373-8520*
Bahamian cuisine
Lunch: Wed.–Mon. noon-5 p.m., entrees $7–$16
Dinner: daily 5–11 p.m.

The name should actually be Fatmen's Nephew, because the owner named it for the two "large" uncles who taught him the trade. Overlooking the Port Lucaya marina, this casual second-floor eatery offers a dozen or so varieties of game fish, cracked conch and other Bahamian dishes. Dine indoors or outside on a watch-the-action terrace. Credit cards: AE, MC, V.

Pusser's Co. Store and Pub ★★★

Port Lucaya Marketplace, Port Lucaya
☎ *(809) 373-8450*
English/Bahamian cuisine
Lunch: 11 a.m.–5 p.m., entrees $5–$16
Dinner: 5–11 p.m., entrees $11–$26

This popular English-y pub with nautical decor, player piano, stained glass, gleaming brass and superb marina views draws crowds to its bar (for Pusser's Painkillers—a concoction more likely to cause pain than kill it), and the dining room for typical English favorites and Bahamian mainstays. If you're view-oriented, shoot for a table on the outside terrace. Credit cards: AE, DC, MC, V.

GRAND BAHAMA

Elsewhere on Grand Bahama

Buccaneer Club ★ ★ ★

Deadman's Reef, Grand Bahama
☎ *(809) 349-3794*
Continental cuisine
Dinner: Tues.–Sun. entrees $17–$29

Stone walls, palm-lined terraces, crystal chandeliers, Alpine tunes and beer hall ambience distinguish this restaurant—one of the island's oldest—situated about a 20-minute drive from Freeport toward the western reaches. It's a fun spot, particularly popular with yachties, offering menu choices such as veal Oskar, wiener schnitzel and a variety of Bahamian dishes. Transportation is available from most hotels. Reservations required. Credit cards: AE, MC, V.

Nightlife in Freeport/Lucaya

Casinos

Lucayan Beach Casino

Lucayan Beach Resort, Royal Palm Way
Lucaya
☎ *(809) 373-7777, (800) 772-1227 in the U.S.*

Freeport/Lucaya's two casinos are about the same size; this one is the draw in Lucaya. More than 550 super slot machines and an equal number of other game tables. Large gambling hall at 20,000 square feet. Beginners can take free lessons at 11 a.m. and 7 p.m. Happy hour from 4 to 7 p.m. Casino open daily 9 a.m.–3 p.m.

Princess Casino

Bahamas Princess Resort
The Mall at W. Sunrise Highway
Freeport
☎ *(809) 352-7811, (800) 422-7466 in the U.S.*

A huge, Moorish-domed building, this is one of nicest casinos in the Bahamas, if not the entire Caribbean. Twenty thousand square feet with 450 slot machines, 40 blackjack tables, eight roulette wheels, eight dice tables and two money wheels. Elevated bar for a great view of the action. Vegas-style stage shows. Gourmet restaurant. Open daily 9 a.m.–4 a.m.

Bars/Clubs/Discos

Club Estee

Port Lucaya Marketplace
Royal Palm Way, Lucaya
☎ *(809) 373-2777*

This is the best disco on the island, and really the only choice if you decide to leave your resort. In its own right, the place is outrageous. Huge dance floor and two bars. One is noisy and sweaty, while the other is smaller and a little less noisy. Throbbing tunes to superb lighting antics makes this the place to dance until you drop. Drinks are reasonable at $3.50, and so is the cover at $5–8. Dress up for this place. Open from 9 p.m.–? Closed Mondays.

Centre Bandstand

Port Lucaya Marketplace
Live calypso music from 8 p.m.–1 a.m. A popular gathering spot in the wee hours.

GRAND BAHAMA

John B.

Bahamas Princess Country Club
☎ (809) 352-6721

Goombay shows and live music at this outdoor lounge and disco.
Open Mon.–Sat. 9 p.m.–2 a.m. Goombay shows Sat. at 6 p.m.

Kaptain Kenny's

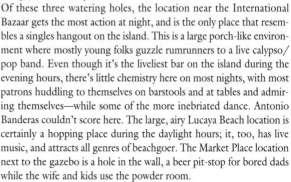

3 locations: next to the International Bazaar, at the Market Place in Port
Lucaya, and on Lucaya Beach.

Of these three watering holes, the location near the International
Bazaar gets the most action at night, and is the only place that resembles a singles hangout on the island. This is a large porch-like environment where mostly young folks guzzle rumrunners to a live calypso/
pop band. Even though it's the liveliest bar on the island during the
evening hours, there's little chemistry here on most nights, with most
patrons huddling to themselves on barstools and at tables and admiring themselves—while some of the more inebriated dance. Antonio
Banderas couldn't score here. The large, airy Lucaya Beach location is
certainly a hopping place during the daylight hours; it, too, has live
music, and attracts all genres of beachgoer. The Market Place location
next to the gazebo is a hole in the wall, a beer pit-stop for bored dads
while the wife and kids use the powder room.

Safari Lounge

Freeport Inn
Freeport
☎ (809) 352-2805

The disco here isn't as nice as the Club Estee, but it's more popular
with the locals. Calypso is featured here.

Sultan's Tent

Bahamas Princess Towers
☎ (809) 352-9661

This place is a little outrageous with its sequined, tacky lounge lizard
shows. Shows at 9 nightly.

Veranda Bar

Clarion Atlantik Beach
☎ (809) 373-1444

Overlooks the hotel's pool; nice setting for live piano music and intimate conversation.

Yellow Bird Show Club

Castaways Resort
International Bazaar
☎ (809) 373-7368

If you want a show complete with fire-dancing and glass-eating, head
over here with the mobs of others into the total Bahamian/Carib steel
drumming thing. Limbo dancers to the beat of congas and calypso.
It's quite a show. And if you've got anything left afterward, the disco
opens after the show. The cover's a little hefty at $20. Shows start
around 8.

Performing Arts

Freeport Player's Guild

Regency Theatre
☎ (809) 352-5533

Four plays a year are produced by this nonprofit theater company. Shows run from September-June.

Freeport Friends of the Arts
☎ *(809) 373-1528*
This groups does musicals and plays from November–May.

Grand Bahama Players
These guys just sort of hop around to varying venues for comedy performances.

Stage Shows

Casino Royale Showroom
Bahamas Princess Resort & Casino
The Mall at W. Sunrise Highway
☎ *(809) 353-6721*
Glitzy Vegas-style cabarets and stage shows, complete with barebreasted showgirls (sometimes), with a Goombay touch. Some soft raunch comedians are also on hand and sometimes, regrettably, get more stage time than the dancers. Shows Tues.–Sun. at 8:30 p.m. and 10:45 p.m. The cost is $25; call for reservations.

Flamingo Showcase Theatre
Lucayan Beach Resort
Royal Palm Way
☎ *(809) 373-7777*
Vegas-style revues and comedy acts, with all the pomp and sequins, that many say are the best in the islands. Performances are twice-nightly Mon.–Sat. About $30 per person. Call for reservations.

Sports in Freeport/Lucaya

Banana Boating

Bahamas Sea Adventures
Box 2545
☎ *(809) 373-3923*
Ten-minute rides cost $10.

Deep-Sea Fishing and Boating

The four major marinas on Grand Bahama are the 77-slip Xanadu Marina and Beach Resort in Freeport, the 66-slip Running Moon Marina to the east, the 150-slip Lucayan Marina inside Bell Channel and the 50-slip Port Lucaya Marina at Port Lucaya. The Running Moon Marina is the base for the island's deep-sea fishing fleet. It's also one of the better for chartering game fishing boats.

Charter rentals cost much the same as they do on New Providence, with full day rentals going for about $600 and half-day outings fetching $300.

If you've got a powerboat, check out the man-made Grand Lucayan Waterway, which cuts through the island to the north side at Dover Sound. Some of the places where you can rent boats or arrange charters include:

Reef Tours
☎ *(809) 373-5880*
Deep-sea fishing charters at cheap prices: $60 for fishermen and $40 for going along for the ride on the company's half-day trips. Departures are at 8:30 a.m. and 1 p.m. daily

Running Moon Marina
208 Kelly Court

Bahama Terrace
☎ *(809) 352-6833*
Half-day deep-sea fishing trips cost $60 a head; a full day costs $120.

Superior Watersports

Box F 837
Freeport
☎ *(809) 373-7863*
The Bahama Mama is a 72-foot catamaran tour boat. The company also has a couple of small subs for touring the depths.

Bowling

Sea Surf lanes

Queen's Highway
Box F 3245
☎ *(809) 352-5784*
$3 a game, which includes shoes.

Scuba Diving/Snorkeling

Local short trips from Freeport include stops at **Ben's Cave**, a beautiful cavern part of the Lucayan Caverns, and at **Gold Rock**, **Pygmy Caves**, **Silverpoint Reef** and **Blair House** for magnificent vistas of spur and groove coral beds. **Theo's Wreck** makes for the best wreck diving off Freeport and offers superb photo ops. The 230-foot freighter, resting on its port side and teeming with Eagle Rays, sea turtles, horse-eye jacks and morays, was intentionally sunk in 1982. Other popular underwater tourist attractions at Freeport include the **Dolphin Experience**, where Atlantic bottlenose dolphins have been trained to follow a boat in 45 feet of water from Sanctuary Bay to an offshore reef to the pleasure of accompanying divers, and **Shark Alley**, a copycat of the Stella Maris shark feed show on Long Island.

Away from the hustle-and-bustle and the camcorders is the West End of Grand Bahama, where live-aboards have ingress to the Mount Olympus wall dive, the spotted dolphins of White Sand Ridge and the Sugar Wreck.

Paradise Watersports

Sunken Treasure Drive
Xanadu Beach
☎ *(809) 352-2887*
A 48-foot catamaran is the base for a day of snorkeling. Snorkeling trips cost $18 and you can rent the equipment at an inflated $9 an hour. Bogus. Or if you don't want to get wet, a 1.5-hour glass-bottom boat ride costs $15 for adults and $8 for youngsters under 12. PW also offers waterskiing ($15 for 1.5 miles or 15 minutes—whichever comes first; lessons are $35 for 30 minutes) and windsurfing. Sailboards go for $15 an hour with a $25 deposit. Windsurfing lessons cost $30.

Pat & Diane

Radisson Hotel and Atlantik Beach Hotel
☎ *(809) 373-8681*
Two-hour trips bring snorkelers out to shallow reefs. Three trips a day. The cost is $18 for adults and $14 for children, equipment included.

Running Mon Marina

Kelly Court & Knotts Boulevard
Box F 2663

☎ *(809) 352-6834*
Sunday snorkeling trips to shallow reefs at 9 a.m. and noon. The cost
is $18 for adults and $9 for kids, equipment included.

The Underwater Explorers Society (UNEXCO)

P.O. Box F-2433
Freeport, Grand Bahama
☎ *(800) 992-DIVE, (809) 373-1244; FAX (809) 373-8956*
U.S. Office
P.O. Box 22878
Fort Lauderdale, FL 33335-5608
☎ *(800) 992-DIVE, (954) 351-9889; FAX (954) 351-9740*
This company's been around for nearly 30 years and it shows. State-
of-the-art facility and one of the better known outfits in the world.
UNEXSO has equipment for rent and offers both NAUI and PADI
certification courses. The firm has seven boats for dive trips and some
15 guides. Some of the specialties are trips to Ben's Cave and Shark
Junction, as well encounters with bottlenose dolphins ("The Dolphin
Experience." See "What to See and Do in Freeport/Lucaya.")
Underwater cameras can be rented here. Three-dive packages cost
$89. A single dive costs $35. A 21-dive (7 days, 3 dives a day) package
costs $299. Snorkeling trips to the reef cost $18. Beginner's packages
start at $89, which includes training in UNEXSO's pools and then a
same-day shallow reef dive.

Xanadu Undersea Adventures

P.O. Box F-42846
Freeport, Grand Bahama
☎ *(800) 327-8150, (809) 352-5856; FAX (809) 352-4731*
U.S. Office
P.O. Box 21766
Fort Lauderdale, FL 33335
☎ *(800) 327-8150, (954) 462-3400; FAX (954) 462-4100*
Xanadu is another reputable dive operation conducting shark and
night dives. There is also a beginner's course offered for $79.

Fitness Centers

Bahamas Princess Resort & Casino

W. Sunrise Hwy.
Box F 207
☎ *(809) 352-6721*
Fitness club with universal gym, aerobics, stationary bicycles, sauna,
facials and massages. Open to both guests and non-guests. Open
seven days from 10 a.m.–6 p.m.

Olympic Fitness Center

Clarion Atlantic Beach
☎ *(809) 373-1444*
Universal gym, free weights, aerobics. Guests and non-guests welcome.

YMCA Scandinavian Fitness Centre

E. Atlantic Drive & Settler's Way
Box F 253
☎ *(809) 352-7074*
Free weights, fitness machines, aerobics.

Golf

Bahamas Princess Hotel & Golf Club

West Side Highway
Box F 207
☎ *(809) 352-6721*

Two courses are featured here. The Dick Wilson-designed Princess Emerald course stretches out to 6679 yards and was once the site of the Bahamas National Open. Lots of water and lots of sand on this par-72 layout, which includes a 545-yard par-5. Long by even John Daly standards. The Princess Ruby course was designed by Joe Hill and reaches 6750 yards. Also a par-72, this has also been the site of professional championships. Both courses cost $63 for 18 holes and $46 for nine holes; non-members pay a slightly higher fee. Electric carts are required and run $48. Club rentals are $21.

Fortune Hills Golf & Country Club

Richmond Park, Lucaya
☎ *(809) 373-4500*

Here is a nine-hole course that never got around to becoming 18. It's a par-36, 3453-yard course. Greens fees are set up for 18 holes and are a relative bargain at $56 ($34 for nine holes), with the cart included. Club rentals are $13 for 18 holes and $8 for nine.

Lucayan Park Golf & Country Club

Lucaya Beach
Box F 333
☎ *(809) 373-1066*

This par-72, 6824-yard course may be the best on the island. Two par-5s stretch more than 500 yards. There's also a clubhouse, pro shop, restaurant and cocktail lounge. The fee for 18 holes is $70 and $35 for nine, both of which include cart rentals.

Horseback Riding

Pinetree Stables

N. Beachway Dr.
Freeport
☎ *(809) 373-3600*

This is a scenic 90-minute ride that includes a trail and the beach with either Western or English saddles Rides are Tues.-Sun. at 9 a.m., 11 a.m. and 2 p.m. The cost is $35. Jumping is also available and lessons cost $35 for about 50 minutes of instruction. Children's group lessons cost $15 an hour.

Kayaking

Erika Moultrie

☎ *(809) 373-2485*

Organizes sea kayaking trips along the north shore. Trips last from 10 a.m.–3 p.m. and cost $60.

Parasailing

Bahamas Sea Adventures

On the beach in front of the Radisson
Box F 2545
☎ *(809) 373-3923*

Five-minute parasail rides cost $25.

Clarion Atlantik Beach

Royal Palm Way
Box F 531
☎ *(809) 373-1444*
A seven-minute ride costs $20.

Sailing

Bahamas Sea Adventures

On the beach in front of the Radisson
Box F 2545
☎ *(809) 373-3923*
Hobie Cats run $30 an hour and Sunfish cost $25 an hour.

Paradise Watersports

Sunken Treasure Drive
Xanadu Beach
☎ *(809) 352-2887*
Hobie Cats run $25 an hour and Sunfish cost $20 an hour; a $25 deposit is required.

Tennis

Bahamas Princess Resort & Casino

The Mall at W. Sunrise Highway
Box F 207
☎ *(809) 352-6721*

Six hard-surface courts at the Princess Country Club. $7 an hour. Lessons available. **The Princess Tower**, ☎ *(809) 352-9661*, offers three hard-surface and three clay courts. $7 per person and $17 per person at night.

Lucayan Beach Resort & Casino

Royal Palm Way
Box F 336
☎ *(809) 373-7777, 373-6545*
Four hard courts here, but none of them are lighted. $10 an hour for non-guests; free for guests.

Radisson Lucaya Beach Resort

Royal Palm Way
Box F 760
☎ *(809) 373-1333*
Four hard courts at $10 an hour for both guests and non-guests.

Xanadu Beach Resort

Sunken Treasure Drive
Box F 2438
☎ *(809) 352-6782*
Three clay courts, one with lights. $5 per hour and $10 per hour at night.

Silver Sands Hotel

Royal Palm Way
Box F 2385
☎ *(809) 373-5700*
Two hard courts at $5 per hour for non-guests. Guests play for free.

Windsurfing

Bahamas Sea Adventures

Box F 2545
☎ *(809) 373-3923*

Rental sailboards at $20 per hour. Lessons run $15 an hour.

Clarion Atlantik Beach

Royal Palm Way
Box F 531
☎ *(809) 373-1444*
Rents sailboards at $10 an hour and $150 per week. Lessons are $25 an hour.

Paradise Watersports

Sunken Treasure Drive
Xanadu Beach
☎ *(809) 352-2887*

Beaches of Grand Bahama

One doesn't picture deserted beaches on Grand Bahama, but there are plenty of them—in fact 60 miles of sand surround the island, most of the beaches only used by locals. Most of the beaches, however, are in the Lucaya hotel zone and are packed with tourists during the winter months.

One of the most popular is the mile-long beach in front of the Xanadu Beach Resort in Freetown, called appropriately Xanadu Beach. Another great stretch of sand is Fortune Beach, considered the best beach on the island. Also in the area, east of Lucaya, is Smith's Beach and Taino Beach.

Beaches preferred by the locals include William's Town Beach, just east of Xanadu Beach and close to Pinetree Stables. Natives also head for Gold Rock Beach in Lucayan National Park farther east on the island. Most tourists don't make a day out of this magnificent beach because there are no facilities.

Shopping in Freeport/Lucaya

Grand Bahama is renowned for its bargains in all sorts of categories. The major shopping destinations are Port Lucaya, the International Bazaar, the Straw Market, the Regent Center and the Art & Craft Goombay Park. See "What to See and Do in Freeport/Lucaya" for descriptions of the centers.

Art and Antiques

Flovin Gallery & Flovin Gallery II

Arcade, International Bazaar
☎ *(809) 352-7564*
II: Port Lucaya
☎ *(809) 373-8388*
A generous selection of fine Bahamian and international art, from oil paintings and sculptures to lithographs, Bahamian straw dolls and coral jewelry. Also other gift items.

Garden Gallery

Arcade, International Bazaar
☎ *(809) 352-9755*
International and Bahamian oil paintings, crafts and other gifts.

Old Curiosity Shop

Arcade, International Bazaar
☎ *(809) 352-8008*
Lithographs, antique clocks and silver and brass objects.

Pusser's Co. Store & Pub

Port Lucaya
☎ *(809) 373-8450*

A truly unique shopping experience. Choose from the latest fashions and the store's own line in a museum-like atmosphere with a nautical motif. There are also ship models and antiques here, as well as a bar and restaurant. For shoppers, not to be missed.

Batik

Androsia House

Arcade, International Bazaar
☎ *(809) 352-6067*
Androsian batik and other fashions.

Coconuts by Androsia

Port Lucaya
☎ *(809) 373-8387*
This is a branch of the famous batik house on Andros. Batiks, cotton sportswear, resort wear, as well as shirts and tops for women.

China & Crystal

Island Galleria
Arcade, International Bazaar
☎ *(809) 352-8194*
Bahamian art, Waterford crystal and china from Wedgewood, Aynsley and Rosenthal.

Midnight Sun

Arcade, International Bazaar
☎ *(809) 352-9515*
Baccarat crystal, dinnerware, Hummel figurines and other gift items from Royal Worcester, Daum and Stratton, among others.

Lladro Gallery

Arcade, International Bazaar
☎ *(809) 352-2660*
Waterford crystal and figurines from Lladro.

Fashion

Androsia House

Arcade, International Bazaar
☎ *(809) 352-6067*
Androsian batik and other fashions.

Far East Traders

Island Galleria
☎ *(809) 352-8194*
Silk coast and hand-embroidered dresses and blouses. Coral jewelry. Exotic fashions and gifts.

Gemini

Arcade, International Bazaar
☎ *(809) 352-4809*
Leatherware and other leather goods. Italian-made shoes for men and women. Wallets, belts and jewelry.

London Pacesetter Boutique

Arcade, International Bazaar
☎ *(809) 352-2929*
European fashions, cashmere sweaters from Braemar and Pringle, swimwear.

Pusser's Co. Store & Pub

Port Lucaya

☎ *(809) 373-8450*

Shades

Arcade, International Bazaar
☎ *(809) 351-4130*
Designer sunglasses at unbelievable bargains, as high as 50 percent than the prices on the same items found in the States.

The Sweater Shop

Arcade, International Bazaar
☎ *(809) 352-8194*
Italian and Scottish sweaters of cashmere, cotton and lambswool.

Jewelry and Watches

Casa Simpatica

Spanish section, International Bazaar
☎ *(809) 351-4130*
Gemstone, gold and silver jewelry. Japanese watches, coral jewelry, semiprecious beads.

Colombian Emeralds International

International Bazaar, South American section
☎ *(809) 352-5464*
Also Port Lucaya
This may be the best place in the Bahamas for sapphires, rubies, diamonds and gold. Also check out the Tissot watches, and other watches from Switzerland and Japan.

Ginza

International Bazaar, Far East section
☎ *(809) 352-7515*
Mikimoto pearls, gold chains, bracelets and rings. Watches from Rolex, Baume & Mercier and others. Cameras and Cartier leather.

John Bull

International Bazaar
☎ *(809) 352-7515*
Great selection of jewelry, cameras, watches, cosmetics and perfumes. Jewelry from Nina Ricci, Yves Saint Laurent and others.

Oasis

International Bazaar
☎ *(809) 352-5923*
Also at Port Lucaya Marketplace
Cosmetics and French perfumes. Also jewelry and leather products.

The Old Curiosity Shop

International Bazaar
☎ *(809) 352-8008*
Great selection of watches. English bric-a-brac, antique engagement rings, Victorian dinner rings.

Sea Treasures

International Bazaar
☎ *(809) 352-2911*
Handcrafted jewelry, gold necklaces and bracelets with pearls, diamonds, topazes and more.

Time Machine

International Bazaar
☎ *(809) 352-5380*

French designer watches and great prices on wide range of other watches.

Leather Goods

Fendi Boutique

International Bazaar
☎ *(809) 352-7908*
Italian leather goods.

The Leather Shop

International Bazaar
☎ *(809) 352-5491*
Leather handbags and briefcases from Fendi, HCL, Vitello and others.

Oasis

International Bazaar
☎ *(809) 352-5923*
Also at Port Lucaya Marketplace
Cosmetics and French perfumes. Also jewelry and leather products.

The Unusual Centre

International Bazaar
☎ *(809) 352-3994*
Eel-skin products.

Music

Intercity Records

International Bazaar
☎ *(809) 352-8820*
Also at Port Lucaya Marketplace
Great selection of reggae, calypso, Bahamian and soca music tapes and CDs.

Perfumes and Cosmetics

Les Parisiennes

International Bazaar
☎ *(809) 352-5380*
All the latest fragrances from Paris as well as Lancôme cosmetics.

Oasis

International Bazaar
☎ *(809) 352-5923*
Also at Port Lucaya Marketplace
Cosmetics and French perfumes. Also jewelry and leather products.

Parfum de Paris

International Bazaar
☎ *(809) 352-8164*
The latest perfumes and colognes from Paris. Huge discounts. Maybe the best selection on the island.

Perfume Factory

International Bazaar
☎ *(809) 352-9391*
Cosmetics, perfumes, lotions from Fragrance of the Bahamas. Gives tours and allows visitors to concoct their own perfumes. Housed in a beautiful replica of an 18th century mansion.

Souvenirs

Bahamian Souvenir Outlet

> *International Bazaar*
> ☎ *(809) 352-2947*
> Inexpensive gifts with a Bahamian theme.

Ye Olde Pirate Bottle House

> *Port Lucaya Marketplace*
> This is the souvenir shop adjacent to a museum specializing in old bottles.

Stamps and Coins

Bahamas Coin & Stamp Ltd.

> *International Bazaar*
> ☎ *(809) 352-8989*
> Uncirculated sets of coins, $100 gold coins, gold jewelry, stamps and British half sovereigns.

Directory

Transportation

Grand Bahama is about 60 miles east of Palm Beach, Florida. It is directly accessible by air from cities in Florida, although many tourists also come in via Nassau. American Eagle and Bahamasair fly into Freeport from Miami, while Comair makes the trip from Fort Lauderdale, Orlando and Tampa. Air Canada flies in from Montreal and Conquest services Freeport from Toronto. Keep in mind that, like Nassau, there is no bus service from Freeport International Airport into either Freeport or Lucaya. Taxis make the journey for about $12 into Lucaya and $8 into Freeport.

By ship, a number of cruise lines call on Freeport (see "Cruise Lines That Provide Service To The Bahamas"). These include Carnival Cruise Lines, Discovery Cruises, Majesty Cruise Line, Norwegian Cruise Line, Premier Cruise Lines, Royal Caribbean Cruise Line and Sea Escape Ltd.

Many cruise ships leave from south Florida for Freeport and return in a single day on gambling junkets. Others leave south Florida for 3- to 7-day cruises of the Bahamas and the Caribbean. The day ships spend only three hours in Freeport. The usual cost of the day trips is in the $80 range, and another $36 in port fees. Cabins are available at an additional cost, usually between $40 and $125. Two of the bigger short trip lines include:

Palm Beach Cruise Line

> *2790 N. Federal Highway*
> *Boca Raton, FL 33431*
> ☎ *(407) 394-7450, (800) 841-7447*
> Cruises to Freeport for day trips from West Palm Beach at 8:30 a.m. and arrives back in port at midnight the same day. Each way takes about five hours. Onboard pool, cabaret show, casino, live entertainment, skeet shooting and video movies. The cruise costs from $70 to $90, plus $36 in port fees, and includes three meals. Activities and drinks are not included.

SeaEscape

> *8751 W. Broward Boulevard, Suite 300*
> *Plantation, FL 33324*
> ☎ *(305) 476-9900*

Sails to Freeport from Fort Lauderdale and departs from the Port Everglades Terminal. The ship has a casino, two bars, three restaurants, a disco, swimming pool and limbo bar. The cost is $119 per person (Mon., Wed. & Sun.) plus $49 in port fees. On Friday the charge is $99 per person plus the $49 ports fee.

Airline Offices

Air Canada
☎ *(800) 776-3000*

American Airlines and American Eagle
☎ *(800) 433-7300*

Bahamasair
☎ *(800) 222-4262*

Delta Airlines and Comair
☎ *(800) 221-1212*

Local Transportation

By Car

Car rentals are readily available at Freeport International Airport but are generally quite a bit more expensive than in the States. The rare find is a car under $50 a day. Expect to pay anywhere between $60–$100 a day and $350–$550 a week. And gasoline is a little outrageous at close to $3 a gallon (at press time). But there are an abundance of rental firms on Grand Bahama. Check out the CDW requirements before choosing a company. Some policies cover the entire damage cost, while others require a $1000 deductible. Also, remember to drive on the left hand side of the road. **Avis Rent A Car** has branches at Freeport International Airport (☎ *[800] 331-2112, [809] 352-7675 locally*), in Freeport (☎ *[809] 352-7666*) and in Lucaya (☎ *[809] 373-1102*). **Budget** (☎ *[800] 472-3325, [809] 352-8844*) is at the airport. As is **Hertz** (☎ *[800] 654-3001, [809] 352-9250*). **Dollar** is located at the Clarion Atlantik Beach & Golf Resort (☎ *[809] 373-1444*). **National** (☎ *[800] 328-4567 or [809] 352-9308 locally*) has offices at the airport. You might also try **Star Rent-A-Car** (☎ *[809] 352-5953*) at the airport. There is no tax on car rentals and you have to be at least 25 years of age with a major credit card and a valid license. You may be able to get away with a cash deposit in lieu of a credit card (what's the flight risk?), but it will be hefty. Call ahead. And don't expect speedy service anywhere.

Insider Tip:
The Bahamas' Bogus Budget

Beware of renting a car in Freeport if you choose Budget. There's a masquerader in town using both Budget's name and logo. They are essentially identical. Budget has been trying to get these bogusmobile renters off the island. They're pretty high-profile, so beware. The cars aren't nearly as well maintained and the insurance safeguards are lacking.

By Taxi

Working meters are required by law in the Bahamas, as are, it seems exorbitant prices. The first 1/4 mile costs $2, and 30 cents for each additional quarter-mile. Throw in another two bucks for each additional passenger. You can also hire taxis by the hour for sightseeing and other purposes. The prices range between $23–$25 an hour. Currently, there are three services on Grand Bahama. Try **Freeport Taxi Co. Ltd.** on Old Airport Road (☎ *(809) 352-6666)*, **Grand Bahama Taxi Union** (☎ *(809) 352-7101)* or **Austin & Sons** on Queen's Highway (☎ *(809) 352-5953)*. Keep in mind you'll find plenty of taxis wherever you find tourists.

By Bus

There are privately owned bus companies on Grand Bahama, and they often travel around downtown Lucaya and Freeport (the fare is 75 cents) and between the two cities ($1). **Franco's People Express** has a twice-daily service to West End from Lucaya Beach and the International Bazaar.

By Moped

Outrageously expensive at $40 a half-day for two-seaters and $35 per day for a one-seater. The deposit is usually $100. and $40 a full-day, motor scooters (or mopeds) are a favored way of getting around Grand Bahama. They're available at most of the hotels or through: **Honda Cycle Shop**, Queen's Highway, ☎ *(809) 352-7035*; **Princess Country Club**, W. Sunrise Highway and the Mall, ☎ *(809) 352-6721*; **Radisson Lucaya Beach Resort**, Royal Palm Way, ☎ *(809) 373-1333*; and **Princess Tower**, W. Sunrise Highway, ☎ *(809) 352-9661*. Mopeds can also be had at the Freeport harbor.

By Bicycle

Bicycles can be rented for about $10–$15 a day and $8–$12 for a half-day. If your hotel doesn't provide bike rentals, try **Princess Country Club**, W. Sunrise Highway and the Mall, ☎ *(809) 352-6721*; **Radisson Lucaya Beach Resort**, Royal Palm Way, ☎ *(809) 373-1333*; and **Princess Tower**, W. Sunrise Highway, ☎ *(809) 352-9661*.

Emergencies

Police

☎ *(809) 919*

Bahamas Air Sea Rescue

☎ *(809) 352-2880*

Rand Memorial Hospital

E. Atlantic Drive
☎ *(809) 352-6735*
Government-operated facility with 92 beds.

Ambulance

☎ *(809) 352-2689, 352-6735*

Drugstore

LMR Prescription Drugs
Mini Mall
1 West Mall, Explorer's Way
☎ *(809) 352-2689*
Open Mon.–Sat. 8 a.m.–9 p.m.

Fire Department

☎ *(809) 352-8888*

Tourist Offices

Ministry of Tourism (Main Office)

E. Mall
☎ *(809) 352-8044*
FAX (809) 352-2714

Ministry of Tourism

Freeport International Airport
☎ *(809) 352-2052*

Ministry of Tourism

Harbour Cruise Ship Port
☎ *(809) 351-4277*

Ministry of Tourism

International Bazaar
☎ *(809) 352-6909*

Ministry of Tourism

Port Lucaya
☎ *(809) 373-8988*

Grand Bahama Island Promotion Board

International Bazaar
☎ *(809) 352-8356*
FAX (809) 352-7849
Carries brochures and is a good source for maps. These guys are also the source for Bahamahosts, trained guides.

Post Office

General Post Office

Explorers Way
Freeport
☎ *(809) 352-9371*
Surface mail is delivered weekly, while airmail is delivered daily. Open Mon.–Fri. 9 a.m.–5:30 p.m.

Banks and Money Changers

Although not as numerous in Freeport as in Nassau, you won't find a problem cashing traveler's checks in Freeport. Barclays Bank is here, as is Royal Bank of Canada, Bank of the Bahamas and Bank of Nova Scotia. Banking hours are Mon.–Thurs. 9:30 a.m.–3 p.m. and on Fri. 9:30–5. Keep in mind that U.S. dollars do not need to be converted into the local currency, as the Bahamian dollar is pegged to the greenback. If you need money in a pinch, contact:

American Express

Mundytours office)
Block 4, Regent Centre, Suite 20
Freeport
☎ *(809) 352-4444*
Open from 9 a.m.–5 p.m. Mon.–Fri.

Newspapers and Magazines

The *Miami Herald* is usually available at the hotels on the date of publication. The *New York Times* is available here as well. The *Freeport News* is the local daily; it's an afternoon paper published Mon.-Sat., except on holidays. Also available are the Nassau papers, the *Tribune* and the *Nassau Guardian*. American periodicals such as *Time* and *Newsweek* are also circulated here the week they're published. The large hotel newsstands are the best places for newspapers and magazines. Also try:

Freeport Book Centre

14 West Mall
☎ *(809) 352-3759*
Open Mon., Tues. and Thurs. 9 a.m.–5:30 p.m.; Wed. 9 a.m.–1 p.m.;
Sat. 9 a.m.–4:30 p.m.

Library

Sir Charles Hayward Library

The Mall
☎ *(809) 352-7048*

Photography

The International Bazaar is a good source for film and other camera
needs, as is the Bahamas Princess Resort & Casino. But all major hotels
usually sell and process film. Also try:

Photo Specialist

Port Lucaya Marketplace
☎ *(809) 373-7858*
Camera and video equipment, accessories and repairs.

Religious Services
Catholic

Mary Star of the Sea

E. Sunrise Highway and West Beach Road
☎ *(809) 373-3300*

Anglican

Christ the King

East Atlantic Drive & Pioneer's Way
☎ *(809) 352-5402*

Baptist

First Baptist Church

Columbus Drive & Nansen Avenue
☎ *(809) 352-9224*

Presbyterian

Lucaya Presbyterian Kirk

West Beach Road & Kirkwood Place
Lucaya
☎ *(809)373-2568*

Methodist

St. Paul's Methodist Church

East Sunrise Highway & Beachway Drive
☎ *(809) 373-1888*

Lutheran

Our Saviour Lutheran Church

East Sunrise Highway
☎ *(809) 373-3500*

Tour Operators

All of the major hotels offer their own guided tour services. Or you can
choose from among the following private operators:

Bahamas Travel Agency

Box F 3778
☎ *(809) 352-3141*

Half-day and full-day island tours that cover most of the attractions. Full-day tours cost about $25 per person and $15 for children under 12. Half-day tours cost about $15 for adults and $12 for children.

Executive Tours

Box F 2509
Mercantile Bldg.
☎ *(809) 352-8858*
Half-day and full-day island tours that cover most of the attractions. Full-day tours cost about $25 per person and $15 for children under 12. Half-day tours cost about $15 for adults and $12 for children.

H. Forbes Charter Co.

Bahamas Princess Country Club
The Mall at West Sunrise Highway
Freeport
☎ *(809) 352-9311*
Half- and full-day bus tours (big, 52-seat buses) that hit most of the island's tourist stops. The half-day Super Combination Tour combines guided visits to the botanical gardens, the harbor, residential areas and parks with shopping. The cost is $16 per person and $12 for children under 12. The full-day tour does much of the same thing but also heads out to the island's West End. It costs $25 per person and $15 for children under 12. You'll definitely need to make reservations in advance. The earlier the better.

International Travel & Tours

Box F 850
☎ *(809) 352-9311*
Half-day and full-day island tours that cover most of the attractions. Full-day tours cost about $25 per person and $15 for children under 12. Half-day tours cost about $15 for adults and $12 for children.

Reef Tours

Box F 2510
Port Lucaya
☎ *(809) 373-5880*
Half-day and full-day island tours that cover most of the attractions. Full day tours cost about $25 per person and $15 for children under 12. Half-day tours cost about $15 for adults and $12 for children.

Sun Island Tours

Box F 2585
☎ *(809) 352-4811*
Half-day and full-day island tours that cover most of the attractions. Full-day tours cost about $25 per person and $15 for children under 12. Half-day tours cost about $15 for adults and $12 for children.

Sunworld Travel and Tour

Box F 2631
☎ *(809) 352-3717*
Half-day and full-day island tours that cover most of the attractions. Full-day tours cost about $25 per person and $15 for children under 12. Half-day tours cost about $15 for adults and $12 for children.

Boat Tours

Mermaid Kitty

Port Lucaya Dock
☎ *(809) 373-5880*

Huge glass-bottom boat tour departs from the Lucayan Bay Hotel three times daily. at 10:30 a.m., 12:30 p.m. and 2:30 p.m. The cost is $15 for adults and $8 for children under 12.

Airplane Tours

Taino Air

Box F 7-4006
Freeport
☎ *(809) 352-8885*
Offers light airplane tours of Grand Bahama, as well as New Providence and some of the accessible Family Islands.

THE FAMILY ISLANDS

Pink Beach on Harbour Island, Eleuthera

Technically, the Family Islands (or Out Islands) consist of every island in The Bahamas with the exception of Grand Bahama and New Providence (as well as Paradise Island, connected by bridge to Nassau). Of the more than 700 Family Islands, perhaps only a dozen are geared up to handle tourists. The name they've been given particularly suits them, as the communities on these relatively isolated and remote islands are much more closely knit than those of the concrete jungles of Freeport and Nassau. Many travelers say the people of the Family Islands are the warmest and most friendly of all the Caribbean, having not yet become jaded by the vices and density of the big cities.

It's something to keep in mind when deciding your Bahamas itinerary. If you've come to The Bahamas to get down and party junkanoo style, dance and gamble the nights away, and then catch a topless cabaret before returning to your air-conditioned room for the "Letterman" show, the Family Islands are certainly not for you.

There are relatively few resorts on the Family Islands, with the exception of the more developed islands: Bimini, Abaco and Eleuthera. And where you can find a resort, you'll quickly discover the pace of life is far slower than at those found in Nassau and Freeport. Many hotels on the Out Islands do not offer air-conditioned rooms, telephones or televisions. Instead, you'll need to rely on ceiling fans and the breezes of the warm Atlantic. Rather than gourmet cuisine prepared by Paris chefs, you can expect the simple, delicious food of the islands, prepared by a Bahamian who may also moonlight as a taxi driver or deckhand—or both.

Gratefully, a trip to the Family Islands will leave the hordes back in the casinos and the cruise ships. You'll find pristine, deserted beaches, unspoiled pine forests and a kind of laid-back ambience that will stun you. You'll befriend Bahamian locals during the simplest of encounters. It may be at the rare gas station, at a village grocery store or at the neighborhood bar. Residents will often invite visitors to social events, dances, beach parties and town gatherings, even to a simple family dinner. These islands are a place to relax. The only nightlife is what you make it. It may be a bonfire on the beach or a cocktail in a cozy beachside thatched hut. It may be simply reading a good book under a full moon to the soft lapping of the surf.

On some of the Family Islands, you may be surprised to find pockets of native caucasian Bahamians in such places as Elbow Cay, Abacos; Spanish Wells, Eleuthera; and Man-O-War, Great Guana. These are the descendents of settlers who migrated from Bermuda in the 17th century or the Loyalists who fled to The Bahamas after the American Revolutionary War

The Family Islands stretch from Walker's Cay, north of Grand Bahama, south to Great Inagua. Up until 20 years ago these islands were simply the domain of the islanders and the rare yachtsman who had carved out his own personal piece of paradise on one of the islands, using it as a base for deep sea fishing or spectacular diving. But that's all changing as airstrips have been built on a number of islands, now readily accessible through Bahamasair. Many of the Family Islands can now be reached directly from Florida and Nassau. Regardless, you'll find few modern conveniences on islands such as Cat Island and Crooked Island, San Salvador and Mayaguana—and even fewer people. In places such as these, it's quite possible to feel entirely isolated from the rest of the world, which is the best reason for visiting these islands.

There are few cars on the Out Islands and you'll notice young Bahamian locals hitching rides to work and other spots on the island. The most common means of transportation in the Family Islands is the bicycle, while some of the resorts maintain small fleets of golf carts. Taxis aren't metered as they are on New Providence and Grand Bahama—when you can find one. They're usually quite old and large (of the Chevrolet Impala variety and vintage). Taxis usually hang out at airstrips and marinas. Negotiate a fare before you get into one. And take solace that most Bahamian cab drivers won't try to rip you off. Their quoted fares won't be much more than Bahamians pay themselves. A little brinksmanship on your part and you'll get it down to what the locals pay.

Of all the Family Islands, the most developed are Eleuthera, Bimini (which sees hordes of tourists on its ribbon of sand), Abaco and Exuma. Though it wouldn't be exactly fair to call these islands "developed," there are quite fancy resorts found here, towns and a number of full-service, modern marinas. North Bimini is virtually a sardine can, while Eleuthera is built up for tourists only on its southern cape and northern tip.

Whichever Family Islands you choose to visit, you'll find an experience unique to that island, whether it be the pink sands of Harbour Town off the coast of Eleuthera, the colorful Out Island Regatta of George Town in Exuma or the sight of 20,000 pink flamingos taking off in one flock on Inagua. Not to mention The Bahamas' hallmarks: perhaps the best sportfishing and scuba diving in the Atlantic, if not the world's oceans.

THE ABACOS

Hope Town Lighthouse, Elbow Cay

Called Habacoa by the early Spanish settlers and shaped like a boomerang, the Abacos (sometimes just called Abaco) is a 130-mile-long string of cays with some 650 square miles of land. It is home to 10,000 people and some of The Bahamas best beaches, including Manjack Cay, Great Guana and Elbow Cay. The Abacos are also considered the sailing capital of The Bahamas.

Ponce de Leon paid a visit here in 1513 in his search for that elusive Fountain of Youth. After the native Lucayans were enslaved by the Spanish in the mid-16th century, the islands were later inhabited in the 1780s by Loyalists and their slaves from New England, escaping the newly formed United States to a British colony that seemed a little more stable. (This helps explain why, in a country that is 85 percent ethnic African, half the population of the Abacos is white.) They were lured by news accounts and brochures touting the Abacos as rich in agricultural and commercial opportunities. In actuality, there was little that could be grown in the rocky, sandy soil, many of the Abacos' settlers turned to "wrecking," or setting up bogus beacons to confuse merchant ships trying to navigate the region's treacherous waters. (The first lighthouse wasn't built until 1836.) Using these false beacons as guides, dozens upon dozens of vessels ran upon shoals and reefs and sank, their cargo being pilfered by the islanders. Of course, many others ran aground by their own means, making the salvaging of cargo a lucrative career for the island's residents. As many as 600 Spanish galleons met their demise on Abacos' reefs. In fact, the Abacos' widely known reputation as a haven for pirates and wreckers was well-founded from the 16th century through the mid-1800s.

In the far north is found Walker's Cay, the northernmost island in The Bahamas, and Hole-in-the-Wall in the southwest. The major islands are Great Abaco and Little Abaco. Wild boar still roam in the Abacos' dense pine forests; yet the commercial center of the islands, Marsh Harbour, is The Bahamas' third-largest city. It has its share of tourist hotels and resorts, gift shops and boutiques, but can hardly be compared with Nassau and Freeport. Yet after New Providence and Grand Bahama, the Abacos are The Bahamas' most touristed destination. The marinas in the area are superb, making the Abacos a major deep-sea fishing and boating mecca. There are no fewer than six major game fishing tourneys held in the Abacos each year, and the largest boating event, the Abaco Regatta, held in late June and early July, attracts hundreds of tourists and participants. The island's naturally protected waters and countless beautiful, isolated coves and inlets make the Abacos perhaps the most popular sailing destination in The Bahamas.

What to See and Do in the Abacos

Great Abaco

Most first-timers to the Abacos immediately head for Marsh Harbour on Great Abaco. If you insist on the creature comforts of home, you won't be disappointed with Marsh Harbour. The capital of the Abacos is a magnet for boaters, sport fishermen and scuba divers, who flock here to resupply and rest for awhile. There are a growing number of shops here catering to the increasing arrivals of tourists. There are supermarkets, banks, department stores, hardware stores, tackle shops, gas stations and decent restaurants. The "city" even has a single traffic light, the only one found in the Family Islands—although it is quite unnecessary. On my first visit to Marsh Harbour, my taxi driver commented to me as we waited at the light: "We come up to the only traffic light in the Out Islands—and it's red. Go figure."

Marsh Harbour is also the hub for many of the fishing tournaments held in the Abacos annually. One of the most popular is the Penny Turtle Billfish Tournament held in late April and early May. This sleepy community then becomes a party town as it does during the Abaco Week Festival held in November. This festival, featuring parades, fairs, fishing, golf and tennis competitions, celebrates the arrival of Loyalists at the end of the American Revolution. (For more information on both events, contact the **Abaco Chamber of Commerce**, Box 20482, Marsh Harbour, Abaco; ☎ [809] 367-2663.)

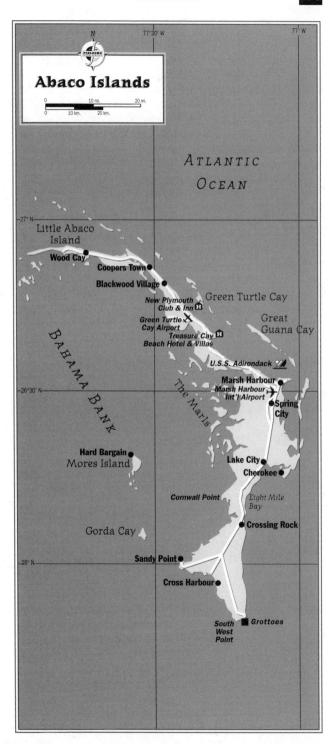

Today, Marsh Harbour is the boat-building capital of The Bahamas, even though tourism has been eclipsing these revenues in recent years. There are a number of full-service marinas in Marsh Harbour, which is considered to be one of the best harbors in The Bahamas. And the marina at the Great Abaco Beach Hotel, according to management, is the largest marina in The Bahamas at 180 slips-plus. Also at Marsh Harbour is an airport. Marsh Harbour itself isn't worthy as a tourist draw, except to use as a base for exploring the area's smaller cays and coves on and around Great Abaco.

Regrettably, the growth of Marsh Harbour—and it's growing extraordinarily quickly—appears to be unchecked. Buildings are going up apparently without any codes saying where they should be located and what they should look like. Service sector investors, in their rush to capitalize on the boom in tourism, have been erecting flimsy, corrugated roof structures—housing everything from grocery stores and boutiques to auto parts stores—which make Marsh Harbour look somewhat like a temporary community for scientists in the South Pole, but without the snow.

Shopping in Marsh Harbour

Although the shopping here hardly rivals that found in Nassau and Freeport/Lucaya, there are some attractions here for tourists. Nassau-based **John Bull** (☎ *[809] 367-2473)* has a store here, where bargains can be had on jewelry and watches. The **Loyalist Shoppe** (☎ *[809] 367-2701)* has a good selection of European leather goods, china and pottery. **Little Switzerland** is also in Marsh Harbour with two stores, one at the Great Abaco Beach Bazaar shopping center and the other near the Conch Inn Hotel. Original bronze works by the Johnstons can be found at the **Johnston Studios Art Gallery** (☎ *[809] 367-3466).*

Boating and Sailing

The Abacos are a meandering mariner's paradise with perhaps the best sailing and marinas in the Out Islands. The marina at the Great Abaco Beach Hotel is said to be the largest in The Bahamas. See "Sports in the Abacos."

Scuba Diving/Snorkeling

A number of scuba diving and snorkeling options are available on Great Abaco, including sightseeing and dive cruises. See "Sports in the Abacos."

Cottman's Miniature Castle

This miniature castle, built by Dr. Evans Cottman, rises from a small hilltop overlooking Marsh Harbour. Cottman was a Madison, Indiana biology teacher who moved to the Abacos in the 1940s and began practicing medicine without a license, but the islanders didn't care. Cottman wrote an acclaimed book called *Out Island Doctor.*

Treasure Cay

20 miles north of Marsh Harbour on Sherben Boothe Highway
This trip makes for a nice drive through the pines to the magnificent Treasure Cay Resort & Marina, with its huge marina, great beach and championship golf course. There is also a 3000-acre farm here that produces winter produce. Treasure Cay is not actually an island, but is connected to Great Abaco by an isthmus of sand. The "cay" was once known as Lovel's Island and actually was separated from Great

Abaco by Carleton Creek until landfill operations joined the two islands.

Bahamas National Trust Sanctuary
Just south of Marsh Harbour
More than 100 species of birds are believed to be fluttering about this national nature preserve, established to protect the endangered Bahamian parrot.

Cherokee Sound
This is a tiny, quaint crawfishing village about 20 miles south of Marsh Harbour. Not much to do or see here other than take in the flavor of fishing village life. The one attraction here is probably **Different of Abaco** (☎ *[809] 366-2150*), a funky little bonefishing club where you can kick back and swill a few cups of Nettie Symonette's bush tea, a rum-based concoction that'll knock your socks off.

Sandy Point
This is another small fishing hamlet, but one with a great beach.

Hole-in-the-Wall
Nobody here on the far southern tip of Great Abaco but the keeper of the lighthouse.

Carleton
Carleton, to the north and a little east of Treasure Cay, contains remnants of a village that doesn't exist anymore. It was founded as the first settlement in the Abacos in 1783 by Loyalists fleeing the newly formed United States and was abandoned around 1795 by its 600 residents after internal bickering over the communal provisions store and a massive hurricane. Most of the settlers moved southeast to found Marsh Harbour. Others scattered to the area around Cocoa Plum Creek. The town was entirely forgotten until 1979, when artifacts were discovered at the former settlement. Near it, in 1983, a plot of land was designated Carleton Point. Today, there is a plaque at the site commemorating the town that died.

Man-O-War Cay
Settled by a single couple, Mammy Nellie and Pappy Ben, in the 1820s, Man-O-War Cay seems stuck in a time warp. This place is about as Victorian as they come. Nearly 230 of the 235 people who resided here during a recent study were direct descendents of the pair. Everyone here is named Albury. Talk about inbreeding. This is the boat-building capital of The Bahamas, although the traditional wooden boats are being replaced by fiberglass vessels, enough to make Mammy and Pappy spin in their graves. No resorts, but a cozy little place to walk around.

Man-O-War Cay is about 45 minutes by boat (water taxi or ferry) from Marsh Harbour. Despite its toss back into time, you might be amazed at the satellite TV and working phones. The cay is an extremely religious community, perhaps even more so than most other communities in The Bahamas. Thus it is quite conservative. No thongs (of the G-string variety) will be tolerated here, folks. Save the skimp for another beach.

There's nowhere really to stay on the island save for **Schooner's Landing** (☎ *[809] 365-6072*)—which is only a few 2-bedroom apartments outrageously priced at $150 per day—and only a handful of restaurants. Most tourists pop over for the day from Marsh Harbour, usually wives in tour groups while their husbands are out on the sea engaged in manly pursuits.

To get out here, take **Albury's** (who else?) **Ferry Service** (☎ *[809] 367-3147 in Marsh Harbour, 365-6010 in Man-O-War)* from the dock next to Great Abaco Beach Resort. The round trip costs $12 for adults and $6 for children.

Shopping & Eating

Don't tell anyone here you'll meet them at Albury's. There's **Albury's Harbour Store** at the harbor for groceries; **Albury's Sail Shop** *(☎ [809] 365-6014)* on the waterfront, with its selections of colorful handmade canvas bags, hats, purses and jackets; and **Albury's Bakery** for conch fritters, pies and baked breads. That's not to mention **Sally's Sea Side Boutique** *(☎ [809] 365-6005)*, for custom-made clothing fashioned from Androsian batik; **Aunt Mady's Boutique**, for resort wear; **Edwin's Boat Yard**, to see sails being repaired; **Joe's Studio**, for ceramics, watercolors, wind socks, T-shirts, nautical souvenirs and jewelry; **Ena's** *(☎ [809] 365-6187)*, for munching on fried conch and coconut pie; and **Sally's Takeaway** *(☎ [809] 365-6240)* for snacks and other munchies. These folks are all undoubtedly Alburys as well. **Island Treasure Gallery** *(☎ [809] 365-6072)* stocks corny souvenirs and you can chow on salads and chicken at **Man-O-War Marina Pavilion** *(☎ [809] 365-6185)*. If you're looking for values on liquor, you're cursed. It's not sold on the island.

Elbow Cay

Wyannie Malone Historical Museum

Elbow Cay was also settled by fleeing Loyalists at the end of the Revolutionary War, and what the Alburys are to Man-O-War, the Malones are to Elbow Cay—and the only safe potential spouses for the Alburys. In the 1900s, the island was home to some of the wealthiest people in the Abacos.

This small island of a few hundred residents and noted for its fine beaches, is also accessible from Marsh Harbour via **Albury's Ferry Service** *(☎ [809] 367-3147* in Marsh Harbour*)* from the dock next to Great Abaco Beach Resort. The round trip costs $12 for adults and $6 for children. The ride is about 20-25 minutes.

Did You Know...

Hurricanes weren't always named after men and women. Back in the 1920s and 1930s they were simply named by the year in which they occurred. And four years during that period were the names of some pretty awesome hurricanes that devastated the Abacos, particularly Elbow Cay. 1926, 1928, 1929 and 1932, although without gender, were particularly lethal hurricanes. After 1932, Hope Town was essentially leveled. By the end of the 1930s, Hope Town's population dropped from 2000 to 200.

Hope Town is the island's center, and the families that live here have been here for generations, mostly Malones. There are few cars here and fewer other connections with the 20th century in this small, Cape Code-like community. The clapboard houses are cheerfully painted in the tropical hues of yellows, greens, blues and purples, alive with bougainvillea. The larger homes are owned by Americans and Europeans who only get here a few times a year. A thin concrete walkway slices between the beautifully preserved older structures, which include a church, a teeny-tiny park, and even tinier museum, the totally out of place swimming pool of the Hope Town Harbour Lodge and the "burial services" building, which looks like an outhouse. The stroll is a delightful way of killing time, because you'll find that once you're out here, there's not much else to do but hang out at the beach or drink Kaliks at one of the half-dozen or so quaint restaurants that line the harbor. Regardless, you'll have a few hours to kill before the next boat heads back, so be creative if you're on a day trip. If you're staying on the island, the Fielding recommendation goes to Hideaways (see below; make reservations early). Proprietor Peggy Thompson is one of the most hospitable folks running a caravansary in the Bahamas—and that's saying a helluva lot, because in the people department, she's got a lot of competition. The beautifully manicured harbor-side property is one of the most tended in the islands. Thompson's villas get my pick as a honeymooner's paradise.

If you're Catholic, you might want to come out here for Sunday Mass, which is celebrated outdoors at the Jarret Park Playground next to the main dock. Some of the worshippers will even sit in the trees.

There is a post office in town (☎ *[809] 365-6214)* as well as a drug store (☎ *[809] 365-6217)*. Ferries leave for Hope Town from Marsh Harbour daily at 10:30 a.m. and 12:15 p.m. on Mondays, Thursdays and Saturdays. There is also a 4 p.m. ferry, but you'll need to spend the night.

The Lighthouse

At Hope Town is a 120-foot-tall lighthouse that's striped like a barber's pole and was built—or completed, rather—in 1838. It took a while for the boys to finish it as it was continually sabotaged by wreckers during its construction. The wreckers weren't comfortable with a beacon that would actually guide ships around disaster rather than directly into it. The lighthouse features only one of four hand-turned kerosene beacons in The Bahamas. You can climb the stairs to the top between 10 a.m. and 4 p.m. weekdays. Keep in mind that the ferry makes a few stops in the harbor. If you get off at one of the docks on the north side, most notably the lower dock, you'll have to take another small boat to reach the lighthouse, swim, or make a two-mile detour walking around the harbor to reach the place.

Wyannie Malone Historical Museum

Purple Porpoise Place

This is a matchbox-sized museum that features photos and other memorabilia of days gone by in Hope Town. Wyannie Malone was the founding mother of the town and came here as early as 1775 with her four children. The museum is kept up by volunteers and is usually locked. It opens only when someone can get a key for it. Approach any of the locals and you'll be steered in the right direction.

Great Guana Cay

Great Guana is the longest of the Abaco cays at seven miles and is also off Marsh Harbour. Only about a hundred people live here (some say 150) and they don't see much of the occasional cruise ship passengers who are shuttled here to take advantage of the spectacular beach. The residents here are mostly white descendents of Loyalists from Virginia and the Carolinas who inhabited this strip of sand after the American Revolution. Like Man-O-Cay and Elbow Cay, the clapboard houses here resemble New England seaside cottages. The central village is tiny, with a church, a couple of stores and a one-room schoolhouse. Kids on the island can only go to school here until they're 14 and have to leave the island if they want to continue their education. Most stay and enter the traditional family trades of boatbuilding, carpentry and fishing.

There are no cars on the island and residents get around by boat, as the isle is so skinny that "inland" is perhaps only a few meters away. There is one resort on the island, **Guana Beach Resort & Marina** (☎ *[809] 367-3590*). In addition to the resort, **Pinder's Gift Shop** is the place for provisions and for boat rentals. Rentals on small sailboats are available for the half day, full day or an entire month.

Great Guana Cay is accessible from Marsh Harbour through **Albury's Ferry Service** (☎ *[809] 367-3147*). The charter cost is $85 one-way for up to five passengers.

Green Turtle Cay

Green Turtle Cay offers shallow reefs, deep bays and great beaches.

Green Turtle Cay, three miles east of Great Abaco and 170 miles east of Palm Beach, Florida, may be the most perfect islet of all the cays surrounding Abaco. There are magnificent shallow reefs, deep bays, magnificent beaches and even a few hills! An added bonus is that there are, with the exception of regatta time, few visitors here, compared with nearby Treasure Cay.

Green Turtle's population center is New Plymouth, which like towns on the other cays off Great Abaco resembles a small beachside New England community. In the 1800s, New Plymouth was considered the most prosperous community in the Abacos, being populated with as many as 1400 Loyalists who fled the American colonies at the end of the Revolutionary War. Today, the population has dropped to about 500, the island's staple industry of boatbuilding collapsing after the emancipation of slaves in 1838. During the Civil War, New Plymouth was a safe port for Confederate ships and blockade runners. Today, most of the residents work for the Abaco Seafood Company, which exports lobster to the States, or by diving for conch. And the quaint streets of New Plymouth remain flanked by tiny, handsome white clapboard houses trimmed in pastel blues, greens, pinks, browns and yellows. The residents are generally cheery, and when the regatta's in town, expect to attend an impromptu backyard barbecue.

A few tourists who visit here rent boats to be taken to the pristine, deserted islands of No Name Cay and Pelican Cay to the south of Green Turtle Cay and Fiddle Cay to the north.

The island has a few resorts and some cottage rentals, making it quite tourist-friendly. The Bluff House is a particularly superb getaway, set up on a hill overlooking the bay toward New Plymouth.

Green Turtle Cay has been "discovered." There's only one taxi on the island and it can be very busy, so be prepared to wait if you're at one of the villas and need to get into town. The roads on the island are generally awful. Most tourists arrive via the Treasure Cay Airport. There, guests take taxis to the 10-minute ferry ride for New Plymouth and the Green Turtle Club.

Albert Lowe Museum

Parliament Street. ☎ *(809) 365-4094. Open Mon.–Sat. 9 a.m.–noon and 1–4 p.m. Admission is $3 for adults and $1.50 for children.*

A beautifully restored 200-year-old clapboard building is home to this museum founded by Alton Roland Lowe, the son of one of the island's original settlers. There are a lot of photos and other memorabilia here chronicling life on the cay during the 19th and 20th centuries, including a shot of New Plymouth after it was sacked by a hurricane in 1932. There are also model ships and paintings done by Alton Lowe, one of the best-known painters in The Bahamas. His work can be found around the world. The backdrops for a number of Bahamian postage stamps are the work of Alton and blow-ups of these can be found in the museum. You'll also see the stone kitchen that was used as a storm shelter during the ravaging 1932 hurricane. Albert Lowe was a historian and boatbuilder of significant renown.

Memorial Sculpture Garden

Across from the New Plymouth Inn in the middle of town.

This pleasant garden, opened at the 1984 bicentennial, is in the shape of the Union Jack and celebrates the Loyalists who migrated to Green Turtle Cay after the American Revolution.

Miss Emily's Blue Bee Bar

Victoria Street

No stop on Green Turtle Cay is complete without a visit to this famous bar, the original home to the Goombay Smash, if we're to believe Emily Cooper, the establishment's proprietor. The walls are covered here with business cards and other mementos left by travelers and dignitaries. The bar keeps odd hours.

Shopping and Eating

The **Loyalist Rose Shoppe** and the **Sand Dollar Shoppe** sell T-shirts and other souvenirs. The island's fanciest restaurants are found at **Bluff House** and the **Green Turtle Club** hotels, outside town. At **Laura's Kitchen**, which sells conch, fish, chicken and ice cream, you can order at the window, then eat on the breezy porch. You can have a bona-fide Bahamian meal at the **Sea View Restaurant**. Patrons' business cards, photographs of visitors, and dollar bills cover the walls of this casual, inexpensive restaurant. Another popular local restaurant is **Rooster's Rest**, where the Gully Rooster band plays on weekends. Stop at **The Wrecking Tree Restaurant & Bar**, when in the mood for pastry, cool drinks or local munchies. A big casuarina grows up through the front porch. Some say this place was named because people used to sit in the shade of the tree and get wrecked on rum libations. Try the conch fritters. Light meals are served between 9 a.m. and 3 p.m. at **Plymouth Rock Liquors & Cafe**, next to **Ocean Blue Gallery**.

Spanish Cay

This small island (three miles long) about 11 miles northwest of Green Turtle Cay, was once the private playground of Texas multimillionaire and former Dallas Cowboys owner Clint Murchinson. This undeveloped island was then transformed into second homes for the rich and famous by a couple of Florida companies after Murchinson died in the early 1980s. There is little more here than a few homes for the elite, and one can observe the well-heeled visitors and residents puttering along in their golf carts on the way to their yachts at the 70-slip marina. There's even a 5000-foot runway to accommodate a mere four homes and 13 guest suites on the island.

Walker's Cay

This is the "Top of The Bahamas" and is well known as a sport fisherman's paradise, although it wasn't always so. The island was a haven for pirates and blockade runners during the Civil War, as well as for rumrunners during the Prohibition. This tiny island, for its size, has had a colorful history. Ponce de Leon paid a visit in 1513 in search of water, only a week before he "discovered" Florida.

Virtually all visitors here stay at the Walker's Cay Hotel & Marina, and the hotel even operates its own airline, which flies daily between the island and Fort Lauderdale (**Walker's International**; ☎ *[305] 359-1400, [800] 925-5377).*

Most of the hotel employees live on nearby Grand Cay and get ferried back and forth daily, where on Grand Cay they hit up Rosie Curry's Island

Club Bar & Restaurant or the Seaside Disco and Bar. The locals on both islands head for Whale Bay Island when they want to hit the beach.

The vegetation on the two islands resembles the southern U.S. more than The Bahamas. Missing are the casuarina trees and other tropical species. And it can get nippy up here during the winter months, as low as the upper 40s when a storm comes passing through.

Aqualife

This is a firm on Walker's Cay that procures and raises tropical fish for sale into U.S. pet shops. Interestingly, most of the fish come from the Pacific. Guided tours are available by asking the resort.

Where to Stay in the Abacos

Great Guana Cay

Guana Beach Resort   **$85–$130**   ★ ★ ★

P.O. Box AB-20474, Marsh Harbour, Abaco
☎ *(800) 227-3366 U.S., (809) 367-3590; FAX (305) 751-9570*
Single: $85–$130; Double: $85–$130

Easy choice for Great Guana Cay because there's nowhere else to stay on the entire island. Relax and kick your shoes off (it's the owners' policy), plop yourself into a hammock, and enjoy one (or more) of the potent rum drinks. Thick foliage, coconut groves, and a divine beach will have to keep you occupied. The restaurant serves noteworthy Bahamian and American-style cuisine (conch burgers are a lunch-time specialty), and not one of the eight rooms or seven villas has a phone or television. Amenities: restaurant, bar, bicycle rentals, swimming pool, dock. Credit cards: MC, V.

Green Turtle Cay

Green Turtle Club   **$120–$150**   ★ ★ ★ ★

P.O. Box AB-22792, Green Turtle Cay, Abaco
☎ *(800) 688-4752, (809) 365-4271; FAX (809) 365-4272*
Single: $125–$150; Double: $125–$150

This 80-acre resort is home-away-from-home for yachties, water-lovers and various celebs seeking to leave their cares behind. Associated with both British Royal Yachting Association and the Palm Beach Yacht Club, this beachfront property is always crowded with yachts anchored at its 35-slip marina. Unless you're a member (in which case you'll have your own water-side villa), you'll be put up in large tree-sheltered bungalows overlooking the harbor. Furnishings are yachtie-gone-troppo elegant, and each unit has its own living and dining area, terrace and deck. The dining room serves excellent meals and fine wines in the same posh style, while the bar (papered in dollar bills) is the focal point for the social snob-snob. The setting is sensational, though it's several miles from New Plymouth—getting into town either means a good walk or a boat ride. Amenities: Swimming pool, restaurant, bar, lounge, exercise room, dock, fishing, diving. Credit cards: AE, MC, V.

Bluff House   **$90–$380**   ★ ★ ★

Green Turtle Cay, Abaco
☎ *(809) 365-4247; FAX (809) 365-4248*
Single: $90–$110; Double: $90–$110; Split level suite: $105–$120; one-bedroom villa: $155–$175; two-bedroom villa: $235–$270; three-bedroom villa: $330–$380

The view is fantastic—White Sound harbor on one side, Sea of Abaco on the other—from this 12-acre property, perched atop the Abaco chain's tallest hill. Plenty of pines, oaks, and palms shelter the resort and its ethereal powdery pink beach. A swimming pool and sun deck allow you to tan with a view. Lunch and snacks are served in the Beach Club, while candlelight dinners with Bahamian and American cuisine (including plenty of fresh seafood) are sequestered in the main Club House. Aside from the beach and pool, action takes place at the 30-slip marina, on the tennis court, or a fishing or snorkeling charter excursion. Complimentary excursions into New Plymouth are scheduled a few times a week, including Saturday night jaunts to the local dance (sound like summer camp?). Regatta time brings a merry junkanoo festival, Bluff House-style, to the resort, as do the traditional junkanoo festivals around Christmas time. Owner Martin Havill's personal style is reflected in every aspect of Bluff House, from the airy tropical architecture to the intimate, yet casual restaurant and bar. Regrettably, he's sold the place—but at least he'll be on another five years to manage it—which will only be to the customers' benefit. He couldn't have a better sense of humor. Accommodations are spacious, woodsy, and wickery villas with tropical ambience and good views, but with no phones or televisions. But amazingly comfortable and roomy with a home-like ambience. Amenities: swimming pool, dining room, lounge, one tennis court, dock, gift shop.

New Plymouth Inn   **$115–$125**   ★ ★

New Plymouth, Green Turtle Cay, Abaco
☎ *(809) 365-4165; FAX (809) 365-4138*
Single: $115–$125; Double: $115–$125

In the center of New Plymouth, this 1830-built two-story inn allows visitors to soak up some history along with the rays. Restored to its New England-Bahamian colonial charm, the inn features breezy verandahs, tropical gardens, a swimming pool and nearby tennis and snorkeling. The restaurant, popular with locals (always a good sign), serves Bahamian and American candlelight dinners, vintage wines, and a can't-wait-until-Sunday brunch. Amenities: swimming pool, dining room, bar. Credit cards: No credit cards.

Hope Town/Elbow Cay

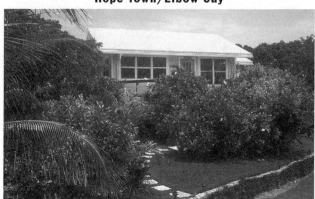

Hope Town Hideaway, Elbow Cay, Abacos

Hope Town Hideaways   **$140–$250**   ★★

One Purple Porpoise Place
Hope Town, Elbow Cay, Abaco
☎ *(809) 366-0224; FAX (809) 366-0434*
Villas: $170–$250, $140–$190 off season

This is our choice when staying in Hope Town. Nestled in a small cove in the Hope Town harbor. You'll need to take a boat to get to this 11-acre hideaway located across the harbor from "greater" Hope Town. The property is planted with flowers, fruits and vegetables, as well as grass you could play golf on. This has undoubtedly got to be the most romantic honeymoon getaway in the Abacos, if not all The Bahamas. The name suits it perfectly. Owners Chris and Peggy Thompson, a thoroughly hospitable couple, will arrange rental boats and various excursions, and may even share a Kalik or two with you when not busy with their two young children. The large, airy villas with high cathedral ceilings feature living areas, two bedrooms, VCRs, large decks and fully equipped kitchens. The villas are furnished with a library of movie videos, but don't expect any new releases. You could have stayed in Peoria to watch a movie. Also a pragmatic and convenient touch is the VHF radio in every villa. There's no restaurant but some local spots are pretty close by. Small skiffs are provided for customer use around the charming harbor. A pool has been built dockside at the resort's own 12-slip marina. A definite Fielding choice. Amenities: VCRs. Credit cards: AE, MC, V.

Sea Spray Resort   **$750–$1000**   ★★★

White Sound, Elbow Cay, Abaco
☎ *(809) 366-0065; FAX (809) 366-0383*
$750–$1000 for one to four persons

This is a good choice for a couple or two. Each of the six villas feature one or two bedrooms, island decor, equipped kitchens and ocean or harbor views. The owners make guests feel at home and love to share tips on places to see, things to do. Various activities include snorkeling, sailing (free rental boats), cycling and deep-sea fishing. Surfers will be happy to find the resort looks out over one of the Bahamas' best surf sites. A casual clubhouse restaurant cooks up local dishes (you can have meals brought to your villa), plus there's a pool table and satellite TV. Situated a few miles south of Hope Town, this six-acre property is kept in immaculate shape. Amenities: swimming pool, restaurant, dock. Credit cards: AE, MC, V.

Abaco Inn   **$115–$145**   ★★★

Hope Town, Elbow Cay, Abaco
☎ *(800) 468-8799 U.S., (809) 366-0133; FAX (809) 355-0113*
Single: $115–$135; Double: $125–$145

The Abaco ranks consistently high with visitors who seek a little sophistication with their island stay. Set amidst palms and sea-grape trees, with the Sea of Abaco to one side and White Sound on the other, the inn offers plenty of lazing space on the beach, in the ocean-front gazebo, or the thatched solarium. Snorkeling and diving are the most popular watersports, while indoor activity centers around the clubhouse with its cool bar and roaring fire. Seafood and vegetarian cuisine, prepared nouveau and nouvelle, are menu headliners in the restaurant. Villas feature high ceilings, open beams, air conditioning, ocean or harbor views, and personal hammocks. Amenities: swimming pool, dining room, bar, lounge. Credit cards: MC, V.

Club Soleil Resort   **$120–$130**   ★★★

Western Harbourfront, Hope Town, Elbow Cay
☎ *(809) 366-0003; FAX (809) 366-0254*
Single: $120–$130; Double: $120–$130

Bring your boat or arrange a ride with the resort to get to this spot across the harbor from Hope Town. Built in the 1990s, this Spanish-style property is nicely secluded among coconut palm and banana groves, in a relatively uninhabited area near some prime secluded beaches. Frolic around the sand and sea, in the swimming pool, or arrange for a diving, fishing, or sailing excursion. The cheery, wood-beamed dining room is a best bet for fresh seafood. Rooms are a bit motel-y but have tile floors, private balconies, driftwood art, small refrigerators, and TVs with VCRs. Amenities: swimming pool, restaurant, bar, dock. Credit cards: MC, V.

Hope Town Harbour Lodge   **$100–$1000**   ★★★

Hope Town, Abaco
☎ *(800) 316-7844 U.S., (809) 366-0095; FAX (809) 366-0286*
Single: $100–$110; Double: $110–$125; Triple: $120–$135; Quad: $135–$145; Butterfly House: $300 ($1000 per week)

On a hill above Hope Town, this renovated former private home offers 14 harbor-view rooms in the main house or seven prefab ocean-view cottages clustered around the swimming pool and garden area. Some of the rooms have views of both the harbor and the ocean on the opposite side. All are colorful, but simply decorated and none has a phone or TV. Take in some diving, snorkeling, fishing or boating, then gorge yourself at the casual poolside restaurant for breakfast and lunch, or the more formal dining room with super views and Bahamian cuisine. Amenities: two restaurants, two bars, swimming pool. Credit cards: MC, V.

Man-O-War Cay

Schooner's Landing   **$165–$190**   ★★★

Man-O-War Cay, Abaco
☎ *(809) 365-6072; FAX (809) 365-6285*
Single: $165–$190; Double: $165–$190

Four two-bedroom condos sit Mediterranean-style atop a rocky outcrop, overlooking crashing surf and a fairly isolated beach. Snorkeling and swimming are premiere beach activities, and fishing and boating can be arranged—a private dock is available if you bring your own boat. Each duplex-type unit contains two bedrooms, two bathrooms, TVs with VCRs (there's no TV reception), rattan and wicker furnishings, and equipped kitchens. The property has no restaurant, but several are nearby as are a couple of grocery stores that will deliver. A minimum three-day stay is required. Amenities: dock. Credit cards: AE, MC, V.

Marsh Harbour/Great Abaco Island

Abaco Towns by the Sea   **$140–$200**   ★★★

P.O. Box AB-20486, Marsh Harbour, Abaco
☎ *(800) 322-7757 U.S., (809) 367-2227; FAX (809) 367-3927*
Beach View: $200; Ocean View: $160; Garden/Pool: $140

This time-share/condo complex is a deluxe choice for this area—white stucco villas hovering like Greek icons above the sparkling sea and sandy beaches, with flowering plants and trees providing bursts of color. The property features a swimming pool, boutique, lighted tennis courts, snorkeling and array of daily activities. Restaurants are within walking distance, and car, scooter, and bicycle rentals can be arranged. Each of the 64 apartments can accommodate up to six people and offers a living/dining area, kitchens with dishwashers and microwaves, two bedrooms and all towels and linens (if you want maid service, you'll have to kick in about an extra $20 per day). Amenities: swimming pool, two tennis courts, boutique. Credit cards: AE, MC, V.

Great Abaco Beach Hotel $105–$175   ★ ★ ★
P.O. Box AB-20511, Marsh Harbour, Abaco
☎ *(800) 468-4799 U.S., (809) 367-2158; FAX (809) 367-2819*
Single: $105–$175; Double: $105–$175
Four miles from Marsh Harbour Airport, gracing a hill above the Sea of Abaco, this hotel—with its 180-slip marina and full docking facilities—is a big favorite with fishers and divers. A variety of charters, trips and tours can be arranged while—resort-side—guests have use of two swimming pools and two tennis courts. Some of Marsh Harbour's better dining takes place in the new gourmet restaurant or the old-favorite Bahamian room. Afterwards action centers around the nightclub and lounge with live local entertainment, or at the two bars. Accommodations are either in roomy units or the six separate two-bedroom villas, each with kitchen and two bedrooms. All accommodations have white-wicker furnishings, tropical decor, TVs, telephones and sea-view balconies. Amenities: two swimming pools, two restaurants, two bars, two tennis courts, dock. Credit cards: AE, MC, V.

Different of Abaco $205–$230   ★ ★
P.O. Box AB-20092, Marsh Harbour, Abaco
☎ *(809) 366-2150; FAX (809) 327-8152*
Single: $205; Double: $230
The home of the Great Abaco Bonefishing Club welcomes bonefishers and others to an eight-room resort located about 18 miles south of Marsh Harbour. Luxury-seekers would do better elsewhere, but environmentally conscious visitors in search of practically untouched reefs and beaches—and, of course, bonefish—as well as some local color, should enjoy it here. Waterfront rooms are simply furnished but immaculate and breezy. Owner Nettie Symonette serves wonderful Bahamian dishes (included in the rates), and evenings tend to be lively occasions. Amenities: dining room, bar. Credit cards: No credit cards.

Conch Inn $95   ★ ★
P.O. Box AB-20469, Marsh Harbour, Abaco
☎ *(809) 367-4000; FAX (809) 367-4004*
Single: $95; Double: $95
Located between downtown Marsh Harbor and the ferry dock, this low-key inn draws yachters and divers to its full-service 75-slip marina—home to the Moorings yacht chartering company. It also tends to be the congregating spot for groups of locals and other visitors. Aside from the marina action, the property has a large swimming pool, harbor-side cafe and a lively bar (especially during happy hour).

Rooms feature predictable nautical decor, TVs and harbor-view patios. Amenities: swimming pool, restaurant, bar, dock, dive shop. Credit cards: AE, MC, V.

Pelican Beach Villas   **$170**   ★★

P.O. Box AB-20304, Marsh Harbour, Abaco
☎ *(800) 642-7268 U.S., (809) 367-3600; FAX (912) 437-6223*
U.S. Office
P.O. Box 644
Darien, GA 31305
☎ *(912) 437-6220, (800) 642-7268; FAX (912) 437-6223*
Single: $170; Double: $170

Five pink cottages tucked away amid casuarina trees share a small oceanfront cove and a lagoon, with 87-foot dock, on the backside. Snorkel, dive or just stretch out in one of the hammocks along the beach. Cottages—all facing the sea—feature two-bedrooms, two-baths, and a fully equipped kitchen, as well a color TV (which only gets a couple of stations). They're all quite comfortable and endowed in the interiors but regrettably resemble a pink army barracks from the outside. No landscaping, so the grounds look a little like a construction site. It's a good thing they sit on an incredible beach. Few frills, but you can do your laundry here. A resident caretaker—Ada Deveaux—is around to help, and grocery stores are nearby. But there is no other staff, at least at our last inspection. Amenities: Dive shop, dock. Credit cards: MC, V.

Lofty Fig Villas   **$75–$95**   ★★

P.O. Box AB-20437, Marsh Harbour, Abaco
☎ *(809) 367-2681; FAX (809) 367-2681*
Single: $75–$95; Double: $75–$95

Located across from the Conch Inn, this family-run grouping of villas overlooks the harbor, offers tropical surroundings, and a pool area with a gazebo and barbecue facilities. It's not much but there are plenty of nearby boat and equipment rentals, shops and restaurants. Each of the six villas offers a sofa bed, queen-size bed, equipped kitchen, dining area and screened-in porch, with maid service on hand every day but Sunday. Guests will enjoy peace, privacy and good value. Amenities: swimming pool. Credit cards: MC, V.

Spanish Cay

Inn at Spanish Cay   **$200–$325**   ★★★

P.O. Box 882, Cooperstown, Abaco
☎ *(800) 688-4752 U.S., (809) 365-0083; FAX (809) 365-0466*
Single: $200–$325; Double: $200–$325

This 200-acre private and very exclusive property sits well off the tourist track in the northern Bahamas. For decades it was a billionaire's hideaway, but now ordinary riff-raff with the bucks to spare can share the beauty and peace of Spanish Cay. Activities include private-island joys such as diving, fishing, boating and exploring nearby uninhabited beaches and reefs, plus there are four tennis courts and a dock. Dining is at either at the casual eatery near the marina, or in the more upscale (and expensive) **Wrecker's Raw Bar**, where the chef will try to please your every culinary desire. Accommodations are in one- or two-bedroom apartments, or in villa suites. Most feature kitchens and private gardens, along with a golf cart for handy transportation. Amenities: dock, two restaurants, two bars, four tennis courts. Credit cards: MC, V.

Walker's Cay

Walker's Cay Hotel and Marina **$110–$160** ★ ★ ★

Walker's Cay, Abaco
☎ *(800) 432-2092 U.S., (305) 359-1400; FAX (305) 359-1400*
Single: $110–$160; Double: $110–$160
This 100-acre island resort—the northernmost in the Bahamas—is so self-contained it even has its own Fort Lauderdale-based airline. Yachties cruise over to use the top-notch, full-service, 75-slip marina, while fishers are pulled by the Annual Billfish Tournament—largest in the Bahamas. Other activities include a wide range of watersports and two all-weather tennis courts. Guests are put up in luxe suites or villas with tropical decor and private patios. The Lobster Trap restaurant serves Bahamian and American cuisine, including fine wines and home-made pastries and breads. The lounge offers booze with views, and occasional disco dancing. Amenities: restaurant, lounge, two bars, two swimming pools, dock, dive shop, two all-weather tennis courts. Credit cards: AE, MC, V.

Treasure Cay

Treasure Cay Resort and Marina **$65–$95** ★ ★ ★

Treasure Cay, Abaco
☎ *(800) 327-1584 U.S., (809) 367-2570; FAX (809) 367-3362*
Single: $65–$85; Double: $75–$95
Oh, do come stay at the very same place where *Day of the Dolphins* was filmed! You'll find plenty to do besides ogle the stale footprints left by George C. Scott. Activities include 18-hole golf (plus golf-cart rentals for putting around the property), eight tennis courts, just about every water sport (including parasailing and wind surfing), bicycle and boat rentals, fishing and snorkeling excursions, and everything that comes with a 150-slip marina. You'll have a restaurant (serving fine international cuisine), snack bar, two bars and occasional live entertainment. Accommodations have TVs (but no phones), rattan and bamboo furnishings, pastel color schemes, and most have colorful marina views. Shops and "city" facilities are nearby. Amenities: swimming pool, restaurant, two bars, lounge, eight tennis courts, 18-hole golf, bicycle and golf-cart rentals. Credit cards: AE, MC, V.

Where to Eat in the Abacos

Laura's Kitchen ★ ★

Parliament Street, Green Turtle Cay
☎ *(809) 365-4287*
Bahamian cuisine
Lunch: daily 11 a.m.–3 p.m., entrees $8–$13
Dinner: daily 6:30–9 p.m., entrees $10–$15
Chicken, cracked conch, fresh fish and simple Bahamian dishes are served in this family-run eatery housed inside a former private cottage near the ferry dock. Reservations recommended. Credit cards: No credit cards.

Rooster's Rest ★ ★

Gilliam's Bay Road, Green Turtle Cay
☎ *(809) 365-4066*
Bahamian cuisine

THE ABACOS

Lunch: Mon.–Sat. 11:30 a.m.– 3 p.m., entrees $4–$8
Dinner: Mon.–Sat. 6:30–9:30 p.m., entrees $10–$16

Located near the school, just outside of town, this spot turns out all the local favorites including conch, lobster and the de rigeur side accompaniments such as peas 'n' rice, potato salad and cole slaw. Yachties and locals fill the place on weekend nights, plus there's live entertainment. Reservations recommended. Credit cards: No credit cards.

Mangoes

Front Street, Marsh Harbour
☎ *(809) 367-2366*
Bahamian/American cuisine
Lunch: daily 11:30 a.m.–3 p.m., entrees $5–$12
Dinner: daily 6:30–9:30 p.m., entrees $16–$25
Closed September through mid-November

At some time or other, most residents and visitors congregate at this harbor-front restaurant. The cathedral ceiling and island-sophisticate decor make it an enjoyable location for fresh seafood, grilled steaks, pasta dishes and lunchtime salads and sandwiches. Reservations required. Credit cards: AE, MC, V.

Wally's ★★★

East Bay Street, Marsh Harbour
☎ *(809) 367-2074*
Bahamian cuisine
Lunch: Mon.–Sat. 11:30 a.m.–3 p.m., entrees $8–$12
Dinner: Mon. 7 p.m., Sat. 6 p.m., $18–$30
Closed September through mid-October

Across from the harbor, this pink colonial residence is a sought-after spot by the doing-lunchers for sandwiches, conch and beef burgers, salads and definitely for its specialty drinks. On Monday and Saturday evenings there's a pseudo-gourmet prix-fixe dinner, well-attended by the locals and visitors in the know (you!). Reservations required for dinner. Credit cards: AE, MC, V.

Harbour's Edge

Elbow Cay (Hope Town)
☎ *(809) 366-0087*
Bahamian cuisine
Lunch: Wed.–Mon. 11:30 a.m.–3 p.m., entrees $8–$15
Dinner: Wed.–Mon. 6–9 p.m.
Closed mid-September-mid-October

There's usually lots of action at this restaurant hovering above the water on piers, near the post office. The lunch and dinner menu offers simple fare—burgers, conch dishes, chicken, steak and such. A pool table, satellite television, bar and water's-edge deck are added attractions. Show up on Saturday night for live music. Credit cards: No credit cards.

Rudy's Place ★★★

Center Line Road, Elbow Cay (Hope Town)
☎ *(809) 366-0062*
Bahamian cuisine
Dinner: Mon.–Sat. 6:30–8:30 p.m., $22–$27
Closed September through October

This restaurant is out of the way—about mid-island in a residence nestled within a valley—but, worry not: the owner will have someone come fetch you. Rudy prepares variations of his grandma's recipes for his admiring and adoring patrons who dine in a paneled room, smacking their lips over three-course shrimp, duck, chicken and seafood extravaganzas. Reservations required. Credit cards: No credit cards.

Nightlife in the Abacos

As you might well imagine there aren't a lot of raves taking place in the Abacos these days and, overall, nightlife is limited to the resorts. But you won't find the throbbing discos of Nassau and Freeport/Lucaya. Instead it might be a local pianist or guitarist softly playing to the backdrop of hushed, romantic conversation. Probably the most "happenin'" place in the Abacos is **Miss Emily's Blue Bee Bar** on Green Turtle Cay. The resorts and some of the villas offer bars and other diversions. The **Conch Out Bar** at the Conch Inn Resort & Marina is the best night spot to head for in Marsh Harbor, particularly if you're not staying at another resort.

Bars

Rooster's Rest Pub & Restaurant

Gilliam's Bay Road
New Plymouth Green Turtle Cay
☎ *(809) 365-4066*
On the weekends, you'll find some cheesy music here and visiting pleasure boaters who've been on the sea too long, so long that anyone with a couple of pine branches and an overturned bucket sounds like a Jimmy Buffet concert. Party on.

Miss Emily's Blue Bee Bar

Victoria Street
☎ *(809) 365-4181*
No stop on Green Turtle Cay is complete without a visit to this famous bar, the original home to the Goombay Smash, if we're to believe Emily Cooper, the establishment's elderly proprietor. The walls are covered here with business cards and other mementos left by travelers, celebrities and dignitaries the likes of Glen Campbell and Lillian Carter, the late mother of former President Jimmy Carter. The bar keeps odd hours but is generally open from 10 a.m. until the last customer leaves.

Sports in the Abacos

Scuba Diving/Snorkeling

The Abacos make for a great dive getaway because most of its islets are quite small, and sparsely populated, allowing the subaquatic environments to remain pristine. Visibility can be particularly keen here as the boomerang-shaped sub-chain lies close to the Gulf Stream. This is also a great area for wreck diving and blue holes.

Certainly the best shark diving in The Abacos is found off Walker's Cay at an area known as Shark Rodeo. Here, hammerheads, bull, nurse, Caribbean reef and blacktip sharks have taken a liking (most would call it a habit) to the frozen chum balls concocted by the local divemasters. Dozens (sometimes more than a hundred) of sharks feed frenziedly on the feast, exciting even divers who've "been there, done that." Off Walker's Cay can also be found Pirate's Cathedral, marvelous underwater caverns teeming with glass minnows, and White Hole, with its myriad coneys and groupers. Spanish Cay features a recently opened resort, giving divers access to numerous shallow reefs.

At Green Turtle Cay, not to be missed are the wrecks Viceroy, an early 20th-century steamship, and the San Jacinto, a Civil War gunboat that sank in 40 feet of water in 1865. The Catacombs are a spectacular set of ledges and caverns, while The Pillars and Tarpon Reef offer divers splendid views of feeding coral and schools of tarpon.

However, most divers in The Abacos flock to Marsh Harbour, where the Fowl Cay Land and Sea Preserve is located. Because the preserve is protected, magnificent shallow reefs are the home to dozens of species of essentially tame sealife. Here it's possible to kiss barracudas and bump-and-grind with a school of blue sharks while shooting your Nikon point-blank at a placid grouper tame enough to make Garfield look neurotic. Notable here are the Towers, a pair of coral towers that rise magnificently from 70 feet to only a few feet from the surface. Huge schools of Silversides move like giant drapes in a breeze at Maxi Cave Bay, and at Maurice Bay can be seen an abundance of Margate snapper, grouper, nurse sharks, turtles and even spotted eagle rays. And be sure to check out the Cathedral, a large cave at about 30 feet known for dazzling shafts of sunlight.

Dive shop, Marsh Harbour, Abacos

Brendal's Dive Shop

☎ *(800) 780-9941*

Daily trips for divers and snorkelers to coral gardens, wrecks and reefs. Instructions available.

Dive Abaco

P.O. Box AB20555
Marsh Harbour
Abaco
☎ *(800) 247-5338, (809) 367-2787*
FAX (809) 367-4004

Scuba trips out to the world's third-longest barrier reef for certified divers cost $65, tanks and weights included. Snorkelers can come along for $35. Instruction at the resorts costs $100. Trips leave daily at 9:00 a.m. Open daily 8:30 a.m.–5 p.m. Also equipment rentals, including underwater cameras.

Great Abaco Beach Undersea Adventures

☎ *(800) 327-8150*

Daily trips for divers and snorkelers to coral gardens, wrecks and reefs. Instructions available.

Spanish Cay Diving

☎ *(809) 365-0083*
Daily trips for divers and snorkelers to coral gardens, wrecks and reefs. Instructions available.

Spanish Cay Watersports

P.O. Box 882
Cooperstown, Abaco
☎ *(809) 365-0083*
FAX 365-0466
Daily trips for divers and snorkelers to coral gardens, wrecks and reefs. Instructions available.

Walker's Cay Undersea Adventures

U.S. Office
P.O. Box 21766
Fort Lauderdale, FL 33335-1766
☎ *(800) 327-8150, (954) 462-3400*
FAX (954) 462-4100
Bahamas ☎ *(809) 352-5252*
Bahamas FAX (809) 352-3301
Daily trips for divers and snorkelers to coral gardens, wrecks and reefs. Instructions available.

Sportfishing

The Abacos are a fisherman's dream, as yellowtail can be plucked off the reefs or marlin wrestled in from the deep waters off the cays. The bonefish fishing is particularly good around the cays off Marsh Harbour. Boats, from 18-foot Boston Whalers to 30-foot Bertrams can be rented anywhere from $40 for a half-day to more than $400 for the full day. See "Boat Charters" in the "Directory." Some of the Abacos' many fishing tournaments throughout the year (the biggest are in May and June) include the Treasure Cay Billfish Championship, the Green Turtle Yacht Club Fishing Tournament, the Boat Harbour Billfish Championship and the Walker's Cay Billfish Tournament. (For more information on all events, contact the **Abaco Chamber of Commerce**, *Box 20482, Marsh Harbour, Abaco;* ☎ *[809] 367-2663.*)

Hope Town, Elbow Cay, Abacos

Boating and Sailing

Both boats with crew and bareboats can be rented daily and weekly. Rates range from $80–$400 a day to $1000–$4000 a week. Boats can be had out of either Marsh Harbour or Hope Town. See "Boat Charters" in the "Directory."

Full-service marinas are in abundance throughout most of the Abacos. Most of the marinas are located at and attached to the cays' resorts.

Boat Harbour Marina
Marsh Harbour
Great Abaco
☎ *(809) 367-2736*

Conch Inn Marina
Marsh Harbour
Great Abaco
☎ *(809) 367-4000*

Marsh Harbour Marina
Marsh Harbour
Great Abaco
☎ *(809) 367-2700*

Guana Beach Resort
Great Guana Cay
☎ *(809) 367-3590, (800) 227-3366*

Green Turtle Club
Green Turtle Cay
☎ *(809) 365-4271*

Hope Town Marina
Hope Town
Elbow Cay
☎ *(809) 366-0003*

Man-O-War Marina
Man-O-War Cay
☎ *(809) 365-6008*

Treasure Cay Resort & Marina
Treasure Cay
Great Abaco
☎ *(809) 367-2570*

Walker's Cay Hotel & Marina
Walker's Cay
☎ *(809) 352-5252*

Golf

Treasure Cay Golf Club
Treasure Cay Resort & Marina
Treasure Cay, Great Abaco
☎ *(809) 367-2570*

This is the only golf course in the Abacos, but it's a passable par-72, 18-hole layout at 6985 yards and designed by Dick Wilson. The cost is $40 for 18 holes and $25 for nine. Carts are required and cost $25 for 18 holes and $15 for nine.

Tennis

There are barely more than a dozen tennis courts found in all of the Abacos, putting the islands off the contention list for the site of John McEnroe's All-Star Summer Tennis Camp. All of the courts are found at resorts and are almost exclusively used—when they're used—by the resort's guests.

Treasure Cay Resort & Marina
Treasure Cay, Great Abaco
☎ *(809) 367-2142*
Eight courts, both hard-surface and clay; four are lit. This is the best place to play in the Abacos, and there are not a lot of other choices, as the islands have only about 16 courts in all. The clay courts cost $18 an hour, while the hard surface courts run $16 per hour.

Abaco Towns by the Sea
☎ *(800) 332-7757*

Bluff House
☎ *(809) 365-4247*
One hard court; guests play for free and non-guests are charged $10 an hour.

Great Abaco Beach Hotel
☎ *(800) 468-4799, (809) 367-2158*
Two hard-surface courts that run for $10 an hour.

Green Turtle Club
☎ *(800) 688-4752*

Walker's Cay Hotel & Marina
☎ *(809) 352-5252, (800) 432-2092*

Water-skiing and Windsurfing

Treasure Cay Resort & Marina
Treasure Cay, Great Abaco
☎ *(809) 367-2142*

Abaco Towns by the Sea
☎ *(800) 332-7757*

Great Abaco Beach Hotel
☎ *(800) 468-4799, (809) 367-2158*

Green Turtle Club
☎ *(800) 688-4752*

Walker's Cay Hotel & Marina
☎ *(809) 352-5252, (800) 432-2092*

Directory

Transportation

Airports in the Abacos are at Walker's Cay, Treasure Cay and Marsh Harbour. Spanish Cay has its own airstrip and has been recently been designated a point of entry, so guests at the resort can fly directly to the island from the U.S. By air, **USAir** (☎ *[800] 622-1015*) flies directly into Marsh Harbour and Treasure Cay from Miami and Fort Lauderdale, as does **Island Express** (☎ *[305] 359-0380*) and **Gulfstream Airlines** (☎ *[800] 992-8532, [305] 871-1200*). **American Eagle** (☎ *[800] 433-7300*) flies daily to the Abacos from Miami. **Walker's International** (☎ *[305] 359-1400, [800] 925-5377*) services Walker's Cay from Fort Lauderdale. **Bahamasair** (☎ *[800] 222-4262*) flies twice daily from Nassau to Marsh Harbour and Treasure Cay.

A great way to reach the Abacos is by mailboat—if you've got the time. The M/V Deborah K II sails from Potter's Cay in Nassau on Wednesdays to Cooper's Town, Hope Town, Marsh Harbour, Green Turtle Cay and Turtle Cay. It gets back into Nassau on Mondays. The fare is $25 round trip for a bunk bed. The trip to Marsh Harbour takes about 12 hours, depending on the weather. The M/V Champion II leaves Nassau on Tuesdays and goes to Sandy Point, Moore's Island and Bullock's Harbor. It returns to Nassau on Fridays. The fare is $30 round trip. Take into account that there often delays, in both departing and out at sea. For the latest info on the mailboat schedules and rates, call the dockmaster's Office at Potter's Cay; ☎ *(809) 393-1064.*

By cruise ship, Premier Cruise Line sails the Majestic to the Abacos from Port Canaveral in Florida on four-day cruises, with stops at Great Guana Cay, Green Turtle Cay, Treasure Cay and Man-O-War Cay. Contact:

Premier Cruise Line

> *P.O. Box 573*
> *Cape Canaveral, FL 32920*
> ☎ *(800) 327-7113, (407) 783-5061*

Ferries from Marsh Harbour take passengers to Elbow Cay, Man-O-War Cay and Great Guana Cay. Those headed for Green Turtle Cay catch the ferry near the Treasure Cay airport. If you plan to explore the Abacos, note that Green Turtle Cay is about a 45-minute powerboat ride from Elbow Cay or an hour from Marsh Harbour, and Treasure Cay is about a 45-minute bumpy drive from Marsh Harbour or a refreshing 60-minute sail away. If you want to rent a boat, check out the following:

Rich's Rentals

> ☎ *(809) 367-2742*

Sea Horse Boat Rentals

> ☎ *(809) 367-2513*
> See "Boat Charters."

Your hotel will have all the latest information regarding rentals and where to get them.

 To get from the Marsh Harbour airport to **Albury's Ferry Station** (☎ *367-3147 or 365-6010*) you'll need to take a taxi (about $12 for two people). Ferries sometimes also depart from Union Jack Dock, which is closer to the airport, so be sure you're clear on which dock to go to. Water taxis depart two or three times a day for Elbow Cay, about 25 minutes away. Passengers are charged $8 one way or $12 for same day round trip (see below). For about the same price, water taxis leave Marsh Harbour for Man-O-War Cay twice a day (about a 15-minute ride). If you arrive after the last ferry (around 4 p.m.), hope that you run into others going your way because you'll have to charter a ferry ($40 and up, per boat). A one-way ride between Marsh Harbour and Great Guana Cay (25 minutes) will cost about $10 per person ($12 for same day round trip). **Guana Beach Resort & Marina** picks up guests twice a day from Mangoes Restaurant in Marsh Harbour. A charter will be about $70–$80 for one to five passengers, plus $12 for each additional passenger. You can also charter boats to Little Harbour, Treasure Cay and Green Turtle Cay, among other islands. Note the "Tips cheerfully accepted" signs in the ferries.

The taxi from the Treasure Cay airport to the dock for ferries to Green Turtle Cay will cost about $8 per couple. Plan to pay about $9 per person for the brief ferry ride. Again, if you arrive after the last ferry your taxi driver will have to radio for a charter, which will run you considerably more.

Taxis are readily available at the airports for transfer to the hotels or the docks. Fares are usually about $1.50 per mile. My choice for friendliness and island lore is:

Drexel "Jackie" & Manuletha Bootle (Taxi Service #74)

> P.O. Box 2141
> Treasure Cay, Abaco
> ☎ (809) 365-8397; FAX (809) 365-8197
> VHF Channel 0.6

Car rentals are available but the prices are steep, usually about $70 a day. They can be arranged at the hotels or you contact:

Agatha Archer Car Rental

> Marsh Harbour, Great Abaco
> ☎ (809) 367-2148

H&L Car Rentals

> Don MacKay Blvd.
> Marsh Harbour, Great Abaco
> ☎ (809) 367-2840

Albury's Ferry Service Schedule

☎ (809) 367-3147, (809) 365-6010, FAX (809) 365-6487, VHF Channel 16

Marsh Harbour to Man-O-War Cay	10:30 a.m. daily 4 p.m. daily
Man-O-War Cay to Marsh Harbour	8 a.m. daily 1:30 p.m. daily
Marsh Harbour to Hope Town, Elbow Cay	10:30 a.m. daily 4 p.m. daily
Hope Town, Elbow Cay to Marsh Town	8 a.m. daily 1:30 p.m, daily 4 p.m. daily

FARES COLLECTED ON BOARD:

Regular ferry fare	$8 one way
Children's fare	$4 one way
Round trip same day	$12
Round trip same day (children)	$6

CHARTERS: One way Marsh Harbour to Hope Town/Man-O-War Cay

1-4 passengers	$50
5 or more (each passenger)	$10

CHARTERS: One way Marsh Harbour to Guana Cay

1–6 passengers	$80
7 or more (each passenger)	$12

Emergencies

Police/Fire

☎ 919, (809) 367-2560 (Marsh Harbour)

Great Abaco Clinic

Steede Bonnet Road
Marsh Harbour, Great Abaco
☎ (809) 367-2510

Green Turtle Cay Clinic

New Plymouth
Green Turtle Cay
☎ (809) 365-4028

Post Offices

Marsh Harbour Post Office

Don MacKay Boulevard
Marsh Harbour, Great Abaco
☎ (809) 367-2571

Green Turtle Cay Post Office

New Plymouth
Green Turtle Cay
☎ (809) 365-4242

This has the only public telephone on the island. Open Mon.–Fri. 9–noon, 1–5 p.m.

Banks and Moneychangers

Barclays Bank

Don MacKay Blvd.
Marsh Harbor, Great Abaco
☎ (809) 367-2152

Open 9:30 a.m.–3 p.m. Mon.–Thurs. and 9:30 a.m.–5 p.m. on Friday.

Barclays Bank

New Plymouth
Green Turtle Cay
☎ (809) 365-4144

Open 10 a.m.–1 p.m. on Tuesday and Thursday only. Limited services.

Tour Operators

Papa-Tango Tours

Marsh Harbour, Great Abaco
☎ (809) 367-3378

Daylong guided tours of the cays near Marsh Harbour that leave from the Boat Harbour Marina. The activities include snorkeling, shopping, sight-seeing and fishing. There's also a five-day island-hopping tour, and the company offers beach picnics. You can also charter a wave runner. Ask for Captain Perry Thomas.

Boat Charters

Abaco Bahamas Charters

Hope Town, Elbow Cay
☎ (800) 626-5690

Island Marine

Parrot Cay, Hope Town
Elbow Cay
☎ (809) 366-0282

Charter boats and Bahamian guides are available here for all kinds of reef, flat and deep-sea fishing. As well, you can take your own rental, for instance a 17-foot Boston Whaler for $80 a day, to a number of pristine beaches and uninhabited cays.

The Moorings

Conch Inn Resort & Marina
Marsh Harbour, Great Abaco
☎ *(809) 367-4000*

The Sawyer Family

c/o The Green Turtle Club
Green Turtle Cay
☎ *(809) 365-4271, or (809) 365-4173 direct*
Deep-sea fishing trips at negotiable fees.

Treasure Cay Marina

Treasure Cay Resort & Marina
Treasure Cay
☎ *(809) 367-2570*
Deep-sea, flats and reef fishing. Sportfishing boats run $395 for a full day and $285 for a half day. A bonefishing cruise costs $190 a day and $130 for a half day. Boats come with experienced fishing guides/captains.

Sunsail

115 East Broward Boulevard
Fort Lauderdale, FL 33001
☎ *(800) 327-2276, (305) 524-7553*
Also in Marsh Harbour
Sunsail is the largest charter operator in the Bahamas and a thoroughly professional operation, The best value is to "bareboat," or charter a boat without crew. You can pretty much go where you choose, but you are instructed to stay away from shoal waters and are required to stay within the line of the outer cays. Prices range from $1000–$5000 per week. You'll have to have some knowledge of and experience in sailing. Complete instruction and equipment familiarization is provided.

Sea Horse Boat Rentals

Hope Town, Elbow Cay, Abaco
Great Abaco Beach Resort
Marsh Harbour
☎ *(809) 367-2513*
FAX (809) 366-0189
VHF Channel 16
This is a better bet for short-term rentals and is not outrageously priced. Twenty-two-foot Boston Whalers go for $120 a day; 18-footers go for $90 a day. A 24-foot Privateer runs $135 a day; a 22-foot Privateer runs $105 a day, a 20-foot Albury Brothers runs $100 a day, and an 18-foot Privateer costs $80 a day. There are even bicycles here for rent at $8 a day.

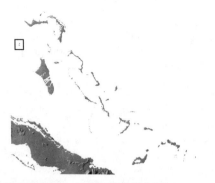

THE BIMINIS

Alice Town, Bimini

Bimini seems possessed with perpetuating the myth that it's the Wild West of the High Seas. Since 1935 when Ernest Hemingway put the island on the map, it has catered to cigar-chomping, beer-bellied macho guys with rod and reel for a six-shooter and a 50-foot Chris Craft for a horse, who would get busted in Miami for most of what they do quite freely in Bimini. In fact, these visitors to the 26-mile-long chain, less then 50 miles east of Miami, try particularly hard to be mistaken for Papa by other guys trying to be mistaken for Papa, but in ways that would get them committed to a rest home back in Pompano Beach.

In the morning, on the docks and away from dusty King's Highway, hung over but with a contrived sense of self-importance, these semi-retired construction company owners and airline executives make certain that all on the docks can see them slowly, exaggeratedly readying tackle and gear for the big fight with an 800-lb. mako or marlin. Leaving Bimini Harbour as the sun starts to climb high is almost anticlimactic, because when they've departed, there will be no one left to observe how cool they are.

For the less-jaded, Bimini is simply a party interrupted by some fishing. The islands (North Bimini and South Bimini) are not exactly magnets for animal-rights activists, nor those looking for a tropical island getaway vacation. There is little solitude here, and even less land. What few acres exist on North Bimini—the focal point of the islands—are bisected by a dusty "highway" flanked by bars and more bars. The drug money that has found its way here— and that's a substantial amount—has been splurged hilariously on German sports cars, which, of course, don't have enough pavement to get out of first gear. Bimini makes for the classic standing quarter-mile.

Of course, Ernest Hemingway spent some time here and worked on a couple of novels in Bimini: *Islands in the Stream* and *To Have And Have Not.* Ernie first heard about Bimini in the early 30s while living in Key West, Florida. Although the writer was primarily responsible for the broad reputation that Bimini has as a rugged individualist's seedy maritime nirvana, sport fishermen had been coming to Bimini well before Hemingway docked the *Pilar* on Bimini in 1935. Hemingway had heard of Bimini in 1933 or 1934 and bought a boat to get there, as there wasn't any air transportation out to the island at that time.

Aboard the *Pilar* cruising toward Bimini in April 1935, Hemingway caught a large shark and reeled it in alongside his 38-foot cabin cruiser. The fish was still alive and with some fight left, so Papa shot it in the head. Then he slipped when a gaff broke and ended up shooting himself in both legs. So began the new lore of Bimini.

While on the island, Papa bagged a 785-pound mako shark and, later, a 514-pound tuna. But it was with the mako that Hemingway established himself on the island as one tough dude. He offered $250 to anyone who could go three 3-minute rounds in the boxing ring with him. He was most enthusiastic with his offers to blacks living on the island, as if they represented some form of African jungle beast prowess. If there were no offers, Papa wasn't reticent about simply finding someone to beat up, as he demonstrated with publisher Joseph Knapp.

Hemingway's aura permeates the Bimini lifestyle today. His favorite watering hole, the **Compleat Angler**, has rooms full of Hemingway memorabilia, and it's hard not feel somehow connected to the whole Bimini/Hemingway thing when sipping on a gin and tonic in the club's bar.

The Bimini islands stretch only about 28 miles. The islands' principal town is slightly seedy but raucous Alice Town on North Bimini with a population of about 1600. Although there's an airport on South Bimini there is very little development on the island, mainly a few private homes. Most who fly into Bimini do so by Chalk's, whose seaplanes splash down in

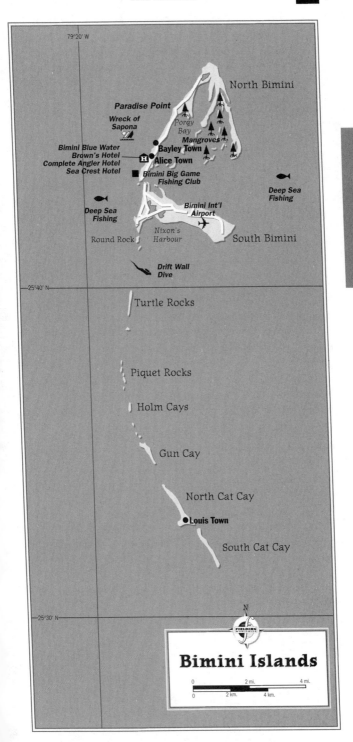

Porgy Bay at Alice Town. The island's capital wears different faces at different times of the day, transforming itself from a whitewashed, hospital-like ghost town during the day—when the only commotion is the arrival of the Chalk's seaplane—into a Barbary Coast by night. The Compleat Angler fills with thirsty fishermen (and with college students during spring break) and the party begins, quickly spreading to the **Bimini Blue Water Resort**, the **End of the World Bar** and the other watering holes lining King's Highway like stalls in an exhibition hall. The calypso music begins blaring, and Bimini becomes the Cabo San Lucas for East Coasters.

Regardless, fishing rules the Biminis. The reason is its location. Off the coast of Florida, Bimini lies where the Gulf Stream meets the Bahama Banks. The deep-sea fishing is considered by most as the best in the world, with giant game fish such as marlin, tuna, swordfish, dolphin, tarpon and grouper visiting the islands' waters at various times throughout the year. With such an abundance of large fish, and so many varieties of them, great sportfishing can be found year-round off Bimini. Perhaps the two biggest sportfishing tournaments in the world—the Hemingway Billfish Tournament and the Bacardi Rum Billfish Tournament—are held every year at Bimini. While north Andros may provide better flats for bonefishing, Bimini's not far behind.

But, quite frankly, more and more visitors are coming to Bimini every year with little or no interest in fishing or scuba diving—or any other sports for that matter.

They're just coming to party.

What to See and Do on Bimini

Hemingway Memorabilia ★
Compleat Angler Hotel, Alice Town
The Compleat Angler Hotel has a roomful of mementos associated with Ernest Hemingway, including manuscripts, photographs and paintings. There are all kinds of photos of Ernie in various poses, mostly with uncomfortable-looking, large fish hanging upside down. Excerpts from his writings (Papa wrote his books standing up, with pen and ink) adorn the walls, as well a photo of the man believed to have been the inspiration for the hero in *The Old Man and the Sea*. There's also a great shot of 1988 presidential contender Gary Hart partying with Donna Rice in the hotel's bar. The rest is history.

Bimini Blue Water Resort
King's Highway, north of the Compleat Angler
This was the former home of shark and dolphin researcher Michael Lerner and is considered to be the setting for Ernie Hemingway's *Islands in the Stream*. Papa wrote most of the book in the Marlin Cottage.

Angler's Hall of Fame ★
Diandrea's Inn, Alice Town
Anglers from around the world, from Joe Smith next door to Hollywood celebrities, pose for photos of themselves and their trophy

THE BIMINIS

catches. If you're a big fish nut, you'll spend a little time here. But we can't help but wonder if there's a subaquatic Fish's Hall of Fame somewhere in the depths of the Gulf Stream, with photos of famous and not-so-famous fish posing with the trophy humans they've munched on.

The Sapona   ★
Between South Bimini and Cat Cay
Automobile tycoon Henry Ford built a large concrete ship, the *Sapona*, during the First World War. For a while during prohibition, it was anchored off South Bimini and used as a private watering hole and brothel for dignitaries and rumrunners. A hurricane in 1929 uprooted the mooring and the ship drifted toward shore, where she rests upright today in 15 feet of water.

Atlantis
Offshore North Bimini
Is it the lost city? Or just a stupid giant turtle pen? Some scientists believe this peculiar 300-foot-long rock formation is 10,000 years old and the remnants of a lost civilization. Others think it's a turtle pen perhaps a century old. Don a tank or your snorkeling gear and you be the judge.

Healing Hole
North Bimini
This is a water hole clearing in the mangrove flats of North Bimini with reputed healing powers for myriad afflictions. It may or may not be true. It didn't cure our scabies on one visit, but tell us your tale.

Where to Stay on Bimini

Bimini Big Game Fishing Club $150–$160   ★ ★
P.O. Box 699, Alice Town, Bimini
☎ *(800) 327-4149 U.S., (809) 347-3391; FAX (809) 347-3392*
Single: $150–$160; Double: $150–$160
The Bacardi Corporation rum-makers own this place, so you know what the house brand is! Bimini's best-loved resort—opened in 1946—provides a full-service, 100-slip marina for its mostly yachtie-and-fisher clientele, plus there's a freshwater swimming pool, tennis court, and nearby beach. The hotel's harbor-side restaurant is the island's best dining spot, and—along with the bars—the area's favorite hangout. Accommodations are roomy and comfortable, with TVs, telephones, and patios or porches. Cottages are available for anyone desiring more room. Amenities: swimming pool, tennis court, marina, two restaurants, three bars.

Credit cards: AE, MC, V

Bimini Blue Water Resort $90   ★ ★
P.O. Box 601, King's Highway, Alice Town, Bimini
☎ *(809) 347-3166; FAX (809) 347-3293*
Single: $90; Double: $90
Hemingway aficionados flock here to be near their hero's 1930s retreat (as well as the main setting for *Islands in the Stream*), and to take part in the annual Hemingway Billfish Tournament. Along with the 32-slip, full-service marina, guests can make use of a lovely beach, and dine and drink in the ocean-view restaurant and bar. Accommodations are in wood-paneled rooms, with white furnishings, TVs and

private balconies. Big-spenders or really-big-on-Hemingway guests can stay in the author's (much-changed) three-bedroom Marlin Cottage. Amenities: marina, swimming pool, restaurant, bar. Credit cards: AE, MC, V.

Sea Crest Hotel and Marina $80   ★

P.O. Box 654, Alice town, Bimini
☎ *(809) 347-3071; FAX (809) 347-3071*
Single: $80; Double: $80
Situated right on King's Highway, this three-story hotel offers a full-service marina, fishing and diving excursions, and a nearby beach. Families tend to seek out this property for its good value and free-for-kids policy. Each of the simply-furnished 11 rooms feature rattan furnishings, TVs, and balconies. Amenities: marina. Credit cards: MC, V.

Compleat Angler Hotel $65–$80   ★★

P.O. Box 601, King's Highway, Alice Town, Bimini
☎ *(809) 347-3122; FAX (809) 347-3293*
Single: $65; Double: $75–$80
This vintage-1930s, somewhat-worn hotel is another site on the Hemingway-was-here list—though he may not have remembered, as this is where he did some memorable *après*-marlin-hunt drinking. The hotel's wood siding is made from Prohibition-era rum barrels. Wood-paneled guest rooms offer simple furnishings and some open onto an exterior verandah. The bar—as might be expected—is the hottest spot on the island, with live weekend entertainment. If you can't get into the swing of things and you're a light sleeper, you should probably stay elsewhere. Amenities: bar, lounge. Credit cards: AE, MC, V.

Where to Eat on Bimini

You'll no doubt be feasting on your own (or possibly someone else's) catch of the day at one of the Bimini's famous fishing lodges. The **Gulf-stream Restaurant** at **Bimini Big Game Fishing Club and Hotel** is one of the top dining choices, while the **Big Fame Club Sports Bar** at the same hotel offers a casual grill menu, burgers, pizzas and such—along with satellite television. **The Anchorage**, at Bimini Blue Water Resort, offers ocean-view lunches and dinners, while **Alice Town's Red Lion Pub** is a good spot for friendly food and camaraderie.

Red Lion Pub

King's Highway, Alice Town, Bimini
☎ *(809) 347-3259*
Bahamian cuisine
Lunch: Mon. 11:30 a.m.–2:30 p.m., $8–$15
Dinner: Tues.–Sun. 6–10 p.m., $14–$18
This simple restaurant, near the center of town, offers a congenial respite from the Bimini fishing lodges. The dining room (add-on to the original pub) has a view of the marina and dishes up tasty local cuisine as well as the catch of the day. For dessert, try the key lime pie. Credit cards: No credit cards.

Nightlife on Bimini

Considering there's nothing to do here during the day (there's plenty to do off shore), Bimini's night scene isn't bad. Not a lot of clubs and numbing heavy metal, but enough bars to play adventurer for a while and show off your tackle jacket. The bars seem to go out of the way to create the impression that Bimini is some thrill-seeker's hell-hole at the end of the Earth (it's also the name of one of the bars), but you're only 50 miles from Miami—and so is Palm Beach—making Bimini the Tijuana of the East Coast.

Bimini Big Game Fishing Club & Hotel

King's Highway
Box 699
Alice Town
☎ *(809) 347-3391, (800) 327-4149; FAX (809) 347-3392*

The large Big Game sports bar here has four TVs and overlooks the marina, a great setting for brewskis and U.S. sports telecasts. Also serves sandwiches and snacks. There are actually three bars at the resort. The poolside Barefoot Bar is only open during the afternoon but a good place for an umbrella drink. The Gulfstream Bar, next to the Gulfstream Restaurant, features live calypso music

The Compleat Angler Hotel

King's Highway
Alice Town
☎ *(809) 347-3122*

The calypso band, planter's punches and Hemingway memorabilia have enough chemistry—and alcohol—to make this one of the island's busiest spots after dark. Mostly guys sitting around talking about fish—big ones. But this place can get crackin', especially during spring break when it's swamped with college students. Live music on the weekends. This is the Señor Frog's of Bimini. Open from 11 a.m. until late.

End of the World Bar

King's Highway
Alice Town

Former U.S. Congressman Adam Clayton Powell made this place a household name back in the late 1960s when he used to hang here while he was being investigated by Congress. The media-types loved the ambience and the beer, so they lined up for both interviews and the grog. The floor is sawdust and the walls are covered with business cards and graffiti, and other odds and "ends." You'll see what we mean.

Sports on Bimini

Scuba Diving/Snorkeling

Wrecks and superb visibility are two of Bimini's hallmarks. The Bimini Barge rests in about 90 feet of water. At 150 feet long, it makes for a large domicile to moray eels, giant groupers and horse-eye jacks. Two 18th-century anchors can be found close to the capsized Bimini Trader. The Sapona can be found at only 15 feet deep. In its holds can be found gray angelfish, grunts and squirrelfish. A massive cliff extends some 2000 feet down off Bimini. This outrageous drop-off marks the continental shelf.

Bimini Undersea Adventures

King's Highway, Alicetown
☎ *(809) 347-3089*
P.O. Box 693515
Miami, FL 33269

☎ *(800) 348-4644, (305) 653- 5572; FAX (305) 652-9148*

The dive trip rates here are the only bargains on the island. One-tank dives cost $30, two-tank dives are $59 and three-tank dives run $79. Night dives cost about $40 and full-day snorkeling trips run about $25. Rentals and instructions available.

Sportfishing

Bimini may well be the sportfishing capital of the world, and anybody who's anybody with a rod and reel has gotten his or her palms bloodied battling marlin, swordfish, sailfish, tuna, grouper and wahoo. Most of the world records were caught off Bimini's shores. And if that's not enough, the seas are also teeming with giant bonefish (15 lbs.!), tarpon, snapper, dolphin, amberjack, bonefish, white and blue marlin, bluefish, bonito, shark, mackerel and barracuda. Bimini has both the deep seas of the Gulf Stream and the Bahama Banks and some of the best bonefish flats in the islands.

If you're serious, you should bring to Bimini your own gear, at least the important stuff, as the bait & tackle shops on the island don't pay the rent selling equipment; they do it selling bait. However, don't fret; some of the charters provide tackle.

Among the tournaments held here each year are:

February

The Hemingway Billfish Championship

March

The Annual Bacardi Rum Billfish Tournament

The Bimini Billfish Championship

May

Memorial Day Weekend Tournament

June

The Big Five Tournament

July

All Billfish Classic

Jimmy Albury Memorial Blue Marlin Tournament

August

Bimini Native Open Tournament

Bacardi Family Open Tournament

September

Bimini Open Angling Tournament (Small BOAT)

November

The Wahoo Tournament

Bimini Big Game Fishing Club & Hotel

King's Highway
Box 699
Alice Town

☎ *(809) 347-2391*

There's a monster 41-foot Hatteras here that charters the full day for about $800 and a half day for around $450. Bertrams at 31 and 28 feet go for about $600 for a full day and $400 for a half day. A 100-slip marina is here, the base for the biggest fishing tournaments of the spring and summer.

Bimini Blue Water Marina

King's Highway
Box 601
Alice Town
☎ *(809) 347-3166*

This 32-slip marina is the accustomed host to the annual Hemingway Billfish tournament. The charters here include gear if you don't feel like lugging along your own. The 28-foot Bertram goes for about $500 a day, plus crew and gear, and about $350 for a half-day

Brown's Marina

King's Highway
Box 601
Alice Town, North Bimini
☎ *(809) 347-3227*

Deep-sea fishing for $350 a day and $225 for a half day; 22-slip marina with all the amenities.

Weech's Bimini Dock

Box 613
Alice Town
☎ *(809) 347-3028*

This 15-slip marina offers Boston Whalers at $90 per day and $50 for a half day.

Tennis

Bimini Big Game Fishing Club & Hotel

King's Highway
Box 699
Alice Town
☎ *(809) 347-2391*

This is the only tennis court on the island—yeah, just one court. No one comes to Bimini to play tennis. It's only available for guests at the hotel and is lighted.

Directory

Transportation

If you're going to fly to North Bimini, then you'll have to land in the water, because North Bimini doesn't have a control tower and North Bimini doesn't have an airport. There's a small airstrip on South Bimini, but it's utilized only for private planes and charter aircraft. **Chalk's International Airline** (☎ *[800] 424-2557*) flies amphibious planes from Miami's Watson Island Terminal to the waters off North Bimini's Alice Town several times daily for about $160 round-trip. The plane takes off from and lands in calm waters, and the flight takes 20–30 minutes. There are also flights from Chalk's base at Paradise Island. The one drag is the 30-lb. luggage restriction, and that includes carry-on, which has to be checked onto the plane and can't be brought into the passenger cabin. There is a substantial overweight levy, so if you're packing your tackle box, be warned. Once off the plane in Alice Town, minibus service is available through the **Bimini Bus Company** for rides into town for $3. If you've landed in South Bimini, there is a taxi-and-ferry service into Alice Town for $5.

By boat, you can get to Bimini from Nassau aboard the *MV Bimini Mack*, a chugger mail boat that leaves from Nassau's Potter Cay Dock with a stop at Cat Island before arriving in Alice Town 12 hours later. The "schedule" changes frequently. Inquire with the dockmaster at **Potter's Cay Dock** (☎ *[809] 393-1064*).

There are no rental cars available on Bimini and everything is pretty much within walking distance along narrow King's Highway. But if you want to rent a moped, one can be had at **Bimini Scooter** (☎ *[809] 347-2555*) across the street from the Bimini Big Game Fishing Club in Watson's Supermarket. The price is an outrageous $50 a day or $10 an hour (plus deposit), whichever drains your wallet the fastest. Also no bargains are the golf carts for rent at **Capt. Pat's** (☎ *[809] 347-3477*) at the Sea Crest Hotel Marina for $100 a day or $20 an hour. Nor the bicycles from **Undersea Adventures** (☎ *[809] 347-3089*) for $17 a day and $5 an hour. When on Bimini, expect to be had by the short hairs.

Emergencies

You're SOL if you get really sick in Bimini. You'll need to be airlifted out to Miami or Nassau. And the occasional chopper you see setting down on the baseball field is doing exactly that for someone. But a doctor and a dentist are available on the island.

North Bimini Medical Clinic

☎ *(809) 347-3210*

Staffed with a doctor and a nurse.

Police/Fire

☎ *919*

Banks and Moneychangers

Royal Bank of Canada

Alice Town

☎ *(809) 347-3031*

Open Monday and Friday 9 a.m.–3 p.m. and Tues.-Thurs. 9 a.m.– 1 p.m.

Immigration

Bahamas Customs & Immigration

Alice Town

☎ *(809) 368-2030*

Post Office

Chalk's International Airline

Alice Town

Hardly a post office, but a much better bet at getting your mail out than a Bahamian post office. The Chalk's office in Alice Town has a basket for outgoing letters, which then are flown to the States and mailed from there. You can even use U.S. postage stamps.

Religious Services
Baptist

Mount Zion Baptist Church
> P.O. Box 645
> Alice Town, North Bimini
> ☎ (809) 347-2056

Anglican

Anglican Church Rectory
> P.O. Box 666
> Alice Town, North Bimini
> ☎ (809) 347-2268

A Warning to Drug Smugglers

Not that we actually want to warn drug smugglers, but there are more undercover cops than conch shells on Bimini these days. Bimini has become, as it was for rumrunners and blockade runners in days past, a major transit point for shipments of illegal narcotics, particularly cocaine from Colombia and heroin from Afghanistan. If you spend any length of time on the island, you will undoubtedly be approached by some dude in shades and a beard seeking to break down your willpower. Kill fish, crack coral, cut up conches, but stay away from the dope.

Telephone Services

There are public phones located along King's Highway. As well, all the hotels and restaurants have phones. Faxes can be found in the better hotels, and some of the worst ones, too.

THE BIMINIS

THE BERRY ISLANDS

The Berry Islands offer miles of white sand.

The Berry Islands, to the east of Bimini and about 150 miles east of Miami and 35 miles northwest of Nassau, have neither the intrigue nor the crowds of Bimini. Beside yachtsmen stopping for a breather in their journeys between south Florida and Nassau, a far different sort journeys to these forgotten, remote jewels. These aren't the cigar-chomping, money-in-your-face types that frequent the Biminis, but a less ostentatious group seeking the solace of miles of deserted white sand. In fact, many of the cays that comprise the rolling hills of the Berry Islands are privately owned. For the most part, residents are fiercely private folks who don't take too kindly to trespassers.

There are only about 600-700 people who call the Berry Islands home all year. The principal settlement is Bullock's Harbour on Great Harbour Cay, which is rather small at about eight miles long and two miles wide, but rambling compared with the other islands. Great Harbour Cay's settlers, broke and homeless ex-slaves, came here in the 1830s but soon discovered that the cay's soil was barely suitable for supporting crops. The Berries' chief resort is also found on Great Harbour Cay, the Great Harbour Cay Yacht Club & Marina. The other resort is the Chub Cay Inn on Chub Cay. Both are townhouse or villa resorts with full-service marinas. The jet-setting, luxurious Great Harbour Cay resort found a lot of publicity when it was learned that Douglas Fairbanks Jr. was one of the investors. The settlement has been frequented by scores of starlets and actors.

Chub Cay, to the south of Great Harbour Cay, is considered one of the great deep-sea fishing and bonefishing venues in the Bahamas (many call its waters the best spot in the world). It is situated near the Tongue of the Ocean and, as such, offers anglers both a deep-sea utopia and huge expanses of bonefish flats. The Chub Cay Club began life as an R&R outpost for a clique of Texas fishermen. Then dormitories were built and an all-out resort was fashioned, complete with a massive, 90-slip marina. Hurricane Andrew devastated the resort in 1992, but it has since been built back up to its former grace.

Fishermen and yachtsmen cruising the waters between Nassau and south Florida use the marina to stock up on liquor, marine gear and other supplies. For divers, there are a number of nearby sites, including Mama Rhoda Rock and Chub Wall.

Cruise liners have started calling on the Berry Islands, at least those islands that are uninhabited. However, Great Stirrup Cay has become a popular mini-stopover between Florida and Nassau, and cruise ship visitors can now expect all the trappings tropical island cruise ship diversions, namely locals dressing up like Tahitians and performing limbo dances—which are about as Bahamian as ice sculptures.

If you can get onto some of the private cays, it's worth it for their isolation. Try Alder Cay and Frozen Cay for bird-watching, especially for seeing flocks of terns. And there's an aviary for tropical birds on Little Whale Cay.

Where to Stay in the Berry Islands

Chub Cay

Chub Cay Club   **$150**   ★★★

Chub Cay, Berry Islands
☎ *(800) 662-8555 U.S., (809) 325-1490; FAX (809) 322-5199*
Single: $150; Double: $150

If you want to stay in Chub Cay, this clubby-type place is your only choice. Yachties appreciate the large 90-slip marina, while escape artists favor the isolation and simple, casual ambience. Fishing is the big game here, followed by diving, snorkeling, tennis and swimming—as well as plenty of doing-nothing. Each of the eight rooms provides refrigerators, cable TVs, minibars and ocean or pool views, while nine larger villas with kitchens are on the beach front. The Harbour House restaurant serves fresh seafood, continental and Bahamian dishes, and three bars (one with big-screen TV) will quench your thirst. Amenities: swimming pool, two tennis courts, dock, bicycle rentals, restaurant, three bars. Credit cards: AE, MC, V.

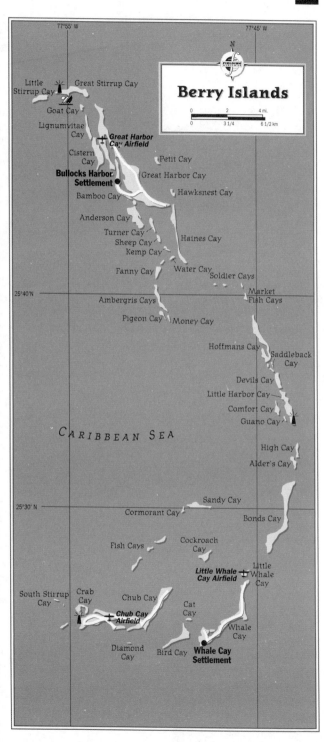

THE BERRY ISLANDS

Great Harbour Cay

**Great Harbour Cay
Yacht Club and Marina**   **$95–$285**   ★★★

> *Great Harbour Cay, Berry Islands*
> *P.O. Box N-918, Nassau*
> ☎ *(800) 343-7256 U.S., (809) 367-8838; FAX (809) 367-8115*
> *Single: $95–$285; Double: $95–$285*
> Aside from the marina, guest facilities include a variety of fishing
> excursions and entry to the yacht club's private club with its private
> restaurant (Wednesdays through Mondays). Two other marina-edge
> restaurants serve meals throughout the day—and throughout the
> week. Accommodations are in large, breezy, two-level townhouses,
> each with two bedrooms, two-plus baths, a fully equipped kitchen,
> TVs, laundry facilities, marina view, and private dock. Privately owned
> villas—studios through four-bedrooms—are also available. Daily
> maid service is tossed in to the rentals. Amenities: swimming pool,
> three restaurants, bar, dock, bicycle rentals. Credit cards: AE, MC, V.

Where to Eat in the Berry Islands

At Chub Cay, you'll be dining on Continental and Caribbean meals at
the **Chub Cay Club's Harbour House Restaurant**. Over at Great Harbour
Cay, opt from the casual pool bar for lunch, the **Wharf Restaurant and Bar**
for breakfast and dinner, or the dinner-only **Tamboo Dinner Club**.

Nightlife in the Berry Islands

There is no nightlife in the Berry Islands other than at the two resorts.

Hilltop Bar

> *Chub Cay Club*
> *Chub Cay*
> *Berry Islands*
> ☎ *(809) 325-1490, (800) 662-8555; FAX (809) 322-5199*
> Not much happening here most nights of the week, but there is a
> pool table and a large-screen TV. There is also a bar in the staff hous-
> ing area that sees more action than the Hilltop Bar. If you want to
> meet the locals, and even dance, check it out.

Great Harbour Cay Yacht Club & Marina

> *Great Harbour Cay*
> *Berry Islands*
> ☎ *(809) 367-8838*
> The club's Tamboo Club, on the west side of the marina, offers the
> only evening diversion; but even then it's mainly for dinner. For those
> insisting on a nightcap with a little conversation and music, in town
> there a number of unassuming watering holes: the **Backside Lounge**,
> the **Graveyard Bar & Grill**, **The Chicken Shack**, **Beulah's Bridge Inn**
> and the **Wayside Inn**.

Sports in the Berry Islands

Sportfishing and Boating

Only Bimini rivals the Berry Islands for an abundance of monster game
fish, found at TOTO (Top of the Tongue of the Ocean). If world records
aren't set around Bimini, they're set here. Light-tackle bottom fishing is superb around here, particularly for grouper, yellowtail, barracuda and snapper. And the bonefishing rivals the flats found off Andros, a mere 25 miles
or so to the south. But it's the deep-sea fishing that's the real "lure" of the

Berry Islands. Spectacular marlin, swordfish, wahoo and dolphin can be yanked out of the waters near the Tongue of the Ocean.

Great Harbour Cay Yacht Club & Marina

Great Harbour Cay
Berry Islands
☎ *(809) 367-8838*
Mailing addresses: Box N 918
Nassau
or 3512 N. Ocean Drive
Hollywood, FL 33019
☎ *(800) 343-7256, (305) 921-9084; FAX (305) 921-1044*
Charters and guides for deep-sea fishing, bonefishing and bottom fishing. Eighty-slip full-service marina.

Chub Cay Club

Chub Cay
Berry Islands
☎ *(809) 325-1490, (800) 662-8555; FAX (809) 322-5199*
or P.O. Box 661067
Miami Springs, FL 33266
☎ *(305) 445-7830*
Ninety-slip full-service marina. Dozens of charter craft (in all sizes) and guides available for deep-sea fishing, bonefishing and bottom fishing.

A variety of diving sites are found around The Berry Islands.

Scuba Diving/Snorkeling

Undersea Adventures

Chub Cay Club
Chub Cay
Berry Islands
☎ *(809) 325-1490, (800) 662-8555; FAX (809) 322-5199*
or P.O. Box 661067
Miami Springs, FL 33266
☎ *(305) 445-7830*

Dive trips to Chub Wall and Mamma Rhoda Rock. Instructions, rentals and snorkeling equipment and trips.

Great Harbour Cay Yacht Club & Marina

Great Harbour Cay
Berry Islands
☎ *(809) 367-8838*
Mailing addresses: Box N 918
Nassau
or 3512 N. Ocean Drive
Hollywood, FL 33019
☎ *(800) 343-7256, (305) 921-9084; FAX (305) 921-1044*

Most divers head for the Chub Cay Club, but fine diving is also found off Great Harbour Cay. Dive trips, instructions, rentals and snorkeling excursions. Arranges for dive guides.

Golf

Great Harbour Cay Yacht Club & Marina

Great Harbour Cay
Berry Islands
☎ *(809) 367-8838*
Mailing addresses: Box N 918
Nassau
or 3512 N. Ocean Drive
Hollywood, FL 33019
☎ *(800) 343-7256, (305) 921-9084; FAX (305) 921-1044*

Nine-hole course designed by Joe Lee. Not particularly challenging but unique in the Bahamas because the terrain is relatively hilly. Check for greens fees.

Tennis

Great Harbour Cay Yacht Club & Marina

Great Harbour Cay
Berry Islands
☎ *(809) 367-8838*
Mailing addresses: Box N 918
Nassau
or 3512 N. Ocean Drive
Hollywood, FL 33019
☎ *(800) 343-7256, (305) 921-9084; FAX (305) 921-1044*

Two hard courts for use by guests and members.

Chub Cay Club

Chub Cay
Berry Islands
☎ *(809) 325-1490, (800) 662-8555*
FAX (809) 322-5199
or P.O. Box 661067
Miami Springs, FL 33266
☎ *(305) 445-7830*

The resort has two hard courts for use by guests and members.

Directory

Transportation

There are a couple of airstrips in the Berry Islands on Great Harbour Cay and Chub Cay. Charter flights are available from **Stanair** *(☎ [407] 586-5748)* and **Island Express** *(☎ [305] 359-0380)*. Stanair flies from Palm Beach to Great Harbour Cay, and Island Express flies about five times a week to the airstrip on Chub Cay from Fort Lauderdale. **Tropical Diversions Air** *(☎ [305] 921-9084, [800] 343-7256)* flies from Fort Lauderdale to Great Harbour Cay. The round trip fares on each carrier are usually under $200. **Trans Island Airways** *(☎ [809] 377-7172)*, at last check, had two flights daily from Nassau to Great Harbour Cay. Transportation to your hotel is provided by the resorts on both islands.

By sea, you can take the mailboat *M/V Champion II*, which departs from Nassau's Potter Cay Dock on either Tuesdays or Thursdays (check for schedule changes) for the Berry Islands. For schedules and fares, contact the dockmaster at **Potter's Cay** *(☎ [809] 393-1064)*.

You'll have to depend on your resort for getting around the islands. The **Great Harbour Cay Yacht Club & Marina** *(☎ [800] 343-7256)* will rent jeeps, boats and bicycles.

Emergencies

Great Harbour Cay Medical Clinic
Bullock's Harbour
Great Harbour Cay
☎ *(809) 367-8400*
Limited services and medicines are available. For serious emergencies you will have to be evacuated to Nassau or Miami.

Police/Fire
Bullock's Harbour
Great Harbour Cay
☎ *(809) 367-8344*

THE BERRY ISLANDS

ANDROS

Small Hope Bay Lodge

Swooping in by plane over Andros, it's hard to tell where the sea ends and the island begins. Andros, the largest of the Bahamian islands is 108 miles long and 40 miles wide at its widest point (2300 sq. miles). There's little distinction between sea and land, and if the islanders are able to get out of bed in the morning and place their feet somewhere, they've got something to be thankful for. This place is as flat as a pancake, which is good for pilots low on fuel and not so good for snowboarders and dudes with mountain bikes. Nonetheless, the approach to the airport at

Andros Town reveals a couple of corpses of Cessnas and Beech-crafts that didn't quite make it to immigration. Carcasses of aircraft a few hundred feet from the runway are a testament to the gamut of folks who have landed here, from drug runners to drunk bonefishermen.

Andros is a great place if you dive or fish, (see "Sports on Andros")—all-around, the best in the Bahamas, for both wall diving and bonefishing. You can take any little skiff (of course, if you know someone it helps) out to barrier reef off the east coast of the island and find all sorts of attractions along its 140-mile length. Twelve-foot waters suddenly plunge to depths exceeding two miles at the Tongue of the Ocean, considered by geologists as a massive underwater canyon, on the scale of Arizona's Grand Canyon. Dozens if not hundreds of drop-offs, coral gardens, blue holes, walls and wrecks await the curious diver off the shores of this, the largest island in the Bahamian chain. Blue holes are a huge attraction here; scientists describe Andros' blue holes as the deepest and longest on the planet. Conch Sound itself has at least 3000 feet of passage; and the inland blue holes of Andros are said to be the dwellings of octopi-like evil spirits called *luca*, and other interesting creatures such as the three-toed chickcharnies.

The Chickcharnie: Goblins or Owls

The Irish have their leprechauns, and Andros has the chickcharnies. For centuries there have been tales on Andros of three-toed devils with red eyes, beards and feathers that stalked on humans by days and nested at the top of palm trees by night. This is the Androsian version of goblins, trolls and bogeymen. And it's uniquely Androsian, for it was only on Andros where these creatures lived. All calamities were blamed on the chickcharnies, and parents used stories of the creatures to frighten their children into good behavior.

The chickcharnie is mired in legend. Some believe chickcharnies are aborigines and descendents of the original Arawak Indians who lived on the islands until being wiped out by the Spanish. The technology of modern times has told us this isn't true, yet still the belief in these feathered fiends persists.

The origin of the chickcharnie myth isn't clear. Some say that the Seminole Indians who settled on Andros in the 1880s to get away from the whites in Florida brought the tales with them. Others think they were simply fabricated by a Nassau duck hunter who wanted to keep away potential trespassers at his coveted duck pond. The conservatory Bahamas Trust Fund has a different explanation: the chickcharnies were actually Tyto pollens, three-foot-tall flightless owls that became extinct in the Bahamas perhaps 200-300 years ago.

As far as fishing goes, Andros is considered the "Bonefishing Capital of the World" by anglers from all over the globe. And Lowe Sound is the bonefishing capital of Andros. Hunters can

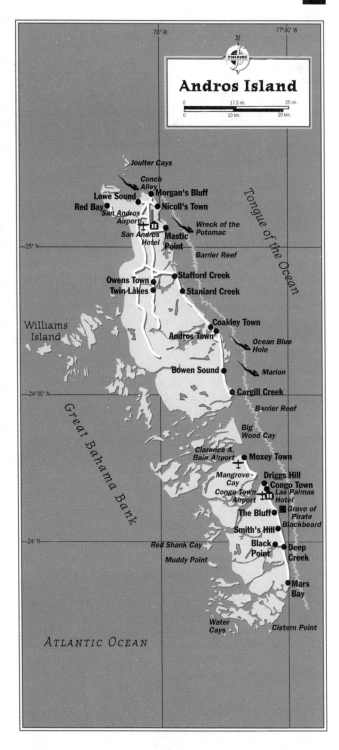

stalk white-crowned pigeons at Green Cay in the Kemp's Bay area about 20 miles east of Deep Creek. September through March is the best time of the year to come to Andros for game. The island's dense forests are filled with partridges, quail and ducks.

Andros is not only a sportsman's paradise, but the center for Bahamian batik, whose bold and richly colorful designs and patterns are sold throughout the world.

Christopher Columbus named Andros "La Isla del Espiritu Santo," or the Island of the Holy Spirit, and it was later named after the British commander Sir Edmund Andros—but other than that, there isn't much historians know about this mysterious island. Seminole Indians from the Florida Everglades made their way here in the 19th century, and their continued existence in the north of the island at Red Bay was only discovered a few decades ago.

Most of the attraction of Andros for tourists lies in the eastern half of the island and off Andros' eastern shores. The western coast is essentially unapproachable by boat (because of the shoals) and shrouded by mangrove swamps. There are only a few settlements on the west coast and an equal number of hotels. There are no roads. The island is separated by North Bight, Middle Bight and South Bight.

Perhaps 5000 people live on Andros today. The island is 170 miles southeast of Miami and 30 miles west of Nassau. On a decent evening the lights of Nassau can be seen dimly on the horizon from Staniard Creek. Near Andros Town, the U.S. Navy runs the Atlantic Underwater Test and Evaluation Center (AUTEC) for testing underwater weapons systems and submarines.

What to See and Do on Andros

Andros Barrier Reef   ★★★

Off the east coast

At more than 140 miles long, this is the third-largest barrier reef in the world, behind the Great Barrier Reef of Australia and Belize's barrier reef in the Caribbean. The Andros barrier reef is far more accessible and equally as spectacular. There are caves and tunnels and all varieties of tropical marine life—and the visibility can get up to 150-200 feet on clear days. The gin-clear waters of the reef stretch in multi-hued ribbons in a kaleidoscope of color as the sun goes behind a cloud, rises or sinks in the west. Depths plunge instantly from 10-15 feet on the western side of the reef to more than two miles deep at Tongue of the Ocean off the eastern side of the reef. Hope Bay Lodge, outside Andros Town, is the island's center for exploring the underwater wonders of this reef.

Blue Holes and Inland Ocean Blue Holes   ★★★

Points throughout the coast and island

Andros offers dozens of blue holes to explore. The offshore freshwater spring blue holes drop hundreds of feet, while the inland variety also drop to phenomenal depths—with as many as thousands of feet

ANDROS

of passage—they are ringed by rims of porous limestone. They are found throughout the island in isolated pockets of pine forest, with few neighbors but the nesting egrets, herons and other wildlife. Small Hope Bay Lodge has a magnificent inland blue hole close by (Captain Bill's Blue Hole), and the resort brings divers out to the numerous ocean variety.

Nicholl's Town Area

Morgan's Bluff ★

North Andros

Local lore says the treasure of the pirate Sir Henry Morgan can be found here. If you're after it, you may have to settle in here for a while. There are a number of caves in the area, and visits can be arranged through the Andros Beach Hotel. Good luck.

Andros Town and Fresh Creek

Androsia Batik Works ★★

At the edge of Fresh Creek

This is the center of the Androsian (in fact, the Bahamian) batik industry. The Batik Works was founded in the early 1970s by Rosi Birch, the former wife of the owner of Small Hope Bay Lodge. Her staff through the years has grown from three to more than 70. You'll get a nice tour here, seeing how the fabric is dyed using the traditional techniques of the ancient Indonesians. The enterprise designs, dyes and sews all types of clothing for both men and women, as well as wall hangings, and maintains a retail outlet in Nassau. The beautiful blues, yellows, purples and greens are known and worn throughout the Bahamas. The fabric can also be purchased by the yard.

Where to Stay on Andros

Andros Town/Fresh Creek

Lighthouse Yacht Club and Marina   **$130**   ★★

Andros Town, Andros

☎ *(800) 835-1019, (809) 368-2305; FAX (809) 368-2300*

Single: $130; Double: $130

The white ducks/blue blazer crowd favor this upmarket resort with its 20-slip marina, located at the mouth of Fresh Creek. Stretch out on the gleamy beach or sign up for a diving, boating or fishing excursion. The resort has its own pool, two tennis courts, a lively cocktail lounge, and a swank restaurant with Bahamian and American cuisine. All 20 rooms feature tropical decor, refrigerators, private patios, TVs and telephones. Amenities: Swimming pool, two tennis courts, restaurant, bar, dock. Credit cards: AE, MC, V.

Small Hope Bay Lodge   **$145–$305**   ★★★

P.O. Box 21667

Fort Lauderdale, FL 33335

☎ *(800) 223-6961 U.S., (809) 368-2014; FAX (809) 368-2015*

Single: $145–$155; Double: $285–$305

The nearby barrier reef draws divers to this notable Bahamian dive resort, developed by Canadian Richard Birch. Aside from the expected dive excursions, you can take in a specialty tour to get up close and personal with a variety of underwater creatures and features. The main lodge is the hang-out spot for lazing by the fire, swapping stories, playing games, drinking at the bar (an old boat) or feasting on the hearty, wholesome meals (included in the rates)—meat or seafood are nightly choices. Accommodations are in 20 rustic, Andros-pine and coral-rock cottages with interesting and artistic decor. Amenities: dining room, two bars, Jacuzzi, lounge. Credit cards: AE, MC, V.

Chickcharnie Hotel　　　　$45–75　　　　★

Fresh Creek, Andros Town, Andros
☎ *(809) 368-2025*
Single: $45–$75; Double: $45–$75

This simple and inexpensive inn—named for Bahamian elves—is situated on the waterfront and a popular spot for fishers. Opt for the higher-priced rooms, unless you don't mind sharing a bath down the hallway. A simple dining room serves meals daily, and the owner runs a grocery store on the main floor. Amenities: dining room, bar. Credit cards: No credit cards.

Cargill Creek

Cargill Creek Lodge　　　　$170–$295　　　★★★

Cargill Creek, Andros
☎ *(809) 368-5129; FAX (809) 368-5046*
Single: $170; Double: $295

Ernest Hemingway wannabes flock to this fishing lodge, mostly for the guided bonefishing outings. Set against the waterfront, the white-stucco, blue-trimmed buildings house large guest rooms with views and tropical decor. Meals, included in the price, are served in a cheery dining room specializing in Bahamian and Continental dishes. Amenities: swimming pool, restaurant, bar. Credit cards: AE, MC, V.

Andros Island Bonefishing Club　　$160–$285　　★★

P.O. Box 959
Wexford, PA 15090
☎ *(800) 245-1950 US., (412) 935-1577; FAX (412) 935-5388*
Single: $160; Double: $285

Situated, seaside, right next to the Cargill Creek Fishing Lodge, this place is for super-serious bonefishers who get to sniff out their prey in the barely fished surrounding flats. The lounge and dining room area are cozy, and the included meals get high praise. Cottage accommodations are well-furnished and modern. Amenities: dining room, bar. Credit cards: MC, V.

Nicholl's Town

Andros Beach Hotel　　　　$95　　　　★★

Nicholl's Town, Andros
☎ *(800) 327-8150 US., (809) 329-2582*
Single: $95; Double: $95

This single-story red-brick hotel, close to top diving spots and right on top of a nice sandy beach, offers 10 cozy units with private patios. The hotel restaurant and dive shop are the best features. Amenities: swimming pool, restaurant, bar, dock. Credit cards: AE, MC, V.

Conch Sound Resort Inn　　　$80　　　　★★

P.O. Box 23029, Nicholl's Town, Andros
☎ *(809) 329-2060*
Single: $80; Double: $80

A short walk to the beach, at the northern edge of Nicholl's Town, this 1980s-built, motel-ish property offers spacious, well-furnished rooms (with satellite TV reception) as well as cottages with kitchens.

ANDROS

The restaurant and bar are open throughout the day, and a variety of fishing and diving excursions can be arranged. Amenities: swimming pool, restaurant, bar. Credit cards: No credit cards.

South Andros

Emerald Palms By-The-Sea $90–$110 ★ ★ ★

P.O. Box 800, Driggs Hill, South Andros
☎ *(800) 742-4276 U.S., (809) 369-2661; FAX (809) 369-2667*
Single: $90; Double: $110

A relaxing, palm tree-studded resort with an informal get-away-from-it-all atmosphere. Black out the world on the white, sandy beach front, or on a hammock amid the palms. For a little more action, rent a bicycle or sign up for a fishing excursion. The property houses a tennis court, freshwater swimming pool, lounge with live entertainment, and a dining room that serves seafood and Bahamian specialties. Accommodations are fairly luxurious, with four-poster beds, mosquito netting, small refrigerators, TVs and VCRs, and private patios. Amenities: swimming pool, tennis court, dining room, minibars, bicycle- and car rentals. Credit cards: AE, MC, V.

Where to Eat on Andros

In North Andros, you'll want to sample local and continental fare at the pier-near Cargill Creek Lodge, or perhaps join guests at the **Andros Island Bonefishing Club**, nearby. In the Andros Town/Fresh Creek area, choose the posh dining room at **Andros Lighthouse Yacht Club and Marina**, the filling salads and seafood at **Small Hope Bay Lodge**, or grab your own groceries at the **Chickcharnie Hotel**'s small store. Around Nicholl's Town, it's a toss-up between **Andros Beach Hotel** and **Conch Sound Resort Inn**. In South Andros, the **Emerald Palms By-the-Sea** offers local dishes in its restaurant as well as occasional buffets and barbecues.

Nightlife on Andros

Nightlife is pretty much limited to falling asleep after a seafood dinner on Andros. Nobody, absolutely nobody, comes here to party and dance till they drop. If you're lucky, you might find a little bit of action in Andros town at:

Chickcharnie Hotel

Fresh Creek
☎ *(809) 368-2025*
The bar here is a magnet for locals and a smattering of visiting fishermen who must get a fix of nightlife, even if it's nothing more than humming a few bars of "Margaritaville" while whetting the whistle with a beer or 10.

Sports on Andros

Scuba Diving/Snorkeling

The diving here is spectacular namely for the area's blue holes, reefs and shipwrecks. At 104 miles long and 40 miles wide, Andros offers an array of attractions, including a massive 120-mile-long barrier reef at the Tongue of the Ocean, which plunges to depths greater than 6000 feet. Barracuda, grouper and giant sea turtles abound. Visibility is often 100 feet or more, but occasionally drops to 40 feet. Over the Wall is a sheer drop from 80 feet down.

On the north end of the island, perhaps the biggest attraction is the wreck of the 345-foot British tanker the *Potomac*, which sank in 1929. The Barge is also popular. It was sunk intentionally in 70 feet of water in the mid-1960s and makes for a superb artificial reef teeming with sealife.

Other attractions off Andros include the Elkhorn corals and majestic sea fans of The Garden and black coral formations that comprise the Back Forest.

Small Hope Bay Lodge

c/o P.O. Box N-1131
Nassau
☎ *(809) 368-2013/4; FAX (809) 368-2015*
U.S. Office
P.O. Box 21667
Fort Lauderdale, FL 33335-1667
☎ *(800) 223-6961*

Andros has undeniably the most dive spots of any island in the Bahamas and Small Hope pretty much has a lock on the activities, at least as far as Andros as a base. The lodge is located in the middle of the island on its eastern shore. Dive trips to all the offshore attractions. Half-day trips for certified divers cost $40 and $10 for snorkelers. Night dives run at $50 per person, with a minimum of six divers. A 6-day, 5-night stay at the hotel and dive package costs $1000, including three dives per day. Instruction is available at no charge. Equipment rentals. If you're not staying at the lodge, but ask nicely, they may fill your tanks.

Andros Undersea Adventures

Andros Beach Hotel
Nicholl's Town, North Andros
☎ *(809) 329-2582*
or P.O. Box 21766
Ft. Lauderdale, FL 33335
☎ *(305) 462-3400, (800) 327-8150*

Full-service dive facility, from rentals and instructions to a slew of dive trips. Specializes in trips to the barrier reef and Tongue of the Ocean. A single tank dive costs $40, two-tank dives at $60 and three-tank dives at $80. Snorkeling costs $25 for a half-day trip. Packages are also available.

Sportfishing

Bonefishing is best in the shallow waters off Andros. The season runs from September to June.

Andros Beach Hotel

Nicholl's Town, North Andros
☎ *(809) 329-2582*
Bonefishing runs.

Charlie's Haven

Behring Point, North Andros
☎ *(809) 368-4087*

North Andros is considered the bonefishing capital of the world and this is one of the best spots in the capital. The specialty here is bonefishing and the resort's guides are some of the best in the Bahamas for smelling out bonefish. Half-day trips cost about $140 and full-day adventures run about $250.

Cargill Creek Fishing Lodge
Cargill Creek
☎ *(809) 368-5129*
Bonefishing trips for about $290 for the boat for a full day.

Chickcharnie Hotel
Fresh Creek
☎ *(809) 368-2025*
Charters available here at $350 per day for a 25-foot reef fishing boat
and $220 for a bonefishing skiff. They have about 10 boats available.

North Bite Bonefishing Service
Behring Point
☎ *(809) 329-5261*
Excellent bonefishing hops in the Cargill Creek area.

Small Hope Bay Lodge
c/o P.O. Box N-1131
Nassau
☎ *(809) 368-2013/4; FAX (809) 368-2015*
U.S. Office
P.O. Box 21667
Fort Lauderdale, FL 33335-1667
☎ *(800) 223-6961*
In addition to dive trips, Small Hope also organizes bonefishing trips.

Directory

Transportation

There are four airports on Andros, if you count the landing strip at Mangrove Cay. The other three are at San Andros in the north of the island, Andros Town in the center and at Congo Town in the south, just south of Mangrove Cay. By air, **Bahamasair** (☎ *[800] 222-4262 in the U.S.*) flies twice daily from Nassau to both Andros Town and San Andros. There are four flights a week to Congo Town from Nassau. From the U.S., **Island Express** (☎ *[305] 359-0380*) flies daily to San Andros, Andros Town and Congo Town from Fort Lauderdale. **Gulfstream Airlines** (☎ *[800] 992-8532*) has daily flights to the same three airports from Miami. Call for current schedules of all three of the airlines. If you're staying at **Small Hope Bay Lodge** (☎ *[809] 368-2014*) at Fresh Creek near Andros Town, and many visitors are, the resort offers a daily charter flight to and from Fort Lauderdale for a cost of about $200 round trip. Andros is a point of entry in the Bahamas.

ANDROS

Insider Tip

Know what part of the island you're going to be staying on when booking flights. At more than 100 miles long, Andros makes a long and expensive taxi ride should you land at Congo Town with hotel reservations in San Andros.

Taxis are usually available at each of the airports, but don't count on it. There aren't many of them and the drivers seem to have their own itineraries. Little Granny Edna's trip to the market in Andros Town will take priority over an incoming Piper Cub, but not over a landing commercial turbo prop. A typical fare from the Andros Town airport into town is $15–$20. The taxis aren't metered. However, bargaining may be useless, as you won't have any choice but to take the taxi you're negotiating for. As a rule of thumb, expect to pay about $1.50 per mile.

No cruise ships call on Andros, but you can arrive by mailboat from Nassau. The *M/V Lisa J II* departs from Potter's Cay Dock in Nassau each Wednesday and makes stops at Lowe Sound (Morgan's Bluff), Mastic Point and Nicholl's Town in the north of Andros before returning to Nassau the following Tuesday. To reach central Andros, catch the *M/V Lady Di* ($25), which leaves Potter's Cay Dock in Nassau on Tuesdays and makes stops at Stafford Creek, Staniard Creek, Blanket Sound and Fresh Creek. It returns to Nassau on Sundays. For reaching the south, catch the *M/V Captain Moxey* ($30), which sets sail from Potter's Cay Dock on Mondays for Kemps Bay, Long Bay Cays and the Bluff before returning to Nassau on Wednesday. Weather may change the schedules, so call the Potter's Cay dockmaster's office at ☎ *(809) 393-1064.*

Car rentals are available in Andros but not from the majors; the roads are bad and the salt air melts the sheet metal—and you count the number of gas stations on your hand. But there are a couple of local-yocals out to make a fast buck (and a big one, too; rentals range from $60–$100 a day!). Try:

AMKLCO Car Rental
Fresh Creek
☎ *(809) 368-2056*

Bereth Rent A Car
Fresh Creek
☎ *(809) 368-2102*

Basil Martin
Mastic Point
☎ *(809) 329-3169*

Cecil Gaitor
Mastic Point
☎ *(809) 329-3043*

When visitors to Andros must get around, a bicycle is the cheapest way. But they're only best for sight-seeing, as there can be dozens of miles between towns on Andros. Going out for a paper and a cup of coffee may be a daylong excursion. But you can try:

Chickcharnie Hotel
Andros Town
☎ *(809) 368-2025*

Longley's Guest House
Mangrove Cay
☎ *(809) 329-4311*

Small Hope Bay Lodge
Fresh Creek
☎ *(809) 368-2014*

Emergencies

If something seriously goes wrong you'll have to be medevac'ed, because health facilities on Andros are extremely limited and medicines are even in shorter supply. So bring your own prescription drugs and other medical supplies you think you might need.

North Andros Medical Clinic

San Andros
☎ *(809) 329-2121*
Government-run; there is a doctor who lives in San Andros.

Central Andros Medical Clinic

Fresh Creek
☎ *(809) 368-2038*
Government-run; there is a doctor and a nurse here.

South Andros Medical Clinic

Mangrove Cay
☎ *(809) 329-4620*
Government-run; only a nurse is available here.

Police

North Andros
☎ *919*

Police

Central Andros
☎ *(809) 368-2626*
South Andros
☎ *(809) 329-4733*

Banks and Money Changers

If you've got any serious banking to do on Andros you're probably going to be seriously out of luck. The only real bank here is open only one day a week, and then only for four hours.

Canadian Imperial Bank of Commerce

San Andros
☎ *(809) 329-2382*
Will cash traveler's checks. Open Wednesdays 10 a.m.–2 p.m.

Post Office

Commissioner's Office

Nicholl's Town, North Andros
☎ *(809) 329-2034*
This isn't exactly a post office, but it will handle mail and parcels. Most of the towns on Andros have a store whose proprietor will handle mail, as will most of the hotels.

Telephone Service

This is almost nonexistent on Andros. You will find a telephone booth at the airports and the occasional one in Andros Town, San Andros and Nicholl's Town. But they may not be working. Usually, the only telephone service available is through your hotel.

ANDROS

ANDROS

ELEUTHERA

Glass Window Bridge, Eleuthera

Besides being one of the best diving destinations in the Bahamas, Eleuthera has another claim to fame. It is the site where the early Eleutherian adventurers made landfall and is thus considered the birthplace of the Bahamas, not unlike how Plymouth Rock is considered the birthplace of America.

The Eleutherian Adventurers were a group of religious dissidents from Bermuda who chose to leave that British colony in 1649 rather than face persecution at home. Many believe they had their sights set on landing at Harbour Island in the north. Other experts question whether Eleuthera was their intended destination at all. Nonetheless, their vessel wrecked on a reef off Governor's Harbour in the middle of the island. (Another group, which had split from the main contingent, wrecked off the northern shore of the island, and the adventurers took refuge in a limestone cave, called Preacher's Cave.) They called their new home Eleuthera, the Greek word for "freedom," and set about the task of somehow trying to subsist on the island. The adventurers later split up and formed settlements on Spanish

Wells and Harbour Island, and today you'll notice the many caucasian descendents of the Adventurers.

Seeing that casting away its unwanted to the sea was a cost-ef-
ficient way of keeping the Crown clean, the Bermudian colonists
decided to send on a slow boat the British island's troublemakers
and rabble-rousers, who were, in most cases, African slaves. During the 18th and 19th centuries, the British purged Bermuda of
many of these troublesome slaves (and, later, freed slaves), who
arrived on Eleuthera as the Bahamas' first black settlers. Throw
in the number of Loyalists who fled the newly formed United
States of America, and you'll see why Eleuthera has perhaps the
most colorful and diverse population mix in the Bahamas.

What the Loyalists did bring to Eleuthera, particularly to Harbour Island, and its population living on a subsistence economy,
was the know-how in many trades that would help Dunmore
Town (on Harbour Island and the original capital of The Bahamas) become The Bahamas' second largest commercial center,
second only to Nassau.

Dunmore Town boomed from the middle of the 19th century
all the way until World War II. It was a major shipbuilding center (producing ships as large as four-masted schooners) and supported a population of nearly 2000 residents—only Nassau had
more. However, by 1943 the population had dropped to about
700 people, and Harbour Island became the quaint little backwater that it is today.

Eleuthera, called "Cigatoo" by the locals, starts about 70 miles
east of Nassau and consists of some 200 square miles. It is bow-
shaped at about 100 miles long and, on the average, two miles
wide. Perhaps 10,000 people call Eleuthera home these days.

The island, with its rolling hills, pink-sand beaches, cliffs and
old villages, was left relatively unexplored by modern travelers
until recent years. Now it is beginning to rival the Abacos in the
number of resorts, most being found on what many call the most
beautiful island in The Bahamas, Harbour Island. Tourism in
the south has taken a dive in recent years, and a number of the
resorts have shut down, notably the Cotton Bay Club and Cape
Eleuthera. (The marina at Cape Eleuthera is still open for fuel
and other basic provisions, but the resort amenities are gone). It
was abandoned by its Arab investors in 1986 and the duplexes
were reportedly sold for $200 apiece—literally. The catch? Buy-
ers had to disassemble the units brick-by-brick and truck them
away. The land wasn't included. Squatters inhabit those still un-
sold.

Eleuthera has arguably the best beaches in The Bahamas, one
of the most incredible sights in the islands (that being the magnificent Glass Window) and one of the most thrilling dives in the
world at the Current.

NORTH ATLANTIC OCEAN

76°50' N
76°30' N
76°10' N
25°30' N
25°10' N
24°20' N
24°30' N
24°40' N

Royal Island
Egg Island
Spanish Wells Harbor Club
Russell Island
The Bluff
North Eleuthera Airport
The Current Cut
Pimlico Island
Boiling Hole
Lower Bogue
Current Island Stlmt.
Current Island
Preacher's Cove
Pierres Island
Man Island
Pink Sands
Dunmore Town
Valentine's Yacht Club
} Harbor Island
Glass Window
Blow Hole
Gregory Town
Budho Caves
Alice Town
Moray Pond
Rainbow Cay
James Cistern
Cupids Cay
Governor's Harbor
Club Med
Finley Cay
Windermere Island
Windmere Club
Marion's Bluff
Tarpum Bay
Winding Bay Beach
Winding Bay
Shooner Cays
Rock Sound Intl. Airport
Rock Sound Club
Cape Eleuthera
Deep Hole
Rock Sound
Ocean Hole
Deep Creek Airport
Greencastle
Deep Creek
Cotton Bay Club
Cotton Bay
Wemyss Bight
Arvinda Bay
John Millars
Millars
Bannerman Town
Eleuthera Point

N
FIELDING

Eleuthera

0   10   20 mi.
0   16   32km

Eleuthera was once a major cattle producing island, and the road (Queen's Highway) in the northern part of the island is flanked by the ruins of concrete grain silos. Also dotting the roadsides are the occasional pineapple plantation.

Harbour Island

Harbour Island is in the far north of Eleuthera, off its eastern shore, about 200 miles from Miami. Many frequent Bahamas visitors say that Harbour Island is the most beautiful of Bahamian islands. The entire eastern shore (the island is three miles long and about a half-mile wide) is adorned with a beautiful pink-sand beach. Swimming is great year-round as the magnificent natural harbour is sheltered by the type of dangerous reefs that did the Adventurers' vessel in.

The local economy is based on fishing and a little farming, but an increasing amount of the islanders are being lured into the tourist industry to cater to the needs of the resorts. The houses are pastel-colored clapboard structures, many of them among the oldest in The Bahamas; some have been magnificently restored. Hibiscus and bougainvillea fringe the white picket fences. The buildings along the harbor here are particularly worth seeing.

Spanish Wells

Most think that Spanish Wells is the name of the island a half-mile off the northwest tip of Eleuthera. Rather, the name of the island is St. George's Cay. Spanish Wells is actually just a small settlement, named after the freshwater well the Spanish dug on the cay during the time of Ponce de Leon, who stopped here to replenish his supplies. The Spanish used St. George's Cay as the last landfall between the New World and the European continent.

The charm of present-day Spanish Wells are its people, most of them direct descendents of the original Eleutherian Adventurers, with their British accents and centuries-old diction. These folks are entirely lost in time. About 700 people live here, most of them rather wealthy due to the booming lobster and fishing businesses most are engaged in. However, they live in simple, Cape Cod-style clapboard houses painted in pastel shades. There really is nothing to do here, other than take in the history of the place, which was started when a group of tattered Bermudian refugees tried to make a new life in the mid-1600s.

Governor's Harbour

Many believe this is the spot where the first group of the Eleutherian Adventurers came ashore after wrecking off the coast. About halfway down the 100-mile long island, this is the largest population center on Eleuthera after Rock Sound. There are a number of wonderful old homes in the area to explore, and an Anglican church on Cupid's Cay and the 150-year-old Cupid's Cay bridge.

Most visitors here, however, remain unaware of the area's attractions, namely because they're staying at the totally inclusive Club Med just a few miles up the road.

Governor's Harbour's past wasn't always as sleepy as its present. After Loyalists began arriving here in the 19th century, this became a major center for shipping pineapple to New York City and Baltimore. The city received in return building supplies and household goods.

Today, though, the local scene is pretty much dictated by Club Med, which has definitely had an influence here—sort of like the first McDonald's in Moscow.

Rock Sound

Two-centuries-old Rock Sound is the largest population center on Eleuthera, which is not saying much—but there is a modern shopping center here. Mainly it's a quiet fishing village that was one of the biggest pineapple producers and canners in the islands. Today, the town has reverted back to most of its sleepiness. But it remains where most everybody in south Eleuthera come to resupply and shop. There are also some 200-year-old homes to check out here.

Nearby Rock Sound (just east) is the less than spectacular and overrated Rock Sound Ocean Hole, a saltwater inland blue hole that links with the sea, but where no one knows. It is called locally The Bottomless Hole. Seawater fish meander on in for a cruise and to be fed by the tourists and others before heading back out to the real sea. Fish as large as grouper and yellowtail used to venture in here to be fed bread by locals and tourists— but none has been seen for some time.

What to See and Do on Eleuthera

Upper Bogue Area

Glass Window ★ ★

This is a fascinating location just south of Upper Bogue, where only a thin limestone isthmus keeps Eleuthera a single island. The view of the contrasts between the deep, dark ocean Atlantic side (east) of Eleuthera and the calm azure shallows off the western shores is a sight to behold. Many a mariner bobbing and tossing in the rough seas to the east off the island have gazed in bewilderment at vessels in the glass-smooth vodka-clear seas off Eleuthera's western shores, only dozens of feet away. This windowlike formation was created by erosion from the sea and the wind. Locals believe that it will take no more than about 100 years for the sea to divide Eleuthera into two islands. Today, storms allow the eastern waters to surge across the rocks and join with the western flats. A storm-battered concrete bridge spans the rift over the isthmus—it's a marvel that vehicles can pass over this bridge at all. Cables dangle from its foundation columns.

The Grotto ★

After a slight rise about 200 feet south of the bridge spanning the Glass Window, head by foot east a hundred yards to the sea across the moonscape limestone. Here is a massive hollowed cave continually battered by the Atlantic. The water table can be seen and the layer of limestone through which rainfall passes. Streams of fresh water drop from the ceiling of the cave, water that the locals call the purest in the world.

Bridge Point Area

Preacher's Cave ★

The Eleutherian Adventurers, after they wrecked here on a reef over 300 years ago, sought shelter in this cave near the tip of the island. A rocky pulpit formation gives a cathedral-like feeling to this cave; thus, its name. The stone altar is still in good shape.

Harbour Island

Historic Churches ★

The oldest church in The Bahamas is located here, St. John's Anglican Church on Harbour Island, which was built in the 1760s. Wesley Methodist was built in 1845, and is the largest Methodist place of worship in The Bahamas. There are also a number of other churches here, giving you the feeling that these people perhaps know something you don't, or perhaps this part of Eleuthera was once visited by a spaceship of aliens, and town fathers swore off booze. Flowers dominate St. Catherine's Cemetery, which is quite close to Wesley Methodist Church.

Hatchet Bay

Hatchet Bay Plantation ★

This plantation was once the center for raising prize Angus cattle. Its present output is poultry and dairy products.

Hatchet Bay Cave ★

It's probably wise to get a guide to explore this mile-long subterranean channel of stalagmites and stalactites, said to have provided shelter and served as a treasure hideout for early buccaneers. The guide will come in handy if for no other reason than he will go first, so you'll know exactly where all of the hundreds of bats in the cave are. The guide will also be good for a few stories, about half of which will have any semblance of truth.

Eleuthera Cliffs

Gregory Town

Hidden Beach

The east coast of Eleuthera in this area features the best surfing found in The Bahamas and all of the Caribbean. In fact, the surfing can be excellent to spectacular here. Surfers used to flock to these beaches from around the world, but weren't particularly welcomed by the locals, as the surfers tended to leave their trash behind. Hidden Beach is south of Gregory Town and is only accessible at low tide.

Governor's Harbour

Mal Flanders' Studio ★

Just east of Governor's Harbour atop a small hill is artist Mal Flanders' house and studio. Flanders is a former American and now Bahamian artist whose bright and colorful oil paintings of Bahamian life and architecture are sold around the world. His works have been seen in numerous publications and Bahamian tourism material. He'll be delighted to step away from his easel for a few moments to give you glimpses of the old Bahamian lifestyle. His works clutter his small studio, and those that aren't commissioned he'll sell to the public from anywhere from $40–$500. Flanders came to The Bahamas from the States in 1972 and has never looked back. He'll be happy to talk about his love for the old Bahamas—the clapboard houses and simple lifestyles.

Rock Sound

Ocean Hole

Just east of Rock Sound on the main road

Nobody is sure just how deep this saltwater lake (blue hole) is. Some say it is as deep as 600 feet. Regardless, the lake is connected to the ocean by underground channels, and ocean fish seem to have found a way to get in here to be fed by the tourists before heading back out into the ocean again for some exercise. I found this spot to be a disappointment. The water at the surface is murky and I saw none of the colorful fish that are always reported to be here taking handouts from tourists. The large grouper that once swam at the surface have since retreated (permanently) to the murky depths. The blue hole is surrounded by a disheveled park. When visiting by car, lock it when seeing the blue hole. Local kids have been known to break into the parked cars here and steal valuables.

Windermere Island ★

This is an ultra-private secured island belonging to and frequented by the rich and famous—including the Queen of England and other British royalty—off the eastern coast of Eleuthera in the Rock Sound area. It is reached via a small bridge after turning east off the Queen's Highway a few miles north of Rock Sound. The turnoff is marked. It is virtually impossible to visit here unless invited by one of the island's illustrious residents. The bridge is manned by a security detail. But take a chance and try getting on the island for a brief visit. It would help to go by taxi, as your driver will no doubt be friendly with the security guards, who might cut the driver some slack and let you both through. The best time to try is during the summer months, when the island is practically deserted. After crossing the bridge, you'll come upon a large white mansion (on the right hand side) where Queen Elizabeth has sought a little R&R. Turn left and take the lone road north to where it is. Turn right and you'll reach a beautiful beach that will give you the feeling you're at the edge of the world. If you drive to the southern tip of the island, you'll pass a few estates—yet few of the houses are visible through the thick junglelike foliage.

Where to Stay on Eleuthera

Governor's Harbour

Club Mediterranee ★★★

P.O. Box 80, French Laves, Governor's Harbour, Eleuthera
☎ *(800) 258-2633 U.S., (809) 332-2270; FAX (809)332-2691*
Single: $800–$1300 per person, per week; Double: $800–$1300 per person, per week

Club Med's Eleuthera Island property, on the Atlantic coast of the island, caters more to families than the usual stalking singles' set. Parents and kids can participate in a variety of family-that-plays-together activities, such as watersports, organized games, day-long picnics, and various entertainments. Kids can sign up for Circus School and learn the basics of tightrope walking, trampolining, greasepaint makeup, and other under-the-big-top fun. The Mini Club teaches older kids how to sail and dive. Other options include tennis, aerobics, sailing, snorkeling, bicycling and scuba lessons. Evening action centers around the dining room, lounge, theater and disco. As with all Club Med's, everything is included in the price—room, meals (with wine and beer), and most activities. Accommodations are Club Med de rigeur—comfortable and cheerfully decorated, with private baths. Amenities: swimming pool, three restaurants, bar, boutique, aerobics, volleyball, eight tennis courts, disco, theater. Credit cards: AE, MC, V.

Cigatoo Inn $50–$85

P.O. Box 86, Haynes Avenue, Governor's Harbour, Eleuthera
☎ *(809) 332-2343; FAX (809) 332-2159*
Single: $50–$85; Double: $55–$75
Overlooking Governor's Harbour from its hillside perch, this motel-style complex offers inexpensive rooms set amid tropical flora. Accommodations are nothing special, but have an island flavor, are decently furnished, and have sea or pool-view patios or balconies. The thatched-roof tropical bar can be rather lively—especially when local entertainment is on tap—while the hotel restaurant specializes in American and Bahamian meals. Guests have use of a pool and tennis court, while the beach is a short walk away. Amenities: swimming pool, restaurant, bar, tennis court. Credit cards: AE, MC, V.

Laughing Bird Apartments $60–$75 ★

P.O. Box EL-25076, Governor's Harbour, Eleuthera
☎ *(809) 332-2012; FAX (809) 332-2358*
Single: $60–$65; Double: $70–$75
These apartments, on the waterfront, convenient to shops and restaurants, are ideal for anyone planning to stay a week or longer. Use it as a base while going off on land or water excursions, or just stay put and enjoy the beach, garden and a snooze in the hammocks. Each of the four beach-front apartments include fully equipped kitchens. Credit cards: MC, V.

Palmetto Shores Vacation Villas $80–$90 ★ ★

P.O. Box EL-25131
Governor's Harbour, Eleuthera
☎ *(809) 332-1305; FAX (809) 332-1305*
Single: $80–$90; Double: $80–$90
Bahamian-style units, set on the waterfront, offer good value for families or couple of couples. Each of the 10 comfortably furnished villas comes with one or two bedrooms, tile floors, equipped kitchens, TVs and a wraparound balcony that opens onto the beach. Guests have use of tennis courts and free Sunflower sailboats, and other sports and excursions are easily arranged. A restaurant and general store are nearby. Amenities: two tennis courts, sailboats, dock. Credit cards: AE, MC, V.

Unique Village $80–$120 ★ ★

P.O. Box EL-25187, Governor's Harbour, Eleuthera
☎ *(809) 332-1830; FAX (809) 332-1838*

Single: $80–$120; Double: $80–$120

Rising above the Atlantic side of Eleuthera, south of Governor's Harbour near North Palmetto Point, this 1992-built cluster offers varied accommodations, a restaurant and bar. The beach is accessed via a wooden staircase, while everything else is a car-drive away. The mainly white group of buildings house a bar and a beach-view restaurant that leans toward fresh seafood and Bahamian dishes. Accommodations are a mix of hotel-type rooms and one- and two-bedroom villas, well-furnished and with satellite TV. Quite simply, this is a spot that offers little other than relaxation. There aren't any watersports activities and the beach is down the side of a cliff. For food, you'll have little choice other than the hotel's expensive restaurant. On one visit, I found the staff rather aloof and uninterested after ordering only an appetizer for my meal. Although certainly comfortable enough, unless total boredom and solitude are what you seek, there are better choices on the island. In fact, if it is boredom you seek, there are still better options on Eleuthera. The bartender is friendly enough, though. Amenities: restaurant, bar. Credit cards: MC, V.

Gregory Town

The Cove Eleuthera   **$79–$139**   ★★★

P. O. Box 2007, P.O. Box 1548
Queen's Highway
Gregory Town, Eleuthera
☎ *(800) 552-5960 U.S., (809) 335-5142; FAX (809) 335-5338*
Single: $79–$119; Double: $89–$129; Triple: $99–$139

Set on almost 30 secluded acres, between two tranquil, vodka-clear coves, this beach-front resort is a couple of miles northwest of Gregory Town and makes for one of the best romantic budget getaways on Eleuthera. It's secluded and unassuming with a gentle, down-to-earth quality, much like the owners, Ann and George Mullin. The villas are a favorite of writers and artists, who come here to work or to forget about it. We won't drop any names. And it's easy to get to know the other guests. Composed of a main clubhouse and various quadraplexes, the property offers superb snorkeling, fishing and boating excursions, a freshwater swimming pool (one of the only on the island), tennis, bicycles, Aqua Eyes and kayaks. Snorkeling equipment is available but limited. The large dining room offers a daily changing menu (though you can always count on fresh seafood to appear), while guests tend to congregate poolside for lunch and cocktails. Rooms feature pastel decor, tile floors, rattan furnishings, and porches or verandahs. Amenities: dining room, two bars, two tennis courts, swimming pool. Credit cards: AE, MC, V.

Harbour Island

Dunmore Beach Club   **$290–$350**   ★★★

P. O. Box EL-27122, Colebrook Lane, Harbour Island, Eleuthera
☎ *(809) 333-2200; FAX (809) 333-2429*
Single: $290; Double: $340–$350

Fronting three miles of sandy pink beach, surrounded by beautifully tended tropical landscaping, this luxury cottage colony pampers its well-heeled guests on the run from the fast lane. Feasting on the delectable and innovative cuisine is a major activity, and meals are included in the rates. The dining room with built-in wine cabinet

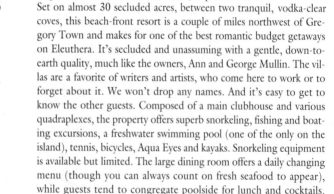

offers a daily changing menu of gourmet cuisine and, to set the tone, men are required to wear jacket and tie in the evening. Breakfast, served on the sea-view garden terrace, is casual. A tennis court is on the property, and the clubhouse functions as a social center with a bar, living room and library area. Guest cottages feature wood paneling, refrigerators, patios, sitting-rooms or areas. Amenities: dining room, bar, tennis court. Credit cards: No credit cards.

Runaway Hill Club $140–$185   ★ ★ ★

P. O. Box 31, Harbour Island, Eleuthera
☎ *(809) 333-2150; FAX (809) 333-2420*
Single: $140–$165; Double: $160–$185
A former private residence built in 1947, this "club" operates as a small inn, offering intimate and stylish accommodations to those who would like to share the upscale-homey environment. The mansion, with its original English colonial dormers, sits atop a bluff above the pink sands amid plants, gardens, a vast lawn and seven acres of beach frontage. Guest rooms, upstairs or in an adjacent wing, are individually decorated. The dining room is a favorite with locals for its fresh seafood and prix fixe meals. Amenities: swimming pool, restaurant, bar, lounge. Credit cards: AE, MC, V.

Romora Bay Club $90–$190   ★ ★ ★

P. O. Box 146, Colebrook Street, Harbour Island, Eleuthera
☎ *(809) 333-2325; FAX (809) 323-2324*
Single: $90–$140; Double: $120–$190
Facing the harbor, this one-time private club features breezy coconut palm and pine trees, divine semitropical plants, and a mood-evoking path down to an even more mood-evoking, pink-sand beach. A variety of sports, including fishing, sailing, and diving, are on the activity roster. The social whirl takes place in the main clubhouse with bar, lounge and dining room that does wonders with Bahamian, continental and American fare—the homemade pastries and breads are noteworthy. Accommodations feature comfy furnishings, private balconies or patios, and harbor or garden views. Amenities: dining room, two bars, Jacuzzi, dive shop, bicycles, scooters. Credit cards: AE, MC, V.

Coral Sands Hotel $100–$150   ★ ★ ★

P.O. Box 23, Chapel Street, Harbour Island, Eleuthera
☎ *(800) 468-2799 U.S., (809) 333-2350; FAX (809) 333-2368*
Single: $100–$125; Double: $110–$150
Positioned above centuries-old Dunmore Town, this casual two-story property—set on 14 acres—offers a gorgeous stretch of sandy, pink beach as well as a night-lighted tennis court, snorkeling, sailboats and rowboats—other watersports and excursions can be arranged. The owners, former wartime flyer/actor Brett King and his wife, Sharon, are known for their welcoming ways and boast a high repeat business—always a good sign. An intimate cafe serves terrific home-style international, American, and Bahamian meals, while a casual beach bar concentrates on lunch fare—or order a picnic lunch to take along on an outing. Guest rooms are adorned with local decor and comfortable furnishings. Amenities: restaurant, three bars, diving, one lighted tennis court, sailboats, rowboats. Credit cards: AE, DC, MC, V.

Valentine's Yacht Club and Inn $75–$145   ★ ★ ★

P. O. Box 1, Harbourfront, Harbour Island, Eleuthera

☎ *(809) 333-2142; FAX (809) 333-2135*
Single: $75–$135; Double: $90–$145

The 40-slip marina at this low-lying, post-Hurricane Andrew renovated complex is the ace that draws yachtsmen and fishermen. The
wood-paneled main building houses a restaurant specializing in Bahamian cuisine, a hopping bar that doubles as the area's social pulse—
often hosting live entertainment, and—out back—a swimming pool.
The marina facilities are extensive, and the dive shop caters both to
beginning and avid divers or snorkelers. The place is usually buzzing
with divers and fishers, along with visiting brought-the-yacht-along
celebrities. Accommodation is in bungalow-type units with private
verandahs. Amenities: swimming pool, tennis court, two restaurants,
two bars, marina, dive shop. Credit cards: AE, MC, V.

Hatchet Bay

Rainbow Inn   **$90**   ★ ★

P. O. Box EL-25053, Governor's Harbour, Eleuthera
☎ *(800) 688-4752 U.S., (809) 335-0294; FAX (809) 335-0294*
Single: $90; Double: $90

This beach-front resort, a couple of miles south of Alice Town, features woodsy bungalow accommodations, a restaurant with excellent
Bahamian cuisine, a popular bar with occasional live entertainment,
and a swimming pool and tennis court. The octagonal-shaped guest
bungalows feature kitchenettes, and plenty of wood beams and paneling. The inn provides free guided tours of Hatchet Bay Caves as well
as free bicycles and snorkeling equipment. Amenities: swimming
pool, tennis court, dining room, bar. Credit cards: MC, V.

Tarpum Bay

Hilton's Haven   **$45–$55**   ★

Tarpum Bay, Eleuthera
☎ *(800) 688-4752 US., (809) 334-4231*
Single: $45; Double: $55

No, not that Hilton—this two-story property is an unassuming ten-
room operation owned by Mary Hilton, a local nurse. Several miles
from Rock Sound Airport, and a couple of minutes from the beach,
these clean, simple rooms provide a satisfying stay for budgeting visitors. Sample some of Mary's home cooking in the small restaurant, on
site. Amenities; restaurant, bar. Credit cards: No credit cards.

Rock Sound

Edwin's Place   **$60–$75**   ★ ★

P. O. Box 30, Rock Sound, Eleuthera
☎ *(809) 334-2094*
Single: $60; Double: $75

This simple Bahamian-owned, waterfront motel offers home-style
hospitality and unpretentious rooms. A small eatery, on site, serves
fresh fish, salads and desserts. Shops and dining facilities are nearby,
and tennis, boating, and water sports can be arranged. Amenities: restaurant. Credit cards: No credit cards.

Where to Eat on Eleuthera

In Northern Eleuthera, **Cove Eleuthera**, in Gregory Town, has a large
sea-view restaurant featuring American and Bahamian specialties plus Saturday buffet dinners—informal dining is available on the outdoor patio. More

local dishes can be sampled at the simple dining room over at Cambridge Villas. At Hatchet Bay, the **Rainbow Inn** dining room offers an extensive dinner menu proclaiming Bahamian and Continental fare. The largest selection of choices is around Harbour Island. Choose a restaurant at any of the resorts and hotels—the **Coral Sands Mediterranean Cafe** is probably the most outstanding, both for cuisine and ambiance. **Valentine's Yacht Club and Inn** offers an English pub-like room, and **Romora Bay Club** offers prix-fixe dinners. For more laid-back dining, try **Angela's Starfish Restaurant**, **Arthur's Bakery and Cafe**, **George's Sports Lounge**, **Seagraves**, and **Ma Ruby's**.

In Eleuthera's mid-section, the restaurant at **Cigatoo Inn** offers Bahamian and American dishes, and the spacious dining room at **Unique Village** is a cheery, sea-view choice for local dishes as well as steaks and seafood. Guests at the all-inclusive **Club Med Eleuthera** eat their fill on premises. **Mate and Jenny's Pizza Restaurant** at Palmetto Point is a popular spot for the ever-fascinating Italian pie and other light meals and snacks.

At the southern end of Eleuthera, **Edwina's Place** and **Sammy's Place** in Rock Sound are two casual favorites serving Bahamian specialties. **Hilton's Haven**, at Tarpum Bay features home-style cooking in a casual tavern-like room.

Nightlife on Eleuthera

Nightlife on Eleuthera is found almost exclusively at the resorts, but there are a couple of pockets on the island where you might wish to hang with the locals.

Cigatoo Inn

> *Haynes Ave.*
> *P.O. Box 86*
> *Governor's Harbour*
> ☎ *(809) 332-2343*
> *FAX (809) 332-2159*

This is a hotel, but with a bar that has live entertainment and great piña coladas and Goombay Smashes.

Mate & Jenny's Pizza Restaurant & Bar

> *Just off Queen's Highway*
> *South Palmetto Point*
> ☎ *(809) 332-1504*

A restaurant with great prices for The Bahamas, but most of the customers are here to drink Kalik beer, rumrunners, piña coladas and Goombay Smashes. A mix of locals and tourists, this place makes for a good break from the resort scene.

Sports on Eleuthera

Scuba Diving/Snorkeling

Arguably the best dive off Eleuthera is at Current Cut, where you'll be blissfully swept away in the currents caused by the funneling tidal flows between two islands. The surge is so great, you'll be accompanied by a wave of tumbling fish, who are along for the ride, as well, as if they had been waiting in line for the adventure. The current is defined by the swift waters moving through the underwater chasm between Eleuthera and Current Island. The current moves at about nine knots and divers are zipped along in a rush of water on a ride that lasts nearly 10 minutes and covers a half-mile. It is considered one of the 10 best dives in the world.

North of Spanish Wells is the site of a number of wrecks, the victims of the Devil's Backbone. The most intriguing is the Train Wreck, a Civil War-era barge that sank here carrying a steam locomotive.

Good news for those headed to Current Cut and Train Wreck is that most visiting divers to Eleuthera head to the reef off the eastern shore near Harbour Island. Groupers and jacks, as well as a huge field of high coral ridges, can be found at the Plateau. Grouper Hole is the place to be on the first full moon of January, when mass amounts of groupers arrive here to spawn. If spotting grunts and barracudas is the order of the day, head to The Arch, a massive underwater grotto that slopes from 65 feet to more than 100 feet beneath the surface.

Romora Bay Club

P.O. Box EL27146
Colebrook Street
Harbour Island, Eleuthera
☎ *(809) 333-2323/5, (800) 327-8286*
FAX (809) 333-2500
Lessons, rentals and dive trips. Scubameister Jeff Cox will be your host. One of the most knowledgeable instructors and divemasters in The Bahamas, he's been here for 15 years. If you're lucky you'll get a chance to see his pair of yellow labs go skin diving as well. They're so good at it, a video was shot of them. They leave most of the human variety of scuba divers in awe. Guided scuba trips at $25 per tank. Snorkelers can tag along for $15 (if permitted) or form their own groups at the same price. Night dives are $36 per tank. A lesson with a half-day dive costs $65. Dive packages are available.

Valentine's Dive Center

P.O. Box 1
Harbour Island, Eleuthera
☎ *(800) 383-6480, (809) 333-2309, (502) 897-6481*
FAX (502) 897-6486
Lessons, rentals and dive trips. Single-tank dives cost $30, two tanks for $55. Night dives cost $45 per person with four-person minimum. Lessons range from introductory to full certification ($350). Half-day snorkeling trips costs $25 per person. Underwater cameras rent for $25 a day and $15 for a half-day. Full range of dive services. Dive packages available.

Boating and Sportfishing

At many of the resorts on the island you'll be able to charter or rent boats for bonefishing, reef fishing, bottom fishing and deep-sea fishing. Bonefishing and bottom fishing rentals run about $75 a half-day. Reef fishing costs about $20 per hour and deep-sea fishing ranges from $300–$650 per day.

Romora Bay Club

P.O. Box EL27146
Colebrook Street
Harbour Island, Eleuthera
☎ *(809) 333-2323/5, (800) 327-8286; FAX (809) 333-2500*
Boston Whalers and Sunfish sailboats for rent; deep-sea fishing charters.

Valentine's Dive Center

P.O. Box 1

Harbour Island, Eleuthera

☎ *(800) 383-6480, (809) 333-2309, (502) 897-6481; FAX (502) 897-6486*

Totally rebuilt (after Hurricane Andrew) 40-slip marina with all the amenities. Charters and rentals available, as well as small boat rentals.

Coral Sands Hotel

Chapel Street

P.O. Box 23

Harbour Island

☎ *(809) 333-2350, (800) 468-2799; FAX (809) 333-2368*

Boat and equipment rentals; bonefish, bottom fishing and deep-sea fishing charters.

Golf

Cotton Bay Club

Rock Sound

☎ *(809) 334-6101*

This 18-hole, 7068-yard, par-72 course remained opened after the Cotton Bay Club resort closed down, and we're glad it did, because, at $40 for 18 holes (including cart) it may be the best golfing bargain in The Bahamas. Lessons available (free clinic); pro shop, 19th hole, bar, snack bar, showers and lockers.

Tennis

Tennis courts can be found at most of the resorts, and these are the only places you'll find them. The **Club Med** at Governor's Harbor *(☎ [809] 332-2270)* has the most courts with eight, but real enthusiasts say the best court to be found on the island is at the **Coral Sands** *(☎ [809] 333-2350)*, which features professional night lighting. Guests are rarely charged for using the courts at their resort, but outsiders will be, if even permitted to use them.

Water-skiing/Windsurfing

Club Med Eleuthera

Box 80

Governor's Harbor

☎ *(809) 332-2270; FAX (809) 332-2855*

Water-skiing and windsurfing.

Valentine's Yacht Club

P.O. Box 1

Harbour Island, Eleuthera

☎ *(800) 383-6480, (809) 333-2309, (502) 897-6481; FAX (502) 897-6486*

Water-skiing and windsurfing.

Romora Bay Club

P.O. Box EL27146

Colebrook St.

Harbour Island, Eleuthera

☎ *(809) 333-2323/5, (800) 327-8286; FAX (809) 333-2500*

Windsurfing.

Directory

Transportation

There are three airports on Eleuthera. North Eleuthera serves the north of the island as well as Harbour Island and Spanish Wells. Governor's Harbour Airport is in the center of Eleuthera and Rock Sound International Airport serves the southern portion of the island. All three airports are points of entry and flights from South Florida directly serve all three airports. Keep in mind when selecting an airport that Eleuthera is more than 100 miles long. A taxi ride from the airport in Rock Sound to Spanish Wells will cost more than $100. And there are no buses on the island.

From Florida, **American Eagle** (☎ *[800] 433-7300*) has daily flights from Miami to Governor's Harbour. From Fort Lauderdale, **Island Express** (☎ *[305] 359-0380*) and **USAir Express** (☎ *[800] 622-1015*) offer daily flights to Governor's Harbour. USAir Express also serves North Eleuthera daily from Fort Lauderdale. Daily flights to both North Eleuthera and Governor's Harbour from both Miami and Fort Lauderdale are offered by **Gulfstream Airlines** (☎ *[800] 992-8532*). **Bahamasair** serves all three airports daily from Nassau. It also flies to North Eleuthera from Miami daily. Schedules change so call for information.

Taxis can be had at all three airports. The typical cost for a ride from North Eleuthera to Spanish Wells and Harbour Island is $8–10, including water taxi fares.

A number of mailboats call on Eleuthera from Nassau's Potter's Cay Dock. The trips take between 5–7 hours and cost $20:

M/V Bahamas Daybreak II
> Leaves on Thursdays for North Eleuthera, including Spanish Wells, Harbour Island and the Bluff, returning Sunday.

M/V Current Pride
> Sails on Thursdays for Current Island, Lower Bogue and Upper Bogue, returning Tuesday.

M/V Harley & Charley
> Sails for central Eleuthera, Hatchet Bay and Governor's Harbour on Mondays, returning Tuesday.

M/V Bahamas Daybreak III
> Departs Mondays for south Eleuthera, including Davis Harbour and Rock Sound, returning Tuesday.

Taxis are the expensive way to get around the island if you're planning on doing some traveling around Eleuthera. They are not metered, but there are usually set rates for frequented destinations. The resorts will be able to get you a taxi, or try the following:

Big M Taxi Service
> *North Eleuthera*
> ☎ *(809) 333-2043*

Reggie's Taxi
> *North Eleuthera*
> ☎ *(809) 333-2116*

To get to Harbour Island from North Eleuthera, take a taxi ($4 per person) to the ferry dock, about a mile from the airport. The ferry to the island costs $4 per person. To get to Spanish Wells, take a taxi from the North Eleuthera airport to the ferry dock. Ferries run constantly to Spanish Wells. The cost is about $12 per person.

Car rentals are available on Eleuthera, and they make more sense than taxis if you're going to traverse the island. Keep in mind there are no national (American or Bahamian) rental companies operating on Eleuthera. So be careful what you get yourself into, and check the insurance carefully. Rentals range in the $60 day neighborhood, sometimes more.

Johnson's Garage

Harbour Island
☎ *(809) 333-4030*

Ross Garage and U-Drive-It Cars

Harbour Island
☎ *(809) 333-2122*

Johnson's Rentals

Governor's Harbour
☎ *(809) 332-2226*

Ronnie's Rent A Car

Cupid's Bay
Governor's Harbour
☎ *(809) 332-2307*

Hilton's Car Rentals

Palmetto Point
☎ *(809) 335-6241*

Cecil Cooper

Palmetto Point
☎ *(809) 332-1575*

Dingle Motor Service

King's Street
Rock Sound
☎ *(809) 334-2031*

Bicycles also make for a great way of getting around. On Harbour Island, contact Michael's Cycles in the Straw Market on Bay Street; ☎ *(809) 333-2384.*

Emergencies

Harbour Island Medical Clinic

Dunmore Town, Harbour Island
☎ *(809) 333-2227*

Governor's Harbour Medical Clinic

Queen's Highway
Governor's Harbour
☎ *(809) 332-2001, 332-2774 for the dentist*
There's also a dentist here.

Rock Sound Medical Clinic

Rock Sound
☎ *(809) 334-2226*
One doctor and four nurses.

Spanish Wells Medical Clinic

Spanish Wells
☎ *(809) 333-4064*

Harbour Pharmacy Health Care & Prescription Service

Harbour Island
☎ *(809) 333-2174*
Over-the-counter and prescription drugs. Open daily 7:30 a.m.–
10:30 p.m.

Police

Governor's Harbour
☎ *(809) 332-2111*
Harbour Island
☎ *(809) 333-2111*
Spanish Wells
☎ *(809) 333-4030*
Rock Sound
☎ *(809) 334-2244*

Post Offices

Governor's Harbour Post Office

Haynes Avenue
Governor's Harbour
☎ *(809) 332-2060*

Banks and Moneychangers

Barclays Bank

Queen's Highway
P.O. Box 22
Governor's Harbour
☎ *(809) 332-2300*
Open Mon.–Thurs. 9:30 a.m.–3 p.m. and Fri. 9:30 a.m.–5 p.m.

Royal Bank of Canada

Near the city dock
Harbour Island
☎ *(809) 333-2250*
Open Mon.–Thurs. 9:30 a.m.–3 p.m. and Fri. 9:30 a.m.–5 p.m.

THE EXUMAS

St. Andrew's Church, George Town, Exuma

From the air, the Exumas appear to be a giant serpent slithering through crystalline waters. They start a mere 35 miles southeast of Nassau and, like stepping stones, extend in a straight line 90 miles south to Great Exuma, the chain's largest island and the site of the largest settlement, George Town. George Town is a tranquil island capital of 900 people and was once in the running for being named the capital of The Bahamas due to its superb natural harbor.

The Exumas are known for the great diving and fishing found off their shores (notably in the Exuma Cays National Land and Sea Park), and for the few people who visit the islands. That's right; not a lot of people visit the Exumas, and that explains why the 3700 or so islanders are so friendly. In few places in The Bahamas will you see people who are so genuinely excited to see strangers. But in the winter, it's not unusual to find scores of yachts moored in magnificent 15-mile-long Elizabeth Harbor at George Town, scene of the Annual Family Island Regatta, which attracts dozens of the most luxurious yachts found in the world.

269

Let the Good Times Rolle

Exumians are some of the friendliest folks in The Bahamas; and that's saying a lot. You'll notice their unabashed charm and hospitality. And you'll instantly notice that most of them are named Rolle. Even the towns are named Rolle. There's a Rolle Town, a Rolleville, you name it. Call it one big happy family.

In the late 18th century, a fortunate Briton, Denys Rolle, was awarded 7000 acres of Exumas real estate on Great Exuma. He brought in cotton and slaves and went to work. His son, Lord John Rolle, followed in his pop's footsteps and eventually oversaw a "community" of some 325 slaves, working on five plantations: in Rolle Town, Rolleville, Ramsey, Mt. Thompson and Streventon.

Whether it's based in truth or not, the locals will tell you that the plantations failed miserably and, when the emancipation of slaves became imminent, John Rolle deeded all his land holdings to his slaves, setting them free. They all took their master's surname and lived happily ever after.

Others tell a different version of events. The actual deed has never been located, and John Rolle wrote in his will a few years after emancipation in 1834 requesting that all of his Bahamian land be sold. Regardless, the former slaves were able to hold on to the land through the years, and even to this day, it is not clear actually to whom the land belongs.

As Rolle's land was given to the slaves as a group, as the islanders have historically contended, no single person could claim ownership. And even if one could, he'd have a lot of opposition—as everyone is named Rolle. Instead of fighting over the land, the Exumians on Great Exuma coexist quite peacefully, heeding the words that can be found in one of the island's bars: "Rest awhile, live longer."

Great Exuma possesses miles of pristine white sand beaches, as does Little Exuma and Stocking Island, a long, thin barrier island off the coast of George Town in Elizabeth Harbour. And, of course, there is the spectacular Exuma Cays National Land and Sea Park, with its beautiful sea gardens and coral reefs.

Fishermen will want to hit the flats on the western side of Great Exuma for the superb bonefishing. Deep-sea types will be impressed with the waters off all sides of Great Exuma, known for their abundance of billfish, including wahoo, sailfish and marlin.

The principal resort in the Exumas is the Club Peace & Plenty in George Town on the water. This was a former sponge warehouse before being converted into a hotel around 1950. Today, it makes for a scenic base for both scuba diving and fishing.

The Tropic of Cancer slices directly through George Town, a cozy little burgh, whose streets are virtually deserted on most days. The majestic government administration building, modeled after Government House in Nassau, dominates the quaint downtown buildingscape. No one bothers with street names here, but there are places to resupply if you're on a yacht. And

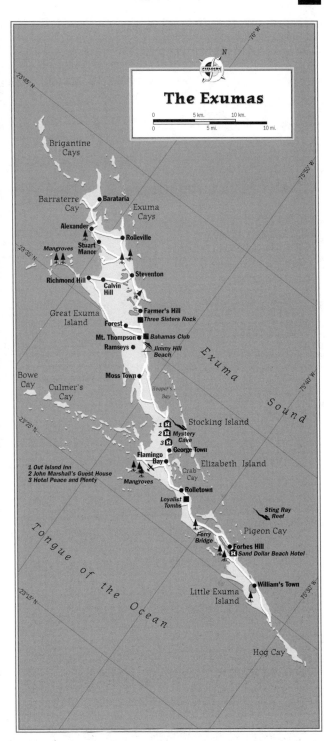

The Exumas

0   5 km.   10 km.
0   5 mi.   10 mi.

Brigantine
Cays

Barraterre
Cay
• Barataria

Exuma
Cays

Alexander •
• Rolleville

Mangroves
Stuart
Manor

Richmond Hill •
Calvin
Hill
• Steventon

Great Exuma
Island
• Farmer's Hill
Three Sisters Rock

Forest

Mt. Thompson • Bahamas Club

Ramseys •
Jimmy Hill
Beach

Bowe
Cay

Culmer's
Cay

Moss Town •

Hooper's
Bay

Exuma   Sound

1 Out Island Inn
2 John Marshall's Guest House
3 Hotel Peace and Plenty

1
2 Mystery
3   Cave

Stocking Island

George Town

Flamingo
Bay

Elizabeth Island

Crab
Cay

Mangroves

Rolletown •

Loyalist
Tombs

Sting Ray
Reef

Pigeon Cay

Ferry
Bridge

Forbes Hill
Sand Dollar Beach Hotel

Tongue of the Ocean

Little Exuma
Island
• William's Town

Hog Cay

those supplies were needed when film crews were in the Exumas shooting the James Bond movies *Thunderball* and *Never Say Never Again*, as well as the Tom Hanks hit *Splash*. Actually, it was at Staniel Cay, north of Great Exuma, where the movies were filmed. Staniel Cay is famed for the clarity and hues of its waters, as well as some magnificent limestone formations, particularly Thunderball Grotto (named after the famous movie), poking from the calm sea off Staniel Cay.

What to See and Do in the Exumas

Snorkeling in Exuma Land & Sea Park

Northern Exuma Cays

Exuma Cays Land and Sea Park   ★ ★ ★

Northern Exuma Cays

Designated a National Park in 1958, this area, about an hour's ride aboard a large powerboat from Staniel Cay, was chosen because of its diversity of land formations (from limestone to mangrove) and its seemingly unlimited varieties of marine life. Accessible only by water, this rambling government-protected land and sea park is one of the most magnificent underwater environments in all of The Bahamas.

The park is maintained and kept running by volunteers and donations, despite that it's run by the government. Students and others come here from abroad to donate their time cleaning the beaches, maintaining the moorings, doing electrical, carpentry and plumbing work, and to provide data entry into the park's computers. Others help by donating money or equipment, such as computers, two-way radios, medical supplies and solar panels, as well as other odds and ends.

Protected as it is, it is now illegal to fish here, as it is to remove coral or any underwater objects and animals. Fortunately, the boys in Nassau protected the place before there was even a hint of environmental damage due to the follies of man. Consequently, the park is in pristine condition. (A few of the islands are privately owned, but aside from a few houses, there has been no development of the cays in the park.) Underwater visibility is virtually unlimited—200 feet on its clearest days. The park claims one of the largest stands of rare pillar coral in

THE EXUMAS

The Bahamas. The park is about 22 miles long and eight miles wide and blessed with miles of deserted beaches, myriad dive and snorkeling sites, marked hiking trails and the remnants of original Loyalist settlements, which can be found on Warderick Wells and Hawksbill Cay. All kinds of wildlife can be observed in the region, including osprey, bananaquits, terns, large iguanas, hawksbill turtles, giant groupers, lemon sharks, crawfish and tropical.

There are marked trails on a number of the small uninhabited cays that poke from the azure sea like electric green lily pads. Superb walks can be done on Hawksbill Cay, Hall's Pond or Warderick Wells, considered by many to be one of the most idyllic islets in The Bahamas. On Shroud Cay, you can climb the hill for magnificent views of both sides of the cay, its excellent beaches on one side and mangrove swamps on the other. At Camp Driftwood, there's a surging current that will carry you to a sandy beach after rounding an outcropping. It's a fabulous ride.

The park's office is located at Warderick Wells; it's where the warden lives, and it's here where you can obtain brochures and printed information about the park and its rules. There's a small library here with a collection of writings about the area as well as a book exchange and a souvenir shop.

Thunderball Grotto ★★★

Off Staniel Cay

The name was given to this unusual grotto as it was used as a setting for two James Bond movies as well as the film *Splash*. In a rocky islet facing the Staniel Cay Yacht Club is this amazing cavern. There is superb snorkeling here as sunlight splashes through holes in the temple-like ceiling of the cave. The light shafts carve the salt air and strike the gin-clear water like a laser. All types of fish, including snapper, parrotfish, queen angels and trumpetfish are found just beneath the surface. It's almost a surreal experience, like an animated canvas on which has been splashed a "motion picture." Dive trips call on the grotto, and you can swim and snorkel here at low tide. It's possible at high tide, but a lengthy underwater swim is necessary to reach the main cavern, so it's not recommended for all but the most in-shape swimmers—and fins are recommended, as well.

Great Exuma Area

Stocking Island ★★★

Across from George Town

This long, narrow island, with three hills in the center, is in the sound off George Town. There are only a few residents here on this seven-mile long island, and because Club Peace & Plenty has no beach of its own, it leases a tract of Stocking Island and provides the ferry there (free to hotel guests; $8 round trip for others) for beach activities, including some superb shelling. There are plenty of secluded areas on the beach and decent bonefishing from right off the pier where the ferry docks. Ask the ferry operator to take you to the southern end of the island to Sand Dollar Beach. A few bucks should be enough to get him to stray from his route down to this beautiful area for swimming out to Elizabeth Island. Divers head straight for Mystery Cave, a 400-foot-deep blue hole teeming with undersea creatures.

St. Andrew's Church ★

George Town

Whitewashed St. Andrew's Anglican Church and its graveyard rest on a small hill across from the Government House. The church, with its distinct blue doors, was built about 1802. Service here on Sunday gives you a great glimpse on how the islanders live and worship. At the rear of the church is Lake Victoria.

The Hermitage ★

Jimmy Hill, down a narrow road off Queen's Highway

The Hermitage, about eight miles from George Town, is a former 19th-century slave plantation that has been converted into a private home. You can see the remnants of the slave quarters close by. Three tombs of slavemasters are found next to the grave of one of their servants. Because the former plantation is technically private property, it may be wise to get permission first before visiting the grounds. A friendly local may also volunteer as a "guide."

Rolle Town & the Rolle Town Tombs ★

Rolle Town

Fruit, such as tamarind, mangoes, bananas, soursop and sugar apple, contribute to the local economy of this small settlement about five miles south of George Town. There is a path that leads to a palm grove and Elizabeth Harbour. At a clearing, you'll discover three tombs of different sizes. The largest looks something like a queen-sized bed, complete with a headboard and footboard. There's a plaque here made of marble, and inscribed into it are the words: "Within this tomb lie interred the body of Ann M. Kay the wife of Alexander M. Kay who departed this life the 8th of November 1792 aged 26 years and their infant child." Ann M. Kay was the wife of an overseer during the slavery years.

Patience House and the Shark Lady of the Exumas

Born in 1917, the Shark Lady of the Exumas is a little old lady septuagenarian with a shock of white hair born Gloria Patience, of Irish and Scottish stock. But she happens to be one of the most prolific shark hunters in the seven seas. First, she traveled around the world, then returned to The Bahamas to raise nine children. She later moved to Little Exuma and started earning a living catching sharks. More than 2000 sharks have met their demise on one of Gloria's hooks: makos, lemon tips, hammerheads and others—most weighing hundreds of pounds. The Shark Lady doesn't need any help. She wrestles the beasts aboard her boat herself. What the lure of tourism dollars will do to people. She turns the spines and teeth into jewelry and sells or eats the meat. Every bit of the shark is utilized. Jaws and other skeletal parts are turned into wall hangings, paper weights or table ornaments. Just what the Brody family would want to decorate the Amity home with.

She turned her home into a jaws boutique, with a mish-mash of shark jewelry, antique china and glassware, sea fans, gold-plated sand dollars, driftwood and paintings by her husband.

Little Exuma

Williamstown Great Salt Pond ★

Williamstown, Little Exuma

This is one of the sites that is a testament to the booming salt industry of days past in the Exumas. To get a superb view of the old salt marsh, there is a small rise marked by a single concrete column. Here is where the best view is found, overlooking the entire salt pond.

Where to Stay in the Exumas

George Town

Coconut Cove Hotel **$80–$155** ★★★

P. O. Box EX-29299, George Town, Exuma
☎ *(800) 688-4752 U.S., (809) 336-2659; FAX (809) 336-2658*
Single: $80–$135; Double: $100–$155

One mile west of George Town, this 10-room hotel offers stylish living combined with tropical landscaping. Snorkeling and diving opportunities are excellent, plus there's a freshwater swimming pool on the beach front. The restaurant serves fresh seafood and gourmet concoctions—casual by day, formal by night—and the bar will prepare your favorite exotic cocktail. Accommodations have TVs, tile floors, minibars, bright quilts, bathrobes, and ocean views. Amenities: swimming pool, restaurant, bar, minibars. Credit cards: MC, V.

Club Peace and Plenty **$90–$150** ★★★

P. O. Box 29055, George Town, Exuma
☎ *(800) 525-2210 US., (809) 336-2551; FAX (809) 336-2093*
Single: $90–$150; Double: $90–$150

This former warehouse and private home was turned into a hotel in the late 1940s, and ever since has claimed fame as the island's unofficial favorite hideaway. Set on blooming and landscaped grounds, facing Stocking Island and fronting Elizabeth Harbour, the two-story pink property holds court to the yachting crowd (Prince Philip, among them), as well as bonefishing enthusiasts. Other activities include sailing, boating, diving, snorkeling and windsurfing. One of the two bars—a former slave kitchen—features nautical memorabilia and a lively crowd, while indoor/outdoor dining centers around Bahamian, American and continental cuisine. Accommodations feature stylish island decor and water-view balconies. Amenities: swimming pool, dining room, two bars. Credit cards: AE, MC, V.

Peace and Plenty Beach Inn **$100–$135** ★★★

P. O. Box 29055, George Town, Exuma
☎ *(800) 525-2210 U.S., (809) 336-2250; FAX (809) 336-2093*
Single: $100–$135; Double: $100–$135

About a mile west of Club Peace and Plenty, this newer sibling (opened in 1991) fronts the white-sand beach and colorful harbour. A free shuttle operates between the two properties for guests who want the whole Peace-and-Plenty treatment. The restaurant and bar provide a great waterfront setting, as do the spacious accommodations, with tile floors, TVs, and balconies. Amenities: swimming pool, restaurant, bar. Credit cards: AE, MC, V.

Three Sisters Beach Club **$90–$115** ★★★

P. O. Box 29196, George Town, Exuma
☎ *(809) 358-4040; FAX (809) 358-4043*
Single: $90–$115; Double: $90–$115

Isolated on a glorious long, white beach, a couple of miles north of the airport, this motel-like property features newly renovated rooms with simple furnishings, TVs and terrific sea views. The open-beam dining room, also with great views, serves both Bahamian and American dishes, and on Friday nights there's usually live music. A swimming pool and lighted tennis court are on-site, bicycles are available, and fishing excursions can be arranged—for any other sport (such as snorkeling), bring your own equipment. Amenities: swimming pool, lighted tennis court, bicycles, restaurant, bar. Credit cards: MC, V.

Regatta Point $105–$140   ★★

P. O. Box 29006, Regatta Point, Kidd Cove, George Town, Exuma
☎ *(800) 310-8124 U.S., (809) 336-2206; FAX (809) 336-2046*
Single: $105–$140; Double: $105–$140
Situated on a cay overlooking Elizabeth Harbour, across the causeway from George Town, this five-unit apartment complex has a small beach and a cool view. The efficiency units are nicely furnished, have fully equipped kitchens, high ceilings and breezy porches. Bicycles and Sunfish are on hand for guests' use, and restaurants and shops are nearby. Credit cards: MC, V.

Two Turtles Inn   ★

P. O. Box 29251, Main Street, George Town, Exuma
☎ *(809) 336-2545; FAX (809) 336-2528*
Single: $70–$90; Double: $70–$90
Well-situated, opposite the village green and overlooking Elizabeth Harbour, this two-story hotel is built around a courtyard graced with a fantastic Norfolk pine tree. This spot is primarily known for its restaurant and bar, popular with locals who descend for barbecues and happy hours. The beach is a few miles away and water sports can be arranged through the other hotels in the area. The simply furnished rooms have wood paneling, satellite TV and balconies. Amenities: restaurant, bar. Credit cards: MC, V.

Where to Eat in the Exumas

Gourmet cuisine, as well as picnic baskets and special dietary needs are catered for at the **Coconut Cove Hotel** restaurant. **Club Peace and Plenty** also offers elegant continental dining. Other dining choices include the Peace and Plenty Beach Inn, Sam's Place at the Exuma dock, and **Ruth's Deli** in George Town. Good American and Bahamian meals are served at **Three Sisters Beach Club**, though its location north of the airport is a bit isolated. The **Sunshine Bar** at Two Turtles Inn is a local favorite for its Tuesday and Friday night barbecues. You might try **Towne Cafe** in George Town, behind Marshall's complex. With prior notice, visiting yachties are welcome to sup with their brethren at **Stanley Cay Yacht Club**.

Nightlife in the Exumas

Club Peace & Plenty

Queen's Highway
P.O. Box 29055
George Town, Great Exuma
☎ *(809) 336-2551, (800) 525-2210; FAX (809) 336-2093*
There are a couple of cocktail lounges here, but it's the poolside, with its live calypso music and cocktails, that keep nighttime revelers busy here.

Cousin's

George Town
Great Exuma
This is where the overflow spills from the Peace & Plenty during the later hours.

Eddie's Edgewater

George Town
Great Exuma
☎ *(809) 336-2050*
The bar gets rather busy at this little restaurant on the weekends.

Gordy's Palace

Gray's Ville, William Town
Little Exuma
To mix with the locals, come to this hopping bar/restaurant on Friday or Saturday nights, when it actually transforms itself from a shack into a disco.

Royal Entertainer Lounge

Happy People Marina
Staniel Cay
☎ *(809) 355-2008*
A party out in the middle of nowhere. Music played by locals two times a week at this lively watering hole at the marina.

Tino's Lounge

George Town
Great Exuma
Quiet most of the time, but does a late-night set. And it doesn't close until the last person staggers out.

Sports in the Exumas

Scuba Diving/Snorkeling

Beautiful, pristine diving can be found at The Exuma Cays Land and Sea Park. The underwater park covers 177 square miles and has been protected from fishing, coral collecting and trapping since 1958.

The two best dives in the Exumas are perhaps the Coral Cut, with its sensational mile-long underwater tidal ride, and the Shark Encounter off Danger Cay. Here can be found a slew of both Nurse Sharks and Caribbean reef sharks. Close to Great Exuma's George Town can be found a couple of nice ocean blue holes, Crab Cay Crevasse, which opens at 20 feet, and the spectacular Angelfish Blue Hole. It starts at 30 feet and dips to below 90 feet. It then becomes an extensive cave network. Also close by is The Pagoda. No, it's not an ancient Buddhist temple caught in the wrong oceanic stream, but is named after a cathedral-like grotto covered by multiple corals. Also from George Town, accessible are the spur and groove coral formations and the Pillar Coral colonies of Dog and Puppy Reef.

Also, near Highbourne Cay, check out the wreck of the *Edwin Williams*, a Bahamian naval vessel that was sunk intentionally in 55 feet of water. At Blacktip Wall are found Blacktip Sharks and large eagle rays lurking in the wall's spacious caves. Hammerhead Gulch is popular for its gray angelfish.

Exuma Fantasea

P.O. Box 29261
Queen's Highway
George Town, Exuma

☎ (800) 760-0700, (809) 336-3483; FAX (809) 336-3483

This is one of the most comprehensive and knowledgeable dive outfits in The Bahamas. You'll get more than simply air from these folks. Dives include lessons and anecdotes in the ecological and topographical make-up and history of the dive sites, as well as local lore and tales from yesteryear. The center offers "specialty" dives (i.e., night dives, underwater photography) and "eco" dives to give divers an even clearer picture of what their seeing before and after they've seen it. Prices vary, but single-tank dives run about $50 and two-tank dives about $80. There is PADI instruction, with the resort course running at $90. Also offered are full certification courses. The center possesses a couple of dive boats as well as a number of customer-operated Boston Whalers which rent for about $100 a day for an 18-footer and $75 for a 17-footer.

Sportfishing/Boating

Game fishermen flock to the Exuma Sound for deep-sea fishing and to the west coast for bonefishing the flats. Most recreational boaters head for the protected Exuma Cays Land and Sea Park (which stretches south from Wax Cay to Conch Cay). The park is more than 20 miles long (177 square miles) and is northwest of Staniel Cay. It makes for superb bird-watching, not to mention the magnificent sea gardens and coral reefs.

George Town transforms from a sleepy little backwater into the French Quarter of New Orleans each April, when it hosts the Out Islands Regatta, perhaps the most popular yachting spectacle of the year in The Bahamas. The streets fill with revelers and Junkanoo parades, and everyone pretty much gets whipped on rum concoctions as contestants battle it out on the low seas in locally made wooden sailing vessels. The hotels are "packed" during this three-day festival, which also features arts & crafts exhibitions. There is also the Annual New Year's Day Cruising Regatta at the Staniel Cay Yacht Club in January and the two Bonefish Bonanza Tournaments held in October and November off George Town. Also at Staniel Cay is an annual bonefishing festival on July 10.

In George Town, facilities include **Club Peace & Plenty** (☎ *[809] 336-2552)* and **Exuma Fantasea** (☎ *[809] 336-3483)* for bonefishing, **Exuma Docking Services** (☎ *[809] 336-2578)* and **Sampson Cay Colony** (☎ *[809] 325-8864)*. On Staniel Cay, facilities include the **Staniel Cay Yacht Club** (☎ *[809] 355-2024)* and **Happy People Marina** (☎ *[809] 355-2008)*.

Kayaking

Ibis Tours

> *Boynton Beach, FL*
> ☎ *(800) 525-9411*
> A great way to explore the Exuma cays is on this eight-person kayaking outing, where you'll paddle/sail by day and spend the nights under the stars for eight days. Most of the trip is centered on the attractions of the Exuma Cays Land and Sea Park. You'll island-hop and have plenty of time for exploring inaccessible caves, tiny cays and for snorkeling and swimming.

Shopping in the Exumas

Straw Market, Georgetown, Exuma

Arts and Crafts

The Sandpiper

Queen's Highway
George Town
☎ *(809) 336-2084*
Across from the Club Peace & Plenty, this shop has a decent selection of straw goods. There are also other odds and ends, including cameras, arts & crafts and silk-screened fashions.

Staniel Cay Straw Market

Staniel Cay
Pleasant little market offering straw baskets, hats and handbags, as well as other slightly unusual offerings.

Batik

Peace & Plenty Boutique

Queen's Highway
George Town
☎ *(809) 336-2551*
Women (usually) come here for the Androsian batik, while men (usually) flock for the fishing equipment.

Directory

Transportation

By air, **American Eagle** (☎ *[800] 433-7300*) flies direct from Miami daily to Exuma International Airport (on Great Exuma Island, just under 10 miles from George Town), as does **Gulfstream Airlines** (☎ *[800] 992-8532*). **Island Express** (☎ *[305] 359-0380*) serves George Town from

Fort Lauderdale, with flights Thursday-Sunday. **Bahamasair** *(☎ [800]) 222-4262)* flies daily from Nassau to George Town. Call for current schedules—they change. There is also a 3000-foot airstrip on Little Staniel Cay; however, this is for the use of private aircraft dropping off American homeowners on the island. There are no scheduled commercial flights here at press time, but flights can be arranged through Island Express. The airport at George Town is an official point of entry.

The island's few taxis are available at the George Town Airport; the ride into town costs about $25 and is usually shared. If you're going solo, the driver will often not leave until there's another customer.

By mailboat, the *M/V Grand Master* leaves Nassau's Potter's Cay Dock on Tuesdays for George Town and returns Friday. The trip takes about 15 hours depending on the conditions and costs between $25–$40. The *M/V Lady Francis* departs from Nassau for Staniel Cay, Farmers Cay, Black Point and Baraterre on Tuesdays, returning Saturday. To Staniel Cay takes about 8 hours and costs about $25. For the latest schedules contact the dockmaster at **Staniel Cay** *(☎ [809] 393-1064)*.

Hotels are able to arrange taxis if you want to set out exploring the island, or you can call **Kermit's Airport Lounge** *(☎ [809] 345-0002)* or Luther Rolle Taxi Service *(☎ [809] 345-5003)*.

Rental cars are available at **BGS Auto Rentals** *(☎ [809] 336-2122)*, **Club Peace & Plenty** *(☎ [809] 336-2551)* and **Exuma Transport** *(☎ [809] 336-2101)*. Rental cars generally cost $60 a day, or about $300 per week. Some of the hotels offer mopeds and bicycles for rent. Expect exorbitant prices.

Emergencies

George Town Medical Clinic

George Town
☎ *(809) 336-2088*
There is a doctor and a nurse at this government clinic.

Police

George Town
☎ *(809) 336-2666 or 919*

Customs Office

Bahamian Customs

Exuma International Airport
☎ *(809) 345-0071*

Banks and Moneychangers

Bank of Nova Scotia

Queen's Highway
George Town
☎ *(809) 336-2651*
Open from 9 a.m.–1 p.m. weekdays, and also from 3–5 p.m. on Fridays.

Religious Services

Baptist

St. John's Baptist Church
Queen's Highway
George Town
☎ *(809) 336-2513*

CAT ISLAND

The Hermitage, Cat Island

Cat Island, 130 miles southeast of Nassau, is about as far off the beaten track as you can get and still have a decent resort to go home to at night. About 50 miles long and an average of two miles wide, this island is said to have been visited by Columbus, but no one's quite sure.

It seems people aren't quite sure about a lot on this remote rock, including how the island got its name. Some say it was named because of its shape: somewhat like a cat from the air—if you imagine real hard and are on drugs. The other story, equally as probable and a little more romantic, says it was named after the pirate Arthur Catt, who was around the same time as Black-beard, a.k.a. Edward Teach. And as the name's origins are foggy, so is the island's history. As such, legends abound. Many say that a West Indian form of witchcraft—*obeah*—was practiced here. And everyone here certainly wants to believe that Columbus was greeted on this island by friendly Lucayan natives—and that it was the first Bahamian island where the explorer made landfall. There definitely are signs that the Arawaks once called Cat Island home, evidenced by the Arawak Indian Caves at Columbus Point.

About 2000 people live on Cat Island; one principal settlement is New Bight in the middle of the island. But most folks will be more familiar with Arthur's Town in the north, the hometown of actor Sidney Poitier.

Of course, there is both splendid fishing and diving in the waters off Cat Island, but its most unusual attraction is perhaps the Hermitage on Mt. Alvernia, an early 20th-century abbey hand-built by the island's most revered resident, the diminutive Father Jerome Hawes, the hermit Catholic priest who holed up here when he wasn't busy building churches. The dollhouse-sized abbey appears as if it were built for gremlins and hobbits. Inscribed in Father Jerome's tomb (he died in 1956) are the words: "Blessed are the dead who die in the Lord." Mt. Alvernai, at 206 feet, is the tallest point in The Bahamas.

The island is densely forested and has superb beaches, some of them pinkish in color. The joy is they're all absolutely deserted; the opportunities for bare-bunned bathing are numerous. This is one of the sleepiest islands in all The Bahamas; the only time it comes awake is for the annual three-day Cat Island Regatta.

What to See and Do on Cat Island

The Hermitage on Mt. Alvernia   ★ ★

Town of New Bight

Father Jerome Hawes built this curious abbey entirely by hand at the summit of Mt. Alvernia, at 206 feet the tallest point in The Bahamas, early in the 20th century. The Hermitage commands a sweeping view of Cat Island, taking in the Bight as well as Fernandez Bay to the north. The structure is a pint-size abbey with three tiny rooms that were used as living quarters, a miniature cloister and a round corner bell tower, all of gray native stone. The steps leading up to the summit were also carved by the priest, as well as the 14 Stations of the Cross. Father Jerome (who was also known as John Hawes) traveled the world before finally settling on Cat Island. He was a hermit priest— who converted to Roman Catholicism from Anglican—who lived until age 80 and died in 1956. Hawes was an extremely short man and this is what characterizes the abbey's odd architecture: it was built with only his diminutive size in mind. It looks more like a lair for hobbits than anything earthly. It is reached by turning off the main road at New Bight and following the dirt road to the foot of the rise next to the commissioner's office. A freestanding arch marks the beginning of the foot path up the hill. It is about a 15-minute hike to the top and to the abbey.

Deveaux Plantation   ★

Town of Port Howe

This old whitewashed plantation mansion was built for Colonel Andrew Deveaux by his slaves when he settled on Cat Island after being given thousands of the island's acres in reward for booting the Spaniards out of Nassau in 1783. Although the mansion was once

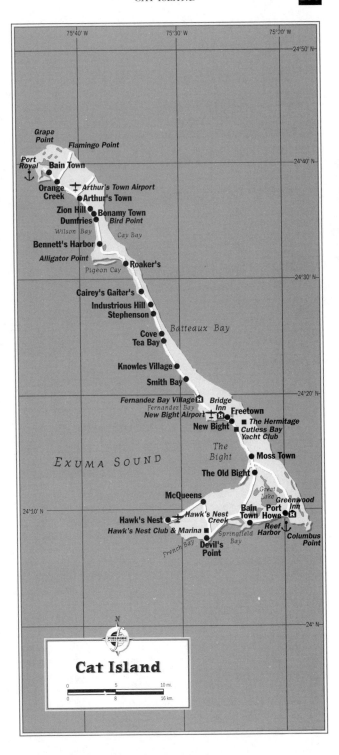

Cat Island

grand and hosted numerous balls and parties, it has been overrun with thick vegetation and now lies in ruins.

Armbrister Plantation   ★

Near Port Howe

This was also once a mighty cotton plantation, but neglect and the elements have taken even a greater toll than on the Deveaux Plantation. All that is left here are portions of crumbled walls and fences.

Richman Hill-Newfield Plantation

10 miles west of Columbus Point

This once-magnificent plantation covered a land area from the Great Lake to the sea, but is also now in a state of ruins. There is little left to see here today.

Fernandez Bay, Cat Island

Where to Stay on Cat Island

Bridge Inn $70–$95   ★ ★

New Bight, Cat Island

☎ *(800) 688-4752 U.S., (809) 342-3013; FAX (809) 342-3041*
Single: $70; Double: $80–$95

This casual, motel-ish inn is near the beach and family-run for family fun. Units, accommodating up to four persons, feature high ceilings, wood paneling and cable TV. Sign up for various watersport activities, or refuel on Bahamian and international dishes in the restaurant, or exotic drinks in the bar. Weekend jam sessions with local musicians are a special treat. Amenities: pool table, restaurant, bar. Credit cards: No credit cards.

Fernandez Bay Village $150–$210   ★ ★

New Bight, Cat Island

☎ *(800) 940-1905 U.S., (809) 342-3043; FAX (305) 474-4864*
Single: $150–$210; Double: $150–$210

On plantation land that's been in the same family since the late 1800s, this secluded and rustic property—a few miles north of New Bight—affords a heavenly escape-from-it-all retreat. The beach is exquisite, there's no charge to use bicycles and Zoom sailboats, and watersports and excursions are easily arranged. Meals (MAP included in tariff)—served either in the open-beam dining room or out on the beach terrace—usually consist of fresh catches for dinner, and buffet lunches.

Afterwards the clubhouse is the place to lounge lizard with other guests to watch videos, sit by the stone fireplace, or do some reading in the small library area. Eight beach-front villas feature kitchens, sea-view terraces, private gardens, and maid service. A general store, on premises, stocks most needed supplies. Amenities: dining room, bar. Credit cards: AE, MC, V.

Hotel Greenwood Inn   **$80–$100**   ★★★
Port Howe, Cat Island
☎ *(800) 343-0373 U.S., (809) 342-3053; FAX (809) 342-3053*
Single $80; Double $100
Stuck away on a glorious span of Atlantic coast, nearly an hour's drive from the airport, this resort features a dive shop and twice-daily dive outings on a 40-foot motorboat. Aside from that, guests can snorkel, fish, sail, dip in the pool or hang out at the clubhouse with its dining room, bar, lounge, and library nook. Renovated rooms have fresh decor and private terraces, and most feature ocean views. Amenities: swimming pool, dining room, bar, dive shop, bicycles. Credit cards: MC, V.

Where to Eat on Cat Island

Bahamian and International cuisine are served at the **Bridge Inn** restaurant, with barbecues scheduled on Friday nights. At **Fernandez Bay Village**, eat in the paneled dining room or out on the beach terrace with nightly Bahamian and continental buffet dinners. **Greenwood Beach Resort** also offers oceanfront dining, along with occasional buffet dinners. Pick up take-away treats at **McKinney Town Bakery**.

Nightlife on Cat Island

Nightlife on Cat Island is what you make it—for the most part. There's actually a disco here.

First and Last Chance Bar
Between New Bight and the New Bight Airport
A very laid-back local watering hole popular with the islanders. It sees some visitors once in a while who come in to admire—and purchase—the handiwork of Iva Thompson, the bar's proprietor. Her items made from straw are superb.

The Sailing Club
New Bight
The only night action on the island. On Saturday nights a local DJ spins disco and island tunes until late for the locals and a smattering of tourists.

Bridge Inn
New Bight, Cat Island
☎ *(809) 342-3013; FAX (809) 342-3041*
Friday nights sometimes see a gathering of local musicians strumming and banging out island music.

Sports on Cat Island
Scuba Diving/Snorkeling

Shrouds of fish can be seen at White Hole Reef. Sharks abound at Tartar Bank, where a spur-and-groove coral plateau strides an 8000-foot-tall pinnacle. A giant wall starts at 80 feet at Big Winding Bay, featuring massive Black Coral trees, tube sponges and beautiful gorgonians. Swim-through tunnels can be found at Tiger Shark Spot and fields of Acropora coral can be viewed only a few feet from the surface at Elkhorn Gardens.

Bridge Inn

New Bight, Cat Island
☎ *(809) 342-3013; FAX (809) 342-3041*
Scuba and snorkeling activities arranged.

Cat Island Dive Center

Hotel Greenwood Inn
Port Howe, Cat Island
☎ *(809) 342-3053, (800) 661-3483; FAX (809) 342-3053*
The center maintains a 40-foot dive boat for dive trips of up to 20 divers at a time (with its own equipment). Twice-daily dives. Resort instruction is available.

Fernandez Bay Village

3 miles north of New Bight
Cat Island
☎ *(800) 940-1905, (809) 354-5043; FAX (809) 354-5051*
Scuba and snorkeling facilities and equipment. Resort instruction available.

Sportfishing/Boating

Surprisingly, there are few yachting facilities available at the island's resorts. Although Fernandez Bay Village has no marina, it is the most visited of the resorts by boaters, who moor in the waters offshore, taking advantage of the general store here to stock up on supplies. Nearby Smith Bay makes for a superb natural harbor, and often boats seek shelter here during storms. There are also fishing trips and boating excursions organized at the resort, as they are at the Greenwood Beach Resort.

Water-skiing

Fernandez Bay Village

3 miles north of New Bight
Cat Island
☎ *(800) 940-1905, (809) 354-5043; FAX (809) 354-5051*

Paddle Tennis

Fernandez Bay Village

3 miles north of New Bight
Cat Island
☎ *(800) 940-1905, (809) 354-5043; FAX (809) 354-5051*

Directory

Transportation

There are two airports on Cat Island, the airport at Arthur's Town and the airstrip at New Bight. By air, there are no direct commercial flights to Cat Island from the United States **Bahamasair** *(☎ [800] 222-4262)* flies into the two airports twice weekly from Nassau. The New Bight area is home to most of the accommodations.

There is no taxi service on Cat Island, but by making arrangements beforehand, you can be picked up at the airport by your hotel. Few travelers arrive on Cat Island by air without previously arranged accommodations. If you haven't booked a hotel and simply want to take a chance on the room and board, hitchhiking is an easy way to get up and down the island, or ask for a ride at the airport. Someone is bound to be going your way, as there's only one road on the entire island.

By mailboat, the *M/V Hauler* leaves Potter's Cay Dock in Nassau for Bluff and Smith Bay on Tuesdays, returning on Sunday. The fare is $35 and the trip takes 10 hours or so. The *North Cat Island Special* departs from Nassau's Potter's Cay Dock for Bennett's Town and Arthur's Town on Tuesdays, returning from the 14-hour trip on Thursday. The trip costs $35. Contact the dockmaster *(☎ [809] 393-1064)* at Potter's Cay for updated information.

Oddly enough, car rentals are available on the island. Contact **Russell Brothers** *(☎ [809] 342-3014)*—sometimes called Jason's Car Rental—at the New Bight Service Station (the Bridge Inn) in New Bight, but expect to pay an arm and a leg—at least $85 a day.

Emergencies

There are three medical clinics on Cat Island, all three with very limited services and medical supplies. Should you be seriously sick or injured, your hotel will have to arrange for evacuation to Nassau or Miami.

Telephone Service

Telephone service is all but nonexistent on Cat Island. Hotels are virtually the only sources of telephones and faxes.

LONG ISLAND

Cape Santa Maria, Long Island

Long Island, about 70 miles long and 1.5 miles wide and located 150 miles southeast of Nassau, is another of the Bahamian islands of which not a lot is known of its past—although there may not be a lot to know. Many historians believe that it is the third Bahamian isle Columbus set foot on. This was the island that the explorer had named Fernandina, after King Ferdinand of Spain.

Loyalists fleeing the newly independent United States of America (specifically from the Carolinas and Virginia) settled Long Island in the late 18th century. They brought their slaves with them and started large cotton plantations. However, after the emancipation of the slaves in 1834, the plantation owners abandoned their holdings and left their former slaves behind., who eked out a marginal living from the soil and sea until the island was "discovered" by the tourist industry in the late 1960s.

Today, about 3500 people call Long Island home, some of whom are employed by the Diamond Crystal Company, a large salt concern. Although most of the islanders live near the island's mid-point at Deadman's Cay, Stella Maris and the northern tip of Long Island are the destinations for tourists.

This area is home to the Stella Maris Resort Club, one of the best dive operations in The Bahamas. The club also has its own airstrip, marina, shopping mall, bank and post office, making it perhaps the most self-contained resort complex in the Family Islands. Deadman's Cay itself remains pretty quiet for most of the year, picking up only with the annual Long Island Regatta in June. Then comes four days of sailboat races and partying.

Cliffs at Columbus Monument, Long Island

What to See and Do on Long Island

Dunmore's Cave ★

Deadman's Cay

These caves were used by pirates as hiding places for cargo and the fruits of their pillaging and plundering. Earlier it is believed that they were inhabited or at least utilized by Arawak Indians.

Dunmore Plantation ★

Deadman's Cay

This was the estate and plantation of Lord Dunmore, an early Bahamian governor. He had a number of landholdings. This one, however, has fallen into ruins. All that remains are the six gateposts at the entrance and the ruins of the house's fireplace.

Deadman's Cay Caves ★

Deadman's Cay

Still yielding discoveries and as yet to be entirely explored, these caves possess fine stalactites and stalagmites and feature Indian drawings on the walls. One of the caves eventually funnels out into the ocean.

Clarence Town and Father Jerome's Churches ★

Clarence Town

Clarence Town is the most scenic hamlet on the island, with its harbor and quaint buildings. Father Jerome Hawes, the revered Cat Island Catholic priest who converted from Anglicanism, built two marvelous churches in this town. St. Peter's Church was built after his conversion and St. Paul's Church, which was constructed while Father Jerome was known as John Hawes and was an Anglican. He also hand-constructed the Hermitage on Cat Island. Both Clarence Town

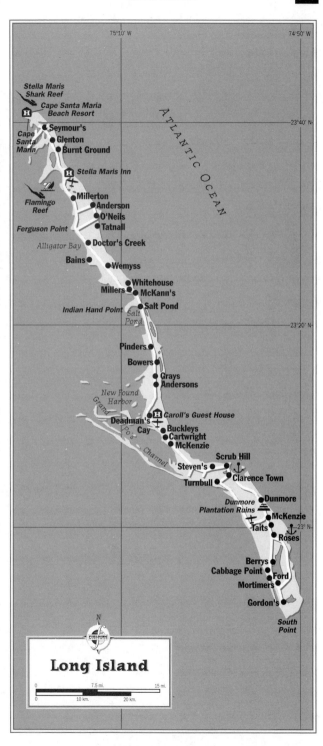

Long Island

churches owe a debt to the architects of the early Spanish churches built in Mexico and California.

Conception Island ★★

Off the town of Stella Maris

This is small island off the northeast coast, protected by The Bahamas National Trust, that's become a magnet for divers. Stella Maris trips often come out here. Being protected, the island offers a safe haven for green turtles and migrating and tropical birds.

Grays Plantation

Grays

There are the ruins of a couple of houses here at this former cotton plantation; one of them with the two chimneys intact.

Adderley Plantation ★

Off Cape Santa Maria, near Stella Maris Inn

This was once a magnificent plantation mansion, but has since fallen into decay. You can still make out the chimney of the manor house as well as the cedar door and window frames. There are three buildings here that are partially intact, minus their roofs. If you don't mind braving the thick vegetation while exploring the property, you'll come upon a burial ground for slaves near the beach and the ruins of the additional structures on the plantation's grounds.

Columbus Point ★

North of Stella Maris

For a little exploring, take the dirt road near the bridge to Newton Cay out to Columbus Point, where the views of the ocean from atop a rocky hill are excellent. You'll pass a good snorkeling site at a small cove. There's a small monument on the top of the cliff that reads: "This monument is dedicated to the Gentle Peaceful and Happy Aboriginal People of Long Island, the Lucayans, and to the Arrival of Christopher Columbus on October 17, 1492."

Where to Stay on Long Island

Stella Maris Inn $95–$260   ★★★

P.O. Box 30105, Ocean View Drive, Long Island
☎ *(800) 426-0466 U.S., (809) 338-2051; FAX (809) 359-8238*
Single: $95–$130; Double: $110–$260

The international set (and particularly Germans) tend to favor this sprawling resort overlooking the Atlantic coast. Emphasis here is on scuba diving and fishing expeditions (including bonefishing), but tennis, water-skiing and other water sports are also available. The superb diving facilities include a saltwater training tank. Guests have use of bicycles and sailboats, three freshwater swimming pools, and can sign up for a variety of land and water excursions. An informal dining room serves continental and Bahamian dishes, and there are plenty of specialty dinners, barbecues, theme parties and other events to keep you entertained at night. Accommodations consist of an array of rooms, studios, apartments and cottages—all have ocean views and most have an rattan furnishings, tile floors and pink accents. Amenities: three swimming pools, dining room, bar, lounge, marina, two tennis courts, bicycles, boating. Credit cards: AE, DC, MC, V.

Cape Santa Maria Beach Resort   **$185–$210**   ★ ★ ★

Cape Santa Maria, Long Island
☎ *(800) 663-7090 U.S., (809) 357-1006; FAX (809) 357-1006*
Single: $185–$210; Double: $185–$210

Located on an unspoiled powdery-white beach near the northern tip of the island, this 12-room luxury resort is composed of a clubhouse and six cottages. The fresh catch of the day is usually the featured menu item in the dining room, and the bar will concoct your perfect tropical cocktail. The large oceanfront cottages feature tasteful decor, marble-tiled floors, rattan furnishings, writing desks, dressing rooms and screened porches. Fishing, snorkeling, sailing and swimming are the routine-away-from-routine. Amenities: restaurant, bar, bicycles. Credit cards: AE, MC, V.

Where to Eat on Long Island

You'll be eating with the other international visitors at the **Stella Maris Resort Club** dining room, unless you're cooking in your own kitchenette or plucking snacks from a mini-fridge. Occasional barbecues, theme dinners, and rum-punch parties alleviate boredom. For more scrumptious cuisine, opt for **Cape Santa Maria Beach Resort** and its excellent clubhouse dining room.

Nightlife on Long Island

Nightlife is confined to the island's few resorts; the most is happening at the **Stella Maris Resort Club**. The resort throws its wild cave parties every week, filled with music and a lot of drinking, as guests boogie the night away in a torch-lit grotto. And the resort is always throwing some kind of rum punch shindig. Whenever you wake up in the morning without recollection of the previous evening's activities, they are classified as nightlife.

Sports on Long Island

Long Island offers a variety of reef and fishing trips.

Scuba Diving/Snorkeling

Virtually all who dive here do it through the Stella Maris megaresort, which sits on 3000 acres and even has its own 4050-foot runway. The resort is best known for introducing The Bahamas' first shark dive in 1973. The best beaches are found in the north on and near Cape Santa Maria.

Of course, most divers here visit Shark Reef, where the shark dive was developed. Divemasters today continue the practice of feeding Caribbean reef sharks into a frenzy. At Barracuda Reefs, the groupers outnumber the barracudas as they do at Grouper Valley. Stella Maris also offers day and overnight trips to Conception Island, which is known for its wrecks. One of the better dives off Long Island is the wreck of the *Comberbach*, a 125-foot freighter that stands upright at 100 feet deep.

Stella Maris Resort

> P.O. Box LI30105
> Stella Maris, Long Island
> ☎ (800) 426-0466, (809) 336-2106, (809) 338-2051;
> FAX (809) 338-2052
> U.S. Office
> 1100 Lee Wagener Boulevard, Suite 319
> Fort Lauderdale, FL 33315
> ☎ (800) 426-0466, (954) 359-8236; FAX (954) 359-8238
> The resort specializes in diving, so it's no surprise that the facilities are full-service and state-of-the-art. There's even a saltwater training tank at the marina. Dives are offered to all sorts of attractions, including coral reefs and heads and drop-offs. Dive trips daily head for the east coast around Rum Cay and Conception Island, the north and Long Island's protected west coast.

Other Activities

The Stella Maris Resort is basically your one-stop sports center on Long Island. The resort offers both reef and bottom fishing trips, and trips to the area's three fantastic bonefishing bays.

Water-skiing is offered through the resort, as is sailing (aboard 12-foot Scorpions and Sunfish, free to guests). Tennis is played on the resort's two hard courts, and bicycles are available for exploring the surroundings. Boaters can take advantage of the resort's full-service marina.

The only other offerings are available through:

Cape Santa Maria Beach Resort

> Cape Santa Maria
> ☎ (809) 357-1006; FAX (809) 357-1006
> This ultra-lux resort offers snorkeling, boating, fishing, windsurfing and bicycling.

Directory

Transportation

Long Island has two airports: one at Stella Maris in the north of the island, and the other at Deadman's Cay in the center of the island. The resorts are centered in the north, around Stella Maris and Cape Santa Maria. Keep that in mind when selecting your airport. If you're staying in the north and land at Deadman's Cay Airport, expect a $100 taxi ride on a bumpy road to your destination. By air, **Island Express** (☎ [305] 359-0380) flies directly to Stella Maris Airport from Fort Lauderdale Thursday-Sunday. **Bahamasair** (☎ [800] 222-4262) usually flies daily from Nassau to Stella Maris and then connects with Deadman's Cay. Call to make sure. Charter flight service is operated by the **Stella Maris Resort Club** (☎ [305]

359-8236, [800] 426-0466, [809] 336-2106), with flights to Stella Maris from Nassau and Exuma.

Taxis are always on hand for arriving flights at Stella Maris and usually on hand for incoming flights to Deadman's Cay. The fare from the Stella Maris Airport to the Stella Maris Resort is about $4. Or you can make arrangements with the resort to be picked up at the airport upon arrival.

By mailboat, the *M/V Mia Dean* from Potter's Cay Dock in Nassau maintains an irregular schedule to Stella Maris, Deadman's Cay and Salt Pond. Sometimes the service is once a week, sometimes every other week. The fare is about $50 and the journey takes 14 hours. The *M/V Ablin* travels to the south end of the island, stopping in Clarence Town, every week from Potter's Cay—usually on Tuesday. The cost is about $50 and the trip takes 18 hours or so, depending on the weather. For the latest schedules, contact the dockmaster's office on Potter Cay *(☎ [809] 393-1064)*.

Rental cars are available from the **Stella Maris Resort Club** *(☎ [809] 336-2106)*, but expect to pay about $85 a day.

Emergencies

Police

> *Clarence Town*
> ☎ *231, (809) 337-0444*

Police

> *Deadman's Cay*
> ☎ *(809) 337-0444*

Police

> *Simms*
> ☎ *(809) 338-8555*

Banks and Moneychangers

Bank of Nova Scotia

> *Stella Maris Resort Club*
> *P.O. Box LI 30105*
> *Ocean View Drive*
> *Long Island*
> ☎ *(809) 336-2106*
> Open Tuesdays and Thursdays 10 a.m.–2 p.m.

LONG ISLAND

SAN SALVADOR
(AND RUM CAY)

Dixon Hill Lighthouse, San Salvador

San Salvador, a mango-shaped cay covered with dozens of lakes about 200 miles southeast of Nassau, makes the most believable claim to have been the first landfall of Christopher Columbus' first journey to the New World. It's generally thought by most historians that Columbus first set foot in the New World near present-day Cockburn Town after having anchored in Fernandez. The explorer is said to have knelt on the sand and prayed, before claiming the island for Spain and enslaving the native Lucayans, who had peacefully inhabited Guanahani (as they called San Salvador) for at least 500 years.

San Salvador's claim to be Columbus' first landfall in the New World was disputed by a fastidiously researched 1986 *National Geographic* article by Joseph Judge, which pointed to Samana Cay, about 60 miles southeast of San Salvador, as the actual landing site of the *Nina*, *Pinta* and *Santa Maria*.

The probable truth of the matter is that we'll really never discover scientifically precisely where the ancient mariner set foot ashore, and as long as we don't, San Salvador continues to bask in its reputation as the start of the New World. What is known for sure is that the 17th century pirate George Watling used San Salvador as a hit-and-run base and built a shelter on the island, although it is unlikely that this structure was what is called Watling's Castle today. He changed the name of the island to Watling's Island, a name which appeared on maps and stood until 1926, when The Bahamas government officially reverted the name back to San Salvador, citing there was enough evidence (gathered namely by Columbus scholar and Catholic priest Father Chrysostomus Schreiner) showing the island to be the first landfall of Columbus.

Although the island is 60 square miles, it is composed of little land. There are numerous land-locked lakes; the largest of these, the Great Lake at 12 miles long, serves as the principal transportation link on the island.

Aside from the island's two resorts, Club Med and the Riding Rock Inn, the biggest attraction on San Salvador, literally, is the 165-foot tall Dixon Hill Lighthouse near Graham's Harbour on the northern tip of the island. It was built in the mid-19th century and its kerosene beacon can be seen for up to 19 miles at sea. It is one of the few remaining hand-operated, kerosene lamps in The Bahamas.

Columbus Monument, San Salvador

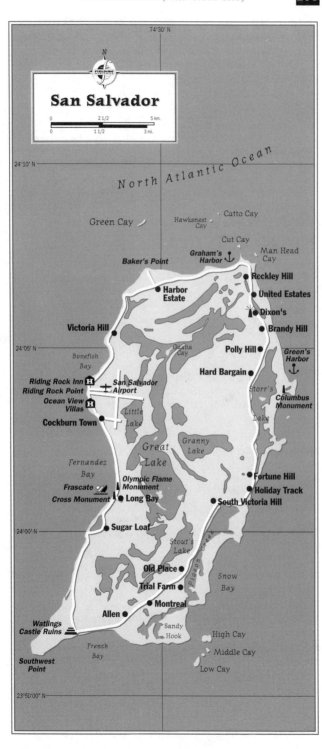

What to See and Do on San Salvador

Tappan Monument   ★ ★

Mile Marker #5, south of Cockburn Town

This is a small obelisk monument to Columbus (also called the Heloise Marker) that was erected February 25, 1951, on the beach at Fernandez Bay by the Tappan Gas Company.

Columbus Monument

Mile Marker #6

This is a simple white cross monument to the explorer that was erected in 1956 by Ruth Durlacher Wolper Malvin, a respected Columbus scholar and wife of the late Hollywood producer David Wolper. The monument is located at the spot where most scholars believe Columbus landed on the island. Yet another monument lies hidden here on the ocean floor and is said to be at the spot where the voyager dropped anchor.

Chicago Herald Monument

Mile Marker #24, Crab Cay, east coast

Yet another monument to the Spanish explorer, this fourth memorial, in a stunning research gaffe for a newspaper, was erected by the *Chicago Herald* in 1892. But it was erected in a spot where it would be almost physically impossible for Columbus to have landed, as the off-shore reef would make approaching extremely hazardous if not impossible without wrecking on the reef. But it certainly is a pretty spot. It's a little tough to get here. Turn off the main road, head out a mile to East Beach. Without a four-wheel-drive vehicle you'll have to get out and hoof it for the next two miles to where the sand path ends. There's a cave on the left at the beach and a path that cuts off to the right. You'll come upon the monument and its inscription, which reads: "On this spot Christopher Columbus first set foot upon the soil of the New World, erected by the *Chicago Herald*, June 1891."

Olympic Games Monument

Long Bay

In 1968, runners carrying the Olympic torch to Mexico took a jog around San Salvador, and, fittingly for this place, put up another memorial to Columbus. Soon, we may see the Great Western Memorial, the American Airlines Memorial or, perhaps more appropriately, the Taco Bell Memorial.

Observation Platform

Near Riding Rock Inn

There is a tall wooden tower about 2 miles from the Riding Rock Inn that affords a magnificent view of the island and its inland lakes. If you pass a junkyard of old rusted cars and trucks you know you're on the right path. At last check, the tower was in disrepair, but still climb-able, so use caution.

San Salvador Museum   ★

Next to the Catholic church, Cockburn Town

Here is a small two-story museum depicting the times of Columbus and the Lucayan Indians. The memorabilia and photos of the old plantations are housed in the island's former jail, which was converted into a museum in 1989 because there just wasn't anyone committing any crimes on San Salvador, or the cops were all asleep. Aside from the occasional drug runner, there hadn't been a prisoner behind bars here since 1967, which seems an awful waste of taxpayers' money. At least there wasn't an overcrowding problem. Arrange to visit the museum through Iris Fernander, the caretaker, who works in the nearby gift shop.

New World Museum ★
North Victoria Hill
Admission: $1
This one-room museum is owned by Columbus historian Ruth Durlacher Wolper Malvin and is part of the Polaris-by-the-Sea estate. When it's open (which it never is; you'll have to fetch someone with a key) you'll see displays of Lucayan Indian pottery and beads, whale bones and an alleged prehistoric skull. Located at Blackwood Rock Point Beach, it is 3.5 miles north of Riding Rock Inn.

Graham's Harbour ★
Northern San Salvador

Sharks pay regular visits to this scenic harbor on the northern hump of the island. Columbus reportedly visited here and is said to have remarked that the harbor was large enough to accommodate "all the ships in Christendome." Every Oct. 12, Discovery Day celebrations take place at this harbor—dinghy races, dances on the dock, kite flying, three-legged races. The Bahamian Field Station, a group of buildings next to the harbor, is a research center where biologists and geologists study the area. The best view of the harbor is from the old helo-pad.

Father Schreiner's Grave ★
Mile Marker #20, near Graham's Harbour
Father Chrysostomus Schreiner, in 1926, was instrumental in changing the name of the island from Watlings to San Salvador. The circular stone platform next to the grave is said to have been used as an auction stand and whipping post during the slavery period. There's a rocky path close to the mile marker; the grave is just up that path. Schreiner died in 1928 inside Cockburn Town's Catholic church. The church's bas relief depicting Columbus was also Schreiner's idea.

Dixon Hill Lighthouse ★★
Dixon Hill, northeast San Salvador
This is a magnificent 160-foot-tall lighthouse built around 1856, which still operates with a kerosene lamp and is still hand-operated by a lighthouse keeper who lives here. Every 15 seconds the snow-white lighthouse sends out a 400,000-candlepower beam that can be seen for 19 miles. There is a fantastic view of the nearby cays from the top, as well as the Chicago Herald Monument to Columbus. Knock on the door and the keeper will more than likely be happy to show you to the top. When leaving, you'll sign a guestbook filled with signatures going back years. A $1 donation is expected, and worth it.

East Beach ★★
Northeast coast
If you want to be transported to the beaches of New England, a trip to the northeast coast is worth it for this sea wheat-spiked, six-mile-long pink beach. Of course, the color of the sand and the many colors of the water will reinforce the fact that you're indeed in The Bahamas

and not in Massachusetts. There have been sightings of sharks in the area, so be warned if you plan on swimming or snorkeling.

Fortune Hill Plantation ★

Mile Marker #25, eastern San Salvador

Plantation owner Burton Williams grew cotton and lived here until 1794, and no one has since. A couple of buildings, though in ruins, are discernible here, namely Williams' study and the manor's outhouse, as well as the tall warehouse which was used for storing cotton. The estate can be reached by taking the rugged path near the mile marker.

Watling's Castle ★★

Mile Marker #9, Sandy Point Estate, Southern San Salvador.

Named after 17th-century buccaneer George Watling (San Salvador itself was once named Watling's Island in honor of the pirate), these vine-covered ruins were more than likely once the foundation for a Loyalist plantation, and not an actual pirate's castle. It is known that Henry Storr, San Salvador's only black plantation owner, lived here and maintained a large labor force of black slaves, as did his white counterparts at the time. The plantation was the last working one on the island, and wasn't abandoned until 1910. Still visible is the manor's cookhouse oven, some of the slaves' quarters and the stone walls around the property. From Queen's Highway, walk up the hill to rise overlooking the sea.

Farquharson's Plantation ★

Pigeon Creek

Charles Farquharson was once San Salvador's judge, and he maintained a large plantation on the eastern side of the island. There are some remnants of the manor house still visible, as well as some of the slaves' quarters. But the place has pretty much gone to the dogs.

Big Well

Sandy Point Estate

This is a 150-year-old freshwater well that can be found south of the Columbus monument at Long Bay.

Dripping Rock ★

Sandy Point

At the southern end of San Salvador are a number of limestone caverns. In this particular cave can be found a freshwater well.

Where to Stay on San Salvador

Club Med—Columbus Isle ★★★★★

San Salvador, the Bahamas
☎ *(800) 258-2633 U.S., (809) 331-2000; FAX (809) 331-2222*
$1050–$1700 per person, per week

Located two miles north of Cockburn Town, this 80-acre property fronting its own two-mile stretch of dreamy beach is touted to be Club Med's most luxurious resort—surrounded by about 1000 Florida-grown palms (to ward off erosion) and constructed around a huge color-of-the-sea, free-form swimming pool. The colorfully painted buildings are lavishly decorated with fine woods, high-end artwork, hand-crafted furnishings, quality tapestries and such that have been imported from all over the world. Guest accommodations are equally swank with tile floors, white walls, bright fabrics and quality artwork and furnishings. Each has a TV, telephone and private patio or balcony. Dining options consist of an Italian restaurant, a grill and a main dining room that specializes in buffets. A lounge, open-air theater and nightclub provide evening diversion, plus there's nightly dancing and live entertainment. This Club Med offers a comprehensive dive facility, 10 tennis courts, a fitness center, aerobics classes, windsurfing, kayaking and a plethora of other activities.Unlike the majority of Club Med properties, this one does not have special camps, schools and activities for children—the target market here is clearly well-heeled couples. In Club Med-style, the weekly tariff includes room, meals (with wine and beer), entertainment and almost all activities. Amenities: swimming pool, three restaurants, lounge, theater, nightclub, 10 tennis courts (three lighted), dive shop, fitness center, aerobics, car rentals, marina. Credit cards: AE, MC, V.

Riding Rock Inn $90–$135
Cockburn Town, San Salvador, the Bahamas
☎ *(800) 272-1492 U.S., (305) 359-8353 (Florida); FAX (305) 359-8254 (Florida)*
Single: $90; Double: $90–$135
The majority of guests at this unpretentious, motel-like inn are divers and underwater types who come to explore the great offshore reefs and take advantage of the diving package deals offered. Two buildings house a restaurant with Bahamian and American cuisine, a bar decorated in diving memorabilia, and a variety of guest rooms ranging from standard to deluxe. The deluxe rooms are a better option with newer decor, telephones, satellite TV and ocean views. Amenities: swimming pool, restaurant, bar, dock, dive center, bicycles. Credit cards: MC, V.

Where to Eat on San Salvador

You'll be feasting at the tres elegant **Club Med-Columbus Isle**, if you're a guest. Otherwise your choice is the Riding Rock Inn with an oceanfront restaurant offering American and Bahamian dishes (the conch chowder with bread is a lunchtime favorite).

Nightlife on San Salvador

Nightlife activities are primarily confined to the island's resorts, although we do recommend a visit to **Rum Cay's Kay's Bar** when the place is hosting parties. They can get to be a lot of fun as boaters off shore are lured into the action by the bar's VHF radio. It'll remind you a little of the CB craze back in the 1970s, or of the current Internet fad—you'll see what we mean.

Because the Club Med is specifically geared to adults, there's plenty of action to be found there. There's a dance hall behind one of the bars, and an open-air theater that can be hilarious some evenings when the staff GOs put on their routines using guests as the butt of jokes.

Sports on San Salvador
Scuba Diving/Snorkeling

If you're looking for shallow reefs, San Salvador will be a disappointment, as the island is the summit of a 13,000-foot underwater peak. But the visibility and wall diving are spectacular. Visibility is regularly at 200 feet. French Bay is the best place to head for clarity. Telephone Pole offers tame Nassau Groupers along a wall that begins in 35 feet of water. Snapshot Reef

Fielding THE BAHAMAS

Resorts of The Bahamas

As the Bahamas emerged in the 20th century, the island chain seemed to have shed its turmoil-laden past. By 1973, with the tourist industry in full swing, the Bahamas gained independence from England. Today, local resorts offer an abundance of activities for visitors, including diving, snorkeling and fishing. The hotels have all the amenities including swimming pools and fine restaurants.

West End

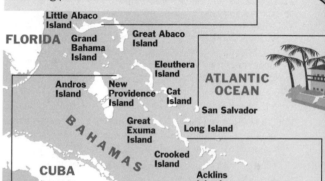

FLORIDA

Little Abaco Island

Grand Bahama Island

Great Abaco Island

Eleuthera Island

Andros Island

New Providence Island

Cat Island

ATLANTIC OCEAN

San Salvador

Great Exuma Island

Long Island

Crooked Island

CUBA

Acklins Island

BAHAMAS

British Colonial Beach Resort

The British Colonial Beach Resort is the island's oldest hotel and was built on top of historic Ft. Nassau. The hotel has 325 guest rooms, equipped with air conditioning, telephones and cable T.V. There are many nearby restaurants that serve traditional Caribbean cuisine, and the Island has a zoo and botanical gardens. For information call (800) 258-4786.

Salt Cay

Love Beach

Lyford Cay

Lake Killarney

St. Augustine's Monastery

Montagu Bay

Eastern Point

Bacardi Distillery

Adelaide Village

SAN SALVADOR (AND RUM CAY)

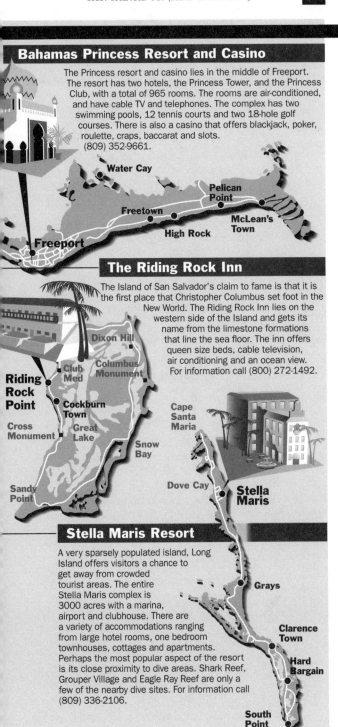

Bahamas Princess Resort and Casino

The Princess resort and casino lies in the middle of Freeport. The resort has two hotels, the Princess Tower, and the Princess Club, with a total of 965 rooms. The rooms are air-conditioned, and have cable TV and telephones. The complex has two swimming pools, 12 tennis courts and two 18-hole golf courses. There is also a casino that offers blackjack, poker, roulette, craps, baccarat and slots.
(809) 352-9661.

Water Cay

Pelican Point

Freetown

McLean's Town

High Rock

Freeport

The Riding Rock Inn

The Island of San Salvador's claim to fame is that it is the first place that Christopher Columbus set foot in the New World. The Riding Rock Inn lies on the western side of the Island and gets its name from the limestone formations that line the sea floor. The inn offers queen size beds, cable television, air conditioning and an ocean view. For information call (800) 272-1492.

Dixon Hill

Club Med

Columbus Monument

Riding Rock Point

Cockburn Town

Cape Santa Maria

Cross Monument

Great Lake

Snow Bay

Sandy Point

Dove Cay

Stella Maris

Stella Maris Resort

A very sparsely populated island, Long Island offers visitors a chance to get away from crowded tourist areas. The entire Stella Maris complex is 3000 acres with a marina, airport and clubhouse. There are a variety of accommodations ranging from large hotel rooms, one bedroom townhouses, cottages and apartments. Perhaps the most popular aspect of the resort is its close proximity to dive areas. Shark Reef, Grouper Village and Eagle Ray Reef are only a few of the nearby dive sites. For information call (809) 336-2106.

Grays

Clarence Town

Hard Bargain

South Point

and Macro Mania are the only shallow reefs of note, and the Frascate makes for about the only wreck diving. The Frascate was a 280-foot steamship that sank in1902. At only 20 feet deep, it offers a lot of bottom time.

Off French Bay, good wall dives are at Sandy Point, Double Caves, Devil's Claw, Dr. John and La Crevice. Here you'll see groupers, barracudas, eagle rays, scalloped hammerheads and horse-eye jacks, as well as beautiful formations of black corals, antler, rope and azure vase sponges.

Riding Rock Inn (Guanahani Dive Ltd.)

Cockburn Town
San Salvador
☎ *(809) 331-2631*
U.S. Office
1170 Lee Wagener Boulevard, Suite 103
Fort Lauderdale, FL 33315
☎ *(800) 272-1492, (954) 359-8353; FAX (954) 359-8254*

Virtually all of the inn's customers have come here to dive, so there are numerous dive packages. Apart from the packages, one-dive trips cost about $40, two-dive trips run at about $60, and three-dive trips cost about $75. The resort offers resort introductory courses for about $100, and full PADI certification can be had for about $475. There is also a fabulous underwater photography facility that rents cameras and even prepares slide shows with guests' photos. Snorkeling trips are available as well.

Club Med-Columbus Isle

2 miles north of Cockburn Town
San Salvador
☎ *(809) 331-2458, 331-2000; FAX (809) 331-2458, 331-2222*
40 W. 57th Street
New York, New York 10019
☎ *(800) 258-2633*

Here is the largest dive facility in the Club Med family. The club uses three 45-foot custom catamarans for its dive trips and even has a decompression chamber at the facilities. The club claims there are more than 40 magnificent dive sites within a 30 minutes of the shore. Even "kayak scuba diving" is offered here.

Boating and Fishing

Riding Rock Inn

Cockburn Town
San Salvador
☎ *(809) 331-2631*
U.S. Office
1170 Lee Wagener Boulevard, Suite 103
Fort Lauderdale, FL 33315
☎ *(800) 272-1492, (954) 359-8353; FAX (954) 359-8254*

Fishing trips are organized here.

Club Med-Columbus Isle

2 miles north of Cockburn Town
San Salvador
☎ *(809) 331-2458, 331-2000; FAX (809) 331-2458, 331-2222*
40 W. 57th Street
New York, New York 10019
☎ *(800) 258-2633*

The resort has an entire fleet of Hobie Cats and other sailing vessels at the disposal of guests.

Other Activities

Windsurfing and kayaking are offered at the Club Med. As well, there are 10 tennis courts here. The resort also organizes volleyball tournaments, guided bicycle tours and water aerobics.

Directory

Transportation

San Salvador's Cockburn Town Airport is on the west coast of the island. By air, **Bahamasair** *(☎ [800] 222-4262)* flies to Cockburn Town from Nassau every day of the week except for Tuesday and Saturday. **Club Med** *(☎ [800] CLUB-MED, [809] 331-2458)* flies charters to Cockburn Town from Miami and Eleuthera. **Riding Rock Inn** *(☎ [800] 272-1492, [809] 359-8353)* flies charter flights directly from Fort Lauderdale on Saturdays. Taxis meet incoming planes

By mailboat, the *M/V Maxine* departs from Nassau's Potter's Cay Dock on Tuesdays or Thursdays for Rum Cay and San Salvador. The *North Island Special* also leaves from Potter's Cay once a week. The trips take a whopping 18 hours. Contact the dockmaster at Potter Cay *(☎ [809] 393-1064)* for precise schedules and fares (which are usually around $40).

Although there is little use for them, car rentals can be had at the **Riding Rock Inn** *(☎ [809] 359-8353)* for about $85 a day. Bicycles rent for about $8 a day and are the best way to explore this small island.

Emergencies

San Salvador Medical Clinic
  ☎ *(809) 331-2105, 207*
  Limited staff, services, supplies and medicines. If you are seriously hurt or sick, you will have to be evacuated to Nassau.

Police
  ☎ *218, 919*

ACKLINS AND CROOKED ISLANDS

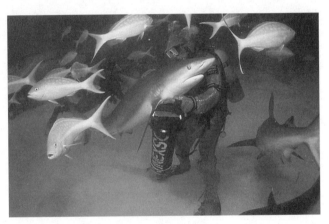

Diving is a favorite sport in The Bahamas

Christopher Columbus sailed the thin Crooked Island Passage between these two small islands located about 230 miles southeast of Nassau. The two islands once served as shelters for pirates attacking ships in the vulnerable channel.

But they weren't truly inhabited until the latter part of the 18th century, when Loyalists fleeing the newly formed United States brought their slaves with them and began cotton plantations. As hard to believe as it is considering the poor soil quality of the islands, there were as many as 40 working plantations on these islands, being worked by more than a thousand slaves. However, no amount of manpower in the world could get the crops to grow out of limestone, and the plantations started to die out in the early 19th century, finally collapsing altogether with the total emancipation of slaves in 1834.

Today, a mere 400 or so folks live on Acklins and Crooked islands, making a meager subsistence on fishing and some scant farming. Some of the former plantations can still be seen, although in ruins.

There are a couple of good resorts on the islands offering diving and other watersports diversion. Crooked Island is ringed by some 45 miles of barrier reef, dropping from 5 to 50 feet, and then to more than 3600 feet in the Crooked Island Passage. And the tarpon and bonefishing ranks with some of the best in The Bahamas.

What to See and Do on Acklins and Crooked Islands

Bird Rock Lighthouse ★

Crooked Island Passage

This is a magnificent, gleaming-white 115-foot-tall lighthouse that was built in 1872 overlooking the Crooked Island Passage. It is still a working lighthouse and is also a popular nesting spot for ospreys.

Crooked Island Caves ★

On Crooked Island can be found some decent caves for exploring, and guides can be arranged through Pittstown Point Landing. Some resemble the ruins of old castles with huge, sunlight-poked chambers and slithering tunnels, the walls of which have regrettably been etched with visitors' names. The Arawak Indians once dwelled in these caverns. Be careful of the bat droppings of the hundreds of these creatures who now make the caves their home.

French Wells Bay ★ ★ ★

Crooked Island

Here is a serene, pristine world of mangrove swamps rich in wildlife, including the many flamingos who come to rest and poke around on the bay's beaches. Not a lot of people get out this way, and you may have the world all to yourself, or seemingly. The water is bathtub clear and warm, and some good snorkeling can be done here. But pay close attention to reports of sharks sighted in the area.

Marine Farms Fortress ★

North end of Crooked Island Passage

This old British fort formerly guarded the Crooked Island Passage against pirates and other foes, and it was the scene of some fighting during the War of 1812. The ruins feature some old Spanish cannons and are protected by The Bahamas National Trust; they can be visited by making arrangements though your hotel.

Fortune Island

Off the coast of Crooked Island, south of Albert Town

This small island can be seen from 12 miles at sea. It got its name from the job-seeking Bahamians who would wait here in the years after World War I for freighters to pick them up for Central America. It is believed that Christopher Columbus named this island Isabella, after the Spanish queen at the time.

Castle Island

Southern end of Acklins Island

A lighthouse stands here that was built in 1867. This is a remote spit of sand south of Acklins Island that was used by pirates to hit ships and other vessels traveling through the Crooked Island Passage.

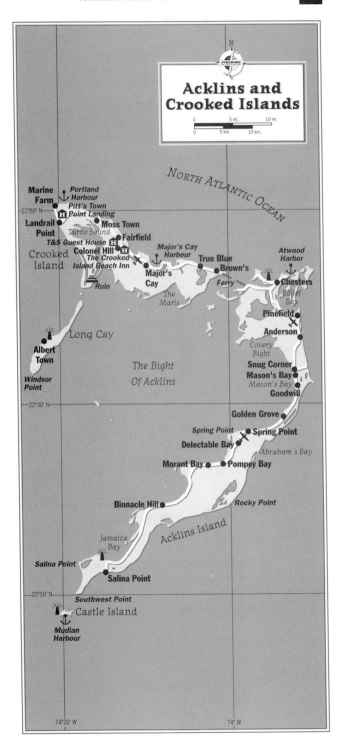

Acklins and Crooked Islands

Where to Stay on
Acklins and Crooked Islands

Caribe Bay   **$165–$220**   ★ ★ ★

Landrail Point, Crooked Island
☎ *(800) 752-2322 U.S., (809) 344-2507; FAX (809) 344-2507*
Single: $165; Double: $220

Located at the very northwestern tip of Crooked Island, this isolated
beach-front hotel (occasionally known as Pittstown Point Landings)
is a favorite with private-plane owners who can put down on the
2300-foot landing strip. Colonel Hill Airport, about 15 miles away,
serves those flying in on commercial craft from Nassau. Escapists are
inspired by the natural features here, including turquoise sea, scrub-
covered terrain, and miles of open beach area. A stone-sided building—dating from the mid-18th century—houses a dining room,
offering fresh seafood, American and Bahamian specialties. Meals are
included in the rates and, often, visiting yachties and fliers drop in as
well. Accommodations face the ocean (some sit right on the beach),
are breezy and functional. Divers need to provide their own gear.
Amenities: dining room, bar, lounge. Credit cards: MC, V.

Crooked Island Beach Inn   **$50–$60**   ★

Cabbage Hill, Crooked island
☎ *(809) 344-2321*
Single: $50; Double: $60

A few minutes north of the Colonel Hill Airport, this waterfront hotel
offers basic accommodations suited to those who don't place much
emphasis on furnishings and amenities. Arrange any meals desired in
advance with the Evangelical minister-owner. Credit cards: No credit cards.

Where to Eat on
Acklins and Crooked Islands

Guests at the all-inclusive **Caribe Bay** (also known as Pittstown Point
Landing), dine in a former naval barracks built in the 1600s. It's also a popular rendezvous for visiting yachties, aviators and local residents. Simple Bahamian dishes are offered at the minister-owned Crooked Island Beach Inn.

The Beaches of Acklins and
Crooked Islands

The beaches in the southwest of Crooked Island are among the best in
the Family Islands and are accessible only by boat. The best bathing beach
would have to be aptly-named Bathing Beach with large parcels of sandy,
rockless ocean floor. Just inland are some fresh water springs. Shell Beach is
where most snorkelers head, with its magnificent coral heads and gin-clear
water. Make arrangements at Pittstown Point Landing to get a boat out to
these beaches.

Sports on Acklins and Crooked Islands

There is some great diving to be found off the shores of Acklins and
Crooked Islands, namely in the 50 miles or so of barrier reefs which surround the islands, with some serious drop-offs from 50 to 3600 feet. The
problem is there aren't many facilities of any note to base your dive excursions. If coming to these islands for diving, it's best if you bring your own
equipment, except tanks and weights).

Caribe Bay (Pittstown Point Landings)
> Landrail Point, Crooked Island
> ☎ *(809) 344-2507; FAX (809) 344-2507*
> *300 Mariner's Plaza, Ste. 303*
> *Mandeville, LA 70448*
> ☎ *(800) 752-2322, (504) 624-3998; FAX (504) 624-9546*
> Diving trips available, but the resort only supplies a boat, tanks and
> weights. Snorkeling is also available, as is some boating.

Directory

Transportation

There are two airports on the islands: one in Spring Point on Acklins Island and the other in Colonel Hill on Crooked Island. There are no direct commercial flights from the U.S. to either airport. By air, **Bahamasair** (☎ *[800] 222-4262*) flies to Spring Point and Colonel Hill twice a week from Nassau. On Crooked Island, there will probably be a taxi or two waiting for passengers. But the best bet is to make arrangements with your hotel for transfer. There are few telephones available (and working) should you get into a jam.

By mailboat, the *M/V Lady Mathilda* or the *M/V Windward Express* leaves from Nassau's Potter's Cay Dock once a week for Acklins and Crooked Islands, with stops also at Mayaguana and Inagua. Call the dockmaster at Potter's Cay (☎ *[809] 393-1064*) for current schedules and fares. They change.

Between Acklins and Crooked Islands, a government-owned ferry service operates daily from 9 a.m.–4 p.m. The cost is about $5. The ferry runs between Lovely Bay on Acklins Island and the southeast tip of Crooked Island.

Emergencies

There are a couple of clinics on the islands, one at Chesters Bay and Spring Point on Acklins Island, another at Landrail Point on Crooked Island. There is a doctor who lives in Spring Point and nurses available in Masons Bay (Acklins) and Colonel Hill (Crooked). For the most part, no one can be reached by phone. Rather, the hotel can call the operator, who will summon assistance by radio. Any serious medical requirement will necessitate evacuation to Nassau.

Police
> *Crooked Island*
> ☎ *(809) 344-2197*

Banks and Money changers

Bring what you need with you. There aren't any ATMs—or banks for that matter—on either island.

MAYAGUANA

Soaking up the sun, Mayaguana

This small island (110 sq. miles; pop. 500) in the far south of The Bahamas chain is the only backpackers' destination in the entire country. And even so, only a smattering ever show up. A good reason why the Hair Club for Men set doesn't venture out here is because there isn't a gift shop at the airport, nor a liquor store at the marina, nor a marina—and nobody takes American Express or African Express or the Downtown Express, and there aren't any TVs to advertise the fact.

Instead, the few travelers who make it to this isolated, blistering rock in the sea just northwest of the Turks and Caicos Islands are Euro-Gauguin wannabes, guys and gals who like to lie around naked on the beach and commune with coconut trees while their art student buddies are freezing their family jewels off back in the Hague, Amsterdam and Munich. Tell someone you're going to Mayaguana and you'll no doubt be mistaken for either a physician with Doctors Without Borders or some guy who pedals a bicycle around Third-World snakeholes wearing a tie and some silly hockey helmet.

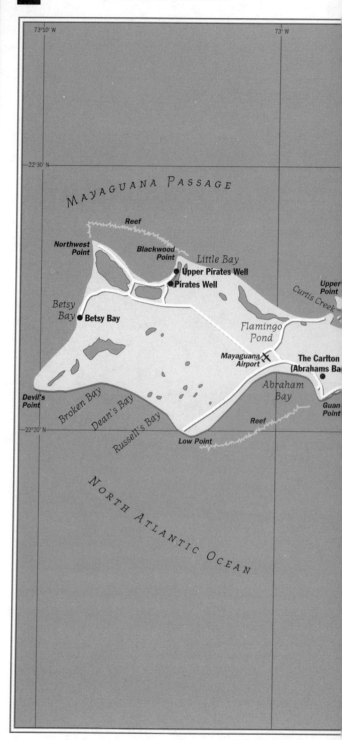

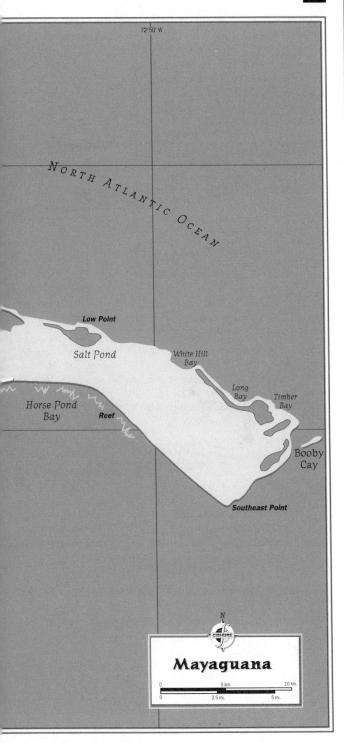

72°50' W

NORTH ATLANTIC OCEAN

Low Point

Salt Pond

White Hill Bay

Long Bay

Timber Bay

Horse Pond Bay

Reef

Booby Cay

Southeast Point

N

FIELDING

Mayaguana

0   5 km.   10 km.

0   2.5 mi.   5 mi.

The place wasn't even settled until the mid-19th century, when some locals from nearby Turks Island got rock fever and decided to head for the mainland, and mistakenly thought Mayaguana just might be it (hardly at 24 miles long and six miles wide at its widest point). Later, when he needed a new missile tracking station, Uncle Sam spun the globe with his eyes closed and, like pinning the donkey's tail, stopped it with a finger that happened to be pressing Mayaguana.

Where to Stay and Eat on Mayaguana

Most of the few people who get here sleep on the beach. You might try heading into Abraham's Bay, the largest settlement on the island. There, one of the locals might put you up and feed you. They're friendly folks, and you've got a good chance if you look any more presentable than Howard Stern. We recommend partially provisioning yourself if on a short stay or buying a fishing boat if on anything longer.

Directory

Transportation

Mayaguana cannot be directly reached from the United States via commercial air carriers. Instead, get to Nassau and catch a **Bahamasair** (☎ *[800] 222-4262*) flight to the lone airstrip (an on/off ramp actually) on the island. Flights, at last check, were three times a week.

But most who get down here do it by mailboat. Life is so painfully slow on Mayaguana, why be in a hurry to get here? The *M/V Lady Mathilda* stops at Mayaguana on its swing through Acklins and Crooked Islands. It departs from Potter's Cay Dock in Nassau on Wednesdays and returns Sunday. For fares and schedule information, contact the dockmaster's office at Potter's Cay (☎ *[809] 393-1064*).

Ragged Island

And if you thought Mayaguana was some asteroid that fell into the Atlantic, come to the Jumento Cays and Ragged Island, specks of exposed coral that see even fewer visitors than Mayaguana and aren't even on most maps of The Bahamas. We mention them here because there are actually a few people living on Ragged Island at a tiny outpost called Duncan Town, which can be reached by mailboat from Nassau.

Off the west coast of Long Island, the Jumento Cays run 100 miles south to Ragged Island. Once in a blue moon a yacht shows up, but usually only for shelter during a storm. There's a 3000-foot airstrip on the island, but no one uses it. And there are absolutely no tourist facilities. If you show up from aboard the mailboat *M/V Emmipt and Cephas* (it leaves Nassau's Potter's Cay Dock on Tuesdays, returning Thursday), expect to be treated like Ace Ventura. Call the dockmaster at Potter's Cay (☎ *[809] 393-1064*) for schedules and fares.

INAGUA

Flamingos at Inagua National Park

Great Inagua, about 40 miles long and 23 miles wide and located 325 miles southeast of Nassau, has two dramatic distinctions as a Bahamian island. First, it serves as the nesting grounds for more than 50,000 pink flamingos, and the few tourists who get down here come precisely for that reason—or to catch glimpses of Bahamian parrots, Great Herons, spoonbills, cormorants or any of the other hundred or so other species of bird life that either migrates through here or call this place home.

The second attraction is the unusual and visually striking salt works at the Morton Salt Company. Huge mountains of salt can be seen, as well the surreal-looking salt ponds. The company employs about a quarter of the island's 1200 or so people.

Other than seeing the birds and the salt, or just to plain get away from it all, there's not much to do on this the southernmost island of the Bahamas. Although it is the third-largest island in the Bahamas, there are only very marginal tourist facilities. One reason may be the beaches: there aren't many of them. There is virtually no rainfall on Great Inagua, and this leaves the landscape comparatively parched. Mature trees and plants rise little

more than a few feet above the ground. And the strong
tradewinds on the island are incessant. But on a clear day, and
there are many, one can climb the Matthew Town lighthouse
and barely see the mountain ridge silhouette of Cuba, a mere 50
miles away.

Great Inagua was first settled (Little Inagua is uninhabited) in
the early 1800s, but not by many. In fact, some records say only
a sole individual lived on the island in 1803. But it is said that the
self-proclaimed king of Haiti, Henri Christophe, built a palace
here during the first years of the 19th century. If true, there are
no physical traces of it on Great Inagua. The population steadily
increased through the 19th century, namely because of the salt
harvesting, and numbered some 1000 people by the 1870s, not
much different from today.

Uninhabited Little Inagua, just to the north of Great Inagua, is
about 40 square miles and sees an occasional fisherman or bird-
watcher. The terrain is also harsh, and not a lot of fun stomping
through. Inland can be found the only natural grove of royal
palms in the Bahamas. Rather than indigenous to the island, it's
thought that birds carried the seeds here from Hispaniola (or
Haiti).

What to See and Do on Inagua

Inagua National Park   ★ ★
23 miles from Matthew Town
This 287-square-mile land & sea park is maintained by the Bahamas
National Trust and is home to tens of thousands of pink flamingos,
which nest here around the first of March through May or June. The
park is also home to roseate spoonbills and other tropical birds. Driving out to the park from Matthew Town, you pass Lake Windsor,
which was once called Lake Rosa by the Spanish for the pinkish color
of the water (caused by the water's salt content). There are a couple
of cabins where you can stay here, with a cooking shed and two showers. But it's best to bring along your own sleeping bag and food. In
March or April, there's a large party here celebrating the nest count,
with usually about 10,000 counted each year. You can arrange for a
car through your hotel or the Inagua Trading Company in Matthew
Town. The cost is about $50 (plus tip for the driver) to see the fla-
mingos.

Morton Bahamas Salt Company   ★
Outside Matthew Town
Salt is the heart of the Inagua economy and Morton's salt crystal factory has been here since 1800, and in Morton's hands since 1934.
This is the largest of the company's solar salt production sites and you
can get a guided tour here to discover how the operation works and
to see the enormous mountains of salt, as well as the surreal-looking,
pinkish salt ponds. More than a million pounds of salt are produced
here each year. There are more than 2000 acres of salt ponds and
nearly 35,000 acres of reservoirs. To tour the facility, make prior
arrangements with either the Ministry of Tourism or the Family

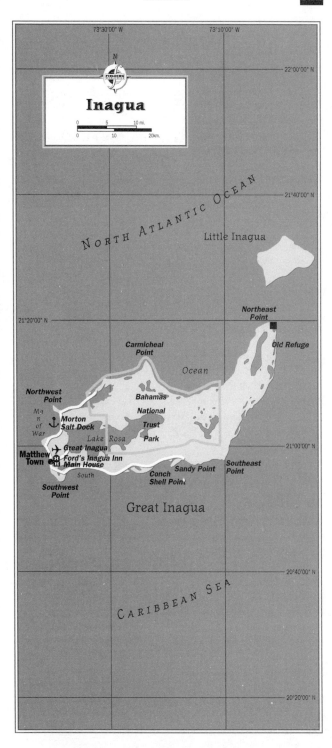

Island Promotion Board. Or call the company's operations office at
☎ *(809) 339-1300.*

Erickson Museum & Library ★

Northern edge of Matthew Town

This is a new museum recently opened by the Morton Salt Company
in the former home of its executive who arrived here to run the company's operations in 1934. The museum houses the relics of the history of Inagua and, of course, Morton's role in it.

Where to Stay on Inagua

Main House $45–$55 ★

Matthew Town, Inagua
☎ *(809) 339-1267*
Single: $45; Double: $55

This modest, two-story, green-and-white guest house (owned by the
Morton salt concern) is set in the center of town, just behind the grocery store. The casual dining room serves local dishes and fresh seafood. Guest rooms are large and clean with wood furnishings, shared
sitting areas, and only two have private baths. A good no-frills budget
choice. Amenities: dining room. Credit cards: No credit cards.

Walk-Inn Guest House $50–$60 ★

Gregory Street, Matthew Town, Inagua
☎ *(809) 339-1612*
Single: $50; Double: $60

This simple family-run, cinder-block guest house, just south of Matthew Town, offers a friendly environment for independent, budget
travelers. All rooms have private baths, TVs, and air conditioning. No
dining facilities are on the premises, but a cozy restaurant is nearby.
Credit cards: No credit cards.

Where to Eat on Inagua

Plan on a simple meal at the **Main House** dining room or over at the **Cozy
Corner Restaurant**, both in Matthew Town.

Nightlife on Inagua

Inagua has the kind of nightlife you'd expect in the remote Out Is-
lands—virtually nothing. But on the weekends it does pick up in Matthew
Town and environs. The bars to check out after the sun sets are the **Hide
Out Cafe** (which features a pool table and a dance hall), **Afterwork Bar &
Restaurant**, **Cozy Corner** (also with a pool table) and **Traveller's Rest** (pool
table), about 10 miles out of town.

Sports on Inagua

Few, if any, journey to Inagua for sporting activities, although if there
were facilities for scuba diving and boating they most assuredly would be
sought after. Rather the island's "resorts" cater more to the crowd that just
wants to get away from it all and relax. The hotels have no facilities for
boating or scuba diving, although snorkelers might be able to scrounge
some fins and a mask (we suggest you bring your own).

Most of the "sporting" activities on the island are confined to nature
walks and birdwatching, which can be arranged through **Great Inagua
Tours** (☎ *[809] 339-1204*) in Matthew Town. The **Bahamas National
Trust** on Great Inagua covers some 287 square miles and is home to more
than 50,000 pink flamingos as well as wild horses, boar and donkeys.

Directory

Transportation

The airport on Great Inagua is at Matthew Town. By air, there are no direct commercial flights from the United States to Inagua. **Bahamasair** (☎ *[800] 222-4262*) flies to Matthew Town Airport from Nassau on Mondays, Wednesdays and Fridays.

Virtually all travelers arriving by air to Inagua have prearranged accommodations, and it's best to make arrangements with the hotel for pickup at the airport. However, taxis do meet arriving flights. If you need a taxi during your stay on the island, arrange for it through the hotel or call ☎ *(809) 339-1284*.

By mailboat, the *M/V Lady Mathilda* (or the *M/V Windward Express*) calls on Matthew Town from Nassau's Potter's Cay Dock. Usually the boat departs Wednesday and returns Sunday after stops on Mayaguana, Acklins Island and Crooked Island. Contact the dockmaster at Potter's Cay (☎ *[809] 393-1064*) for the latest schedule and fares.

Car rentals are available through the **Inagua Trading Company** in Matthew Town. There is no phone number; there doesn't need to be.

Emergencies

Inagua Hospital
> *Matthew Town, Great Inagua*
> ☎ *(809) 339-1249*
> Very limited services, supplies and medicines. If seriously hurt or sick, you will have to be evacuated to Nassau.

Police
> *Matthew Town, Great Inagua*
> ☎ *(809) 339-1263*

Banks and Money changers

Bank of the Bahamas
> *Matthew Town, Great Inagua*
> Open Mon.–Thurs. 9:30 a.m.–2:30 p.m. and Fri. 10 a.m.–5:30 p.m.

Tour Operators

Great Inagua Tours
> *Matthew Town, Great Inagua*
> ☎ *(809) 339-1204; FAX (809) 339-1204*
> This small operation can handle car rentals and accommodations and arrange fishing trips. It also puts together hikes and wildlife walks, including birdwatching and flamingo-viewing trips. They also rent out a modest 4-bedroom house on the beach in the northwest of Great Inagua for about $150 a day.

CRUISING TO
THE BAHAMAS

Cruise ships bring hordes of tourists to The Bahamas.

Ships bound for the Bahamas invariably leave from Miami, Fort Lauderdale, West Palm Beach and Port Canaveral in Florida and sometimes from other ports, such as New York, San Juan and Los Angeles. An increasing number of ships depart Florida for three-day cruises (even single-day cruises!) to the Bahamas. These are primarily gambling and shopping junkets to Nassau and Freeport. Some of the short hops, such as those offered by Premier Cruise Lines on The Big Red Boat, are offered in conjunction with land tours, such as Disney World in Orlando.

The key to getting a good fare is to book early, as far in advance as possible. However, those deciding on a cruise on a whim may benefit in a late booking if the ship isn't full.

Some of the ships are highly regimented and activities, events and meals are carefully choreographed. Others offer a far less formal environment. For instance, Carnival Cruises attracts a younger, more budget-conscious crowd. The dress is casual and the pace relaxed and easy-going. Whereas Princess Cruises often requires formal dress for evening meals and other huffy establishment trappings. In other words, if you can't stand to wear a tie, these ships aren't for you. Our guide here to the ships that call on the Bahamas should make the selection process a lot easier.

CRUISE LINES THAT PROVIDE SERVICE TO THE BAHAMAS

Cruise Line	Destination	Passengers	Facilities	From
American Canadian Lines *P.O. Box 368* *Warren, RI 02885;* ☎ *(401) 247-0955, (800) 556-7450*				
New Shoreham II	Nassau	72		Caicos
Canaveral Cruise Line, Inc. *751 Third Avenue* *New Smyna Beach, FL 32169;* ☎ *(904) 427-6892*				
Dolphin IV	Nassau	588	OP, C	Miami
Carnival Cruise Line *3655 N.W. 87th Avenue* *Miami, FL 33166;* ☎ *(305) 599-2600*				
Fantasy	Nassau, Freeport	2044	3 OP, S, C, TK	Miami
Ecstasy	Freeport, Nassau	2044	3 OP, S, C, TK	Port Canaveral
Celebrity Cruises *5200 Blue Lagoon Drive* *Miami, FL 33126;* ☎ *(305) 262-8322, (800) 437-3111*				
Century	Nassau	1750	OP, TK, S, C	Fort Lauderdale
Chandris Fantasy Cruises *900 Third Avenue* *New York, NY 10022;* ☎ *(800) 621-3446*				
Britanis	Nassau	960	OP, C	Miami
Costa Cruises *80 S.W. 8th Street* *Miami, FL 33130;* ☎ *(305) 358-7325*				
CostaRomantica	Nassau	1356	OP, C, S	San Juan
CostaVictoria	Nassau	1928	OP, IP, C, S	Miami
Crown Cruise Lines *2790 N. Federal Highway* *Boca Raton, FL 33431;* ☎ *(800) 841-7447*				
Crown del Mar	Nassau	486	OP, C	Palm Beach
Dolphin Cruise Line *901 South American Way* *Miami, FL 33132;* ☎ *(305) 358-2111*				
OceanBreeze	Nassau	776	OP, C, S	Miami
SeaBreeze	Nassau	840	OP, C	Miami

CRUISE LINES THAT PROVIDE SERVICE TO THE BAHAMAS

Cruise Line	Destination	Passengers	Facilities	From
Holland America Lines, Westours				
300 Elliott Avenue West				
Seattle, WA 98119; ☎ *(206) 281-3535, (800) 426-0327*				
Westerdam	Nassau	1494	2 OP, S, C	Fort Lauderdale
Statendam	Nassau	1266	2 OP, S, C	Fort Lauderdale
Majesty Cruise Line				
901 South American Way				
Miami, FL 33132; ☎ *(305) 536-0000, (800) 532-7788*				
Royal Majesty	Nassau	1056	OP, S, C	Miami
Norwegian Cruise Line				
95 Merrick Way				
Coral Gables, Fl. 33134; ☎ *(305) 445-0866, (800) 327-7030*				
Dreamward	Pleasure Isle	1246	2 OP, C, S	Fort Lauderdale
Leeward	Nassau, Pleasure Isle	974	1P, 2 OP, C, CPh	Miami
Norway	Pleasure Isle	1864	1P, 2 OP, C, CPh	Miami
Princess Cruises				
10100 Santa Monica Boulevard				
Los Angeles, CA 90067; ☎ *(310) 553-1770, (800) LOVE-BOA(T)*				
Crown Princess	Nassau	1590	2 OP, C, S	Fort Lauderdale
Sky Princess	Nassau	1212	3 OP, C	Fort Lauderdale
Star Princess	Nassau	1490	3 OP, C, S	Fort Lauderdale
Premier Cruise Lines				
400 Challenger Road				
Cape Canaveral, FL 32920; ☎ *(407) 783-5061, (800) 327-7113*				
Star/Ship Atlantic	Nassau, Port Lucaya	1550	2 OP, IP, C, S	Port Canaveral
Star/Ship Oceanic	Nassau, Port Lucaya	1800	2 OP, C	Port Canaveral
Royal Caribbean Cruise Line				
1050 Caribbean Way				
Miami, FL 33132; ☎ *(305) 539-6000*				
Majesty of the Seas	Coco Cay	2744	OP, C, S, YC	Miami
Nordic Empress	Nassau	1610	2 OP, C, S	Miami
Sovereign of the Seas	Nassau, Freeport	2524	2 OP, S, C, YC	Miami

CRUISE LINES THAT PROVIDE SERVICE TO THE BAHAMAS

Cruise Line	Destination	Passengers	Facilities	From

SeaEscape, Ltd.
1080 Port Boulevard
Miami, FL 33132; ☎ *(800) 327-7400*

| | 1-day cruises Miami, Fort Lauderdale | | | Freeport |

Facilities Key

IP	Indoor Pool	YC	Youth Center
OP	Outdoor Pool	T	Theater
C	Casino	W	Whirlpool
CPh	Cashphone	TK	Track
S	Spa or Exercise Facilities		

CANAVERAL CRUISE LINE, INC.

751 Third Avenue, New Smyrna Beach, FL 32169
☎ *(904) 427-6892*

Stunning Bahamian sunsets are a treat for cruise passengers.

History ....

The *Dolphin IV* was purchased from Dolphin Cruise Line by Kosmas Shipping Corporation in July 1995, to be repositioned to Port Canaveral for two-day cruises to the Bahamas as part of a week-long Florida land/sea package. Kosmas named its new line Canaveral Cruise Line, Inc.

Dolphin IV

The ship, built in 1955 as the *Zion* for Zim Israel Line, was turned into the *Amelia de Mello* for Lisbon-Canary Islands service in 1966, laid up in 1971, sold to a Greek company in 1972 and renamed *Ithaca*, then sold again in 1979 to operate as the *Dolphin IV* under a joint agreement between Ulysses Cruise Line and Paquet. In 1984, Dolphin Cruise Line was formed to operate the vessel, which made three- and four-day cruises to the Bahamas out of Miami. At present, it makes short cruises from Port Canaveral to Grand Bahamas Island.

Cabins & Costs

Fantasy Suites: .... NA

N/A

Small Splurges: .... C-

Average Price PPPD: $238 cruise-only.

There are some modest suites on the ship, five of them on the top-most passenger deck and four of them on the deck below the major public areas. Suites 500 and 501 are rather cramped, with double beds against the wall on one side and a sofa, coffee table and closet so close together you have to clamber over the coffee table to put clothes in the closet or sit on the sofa. Suites 513 and 515 are a little larger, but the view is partly obstructed from hanging lifeboats. In all the suites, the sofa makes into a bed, but we can't imagine how it opens up—there's no room.

Suitable Standards: .... D

Average Price PPPD: $198 cruise-only.

Most of the cabins are just big enough for two lower beds, a dresser and bathroom with shower, but some also have upper berths.

Bottom Bunks: .... **D-**

Average Price PPPD: $105 cruise-only.

The lowest-priced are inside cabins with upper and lower berths, five of them deep down into the ship and forward, where the ride is bumpier.

Where She Goes

The vessel sails from Port Canaveral to Grand Bahamas Island on two-night cruises, sold as part of a land package that also includes three days in Orlando theme parks and two days at the beach.

The Bottom Line

It's a high-density ship with long lines for buffets, for teatime, or any other time food is set out. Still, it has a pleasing personality, and the large numbers of first-time cruisers aboard always seem to be having a wonderful time. We do hope the new owners will refurbish the deck areas, which really need work. The teak is badly worn and oil-spotted. And the self-service buffet, which is tucked into a niche just inside from the pool area, is laid out very inefficiently, forcing the lines to circle the room and come back out the same narrow door. At breakfast, they add a second outdoor buffet on deck which cuts down some on the traffic.

Fielding's Five

Five Favorite Places

1. The main lounge has a large metal dance floor and chrome-framed tub chairs that supplement long banquettes around the outside perimeters.

2. The library, with locked cases of books, a strip mirror wall and movable chairs, doubles as a film-screening room.

3. The casino, with one roulette wheel, three blackjack tables, a Caribbean stud table and 71 slots.

4. Two small plunge pools surrounded with tiny blue tiles ornament the aft end of the public rooms deck.

5. A disco buried deep in the bowels of the ship has a shiny, sunken dance floor and mirrored posts.

Five Things You Won't Find On Board

1. Elbow room at your dining table when the ship is full.

2. A peaceful game in the video games room; all 11 are about shooting, wrestling, fighting or car chases.

3. A performers' dressing room; they have to change in the card room off the main lounge. (At that, it's better than the old Royal Viking ships, when dancers used the public ladies' room to change costumes.)

4. Space to swim a lap in the swimming pools.

5. A cabin designated wheelchair-accessible.

)l Carnival.

3655 NW 87 Avenue, Miami, FL 33178
☎ (305) 599-2600, (800) 327-9501

Carnival designer Joe Farcus stands amid the flash and dazzle of his signature atrium lobby.

History . . . .

"The most popular cruise line in the world," as the slogan goes, was founded by Ted Arison, who had sold an air-freight business in New York in 1966 and headed back to his native Tel Aviv to retire. According to Arison's son Micky, now chairman and CEO of Carnival, his father never intended to go into cruising, but once he was back in Israel, he took over the management of a struggling charter cruise operation and turned it into a success.

CARNIVAL CRUISE LINES

When that vessel, a ship called *Nili*, was returned to the Mediterranean because of the owner's continuing financial difficulties, Arison had several cruises booked but no ship. As Micky tells it, "Ted heard the *Sunward* was laid up in Gibraltar, so he called (Norwegian shipping executive) Knut Kloster and said, 'You've got a ship, I've got the passengers, we could put them together, and we'd have a cruise line.' So in effect, they started NCL (Norwegian Cruise Line) that way."

When that partnership dissolved in 1972 after some disagreement between the principals, Arison went out and bought the *Empress of Canada*, renamed it *Mardis Gras* and started Carnival Cruise Lines. The line's first sailing with 300 travel agents aboard ran aground. There was nowhere to go but up.

Today Carnival Cruise Lines operates a fleet of 10 ships with five more scheduled to arrive by 1998. Parent company Carnival Corporation also owns all or part of three other cruise lines, Holland America, Windstar and Seabourn. Founder Arison, an intensely private billionaire and philanthropist, has retired to Israel but still keeps an active eye on the company. *Mardi Gras* and *Carnivale* have also retired from the fleet; both were sold to Greek-owned Epirotiki Lines.

Carnival went public in 1987 and is traded on the New York Stock Exchange.

—The largest cruise line in the world, based on the number of passengers carried.

—Claims the largest staff of trained and qualified youth counselors in the industry (80 full-time employees) to handle some 100,000 kid cruisers a year.

—First cruise line to build a dedicated performance stage in the show lounge (*Carnivale*, 1975).

—First cruise line to use TV commercials on a saturation schedule during the network news hour around the country (1984).

—Pays off a $1,065,428.22 "MegaCash" jackpot to two cruisers from Alaska (aboard the *Jubilee*, March 1994).

—Introduces the world's largest passenger ship, the 100,000-ton, $400 million *Carnival Destiny*, in November 1996.

Concept. . . . .

The fledgling company took off when Arison and a young vice president of sales and marketing named Bob Dickinson created a new concept. They cut prices and added casinos and discos to attract more passengers. By loosening the traditional structure of the cruise market with its formality and class distinctions, they created the "Fun Ships" concept for a vast new cruise audience, a segment of the population that had never cruised before. The company calls itself a "contemporary product" aimed at a mass market, and the cruises are meant to tap the fantasy element to stimulate passengers rather than soothe them, turning the ship into a theme park for adults. Carnival's architect, Joe Farcus, the Michael Graves of the cruise industry, says, "The ships give people a chance to see something they don't in their ordinary lives…Instead of sitting in a theater watching, they're in the movie."

Signatures . . . .

Carnival's distinctive winged funnel painted in bright red, white and blue is instantly recognizable in warm-water ports all over the Caribbean and Mexico, as well as Alaska. Chosen originally as a design statement, the funnel, which vents the smoke off to each side, surprised everyone when it actually worked.

Almost as recognizable is the bright blue corkscrew slide into the amidships pool on every "Fun Ship."

Splashy, fog-and-laser shows with contemporary pop music and spectacular dancing are a regular feature aboard Carnival ships; the bigger the ship, the bigger the show.

Gimmicks . . . .

Smiling waiters in tropical colors circulate around the decks on embarkation day with trays of Technicolor drinks in souvenir glasses, which first-time cruisers sometimes accept without realizing they have to pay for them. And kids in the $1 million virtual reality entertainment complex aboard the *Holiday* can activate the high tech games by using their passenger I.D. cards; they don't need to go get money from Mom or Dad, once the initial use has been approved.

Who's the Competition. . . . .

In the Caribbean, Carnival competes with Royal Caribbean and Norwegian Cruise Line for under-40 couples and singles in the seven-day market and goes head-to-head with both in the mini-cruise market out of Miami and Los Angeles, as well as competing with Premier Cruises out of Port Canaveral. The line still perceives land-based resorts as its primary competition, and exerts a lot of effort to entice first-time cruisers. Dickinson himself says the former competitors are all "moving upscale" and leaving the field to Carnival and what he flippantly calls "the bottom feeders," low-budget cruise lines with old ships.

Who's Aboard. . . . .

Despite the line's early reputation for swinging singles' party ships, Carnival attracts a broad spectrum of passengers from newlyweds to families with small children to middle-aged couples to retirees. About 60 percent are first-time cruisers, down from 80 percent in the 1980s, and some 23 percent have taken a Carnival cruise previously, up from nine percent in the 1980s.

Families comprise a large part of the line's mini-cruise business.

Who Should Go

Families with children and teenagers will find plenty of diversions for the kids aboard, but there's also a well-thought-out Camp Carnival program with youth counselors that divides them into four age groups—toddlers two–four (on all ships except the *Tropicale* and *Festivale*), intermediates five–eight, juniors nine–12 and teens 13–17. They'll find playrooms stocked with games and toys, a full program of daily activities at sea including special aerobics classes and karaoke parties, a kiddies' pool tucked away on its own deck area and the trademark slide at the adult pool (see "Signatures"). Baby-sitting is usually available as well.

Plus: Anyone who likes to spend a weekend in Atlantic City, Nassau or Las Vegas, anyone who wants to show off some new clothes and stay up late dancing, or anyone who adores glittering high-rise resorts.

Who Should Not Go

People whose favorite cruise line was Royal Viking; early-to-bed types; or anyone allergic to twinkle lights and neon.

The Lifestyle

About what you'd expect if you've seen the Kathy Lee Gifford commercials—you know, "If they could see me now…" (Gifford says that when she auditioned for the job she almost didn't get it; she was sixth down on the list of performers they wanted to see.)

While the ships are glitzy, they are also very glamorous if you like bright lights and shiny surfaces, and the humor and whimsy Joe Farcus brings to the designs comes closer to *gee-whiz*! than *omigod*! The casinos and the spas are among the biggest at sea, the disco stays open very late, there's often an X-rated midnight cabaret comedy show, singles get-togethers, honeymooner parties, around-the-clock movies on the in-cabin TV set, plenty of fitness classes, trap-shooting, shuffleboard, knobby knees contests, ice carving demonstrations, bridge and galley tours and all the other usual shipboard folderol.

Wardrobe

While Carnival ships are a bit less dressy than more traditional lines, many of the passengers look forward to dressing up on the one to two formal nights a week, when formal dress or a dark suit is suggested. You will see more sequins and tuxedos those nights than sport coats without a tie. The pattern is usually two formal nights, two informal nights (the line suggests sport coat and tie for men) and three casual nights that call for resort wear. For daytime, almost anything goes (or almost nothing, if you opt to sunbathe in the secluded upper deck topless sunbathing area). To go ashore, casual, comfortable clothing and good walking shoes are best. Don't forget to take a sun hat and sunblock.

Bill of Fare . . . . B+

From a predictable mainstream seven-day menu rotation on its ships featuring Beef Wellington and Surf 'n Turf several years ago, the line has made some changes in its menus after finding a 300 percent increase in the number of vegetarian entrees ordered and a 20 percent rise in chicken and fish. Fewer than half the passengers order red meat these days, says Carnival's food and beverage director; a popular fresh fish "catch of the day" is now offered on every dinner menu.

That's not to say Beef Wellington and Surf 'n Turf have disappeared—they haven't—but rather that menus have moved a little closer to the cutting edge without scaring diners with huitlacoche mushrooms or fermented soybean paste; "Fun Ship" fans will still encounter those ubiquitous theme nights (French, Italian, Caribbean and Oriental) and flaming desserts parade, and children can order from their own special menus of familiar favorites.

Three-quarters of all the passengers opt for buffet breakfast and lunches rather than going to the dining room to their assigned seating, so a much wider range of casual, self-service options has been added, from a 24-hour pizzeria on the new *Imagination* to across-the-fleet salad bars, hot daily breakfast and lunch specials, made-to-order pasta stations and spa cuisine. Table service has been upgraded in the buffet areas as well.

All the shipboard dining rooms are smoke-free on Carnival. You can breakfast in bed and order simple menu items such as sandwiches and fruit and cheese 24 hours a day from room service. Big midnight buffets are followed by a second mini-buffet at 1:30 a.m. on these late-night ships.

Showtime . . . . A+

Lavishly costumed, fully professional entertainment as good as (often better) than you'd see in Las Vegas is one of the line's hallmarks. The company produces its own musical shows in-house with high-tech lighting, sound and special effects. Different shows are featured on different ships (much as the Broadway shows on Norwegian Cruise Line ships vary from one vessel to another) so if you're a fan of big production shows, you'll want to cruise them all sooner or later.

Three different live bands and a piano bar are usually playing around the ship in the evening, along with a steel drum or calypso band on deck at midday.

The only lecturers you'll run across on the "Fun Ships" to the islands are the people who tell you where to shop.

Discounts . . . .

Deduct up to $1200 per cabin from the listed brochure rates if you book early. Savings amounts are reduced over time based on demand, so earliest bookings get the lowest rates. Some restrictions apply.

Sister ship **Fascination**

Ecstasy   ★★★★★

Fantasy   ★★★★★

The *Fantasy*-class ships are all virtually identical in superstructure and deck plan, but each is dramatically different inside. We find ourselves doing a lot of standing by the rail looking down, both inside from the upper atrium levels down into the lobby, watching the glass elevators glide up and down, and outside from the upper decks down into the amidships pool deck with its acres of bronzing bodies in all shapes and sizes, at kids (and adults) trying out the bright blue water slide, at the impromptu dancers in bathing suits who always begin to gyrate on deck when the band comes out on the raised stage.

On the topmost deck is a rubberized jogging track, then down one deck on Veranda Deck is the huge Nautica spa with one of every exercise machine known to man, 26 suites with private verandas and on the aft deck, a sunbathing area and pool with two Jacuzzis.

One deck down on Lido is a large glass-walled self-service cafe with indoor and outdoor dining and the amidships pool area with its stage.

The Promenade Deck and Atlantic Deck contain most of the bars, lounges, showrooms and dining rooms, along with a galley on Atlantic Deck that makes the aft dining room a you-can't-get-there-from-here proposition. Directly behind that dining room is the teen club and children's playroom, and on the deck just above, the wading pool, all completely removed from the adult areas of the ship. Forward on the same deck is a second dining room, a small lounge and library, the atrium, shops and the main level of the showroom. One deck up on Promenade is the showroom balcony, the atrium, a vast casino on port side and an enclosed "avenue" on starboard side with sidewalk cafes and bars, another lounge and a disco, then still another lounge and a cabaret showroom aft.

The remainder of the cabins are on four decks below Atlantic; the base of the atrium with the ship lobby and information desk is one deck down on Empress. Three banks of elevators and three sets of stairs access the cabins.

These are "get up and get out and have fun" ships; the cabin TV runs the same daily feature over and over in any 24-hour period, and with only a minimal library of books, you mustn't expect to snuggle down and read.

The Brochure Says

"The best vacation on land or sea! Children have plenty to do on a 'Fun Ship' cruise. Relax on acres of sun splashed decks. Kick up your heels to one of our many live bands. Pamper yourself with our Nautica Spa program. Our attentive staff will wait on you 24 hours a day. Savor a fabulous array of food from around the world. We bet you'll have a great time in the largest casinos at sea. Enjoy lavish Las Vegas-style entertainment."

Translation

Every sentence is accompanied by a picture making the intent very clear—"Children" are eating pizza with a youth counselor serving them and no hovering parents in the background. "Relax" shows rows of sunbathing bodies holding flower-garnished drinks. "Kick up" depicts a pair of sedate middle-aged couples doing what kids today call close-dancing, meaning they're dancing while holding each other in their arms, like people over 50 do sometimes. "Pamper" shows shapely young bodies, mostly female, on gym machines with smiling male instructors. "Our attentive staff" is a waiter serving breakfast in bed to a happy couple. "Savor" shows a table of six-plus passengers (the table edge is cropped, but a six-top is the small-est table you can usually find on these vessels). "We'll bet" is a croupier at the roulette wheel with a lot of happy couples, all of whom seem to think they're winning. "Enjoy lavish Las Vegas-style entertainment" depicts a bevy of chorines in pink feathers and towering headdresses. Altogether, it's Cruising 101 Illustrated for first-timers.

Cabins & Costs

Fantasy Suites: . . . . A

Average Price PPPD: $348 including airfare.

The *Fantasy*-class ships have some of the best veranda suite buys at sea, with 28 Upper Deck veranda suites and 26 Veranda Deck demi-suites. But opt for the top—one of the Upper Deck suites with sepa-rate sitting area is big enough for entertaining and furnished with an L-shaped sofa, two chairs, coffee table, cocktail table, built-in wood cabinetry that includes a mini-refrigerator, glassware and TV with VCR, and a teak-floored private veranda with lounger, two chairs and a small table. The bedroom area has twin beds that can convert to queen-sized bed and marble counter desk/dresser with five drawers. The bath is fairly large with a marbleized counter, inset porcelain sink, Jacuzzi tub and tile walls and floor. There's an entry with walk-in closet, one full-length and two half-length hanging spaces, shelves and a large safe.

Small Splurges: . . . . A

Average Price PPPD: $320 including airfare.

The demi-suites on Veranda Deck have twin or queen-sized beds, big windows, private veranda with two chairs and a table, sitting area with sofa, table and chair and a bath with tile shower. Some have partially obstructed views due to hanging lifeboats.

Suitable Standards: . . . . B

Average Price PPPD: $251 including airfare.

Carnival's standard cabins are consistent throughout this class, 190 square feet with twin beds that convert to queen-sized, dark gray car-peting thinly striped in bright colors, an armchair and matching stool, a built-in corner table, wall-mounted TV set and desk/dresser with four drawers. The closets have one enclosed and one open full-length hanging space plus shelves. The tile bath has a big shower, a counter around the sink and a glass-doored medicine cabinet.

Bottom Bunks: . . . . D

Average Price PPPD: $200 including airfare.

The lowest category cabins are insides with upper and lower berths placed perpendicular to each other, considerably smaller than the standards (the brochure calls them "cozy"), similar closet space and a tile bath with shower. There are only nine of these on each ship, plus 28 more with upper and lower berths in higher price categories than are slightly roomier.

Where She Goes

The *Ecstasy* sails from Miami every Friday on three-day cruises to Nassau.

The *Fantasy* sails every Thursday and Sunday from Port Canaveral on three- and four-day cruises calling in Nassau; the four-day sailing also visits Freeport.

The Bottom Line

These ships come to life at night when the dramatic colors and lighting are highlighted against the many glass surfaces. They are tactile (touch the surfaces of the chairs, tables, walls and floors on *Imagination*), aural (changing sounds of nature—the surf, rain, wind and chirping birds—wash by on *Sensation's* Sensation Boulevard) and intensely visual (fiber optics and neon panels "jump off" the walls as passengers walk by on the *Sensation*).

We call the *Fantasy* a lava lamp for the 1990s, but we mean it in a fond sense. This series of ships is constantly amazing and amusing, thanks to the ingenuousness and genius of Joe Farcus, whose own innocence and clarity of image keep them from being vulgar.

Are they gaudy? Sometimes. Do they tread dangerously close to maxing out? Perhaps. But they can match the much-praised pair of Crystal ships in marble, crystal and glove leather, dollar for dollar, ton for ton. Whether they strike you as glitzy or glamorous depends on your own individual taste, but they're never boring. Carnival delivers precisely what it promises, and if you've seen its advertising, you should already know whether it's the right cruise line for you.

Fielding's Five

Fabulous Spaces

1. The Universe show lounge aboard the *Fantasy*, which in the words of one passenger "looks like it's ready to blast off" with its carpet covered with comets and swirling ringed planets, its black upholstery flocked with tiny, intensely bright metallic microchips in red, blue, silver and gold, and its ability to turn from a gigantic stage with a 33-foot turntable in the center to a ballroom closed off by a wall of beveled gold mirrors with a sunken orchestra pit that rises to eye level.

2. The 12,000-square-foot Nautica spas on both ships with Steiner of London beauty services from facials to aromatherapy and massage, an abundance of state-of-the-art exercise machines facing a glass wall overlooking the sea, sauna and steam rooms, fully mirrored aerobics room and big twin Jacuzzis lit by the sun through an overhead skylight.

Off-the-Wall Places

1. Cleopatra's Bar on the *Fantasy*, patterned after an ancient Egyptian tomb, with stone floor, hieroglyphics on the walls, gilded sarcophagi

and full-sized seated and standing Egyptian gods and goddesses. In the center of the room is a glossy black piano bar, and as random laser lights spotlight details around the room, you half expect to hear a chorus of "My Mummy Done Ptolemy."

2. Cats Lounge on the *Fantasy*, inspired by the set for the musical of the same name, with oversized tin cans and rubber tires, bottle cap and jar lid tabletops, and walls lined with soap and cereal boxes; you enter through a giant Pet milk can and the band plays atop a giant rubber tire laid on its side.

Five Good Reasons to Book These Ships

1. To have fun in an unintimidating, relaxed atmosphere without worrying about picking up the wrong fork or wearing the wrong clothes.

2. To try to win a million dollars.

3. To eat, drink, gamble, dance and watch movies all night long if you want to; it's your vacation.

4. To show the snapshots of the ships to your neighbors back home "so they can see you now..."

5. To get married on board (the line can arrange it) and spend your honeymoon at sea, all for less than a formal church wedding at home would probably cost; call Carnival's Bon Voyage Department at ☎ *800-WED-4-YOU* for details.

Five Things You Won't Find On Board

1. Lavish gift toiletries, even in the suites; all you get is a sliver of soap.

2. A table for two in the dining room.

3. A lot of books in the library.

4. A cruise director who spells Knobby Knees (as in the contest) with a "k"; every program we've seen calls it "Nobby Knees."

5. An atrium sculpture that doesn't move; some of them are inadvertently hilarious.

Celebrity Cruises, Inc.

5201 Blue Lagoon Drive, Miami, FL 33126
☎ (305) 262-8322, (800) 437-3111

*A passenger volunteer assists executive chef Walter Lauer in a cooking demonstration aboard the **Meridian**.*

History . . . .

The Greek-based Chandris Group, founded in 1915, began passenger service in 1922 with the 300-ton *Chimara*, and by 1939 had grown to a 12-ship family-owned cargo and passenger line. In the post-World War II years, the company acquired a number of famous cruise liners, most of which have been retired. Under the Fantasy label (see "Fantasy Cruises"), the company operates the *Amerikanis* but has retired the *Britanis*.

In April 1989, Chandris formed Celebrity Cruises with the intention of creating an upscale division with a premium cruise product. The *Meridian*, a massive makeover of the classic liner *Galileo Galeilei*, debuted in April 1990, followed the next month by the all-new *Horizon*. In April 1992, sister ship *Zenith* followed.

In October of that same year, Chandris formed a joint venture with Overseas Shipholding Group (OSG), a large publicly-held bulk-shipping company, and entered into the next expansion phase, ordering three 70,000-ton ships to be constructed by Joseph L. Meyer in Papenburg, Germany. The first of these, the innovative *Century*, debuted at the end of 1995, followed in the fall of 1996 by sister ship *Galaxy*.

—Chandris introduced the fly/cruise concept in the Mediterranean in the early 1960s.

—Pioneered fly/cruise packages in the Caribbean in 1966.

—Celebrity pioneered affiliations with land-based experts from London's three-star Michelin restaurateur Michel Roux to Sony Corporation of America to create innovative onboard products and programs.

Concept . . . .

Celebrity from its beginning has aimed at presenting the highest possible quality for the best price, and offers luxury service and exceptional food with a very solid value for the money spent. These stylish ships illustrate the decade's new values—luxury without ostentation, family vacations that don't just cater to the kids and close-to-home getaways that provide pure pleasure.

Signatures . . . .

Perhaps the single best-known feature of this fleet is its superlative cuisine, created and supervised by London master chef Michel Roux, a longtime *Guide Michelin* three-star chef, who takes a hands-on approach, popping in for surprise visits to the ships, training shipboard chefs in his own kitchens and sending key supervisory personnel for regular culinary check-ups.

Gimmicks . . . .

The Mr. and Mrs. icebreaker game. At the beginning of each cruise, a man and a woman on board are chosen to represent Mr. and Mrs. (*Horizon, Zenith, Meridian, Century*). During the cruise, passengers are encouraged to ask individuals if they're the Mr. and Mrs. selected, and the first to find them gets a prize. In the meantime, everyone gets acquainted. Anyone for musical chairs?

Who's the Competition . . . .

In its brief six years of service, Celebrity has managed to virtually create a class of its own by providing a product priced competitively with Princess and Holland America but with a level of food, and sometimes service, that approaches Crystal Cruises. Previously, the line limited its itineraries to Caribbean and Bermuda sailings, but has expanded to include Alaska and Panama Canal sailings, and very likely will enter the Mediterranean in 1998 with its mid-sized *Meridian*, oldest vessel in the fleet.

Who's Aboard

Young to middle-aged couples, families with children, and, aboard the *Meridian* on certain early-season Bermuda sailings from southeastern ports, groups of senior citizens from Florida retirement communities who request early sitting dinners that start at 5:30 instead the normal 6 or 6:30 p.m. In winter season, Celebrity attracts some European and French Canadian passengers as well. Although the line is only six years old, it has many frequent cruisers with double-digit sailings.

Who Should Go

Anyone looking for a good value for the money; discriminating foodies who will find very little if anything to complain about; families with children; couples of all ages. When the line was first introduced in 1990, Al Wallack, then Celebrity's senior vice president for marketing and passenger services, had several suggestions: "People who are joining country clubs but not necessarily the most expensive or exclusive country club on the block;" passengers of the former Home Lines and Sitmar ships who did not merge into Princess and who like "ships that look like ships, ships that have a European quality."

Who Should Not Go

Anyone who calls for catsup with everything or after perusing the menu asks the waiter, "But where's the surf and turf?"

The Lifestyle

Upscale without being pretentious, sleek and fashionable without being glitzy, the Celebrity ships offer a very comfortable seven-day cruise that is outstanding in the areas of food, service and surroundings. Evenings aboard are fairly dressy, with jacket and tie for men requested on both formal and informal nights; only casual nights suggest a sports shirt without jacket. Meals are served at assigned tables in two seatings.

Book a suite and you get all-day butler service; take the kids along during holiday and summer sailings and you'll find well-trained youth counselors on board. Ladies looking for a dancing partner will find social hosts on many sailings.

Evenings the ships present musical production shows and variety shows (except when they are docked in Bermuda, which does not permit professional entertainment other than live music on cruise ships in port), recent feature films, and duos or trios playing for dancing or listening in small lounges around the ships. Daytimes bring popular culinary demonstrations by the executive chef, arts and crafts lessons, trapshooting, napkin folding, golf putting, lectures on finance or current affairs, a trivia quiz, basketball, exercise classes and bingo.

Wardrobe . . . .

A seven-night cruise normally schedules two formal nights, in which the line suggests "both men and women may prefer more dressy attire, such as an evening gown for women and a tuxedo or dress suit for men." In our experience aboard the line's ships, a cocktail dress or dressy pants suit for women and a dark suit or blazer with tie will be acceptable. There is also a tuxedo rental service aboard the *Zenith*.

Two nights are designated informal, and men are asked to wear a jacket and tie, women a suit or dress, and three casual nights when a sport shirt and slacks are acceptable for men, dresses or pantsuits for women.

Daytime wear is casual, with good walking shoes a must. Bahamas-bound passengers in spring and fall should take a jacket or sweater, hat or scarf, for going ashore; there's often a cool breeze blowing.

Bill of Fare . . . . A+

Celebrity's executive chef, Vienna-born Walter Lauer, who goes from one ship to another constantly checking quality, describes it as "creating something new, where you can't cook everything in advance. Here there is the chance to do something new, more of the high standards in cuisine." One example: All the stock for soups is made from scratch on board rather than using prepared bases as many cruise kitchens do.

Lauer's mentor, Michel Roux, says, "The most important thing is to have a very good quality product and to rely on cooking skill more than the richness of the product." Fresh ingredients cooked to order figure prominently, and the menus are changed every six months.

Basically, the idea of serving simple but sophisticated dishes prepared from fresh ingredients as close as possible to serving time was revolutionary in the basic banquet/hotel catering kitchens of big cruise ships. But it succeeds splendidly. Usually if we find two or three dishes a meal that tempt us we're happy, but we could cheerfully order one of everything straight down the menu on these ships.

For lunch you might find a vegetable pizza or minestrone to start, then a main-dish salad of romaine with Mediterranean tabouli, hummus and pita bread garnished with garlic chicken; a piperade omelet with ham, tomatoes, peppers and onions; broiled ocean perch; roasted chicken with Provencale potatoes; spaghetti with fresh tomato sauce; grilled calf's liver with bacon and onions.

Dinner could begin with New England clam chowder or a pasta tossed with cilantro, oregano, ancho chile and fresh cream; a low-fat version of coquilles Saint-Jacques on vegetable tagliatelle; a pan-seared darne of salmon; roast lamb with garlic, thyme, fresh mint and olive oil with country roasted potatoes; broiled lobster tail or prime rib of beef. The dessert menu always includes one lean and light suggestion, along with fruit and cheese, pastries, ice creams and sorbets and a plate of showcase sweets presented to each table by the waiter, who describes them in mouth-watering detail. Full vegetarian menus are offered at every lunch and dinner.

A substantial 24-hour room service menu, gala midnight buffets, Caribbean barbecues on deck, continental breakfast in bed, late morning bouillon and afternoon tea are other meal options during a typical cruise.

Lunchtime buffets are reminiscent of Impressionist paintings, with displays of fresh fruits and vegetables, woven baked baskets holding bread and wonderfully crunchy homemade breadsticks, fresh and crisp salads, a huge display of fresh vegetables, a rolling cart of wines by the glass, cold and hot main dishes and plenty of desserts.

Showtime

The production musical shows have a lot of verve and are well-performed and well-costumed; they follow the usual musical revue formats with salutes to Broadway and/or Hollywood, but with fresh looks at vintage shows like "Hair" and "Jesus Christ Superstar." Variety performers, musical soloists and duos and a Caribbean band round out the evening entertainment. Daytimes are chock-a-block with games, movies, lectures and exercise classes. The new *Century* and *Galaxy* introduce still more technological marvels from rooms with "video wallpaper" to a nightly light-and-sound spectacular.

Discounts

Special advance purchase fares save up to 45 percent for passengers who book well ahead of time; ask a travel agent for details.

Century   ★★★★★

   Celebrity's chairman John Chandris calls his new pair of babies
"the ships I've always wanted to build…ships for the next century" and tags them super-premium, saying they are for "discriminating consumers who demand the highest quality experience at
the best possible value." There are a lot of exciting new features
on board. Take the state-of-the-art spa with its hydropool underwater "air beds" to give the body a weightless sensation and
jets of water that provide neck massages as well as another spa
area with jets of water at different heights that are similar to a
standup Jacuzzi. Along with the usual hydrotherapy and thalas-
sotherapy is a seagoing first—a mud, steam and herbal treatment
called rasul. All the AquaSpa programs can be booked in advance
with a travel agent.

   A lounge called Images utilizes "video wallpaper," hundreds
of changeable, custom-designed backgrounds that can be
punched up on a wall-sized video display system to change the
room's ambiance from tropical palms to low-light jazz club to
sports bar or wine cellar, whatever background fits the activity of
the moment. Around one end is a series of interactive gaming
booths big enough to seat several people at a time. For showtime, there's a Broadway-style theater with row seating, orchestra pit and four-deck fly loft for scenery. A glazed dome in the
Grand Foyer changes in a slow transition from dawn to daylight
to sunset to night, when astronomically correct "stars" appear in
the dome "sky." Sony Corporation of America has created exclusive interactive guest services, touch-screen information
kiosks, in-cabin entertainment systems, telephonic video service
and special teleconferencing equipment for meetings.

The Brochure Says

"Welcome to the new *Century*, a vessel that recaptures the golden age of cruising blended with modern sophistication."

Translation

Perhaps too much emphasis was initially put into the joint venture between Celebrity and Sony. While we think passengers will certainly note the two dozen technological additions from Sony, they will be even more impressed by the elegant dining room, theater, casino, Michael's Club and the Crystal Room nightclub than electronic gadgetry.

Cabins & Costs

Fantasy Suites: .... A

Average Price PPPD: $856 including airfare.

A pair of lavish penthouse suites measuring 1173 square feet offer a private veranda with its own outdoor hot tub, a living room, dining room, butler's pantry and 24-hour butler service, master bedroom with walk-in closet, living room with wet bar and entertainment center and a guest powder room supplementing the marble bath with spa tub.

Small Splurge: .... A

Average Price PPPD: $585 including airfare.

The eight Royal Suites are spacious inside although the private verandas are fairly narrow. The living rooms have sofa and two chairs, dining table with four chairs and a separate bedroom. Museum "art boxes" in each suite displays themed pieces of art; the suite we saw featured African carvings.

Suitable Standards: .... B+

Average Price PPPD: $342 including airfare.

A typical cabin is furnished with a queen-sized bed under a large window with a striped Roman shade, a marble-topped desk/dresser, two armchairs, a cocktail table, TV set, minibar and big hinged mirror covering shelves and a safe in the wall behind it. The bathroom has a very large white tile shower (chairman John Chandris is very big on spacious shower stalls) with excellent shower head, marble counter and lots of storage.

Bottom Bunks: .... B

Average Price PPPD: $268 including airfare.

All the cabins contain safes, mini-bars, hair dryers, direct dial telephones and color TV sets, and the smallest is 171 square feet. The bottom units still contain two lower beds which can convert to a queen-sized bed, bath with spacious shower and all the amenities listed above.

Where She Goes

The *Century* sails alternating Eastern and Western Caribbean itineraries from Fort Lauderdale every Saturday. The Eastern Caribbean sailing calls in San Juan, St. Thomas, St. Maarten and Nassau.

The Bottom Line

A lot of the public rooms strive mightily to look like Tomorrowland, especially the lounge called Images that combines elements of both video games and sports bars with a massive video wall and intimate high-backed booths with game screens inset into the tabletops. The overall design also skimps on the deck space, making the pool deck and sun walk above seem crowded when the ship is full. At the same time, only 61 cabins and suites have private balconies, so that means more people are out on deck. The suites aboard are lovely, well worth the splurge—and having your own private veranda means you can skip the deck sunbathing.

Fielding's Five

Five Good Reasons to Book This Ship

1. The exceptional AquaSpa from Steiners with an elaborate program of beauty and spa appointments that can be booked from home before the cruise via your travel agent.

2. To get a souvenir digital photograph that sets you against an unlikely backdrop of jet skis, yawning alligators, a painter's perch dangling from the bow or on the bridge with the captain.

3. To play video games almost anywhere and use interactive cabin TV service to order food, watch pay-per-view movies or wager on a few hands of video poker.

4. To dine in the elegant two-deck Grand Restaurant that evokes the dining room from the Normandie.

5. To watch a production show in a theater where there are no bad sightlines.

Five Things You Won't Find Aboard

1. Obstructed sightlines in the showroom; the view is perfect from every seat.

2. Visitors.

3. Pets.

4. A golf cart at the simulated golf links.

5. A thoroughly worked-out low-fat, low-calorie menu program; the super light and lean menu is mysteriously heavy in fat and sodium on several suggested dishes such as chicken fajitas and some pork entrees.

C O S T A *Italian Style* C R U I S E S

80 Southwest 8th Street, Miami, FL 33130
☎ (305) 358-7325, (800) 462-6782

Costa's distinctive bright yellow stack with a blue "C"

History . . . .

The parent company of Miami-based Costa Cruises is Costa Crociere of Genoa, which started back in 1860 with a family business that imported olive oil from Sardinia, refined it and exported it all over Europe. When patriarch Giacomo Costa died in 1916, his sons inherited the family business and bought a freighter to transport their oil themselves. By 1935 they had eight freighters.

They started passenger service after World War II with the 12,000-ton *Anna "C"* cruising between Genoa and South America. A fleet of three others was added in just four years—the *Andrea "C"*, *Giovanna "C"* and *Franca "C"*.

The first new ship came in 1957-58 when Costa constructed the 24,000-ton *Federico "C"*, now sailing as Dolphin's *SeaBreeze*. In 1959 they moved the *Franca "C"* to Florida and entered seven-day Caribbean cruising. It wasn't long before their entire fleet began spending winters in the Caribbean.

Today, with one of the youngest fleets in the Caribbean, Costa markets tropical cruises in winter and Mediterranean cruises in summer. The line's present fleet (including the *Mermoz*) numbers 10 with the *CostaVictoria*.

—Introduced three- and four-day cruises to the Bahamas from Miami (*Anna "C"*, 1964).

—Based a cruise ship in San Juan and began the first air/sea program between the U.S. mainland and Puerto Rico (*Franca "C"*, 1968).

—Launched "Cruising Italian Style" with toga night parties (*CostaRiviera*, 1985).

Concept.........................

"Italian Style by Design," Costa explains as "a product that combines the sophisticated elegance of a European vacation with the fun and spirit of the line's Italian heritage."

Signatures......................

The distinctive bright yellow stack with a blue "C" and a blue band across the top makes a Costa ship easily recognizable in any port in the world, especially on the new ships, with their clusters of three narrow vertical yellow stacks.

The use of "C" (meaning Costa) following the ship's name in earlier days and the present use of the ship's name following the Costa name in one word, as in *CostaClassica*, emphasize the fact that this is still a family-owned, family-run company.

The piazza, or town square, comparable to the lobby in a major hotel, is the heart of every Costa ship.

Gimmicks ....

Roman Bacchanal, better known as "toga night," has progressed from a fairly primitive form—passengers tying on sheets taken from their beds—to a very sophisticated routine—ready-made togas handed out by cruise staffers who also pass around gilded laurel wreaths and such. From its very inception it's been wildly popular with North American passengers (they don't usually do it in Italy but offer a Venetian Carnival night instead). It used to be that on masquerade night, you often cringed in embarrassment if you had put on a costume and were one of the few—on toga night, you're embarrassed if you're wearing street clothes because you're very conspicuous. It's usually held the last night of the cruise, simplifying the what-to-wear question for people who pack before dinner. Also, at least one cruise director warns reluctant toga-wearers, "No sheet, no eat."

Who's the Competition.

Costa used to face a lively competition from Sitmar and Home Lines, both Italian cruise lines that are now defunct, but doesn't really have to duke it out with Princess, despite Princess owning the former Sitmar ships; they appeal to different people.

Because of the stylish new hardware both lines have, we'd say Costa and Celebrity might compete in the Caribbean, since both are major names on the east coast. But in the Mediterranean, Costa dominates the upper price market, Epirotiki the lower price market.

Who's Aboard.

Costa has always attracted a large segment of cruisers from the northeastern U.S., especially those with an Italian-American heritage. In both the Caribbean and Europe, French and Italian passengers are numerous, especially since Costa added the *Mermoz* from Paquet French Cruises to its roster. Young to middle-aged couples, young families, retirees and often three generations from the same family may all be seen cruising Italian style.

Who Should Go.

More young couples, especially anyone wearing an Armani label, would love the newest Costa ships, because they have the same spare elegance with their chic Italian furniture and uncluttered cabins. Opera fans will enjoy the bigger-than-life dining rooms with their strolling musicians and La Scala-painted murals that change by the evening from a medieval street to an Italian garden. Anyone who wants to travel in Europe with more Europeans than fellow Americans. Anyone who never said "*Basta!*" ("Enough!") to pasta.

Who Should Not Go

Cunard first-class transatlantic passengers who might find the energy and noise level a little high; anyone who dislikes pasta and pizza; anyone unwilling to don a toga when everyone else on board does; anyone who doesn't want a multi-cultural experience on a European itinerary or can't stand to hear shipboard announcements broadcast in five languages.

The Lifestyle

Traditional cruise programs with an Italian accent characterize the Costa ships, with the usual dress code requests, two meal seatings, and a full onboard and shore excursion activities program. Lavish spas imitating Roman baths are

COSTA CRUISES

on board the newer ships, and the pool decks encourage spending all day outside with cocoon cabana chairs, sidewalk-cafe tables and chairs, splashing fountains and lounge chairs with pale blue-and-white striped cushions. Overall, there's a lighthearted good humor on these ships, especially when a lot of unflappable Italians are aboard.

Because of the number of Europeans aboard in summer, Costa adds an American hostess program to perform as special liaison for the English speakers on board, usually a minority on European sailings.

Wardrobe . . . .

Costa says it would like its passengers to wear on gala evenings tuxedos or dark suits for gentlemen, evening gowns or cocktail dresses for ladies; there is at least one gala evening a cruise. On other evenings, men wear sports coats and slacks, ladies resort attire. In the daytime, casual resort wear is in order, including light cotton clothing and swimwear. Don't worry about toga nights if one is scheduled (they don't usually do it in Europe); the cruise staff delivers the costumes.

Bill of Fare . . . . B+

Meals are served at two seatings, with early or main seating at noon for lunch and 6:15 p.m. for dinner, and late or second seating at 1:30 p.m. for lunch, 8:30 p.m. for dinner. All dining room breakfasts and occasional lunches are designated open seating, which on these ships mean any passenger may arrive within a set time and be seated at whatever table has space. It's not unusual on the larger *Classica* and *Romantica* to find a queue forming 15 or 20 minutes ahead of time; some Costa passengers always seem to be worrying needlessly about when their next meal is arriving.

Food and service are usually good to excellent, with a captain or maitre d'hotel always willing to toss a salad or pasta especially for you at tableside. While the chef may be an Austrian and the waiters Croatian or Honduran instead of Italian, the spirit is there. "They're all Italians at heart," says Costa's president.

Whoever's in the kitchen, we've found the pastas generally outstanding, along with vegetarian eggplant dishes, flambé shrimp, breadsticks, salads, cheeses, fresh fruits, grilled veal chops and pasta-and-bean soups. Less successful on most ships are the pizzas (with the notable exception of the *CostaRiviera*, which has a fine pizzeria on board), some of the meats and the desserts. We particularly miss the Italian-style gelati that has been replaced with American commercial ice creams on several ships.

A fresh fish "catch of the day" is sometimes on display on a decorated cart at the entrance to the dining room on the *CostaClassica* and *CostaRomantica*.

Showtime . . . . B-

Because passengers on board speak several different languages, Costa ships rely more on musical programs or variety performers like magicians, jugglers and acrobats rather than comedians or production shows that need an English-language narrative. The production shows we have seen aboard are produced by a British company and are handsomely costumed and well choreographed but seem dated beside some of the state-of-the-art shows coming out of Carnival, Princess and RCCL these days.

Films are shown on cabin TV sets throughout the day and evening on an alternating basis, and a late-night disco promises to keep going until the wee hours. Live music for listening or dancing is performed throughout the ships before and after dinner. In Europe, a small company of opera singers may be brought aboard to entertain for the evening.

Discounts . . . .

Passengers who book 90 days ahead of time get early booking discounts.

CostaRomantica ★★★★★

These sister ships are sleek and stylish with marble, tile, brass, polished wood, fountains and sculptures. So much hard surface lends a cool rather than warm ambience.

The ships have an angular bow, a boxy midsection and a rounded stern, with a vertical cluster of bright yellow funnels aft balanced by a forward glass-walled circular observation lounge set atop an all-glass deck housing the Caracalla Spa and amid-ships pool.

Two stairwells with bare stone floors and no risers provide the main vertical traffic flow through the ship, and on busy occasions like the lifeboat drill, sounds like changing classes at Woodrow Wilson Junior High.

Decks are handsome and well-designed. One pool is amid-ships, a second one aft, along with two Jacuzzis and several levels of teak decking for sunbathing.

The Brochure Says

"Created for those with a sense of adventure and an appreciation for style…(with) Italian hospitality, European charm and American comforts."

Translation

You can expect to find pasta and pizza; a cabin with TV, radio, hair dryer and safe; and a charming waiter who may just as likely come from Riga or Rijeka as Roma.

Cabins & Costs

Fantasy Suites: .... A+

3 Day Average Price: $995.

Among our very favorite suites at sea are the 10 veranda suites on each ship, particularly those on the *Romantica* named for operas. Each is 580 square feet with private veranda, living room with burled brier-wood furniture, a kidney-shaped desk, a small round table, two tub chairs and a long sofa; a separate bedroom with queen-sized bed, ele-gant wood dresser with round brass-framed mirror; floor-to-ceiling white window shades operated electronically, gauzy white undercur-tains and a tied-back sheer green curtain at the windows; large whirl-pool bathtub, stall shower and double lavatories in a wide counter. Butler service, mini-bar, terrycloth robes and reclining deck chairs on the veranda. Romantic? Yes!

Small Splurges: ....A

3 Day Average Price: $745.

Mini-suites, on the *Romantica* only, measure 340 square feet and contain a couch, two chairs, desk and chair, floor-to-ceiling windows, queen-sized bed, single trundle bed, bath with Jacuzzi tub, stall shower and double lavatories. Butler service, mini-bar and terrycloth robes.

Suitable Standards: .... B+

3 Day Average Price: $365.

More spacious than on many ships, the standard outside cabins mea-sure 200 square feet and contain two lower beds, most of which con-vert to queen-sized; a few designated cabins have fixed queen-sized beds only. White marble counters and built-in hair dryers are in all bathrooms, hanging and storage space is generous and the room has a dresser and a sitting area with two chairs and a table. Several inside cabins (cheaper than the price below) are designated wheelchair-accessible with extra-wide doors, bathrooms with pulldown shower seats and generous turning space.

Bottom Bunks: .... *C*

3 Day Average Price: $195.

The cheapest cabins aboard are insides with a lower bed and upper berth, with two chairs, small table, dresser, TV set and bath with space-age shower. There are only six on each ship and they are sometimes assigned to staff. The next category up has two lower beds and is only marginally higher in price.

Where She Goes

The *CostaRomantica* in winter makes alternate Eastern and Western Caribbean cruises out of San Juan, calling in San Juan, St. Thomas, Serena Cay and Nassau on the eastern itinerary.

The Bottom Line

The "Italian by Design" theme emphasizes the architecture and decor of the ships and stresses Costa's Italian heritage, but most of the Italian waiters are gone, replaced over the years by other Europeans, many from the newly independent eastern countries and some of whom are still awkward with English.

Furnishings aboard are beautiful, with one-of-a kind high-style Italian chairs set about here and there like pieces of art.

In the dining room, despite the dangerous marble floors, meals are served on Limoges china and double-skirted Pratesi linen tablecloths while strolling musicians play. The food is most often very good.

Many standard cabins on the *Classica* have large wooden room dividers that steal floor space without adding any useful storage area; a better bet for couples are the cabins with fixed queen-sized beds and no room divider, the same size as the others but they seem much bigger.

Fielding's Five

Five Easy Places

1. With a pool, an Italian sidewalk cafe, beach cabanas with striped blue-and-white curtains, a striking blue marble "Trevi" fountain and a thrust overhead runway from the jogging deck above overlooking all the action, it's La Dolce Vita time.

2. The heart of each ship is the piazza—on the *Classica* the Piazza Navona, on the *Romantica* the Piazza Italia—where everyone seems to gather, with an all-day- and-evening bar and lounge and music for dancing before and after dinner.

3. The dining rooms aboard change their looks on special evenings when the staff unfurls background scenery to turn it into an Italian garden or medieval city, ancient Pompeiian villas or Renaissance town; the backgrounds are painted by a scenic designer for the La Scala Opera House in Milan.

4. The big open-air cafe aft on each ship is covered with a sweeping white canvas awning and furnished with apple green wicker chairs and marble-topped tables, just like the Via Veneto.

5. The glass-walled discos high atop the ship and forward, like see-through flying saucers, double as observation lounges in the daytime.

DOLPHIN CRUISE LINE

901 South American Way, Miami, FL 33132
☎ *(305) 358-5122, (800) 992-4299*

History . . . .

Dolphin Cruise Line came about through a marketing agreement in 1979 between Peter Bulgarides, who formed Ulysses Cruise Line, and Paquet to operate the *Dolphin IV*. That agreement was terminated in 1984, and Dolphin Cruise Line was born to handle the ship.

A second ship, the former *Star/Ship Royale* from Premier Cruises, was acquired in 1989, and renamed the *SeaBreeze*, and when Admiral Cruises was disbanded by its parent company Royal Caribbean Cruise Line in 1992, Dolphin acquired the former *Azure Seas*, which it named *Ocean-Breeze*. The latter ship had been based in Los Angeles for more than a decade, making highly successful three- and four-day cruises to Baja California.

For three years, the company operated its trio of vessels, using the *Dolphin IV* for short cruises to the Bahamas and the other two for seven-day Caribbean sailings. In August 1995, Dolphin sold its *Dolphin IV* to Kosmas Shipping Group, Inc., a Florida-based company (see Canaveral Cruise Line, page 329). The *OceanBreeze* was redeployed to Miami to take over the three- and four-day cruises to the Bahamas and Key West.

In 1996, Dolphin acquired the former *Festivale* from Carnival which became the *IslandBreeze*.

Majesty Cruise Line, which operates the *Royal Majesty*, is also affiliated with Dolphin Cruise Line. Both lines are headed up by Captain Paris Katsoufis. Peter Bulgarides resigned as chairman of the board in 1994.

Concept............................

Dolphin feels it established itself as a leader in the three-and four-day cruise market early on by providing quality and value, as well as offering "quality service and gourmet dining" on all of its ships. The vintage Dolphin vessels still carry details from their ocean liner days such as teak decks, wood paneling, etched glass and polished brass.

Signatures............................

The distinctive blue dolphin on the ships' white stacks makes an easily recognized and identified logo.

Theme cruises abound, such as Country Western sailings, '50s and '60s cruises, Motown, Oktoberfest, Big Band and Nostalgia.

On-board weddings were popularized by Dolphin and frequently take place on the ships.

Gimmicks............................

As the Official Cruise Line of Hanna-Barbera, Dolphin and Majesty ships are animated with cartoon characters such as Yogi Bear, Fred Flintstone and Scooby Doo.

Who's the Competition...............

Dolphin has long been a leader in the budget cruise arena and competes primarily in the price-driven market that also includes Commodore Cruise Line and Regal Cruises.

Who's Aboard......................

A great many first-time cruisers, family groups, singles, couples, many passengers in their 20s and 30s.

Who Should Go......................

Anybody who wants to sample a cruise to see what it's all about without having to make a big commitment in time and money should try one of the mini-cruises out of Miami.

Who Should Not Go...................

Fussy veteran cruisers will not like the very long lines that form anywhere food is being arranged, served or set out.

The Lifestyle.......................

The three- and four-day cruises are a little more hectic than the seven-day sailings, just because Dolphin tries to work in as many special activities as possible. The usual daily pattern always offers plenty of chances to eat, plus as many as eight shore excursions in port. Sports and exercise classes, movies, ping pong, dance classes, beauty salon demonstrations, napkin folding, fruit and vegetable carving, pool games, horseracing, tours of the navigation bridge, Name That Tune, captain's cocktail party, shore excursion sales, dance music, game shows led by the cruise director, a deck party under the stars, ice carvings, midnight buffet, disco and night owl movie—and that's just one day! Children's programs offer a variety of options from dolphin encounters to sand castle building and treasure hunts. The atmosphere on board is friendly, even ebullient, because people worried about whether they were going to have a good time realize they're having a great time.

Wardrobe.......................

Dolphin is very kind to its first-time cruisers on the three- and four-day sailings, requesting that they dress up for formal night to meet the captain and go to dinner, then letting them change back to casual garb for the rest of the evening. Not many cruise lines do that.

Generally, they expect men to wear at least a jacket and tie for formal nights; a lot of men bring tuxedos or dinner jackets. They do not permit shorts in the dining rooms after 6 p.m. On evenings designated semi-formal, they also expect men to wear a jacket. On Tropical and Casual dress code nights, almost anything goes.

Bill of Fare..................... B

Dolphin has always impressed us with the quality and quantity of its embarkation day buffets when many more-expensive cruise lines are doling out sandwiches. Breakfast buffets on the pool deck usually include bacon, eggs, potatoes, French toast, fruit and pastries. Dinners are fairly predictable hotel banquet-type meals, but the homemade breadsticks are delicious and there are always a lot of rich, elaborate desserts that seem to please the multitudes. Menus rotate on a fixed basis and are changed "every couple of years." Midnight buffets are especially big on the three- and four-day sailings, with a themed version scheduled every night, Italian Buffet, Fruit Buffet and Farewell Buffet, plus the Magnificent Buffet on four-night sailings. There's usually a diet dish on every lunch and dinner menu.

Showtime..................... C

The three- and four-day sailings depend a lot on audience participation games including "The Newlywed and Not-So-Newlywed Game," along with disco and casino action, male nightgown competitions and cash bingo. On longer sailings there are mini-musical revues, variety shows and karaoke contests. The ship's orchestras play quite well for dancing.

Discounts......................

Dolphin's SaleAway Program promises, "The earlier you book, the more you'll save!"

OceanBreeze

A very young Queen Elizabeth II christened this ship as the *Southern Cross* in 1954, when it made the Australia/New Zealand run from Great Britain. It featured several design innovations, including the placement of the funnel and engines at the aft end and the elimination of cargo holds; both features have become commonplace on nearly every passenger ship constructed since. The ship was laid up in Southampton in 1971, then sold to a Greek company in 1973 to be refitted as a cruise vessel named *Calypso*. She sailed the Mediterranean for five years, primarily with British vacation package tourists aboard, then was sold in 1980 to Eastern Steamship Lines and renamed *Calypso I*. In 1981, she was sold to the company's West Coast associates, Western Steamship Lines, named the *Azure Seas* and began sailing on three- and four-day cruises out of Los Angeles to Ensenada, Mexico. Eastern and Western Steamship Lines merged to become Admiral Cruises in 1986, which was subsequently acquired by Royal Caribbean Cruises and disbanded in 1992.

Still handsomely maintained, the *OceanBreeze* shows more than a bit of her art deco background as well as a touch of glitter and glamour from recent makeovers. Cabins are larger than on many ships in this price and age range.

The Brochure Says

"Sit back. Relax. Sip a colorful, tropical cocktail and get to know some new friends. Or get to know each other even better. There isn't a better time or place to do all the things you haven't done in years. This is the cruise to do it all. Or nothing at all."

Translation

Try it, you'll like it.

Cabins & Costs

Fantasy Suites: .... B+

Average Price PPPD: $248 plus airfare.

One of the 12 new penthouse suites they added on Boat Deck during a recent refit is called the owner's suite, and faces forward for a great view. With two big rooms—a living room with sofa and chairs, coffee table, minibar and TV, and a bedroom with queen-sized bed and plenty of storage, plus a bath with tub and shower—it's large enough to live in. The sofa makes into a double bed if you want to bring the kids along to share.

Small Splurges: ....B

Average Price PPPD: $198 plus airfare.

The spacious Category 2 double outside cabins on Barbizon Deck are bigger, cheaper and more private than the pricier category 1 cabins on Atlantis Deck, a promenade deck where you have people going past your window all the time. Most have two lower beds or double, and many have a third pulldown berth. The bath has shower only.

Suitable Standards: .... B

Average Price PPPD: $188 plus airfare.

The Category 3 outside double cabins on Caravelle and Dolphin Decks are adequate, although if you worry about motion sickness, we'd suggest avoiding the ones on Caravelle Deck, which are all forward from the dining room. A deck lower they're amidships for a smoother ride. Most of these have two lower beds but some of the choicest locations—# 239-244—have double beds instead and are near the elevators. Your bathroom will have a shower instead of a tub.

Bottom Bunks: C

Average Price PPPD: $108 plus airfare.

The cheapest cabins aboard are the Category 10 inside doubles on Emerald Deck, and there are only two of them. They have two lower beds or a double and a shower in the bathroom.

Where She Goes

The *OceanBreeze* makes three- and four-day cruises from Miami to the Bahamas and Key West, sailing on Fridays and Mondays.

The Bottom Line

A graceful and dignified ship, the *OceanBreeze* offers a good, medium-priced vacation at sea for first-time cruisers or anyone who wants to get away for a few days. Larger and smoother riding than the *Dolphin IV*, she's ideal for the three- and four-day mini-cruises out of Miami.

Fielding's Five

Five Unforgettable Places

1. The elegantly refurbished two-deck casino with its art deco brass railings and light fixtures.

2. The Cafe Miramar, where buffet breakfasts and lunches are served and late-night cabaret shows sometimes happen.

3. The Mayfair Lounge with its wicker furniture, potted palms and ceiling fans evokes the past. Sunlit during the day, the bay windows offer pleasant sea views; softly lit at night with a pianist playing, it's an appealing spot for a quiet rendezvous.

4. On the other hand, the Rendezvous Show Lounge glitters and sparkles with the evening's main entertainment, which you watch from comfortable swivel tub chairs upholstered in a tight red-and-blue

check that looks mauve from a distance. Don't sit behind a post or you'll miss some of the show.

5. The hard-to-find library has always been one of our favorites because it doesn't get much through traffic; books are locked in wood-and-glass bookcases and there are plenty of comfortable dark blue chairs and sofas.

Five Things You Won't Find On Board

1. TV sets in cabins that are not suites.

2. Windows in the dining room.

3. Windows in the disco—it's below the waterline.

4. Cabins designated wheelchair accessible.

5. A passenger that knows the difference between a boat and a ship.

SeaBreeze ★★★

The *SeaBreeze* was built as Costa's *Federico C* in 1958 as a two-class ship, then became Premier's *Royale* in 1984. Dolphin acquired her in 1989. There are nine passenger decks, with cabins located on all but two, the topmost deck, where there is a buffet setup, and the bottom-most, where the disco is located. During its ownership of the vessel, Premier increased the density both by adding cabins in former deck areas and adding third and fourth berths, so that almost any cabin you book is likely to have additional overhead bunks. The idiosyncratic cabin layout means the configuration of the cabins varies; some have twin beds, some double beds, some bathrooms have tub and shower, some shower only.

The Brochure Says

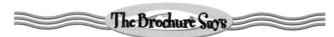

"As you'll find out, almost everything's included on Dolphin Cruise Line. So stop dreaming and wake up to Dolphin. One of the world's best cruise lines. And the best value in cruising."

Translation

The appeal is to first-time cruisers, reminding them that many more things are included in the basic fare on ships than they are accustomed to in resort hotels.

Cabins & Costs

Fantasy Suites: .... B+

Average Price PPPD: $206 plus airfare.

Seven suites on board are spacious, pretty rooms with king-sized bed, sitting area with sofa and chair, and a long built-in desk/dresser, along with two windows.

If you get B4, you'll have a view forward, a tile bath with tub and a frosted window in the bathroom, the last really rare on ships.

Small Splurges: .... B

Average Price PPPD: $171 plus airfare.

Category 2 outside superior cabins are fairly spacious, some of them (# D8, for example) with built-in cabinetry from the 1960s, lovely old coatracks fitted onto the cabin walls with pull-out hangers, brass temperature gauges made in Milan with all the instructions in Italian, left over from the *Federico C* days. We like the cabin despite its obstructed view and its two additional overhead berths.

Suitable Standards: C

Average Price PPPD: $156 plus airfare.

Category 4 cabins are outsides on the lower passenger decks with two lower beds or a double bed (specify which one you want when booking), bathrooms with shower and portholes instead of windows.

Bottom Bunks: .... D

Average Price PPPD: $99 plus airfare.

The very cheapest cabins on board are two very tiny Category 11 inside cabins with upper and lower berths forward on Isolde Deck, the lowest deck with passenger cabins. (The only one lower is the Juliet Deck, where the disco is located.)

Where She Goes

The *SeaBreeze* sails from Miami every Sunday on alternate seven-night itineraries to the Eastern Caribbean and the Western Caribbean. In the Eastern Caribbean, she visits Nassau, San Juan, St. John and St. Thomas, and in the Western Caribbean, she stops at Playa del Carmen/Cozumel, Montego Bay and Grand Cayman.

The Bottom Line

When we were last aboard the *SeaBreeze*, we were tremendously impressed at how clean and fresh she looks, especially given her age and her background as a veteran of the children's crusades over at Premier, when she was the *Royale*. Frankly, this ship is kept more spic-and-span than a lot of fancy new vessels built in the 1980s. It's a good economy-priced vessel for first-timers who want to sample a lot of Caribbean islands in a non-intimidating atmosphere.

Fielding's Five

Five Special Places

1. The Water Music Whirlpool, a trio of Jacuzzi pools surrounded by rows of plastic loungers, is on the aft end of the Boheme Deck.

2. The Prelude Bar is an intimate little lounge with very comfortable swivel rattan barstools, a varnished teak floor and latticework walls, plus lots of healthy fresh green plants.

3. The Casino, with some rare five-cent slot machines among the 99 one-armed bandits, plus four blackjack tables, one Caribbean stud and one roulette.

4. Royal Fireworks Lounge, wide rather than deep, with curved sofas, wood tables, blue and mauve chairs and an oval dance floor in wood parquet.

5. The Carmen Lounge, a show lounge filled with swivel tub chairs in rose or sage, round wooden cocktail tables, bar with eight stools, and very poor sightlines.

Five Good Reasons to Book This Ship

1. The price is right.

2. The itineraries alternate from week to week—the Eastern Caribbean one week, the Western Caribbean the next—so you could add them together for a great 14-day full Caribbean tour, and take a substantial discount on the second week's price as well.

3. Let your kids meet Yogi Bear and Fred Flintstone.

4. To be one of the displays at Pictures From An Exhibition.

5. You could get married on board—and sail away on a wonderful honeymoon. Have your travel agent contact the Wedding Coordinator at Dolphin to find out about five different wedding packages from $275 to $750.

Five Things You Won't Find On Board

1. A chair apiece if you're not in a suite; in the cabins, you get one to share.

2. A look at the bottom halves of the chorus girls in the Carmen Lounge unless you're in the front row.

3. A table for two in the dining room; you'll be seated at a table for eight to 10. But look at the upside—you'll meet that many more people.

4. A movie projected on film; in the ship's cinema, videocassettes are what you get.

5. A horse in the Light Cavalry Arcade, which is occupied by 12 coin-operated video games.

HOLLAND AMERICA LINE

300 Elliott Avenue West, Seattle, WA 98119
☎ *(206) 283-2687, (800) 426-0327*

String trios play for teatime and after dinner, as here, aboard the
Statendam.

History ....

One of the oldest and most distinguished of the cruise lines,
Holland America was founded in 1873 as the Netherlands-
America Steamship Company, a year after its young co-
founders commissioned and introduced the first ship, the
original *Rotterdam*, a 1700-ton iron vessel. The new ship
left the city it was named for on Oct. 15, 1872, and spent
15 days sailing to New York on its maiden voyage. It carried
eight passengers in first class and 380 in steerage. Only a
few years later, because all its sailings were to the Americas,
it became known as Holland America Line.

—A leading carrier of immigrants to the United States, Holland America transported nearly 700,000 between 1901 and 1914 alone; a steerage fare cost $20.

—After World War II, when middle-class Americans began touring Europe in large numbers, HAL concentrated on offering moderately priced tourist class service with two medium-sized ships that carried 836 tourist class passengers and only 39 first-class passengers.

—The line introduced educational and pleasure cruises to the Holy Land just after the turn of the century, and in 1971, suspended transatlantic sailings in favor of cruise vacations.

—The first line to introduce glass-enclosed promenade decks on its ocean liners.

—First line to introduce a full-service Lido restaurant on all its ships as a casual dining alternative.

—First cruise line to introduce karaoke, a sort of high-tech singalong (on the *Westerdam* in 1990).

—Through its subsidiary Westours, Holland America retains a strong tour profile in Alaska, and with another subsidiary company, Windstar, offers small-ship sailing vacations in Tahiti, the Caribbean and Mediterranean.

—In 1989, Carnival Cruise Lines acquired Holland America and its affiliated companies, but retains HAL's Seattle headquarters and separate management.

Concept...............................

With its slogan "A Tradition of Excellence," Holland America has always had a reputation for high quality and giving full cruise value for the money, along with a strong program of security and sanitation. Since its acquisition by Carnival, the line has worked to upscale its product and sees itself now firmly entrenched in what is called the "premium" segment of the cruise industry, a notch up from mass-market lines such as Carnival but not in the highest-priced luxury segment.

HAL defines its premium status with such details as adding suites with private verandas to its four newest ships, *Statendam, Maasdam, Ryndam* and *Veendam*, along with more elaborate spas and advanced technology showrooms. The new vessels have also been designed to handle both short and long cruises equally well, with generous closet space and more-spacious staterooms.

There's also a strong undercurrent of "politically correct" behavior, consistent with its Pacific Northwest base, from specially packaged, environmentally safe cabin gift toiletries to taking a stand against the proposed Alaska aerial wolf-hunting program several years ago. The company also makes frequent, generous contributions to Alaskan universities and nonprofit organizations such as the Alaska Raptor Rehabilitation Center in Sitka.

Signatures . . . .

A "No Tipping Required" policy means that while tips are appreciated by crew members, they cannot be solicited. However, very few passengers disembark without crossing more than a few palms with silver.

The line's longstanding tradition of hiring Indonesian and Filipino crew members and training them in its own Jakarta hotel school results in consistently high-quality service.

The continuing use of museum-quality antiques and artifacts from the golden days of Dutch shipping adds dignity and richness to the ship interiors.

The classic ship names, taken from Dutch cities, are always repeated in new vessels, with the present *Statendam, Maasdam* and *Rotterdam* each the fifth to bear the name, the *Veendam* the fourth, the *Nieuw Amsterdam, Noordam* and *Ryndam* the third namesakes, and the *Westerdam* the second in the line with that name.

Gimmicks . . . .

The ubiquitous Holland America bag, a white canvas carryall embellished with the company's logo and names of all the ships, can be glimpsed all over the world. Each passenger on each cruise is given one of these, so you can imagine how many frequent cruisers manage to amass. They're washable and last forever. "It's the single best investment we ever made," said one HAL insider.

Passport to Fitness, a folded card that has 48 separate areas to get stamped as the holder completes a qualifying activity, from the morning walkathon to aerobics class or a volleyball game. The prizes vary by the number of stamps, but are usually a Holland America logo item such as a T-shirt, cap or jacket. (We heard one eager-to-win passenger ask the librarian to stamp her passport for checking out a book about sports.)

Five Special Touches

1. Beautiful red plaid deck blankets.

2. Toiletries in each cabin wrapped in replicas of period Holland America posters and advertising art.

3. Museum-quality ship and seafaring artifacts in special display cases, along with antique bronze cannons and figureheads.

4. Fresh flowers flown in from Holland all over the ship.

5. Trays of mints, dried fruits and candied ginger outside the dining room after dinner.

Who's the Competition . . . .

Princess is the closest head-on competitor, vying to be top dog in the Alaska cruise market. The two lines can claim the two largest land tour operators, HAL's Westours and Princess's Princess Tours. For the past couple of years, Princess has had more ships in Alaska than Holland America, but Westours claims more tour departures. In the Caribbean, Celebrity Cruises is a major competitor with Holland America. HAL is also in the league to compete in the premium market with Princess for senior couples and singles.

The line's classic ocean liner *Rotterdam* on its long cruises competes head-on with Cunard's *QE2*, *Royal Viking Sun* and *Vistafjord*. The Rotterdam retires in 1997.

Who's Aboard . . . .

Holland America's basic passengers can still be defined as middle-aged and older couples who appreciate solid quality in food, surroundings and service.

Perhaps the most interesting are those who sail on the *Rotterdam's* long cruises, many wealthy, set-in-their-ways dowagers who cruise together year after year, throwing lavish cocktail parties and luncheons and competing to see who brings the most gorgeous gowns (and the most agreeable rent-a-male escorts).

Who Should Go . . . .

More younger couples and families should be aboard Holland America's shorter sailings, especially to Alaska, where the line excels in the scope and variety of its land/cruise packages. Single women and families with children will find HAL is thinking of them—youth counselors coordinate activities for each age group, from an ice cream sundae party for the 5-to-8 set to teen disco parties and contests, and social hosts to dance with unattached women on all cruises 14 days or longer. Physically challenged passengers will find suitable accommodations on board all the new ships, plus extra assistance from the attentive staff, who also lavish special care and attention on the elderly and small children.

Who Should Not Go . . . .

Young swinging singles looking to boogie all night or meet the mate of their dreams.

Nonconformists.

People who refuse to dress up.

The Lifestyle . . . .

A surprising amount of luxury and pampering go on aboard these ships, with string trios (two of them usually work each ship now) playing at teatime, white-gloved stewards to escort you to your cabin when you board, vases of fresh flowers everywhere, bowls of fresh fruit in the cabins, and most of all, what the Dutch call *gezellig*, a warm and cozy ambiance, defined with curtains in the cabins that can separate the sleeping area from the sitting area, friendly Dutch officers and caring Indonesian and Filipino crew members, who make it a point of pride to remember your name.

Kodak ambassadors are on board designated cruises to assist passengers with photo problems and show examples of good slide photography from the area. Movies are shown at three or four daily screening times, as well as on cabin TV, and shore excursions emphasize sightseeing and flightseeing, with floatplane and helicopter glacier flights, kayaking, raft trips and visits to cultural (Native American) areas and historical city tours.

Wardrobe . . . .

Dress code follows a traditional pattern, with a week usually calling for two formal nights (and they do dress up on these ships, even in Alaska), two informal nights when men are expected to wear a jacket but a tie is usually optional, and three "elegantly casual" nights with no shorts, T-shirts, tank tops, halter tops or jeans permitted. During the daytime, comfortable, casual clothing—jogging outfits, shorts or slacks, T-shirts, bathing suits and cover-ups—are adequate deck wear.

Bill of Fare . . . . A

"Genteel tradition" is important to Holland America, from a chime master who announces dinner to the Indonesian bellman in the bellboy outfit (similar to the doormen in white at the Peninsula Hotel in Hong Kong) who holds open the doors between the Lido buffet and the deck for every passenger.

Holland America consistently produces some of the tastiest and most appealing buffets at sea, from the lavish Dutch-style breakfasts to wonderfully varied luncheons. In addition to a full hot-and-cold buffet in the Lido restaurants, chefs on deck will grill hot dogs and hamburgers to order, serve up make-your-own tacos, stir-fry-to-order and pasta of the day, plus a very popular make-your-own-ice-cream-sundae counter with a bowl of homemade cookies.

Because of the scope and popularity of the buffet service, dining room breakfast and dinner are served open seating, which means you can arrive within a specified time and sit with whom you wish.

Dinner menus have grown increasingly sophisticated. A typical dinner might include six appetizers (among them warm hazelnut-crusted Brie with apple and onion compote and French bread, bay shrimp coupe with cocktail sauce, smoked king salmon with horseradish cream and herb crostini), two soups (one may be five-onion cream with frizzled onions), three salads (including field greens with smoked duck, Asian pears and toasted pecans), six entrees, from a low-calorie, low-fat sautéed Alaskan snapper teriyaki or fresh halibut with asparagus and lemon pepper mashed potatoes to a parmesan-crusted chicken breast or a grilled New York steak with baked Idaho potato and onion rings. A cheese and fresh fruit course follows, then a choice of four desserts plus pastry tray, ice creams and frozen yogurts, and sugar-free desserts. Chocoholics will adore the Chocolate Extravaganza late show, served once during each cruise as a midnight buffet.

Children's menus offer four standard entrees—hamburger and fries, hot dog, pizza or chicken drumsticks—plus a nightly chef's special, perhaps beef tacos, fish and chips or barbecued ribs. The more urbane kid may prefer to order from the regular menu, but he can't sample the following winner for the line's executive chef in the seventh annual International Cruise Ship Recipe Competition:

Salmon Tart Scotch Mist

4 servings

1 pound thinly sliced salmon fillets

4 five-inch puff pastry discs, already baked (can use frozen ones)

1 ounce butter, melted

Sauce:

1 ounce butter

3 finely chopped shallots

1 ounce Scotch whisky

1/4 pint heavy cream

4 ounces unsalted butter cut into cubes

2 TB chopped fresh dill

Melt one ounce of butter in saucepan; add shallots and simmer until soft. Add whisky and reduce by half. Add heavy cream, bring to a boil. Whisk in the butter cubes a couple at a time. Add chopped fresh dill and salt and pepper to taste. Keep warm until serving time.

On each pastry disc, overlap slices of salmon, then brush with melted butter and place under a hot broiler for two to three minutes.

To serve, spoon a little of the sauce onto each plate, place the salmon tart near the center, and garnish with steamed baby vegetables, dill sprigs and rosemary sprigs.

Showtime . . . . B+

A more sophisticated level of production shows was introduced recently, with each ship featuring its own specially tailored programs. On the line's long cruises and world cruises, headliner entertainers such as Rita Moreno, Roy Clark, Victor Borge and Vic Damone, plus noted lecturers and even a Las Vegas-style ice skating spectacular, may show up on the program.

Discounts . . . .

Early booking savings can take off 10 to 20 percent for passengers who book and make a deposit on a specified timetable, which may mean anything from one to six months ahead of time. Passengers who book earliest get the lowest prices, and if a new money-saver is introduced after they book, their fare will be adjusted on request and verification. Past passengers also get added discounts and special mail offers on certain cruises.

Westerdam

The distinctive Sun Deck pool area with its sliding glass roof and enclosed glass-walled veranda offers optimum comfort when it gets hot and muggy. The same walls and roof that let in the sun and keep out the rain also hold in the air conditioning.

Nine passenger decks, two separate self-service buffet restaurants, two outside swimming pools, a two-deck showroom and a number of lounges keep the 1494 passengers well dispersed around the ship, while a wood-and-plexiglass dome with special lighting brightens the lower-deck dining room.

Perhaps a little less formal than the line's other ships, the *Westerdam* offers some competitive prices on seven-day cruises. The Big Apple teen disco and video center make this a good ship for families.

The Brochure Says

"It is a balmy Saturday afternoon as the *Westerdam* charts an easterly course through the Caribbean...First there will be two full days at sea. Great!"

Translation

Veteran cruisers treasure days at sea, lazy times when the ship is the destination and there's no getting up early to catch a shore excursion or rushing up and down the gangway in the tropical heat. Days at sea develop their own rhythms.

Cabins & Costs

Fantasy Suites: .... B+

Average Price PPPD: $464 plus airfare.

The five top suites on board are located on Lower Promenade Deck amidships, the traditional place for the most expensive cabins on classic vessels because the ride is smoother. Larger than two standard cabins, each of the suites has a separate bedroom with two lower beds that can convert to king-size, a living room with sofa bed that can sleep an additional two persons, as well as several comfortable upholstered chairs, a bathroom with tub and shower and some handsome cabinetry.

Small Splurges: .... B

Average Price PPPD: $283 plus airfare.

Deluxe double cabins in C category are long rooms with separate sitting area which has sofa and matching chair, plus a sleeping area that can be set off with curtains that close. The entry hallway is lined on one side with two closets, on the other with tile bathroom with tub/shower combination. A desk/dresser with stool and a coffee table round out the furnishings.

Suitable Standards: C

Average Price PPPD: $257 plus airfare.

Standard outside cabins with two lower beds are somewhat smaller than the deluxe, without the sofa and sitting area, and bathrooms have shower only. There is a desk/dresser with good storage drawers and a mirror over and stool underneath.

Bottom Bunks: C

Average Price PPPD: $221 plus airfare.

The cheapest standard inside cabins, which are N category, have two lower beds that can convert to queen-sized bed, a nightstand, desk/dresser, TV set and bath with shower only, but are surprisingly spacious for bottom-of-the-line. However, there are only nine of these, so don't expect to nab one right off the bat. You may have to move up a grade or two on a popular cruise, but HAL has always been good about upgrading passengers when space permits.

Where She Goes

The *Westerdam* cruises the Eastern Caribbean in winter from Fort Lauderdale on seven-day itineraries, calling in St. Maarten, St. John, St. Thomas and Nassau.

The Bottom Line

While the *Westerdam* is the only vessel in the fleet not built from the hull up by Holland America, she still has been rebuilt to fit almost seamlessly into the fleet. (A hint: If you're looking for her "stretch" marks, begin in the smaller dining room addition amidships on Restaurant Deck, the Bookchest library on Promenade Deck, the self-service laundries on Upper Promenade and Navigation Decks or the Veranda Deck and restaurant on Sun Deck.)

A very good value for the money, *Westerdam* provides bigger-than-average cabins and a sense of comfort throughout.

Fielding's Five

Five Favorite Places

1. The beautiful Veranda restaurant with live music during luncheon and tea is one of the prettiest self-service cafes at sea; there's a second Lido Cafe two decks below.

2. The amidships Veranda pool area adjacent, with a sliding glass dome so you can sit comfortably in a lounge chair, loll in the Jacuzzi or swim in the heated pool even on a chilly day.

3. The 127-seat Admiral's Terrace balcony overlooking the main stage has some good sightlines for the evening's entertainment, but late arrivals have to stand to see the show. The 680-seat Admiral's Lounge below provides big, cushy theater-type seats and couches and is probably a better bet.

4. The volleyball and paddle tennis courts on Sports Deck, covered at the sides and top with nets, get a good workout on short cruises.

5. The 17th-century bronze cannon, cast in Rotterdam in 1634, once defended a Dutch admiral's warship, then lay at the bottom of the sea for 300 years until a Dutch fisherman dragged it up in his nets.

Five Good Reasons to Book This Ship

1. It sails to some of the most popular ports in the Eastern Caribbean—Phillipsburg, St. Maarten; Nassau, Bahamas; and St. Thomas and St. John in the U.S. Virgin Islands.

2. To try and find the seams from the "stretch," which added 130 feet in length, 13,872 more gross registry tons and capability for 494 more passengers.

3. Because four laps on the all-around-the-ship Upper Promenade Deck make one mile.

4. Because for the price range the cabins are unusually spacious.

5. The little hideaway Saloon with a Victorian accent and singalong piano bar.

Five Things You Won't Find On Board

1. Private verandas.

2. An indoor swimming pool.

3. A single cabin.

4. Skimpy cabins for wheelchair users; designated mobility impaired cabins E002, D068, J021 and D087 are all on upper decks with plenty of extra turning space.

5. A long walk to an elevator; with four different locations along each deck, it's an easy stroll to a lift.

MAJESTY®
CRUISE LINE

901 South America Way, Miami, FL 33102
☎ *(305) 530-8900, (800) 645-8111*

History . . . .

Majesty Cruise Line, an upscale spin-off of Miami-based Dolphin Cruise Line, inaugurated its $220 million, 1056-passenger *Royal Majesty* in July 1992 when it was christened in New York by actress/singer Liza Minelli. The new line came up with some fresh ideas, including a totally non-smoking dining room and a number of nonsmoking cabins and was built in less time than normal because the hull had already been completed for a ship that was never finished at Kvaerner-Masa Yard in Finland.

—The first Miami-based ship in the mini-cruise market to split itineraries between the Bahamas and Mexico, so a passenger could book two back-to-back cruises with different itineraries (1993).

Concept . . . .

After years of sailing the popular *Dolphin IV* from Miami on three- and four-day budget cruises, Dolphin Cruise Line decided to start up a sister company to operate a new, upscale ship offering to an increasingly younger market cruises that were elegant but still affordable, with an emphasis on hospitality and service.

Signatures . . . .

The distinctive crown logo is visible on the ship's superstructure.

The most attention-getting detail about *Royal Majesty* is the nonsmoking rule—no smoking in the dining room, show lounge or in 132 designated cabins, 25 percent of the total.

"It's a unique selling point," commented one of the travel agents on the inaugural sailing. "A few clients out there among the smokers won't like it, but for every one of them you lose, you'll pick up three others that are thrilled to be in a dining room without any smoking."

Gimmicks . . . .

The Hanna-Barbera costumed characters aboard are equally popular with kids and adults, and when they appear, which they do frequently, video and still cameras pop up all over the ship as loved ones run to be photographed with Fred and Barney.

Who's the Competition . . . .

One prominent travel agent said he did not see that the *Royal Majesty* was competing with Carnival's *Fantasy* in the three-day market but that it would compete with RCCL's *Nordic Empress.* In the seven-day Bermuda market, it does compete head-to-head with Celebrity's *Meridian* and *Horizon.*

Who's Aboard . . . .

Younger couples and singles, a lot of families with small children on holidays and, in summer, around 200 non-U.S. citizens from Canada, Latin America and the United Kingdom are on each cruise. Also in summer, a number of yuppie couples and as many as 300 children. In winter, many of the cruisers are older Florida residents, but once spring and summer arrive, the ship fills with yuppies, singles, couples and families with kids.

Who Should Go . . . .

It's a good ship for seniors because it's not too large, has a warm atmosphere and a caring cruise staff. Children love the Hanna-Barbera characters, of course, and families have enough options to be together when they wish or apart and still have a good time. But it's also a happy hunting ground for single guys looking for great-looking, single, thirty-something women.

Who Should Not Go . . . .

Dowager veterans of the world cruise, and anyone who would be a party-pooper with a lot of families with children, yuppies and singles having a really great time.

The Life-style . . . .

It's a young, active ship with exercise classes such as tai chi, aerobics and stretch-and-tone scheduled before 9 a.m., plus quiz, Scrabble and ping pong competitions, dance and golf lessons, ice-carving demonstrations and art auctions. A Medieval Royal Fest with knights and jesters, face painting and fun and games is held on board during most cruises. A Club Nautica watersports program provides optional shore excursions with deep-sea fishing, snorkeling, scuba and sailing. Besides the daily program for adults, children are issued their own colorful activities booklets with Fred Flintstone on the cover. Particularly during spring and fall, *Royal Maj-*

esty will have conference and incentive groups on board wearing badges and going to meetings in the ship's conference rooms.

Wardrobe......................

Because there are usually a number of first-time cruisers aboard, some of them group and incentive travelers, dress codes are not as strictly adhered to as on some ships. But the line does observe two formal nights when men are asked to wear "proper attire," and two semi-formal nights that usually call for jacket and tie. Casual-dress evenings call for resort-wear rather than shorts, T-shirts or jeans.

Bill of Fare...................... B+

In the dining room, dinner menus usually offer a choice of four or five main dishes, say, Cornish game hen, steak, veal, grilled fish and a vegetarian pasta dish. A choice of three or four appetizers, two soups, two salads and a range of desserts presented at the table fills out the menu.

The buffet breakfasts are copious, with ready-made omelets, scrambled eggs, bacon, sausage, ham, potatoes, herring, smoked salmon, bagels, fruits, cereals and all kinds of freshly made pastries.

A "Light at Sea" menu lists calories, cholesterol and sodium count (but not fat grams). We tried the low-calorie pita pockets with chicken, cucumber, tomatoes and onions that were delicious. Other lunchtime options that day were a California frittata, sauteed ling cod, mignons of turkey supreme Cacciatore, braised round of beef, plus an onion, tomato and white bean salad garnished with black olives.

One of our favorite food venues on board is the Piazza San Marco out on deck, serving pizza, hot dogs, ribs, hamburgers, french fries and ice cream, along with optional wine, beer and soda on ice. Steps away are tables with umbrellas and red-checkered cloths, like an Italian sidewalk cafe with a big stretched canvas canopy overhead in a sort of Sydney Opera House sail shape. (OK, like an Australian sidewalk cafe, then.)

Dining room service is friendly and generally efficient, except for the open-seating breakfasts. One morning every order delivered to our table of six was confused. There's also 24-hour room service with cold plates, desserts, coffee tea or milk.

Showtime...................... B+

Royal Majesty presents live theatrical productions such as "Star-Spangled Girl" and "Murder at the Howard Johnson's" during each cruise by a resident acting company. A Medieval Feast highlights one evening during each cruise, and a "Big Chill" '50s and '60s party, karaoke sing-alongs, fun and games with the cruise staff and some musical production and variety shows round out the programs.

Discounts . . . .

The AdvanSaver promises that the earlier you book, the more you'll save.

Royal Majesty ★★★★

It's an elegant ship with some of the most distinctive fabrics and carpeting we've seen anywhere, along with a generous use of wood that lends a warm ambiance.

Cabins are located on six of the nine passenger decks, with a top deck sunning area, below which is the Majesty Deck pool and spa area. Deck 5, the Countess Deck, is where most of the public rooms are located, starting from the forward observation deck and lounge and moving back through a series of small rooms that double as meeting areas when a conference is on board and bars, card rooms and such when there's no group. Amidships is the Crossroads lobby area, directly below the casino, and the dining room is aft. The show room is conveniently located one deck above the dining room, making it an easy progression from dinner to entertainment.

The Brochure Says

"From the beginning a ship designed for conferences."

Translation

We met a lady in the elevator who was wearing a name tag on her bathing suit.

Cabins & Costs

Fantasy Suites: .... A

Average Price PPPD: $439 plus airfare.

Two royal suites are the top digs aboard, two large separate rooms with floor-to-ceiling bay view windows, a living room with paisley sofa, coffee table, two chairs, glass dining table with four chairs and long built-in granite counter, and a bedroom with queen-sized bed, covered in a paisley print bedspread, nightstands, desk/dresser with chair, TV/VCR, minibar, safe, hair dryer, ironing board, bathrobes and 24-hour butler service. There's also a marble bath with long tub and a big walk-in closet/dressing room with good hanging storage.

Small Splurges: .... A

Average Price PPPD: $359 plus airfare.

The 14 deluxe suites have twins or queen-sized beds, a granite-topped built-in desk and dresser with blue tweed chair, a granite-topped nightstand with four drawers, a big window in the bedroom side and a sliding fabric panel in strips of beige fabric that can be pulled across the room to separate the bedroom from the sitting area. The latter has a large sofa and two chairs, plus a wood-and-glass coffee table. A built-in wood console has TV/VCR and underneath is a wooden cabinet with glassware and minibar. In the marble bathroom is a tub, sink with marble counter and big mirror with good makeup lights, a built-in hair dryer, shower over the tub and complimentary toiletries. There is a glass bay window in the sitting area, and the art-work in the cabin consists of three pleasant watercolors. You also get 24-hour butler service in these suites.

Suitable Standards: .... B

Average Price PPPD: $243 plus airfare.

The outside standard cabins are very attractive because of the elegant fabrics used throughout the ship. These are crisp brick red, apple green and black plaids with a smaller patterned carpet in the same col-ors. You can request queen-sized, double or twin beds, and also get a picture window, color TV, safe, hair dryer, ironing board (ingeniously built into a dresser drawer) and signature kimonos for use during the cruise. The bath is adequately sized with shower only, and there's also a pair of nightstands with drawers, a desk/dresser with chair and a closet with two full-length hanging spaces and one half-length hang-ing space with four drawers under, quite adequate for a week's cruise. Four cabins are designated wheelchair-accessible.

Bottom Bunks: .... B

Average Price PPPD: $146 plus airfare.

Even the lowest-priced inside doubles have two lower beds, and a handsome mirror wall where the window would be successfully pre-sents the illusion of light and space, brightening the room inside. There's a nightstand with drawers, a desk/dresser with chair, bath with shower only, adequate closet and wall-hung TV set. Some of these cabins have upper berths as well.

Where She Goes

Royal Majesty makes three-day cruises to the Bahamas and Key West every Friday from Miami, and four-night cruises to Mexico and Key West every Monday during the winter season. In spring the ship repositions to Boston for seven-night roundtrip sailings to Bermuda during the summer.

The Bottom Line

This is a classy ship and the prices are right. The deck sunbathing areas are a bit small and can be crowded when the ship is jam-packed full, as it was on an Easter weekend last spring when we were aboard, along with some 200 children.

The *Royal Majesty* is one of the rare new ships that offers a full promenade around the ship for inveterate walkers and joggers. Rubberized red matting covers the entire deck, with a special track laid out in green in the center; five laps around is a mile.

It's a good vessel for fitness-conscious people, with plenty of exercise options on board and ashore, including walking tours with cruise staff members. The only thing that surprises us is, for a ship with such an active nonsmoking policy, there are an awful lot of smokers aboard and it's hard to get completely away from the smell of it in the corridors, even when you book a smokefree cabin, eat in a smokefree dining room and watch the show in a smokefree lounge.

Fielding's Five

Five Special Places

1. The dining room, one of the first nonsmoking cruise dining rooms at sea in 1992, now one of many, has lights bright enough to see but not flat cafeteria lighting, and there is enough sound baffle on the ceiling to reduce the room noise a bit.

2. Body Wave, the really hot gym on board with every imaginable kind of equipment, plus an adjacent exercise room with wood floor, windows, mirrors, barre and sauna.

3. Royal Fireworks, where a resident theater company performs two one-act comedies each cruise, with two-seat sofas and swivel chairs in autumn leaf tones, a wood parquet dance floor and bandstand, and elegant blond-burled wood-covered walls.

4. Royal Observatory, with striped red-and-black tub chairs, antique ship models and drawings, a curved wood bar with brass rail and curved glass walls facing forward.

5. The Polo Club, one of the most sophisticated bars at sea, with excellent music, whether a late-morning jazz session with some of the musicians from the ship's orchestra or a cocktail-hour classical guitarist playing music you can hear and converse over at the same time.

NORWEGIAN CRUISE LINE

95 Merrick Way, Coral Gables, FL 33134
☎ *(305) 445-0866, (800) 327-7030*

The sports bar on the Windward *underscores NCL's emphasis on active and theme cruises.*

History

Norwegian Caribbean Lines was founded in 1966 by Knut Kloster and Ted Arison (see Carnival Cruises, History, above) to create casual, one-class cruising in the Caribbean in contrast to the more formal, class-oriented tradition of world cruises and transatlantic crossings. That partnership soon broke up, however, leaving Kloster to begin a rapid expansion of the line while Arison went off to found Carnival Cruise Lines.

NCL's first ship was the *Sunward*, but the fleet soon grew to include the *Starward* (1968), *Skyward* (1969), *Southward* (1971) and, also in 1971, a replacement for the original *Sunward* called *Sunward II* (the former *Cunard Adventurer*).

But the real coup came in 1979 when the Kloster family bought French Line's *France*, which had been laid up in Le Havre for five years, made a major rebuilding to convert the former ocean liner into a cruise ship and renamed her *Norway*. From her debut in 1980, she was the flagship of the line, and the other four vessels came to be called "the white ships" for their white hulls that contrasted sharply with the dark blue hull of the *Norway*. (All the original "white ships" have been retired from the fleet, the last in September, 1995.)

In 1984, Kloster Cruise Limited, the parent company of Norwegian Cruise Line, bought Royal Viking Line, promising to make minimal changes to the highly respected company. Two years later, Kloster changed the Norwegian registry of the RVL ships to Bahamian, then a year after that closed down the long-time San Francisco headquarters and moved the entire operation to Florida.

In 1987, the former Norwegian Caribbean Lines changed its name to Norwegian Cruise Line with an eye to long-range marketing of Alaska, Bermuda and European cruises, and in 1989 acquired San Francisco-based Royal Cruise Line. This time, however, Kloster left the company in San Francisco with most of its executive roster intact.

The dismantling and sale of RVL happened in the summer of 1994, with the flagship *Royal Viking Sun* and the Royal Viking name, logo, past passenger list and general goodwill sold to Cunard, who promptly (but only briefly) named their new division Cunard Royal Viking Line (see Cunard, above). The *Royal Viking Queen* was soon transferred over to Royal Cruise Line and renamed the *Queen Odyssey*. Two earlier RVL ships, *Royal Viking Star* and *Royal Viking Sea*, also went to Royal to become *Star Odyssey* and *Royal Odyssey*.

In 1996, Royal Cruise Line was dismantled, the *Crown Odyssey* becoming NCL's *Norwegian Crown*, the *Queen Odyssey* becoming *Seabourn Legend* and the *Star Odyssey* becoming the *Black Watch* for Fred Olson Lines.

In the late 1980s, Knut Kloster began taking a less active role in the company in order to pursue his dream of building the world's biggest passenger ship, the 250,000-ton, 5600-passenger *Phoenix World City*. Despite its detractors who say the project's dead, the giant ship may still be a viable possibility, pending funding.

—The first three- and four-day cruises to the Bahamas incorporating a private island beach day.

—First line to restage hit Broadway musicals aboard cruise ships; the *Norway*'s first production was "My Fair Lady."

—The official cruise line of the National Basketball Association, the Basketball Hall of Fame and the National Football League Players Association; NCL presents a number of sports theme cruises throughout the year.

—First cruise line to broadcast live NFL and NBA games live aboard its ships.

Signatures

Theme cruises—especially the annual *Norway* jazz festival, now in its 14th year, and the sports theme cruises which are aboard all the ships.

The "Dive-In" program—the first and perhaps most successful of the watersports packages found on cruise ships combines onboard instruction and equipment rentals with shore excursions to snorkel and dive spots. A Sports Afloat T-shirt is given to participants in designated activities who accrue seven tickets by the end of the cruise.

Gimmicks

The line's award-winning advertising campaign built around a sexy young couple who look like they might star in lingerie or perfume ads and the slogan, "It's different out here." The campaign itself is great, but it could be argued they're barking up the wrong mast, because we've never seen that couple on an NCL ship.

Who's the Competition

The main competitors in all its cruising areas (now that Carnival has entered Alaska) are the ships owned by Kloster's old nemesis Arison and the rapidly-growing Royal Caribbean Cruise Line. The *Norway*, unique in the otherwise modern fleet because of her history as the famous ocean liner *France*, should be competing with other classic ships like the *Rotterdam* and the *Queen Elizabeth 2*, but with a year-round, seven-day Caribbean itinerary and the same food and entertainment as the rest of the NCL fleet, she doesn't.

Who's Aboard

A lot of sports-oriented young couples from the heartland; yuppies and baby boomers; jazz fans for two weeks every autumn on the *Norway*; people who want to see a Broadway show without actually having to set foot in Times Square.

Who Should Go

Young couples and singles looking for a first-time cruise; music fans who'll enjoy not only the two-week annual jazz festival but the annual blues festival and two country music festivals; TV quiz show fans to take the annual "Wheel of Fortune" cruise; comedy aficionados for the summer comedy cruise; rock 'n rollers for the '50s and '60s cruise; Big Band devotees for the November sentimental journey; and fitness buffs for the annual fitness and beauty cruise each fall aboard the *Norway*.

Young families who will appreciate NCL's "Kids Crew" program for kids 3 to 17, with special kids-only activities onboard and ashore. They're divided into four different age groups: Junior Sailors, 3–5; First Mates, 6–8; Navigators, 9–12; and teens, 13–17.

Who Should Not Go ....

Longtime cruise veterans looking to check out a new line, senior singles, and urban sophisticates who've "been there, done that."

The Lifestyle ....

"Elegant, yes; stuffy, never," was the way they described themselves a couple of years ago, and it's fairly apt. NCL's ships offer traditional cruising, with themed sailings (see Who Should Go, above), international themed dinners several times a sailing, live calypso music on deck, and something going on around the ship every minute. Not long after boarding, passengers are offered free spa demonstrations, free casino lessons, a rundown on the children's program for the week, a free sports and fitness orientation, dive-in snorkeling presentation and as many as three singles parties—one each at 8 p.m. for college-aged spring break celebrants and over-30 singles (a Big Band dancing session is usually scheduled at the same time for the over-50s set), plus a third at 11:30 for any singles that couldn't find a friend at the first two parties.

In other words, you'll stay busy aboard—and that's before the dozen or so shore excursions offered in each port of call!

Wardrobe ....

NCL calls for less stringent dress codes than its competitors, good news for guys who hate to wear ties. A seven-day cruise usually calls for two formal outfits, two informal outfits and a "costume" for a theme country/western or Caribbean night if you wish. Short cruises schedule one formal night and two informal nights. Formal garb is described by NCL as "cocktail dresses or gowns for the ladies and the men wear a jacket and tie or tuxedo." On informal nights, "just about anything but shorts is fine." For daytimes, take along some exercise clothing, bathing suits, shorts, T-shirts and sandals, plus light cotton clothes and walking shoes for going ashore. NCL also reminds passengers not worry about clothes—if they forget something, they can buy anything they need in the shipboard shops.

Bill of Fare . . . . B

The food is big-ship cruise fare with some new cutting-edge options.

The dinner menu usually provides five appetizers, three soups, two salads, a pasta and four main dishes, one of which is fish, along with a full vegetarian menu offered nightly. There are four desserts plus ice cream and fruit, and low fat, low calorie dishes are indicated on the menus with an asterisk. Dinners are served in two assigned seatings at assigned tables, with first seating 6:30 p.m. and second seating 8:30 p.m.

A welcome-aboard buffet is typical of lunchtime self-service offerings—a make-your-own taco table and a vegetarian buffet with hot and cold selections, plus carved roast beef, turkey goulash with rice and pre-cooked hamburgers, along with a dessert table and separate beverage service area.

An alternative restaurant called Le Bistro, on board the *Norway, Seaward, Dreamward* and *Windward*, requires an advance reservation and a tip to the waiter but makes no surcharge for the food. The menu, described as "South-Beach style" by the Miami-based line (meaning Miami Beach's trendy art deco district), offers for starters a Norwegian seafood medley, escargots, French onion soup or clam chowder, three salads including Caesar and a warm spinach, then a vegetable main course, two pastas and three main dishes—chicken Provençale, pepper steak Madagascar and veal medallions with a wine/herb sauce and polenta. Dessert choices include a warm apple tart, a chocolate dessert and a selection of fruit and cheese.

Showtime . . . . A

NCL was the first cruise line to create a buzz about its onboard entertainment, presenting shipboard versions of popular Broadway shows from "My Fair Lady" to the relatively current "The Will Rogers Follies" and the popular revival "Grease." In addition to the Broadway shows, each ship presents a song-and-dance Sea Legs revue as well as variety performers on other evenings.

Also aboard: Q and A sessions with sports stars, several different lounges offering live music for dancing, art auctions, games, dance lessons, and pop psychology lectures about astrology or fashion colors.

Discounts . . . .

Early booking discounts knock off as much as 15 percent of the cruise price.

Children under two sail free; a maximum of two adults and two children per cabin is the limit for this offer.

Leeward

This joint-venture ship owned by Finland's Effjohn International and operated by NCL is far more attractive in total than the sum of its component parts. The size, 25,000 tons carrying 950 passengers, seems ideally human-scale in these days of megaliners, and the decor, evocatively art deco-style, smudges most of the outline of the former Baltic ferry Sally Albatross.

The Brochure Says

"Your heart is saying, 'Go ahead, take a long vacation.' Unfortunately, your schedule is saying, 'Uh-uh, just a few days.' Oh boy, have we got a cruise for you.'"

Translation

As a mid-sized ship in the three- and four-day market, Leeward offers a more intimate, refreshing change from the big ships of Carnival and RCCL.

Cabins & Costs

Fantasy Suites: .... A

Average Price PPPD: $553 including airfare.
A pair of owner's suites, one dubbed the Presidential Suite because ex-President George Bush once stayed there, provides large private balconies with outdoor hot tub, living room spacious enough for a modest party, separate bedroom with two lower beds, picture windows, mini-refrigerator, walk-in closets and bath with tub and shower.

Small Splurges .... A

Average Price PPPD: $470 including airfare.
Eight deluxe penthouses with small private verandas and living rooms with sofa and large picture window, mini-refrigerator, queen-sized

bed in separate bedroom area, wall-mounted TV, and generous storage space.

Suitable Standards .... B

Average Price PPPD: $306 including airfare in category E.
We deem categories D and E as "suitable," but not categories F and G, outsides with partially or fully obstructed views because of hanging lifeboats. You'll find two lower beds, some sitting areas, and, in many, very handsome black-and- white tile bathrooms with shower. All passengers get a basket of toiletries in the bathroom and a silver dish of fresh fruit in the cabin. Nonsmoking cabins are available on request.

Bottom Bunks .... B

Average Price PPPD: $226 including airfare.
This quartet of small outsides on Promenade Deck are the lowest-priced accommodations on board. While most of the inside cabins priced slightly higher have two lower beds, these upper and lower berth cabins have a window and a good location just steps away from the open deck.

Where She Goes

The *Leeward* makes year-round three-day cruises every Friday, with alternate itineraries from Miami to Nassau and Great Stirrup Cay, the line's private island, or from Miami to Key West and Great Stirrup Cay.

The Bottom Line

All in all, this is a handsome and winning ship. We only wish we couldn't glimpse so much untreated steel superstructure under the cosmetic surface.

Fielding's Five

Five Fabulous Places

1. The Sports Bar and Grill aboard means nobody has to miss any important play of a televised sports event.

2. Gatsby's Piano Bar with angled glass walls, raised curved banquettes and tapestry-covered seating offers a nightclub ambiance.

3. Le Bistro, an alternative restaurant for couples who want to dine alone or with new friends they met aboard.

4. The Stardust Lounge with its entrance that is reminiscent of an art deco movie house.

5. The Four Seasons Dining Room, with a shipboard art deco entrance that reinforces the sense of being at sea.

Five Good Reasons to Book This Ship

1. If you're an art aficionado, you'll find plenty to admire aboard.

2. To dine in one of the two dining rooms that seem no larger than your favorite upscale restaurant.

3. To hang around the Sports Bar amid museum cases of vintage sports equipment.

4. To enjoy a rousing production of "Pirates of Penzance."

5. To visit the super port of Key West.

Norway   ★★★★

On our most recent *Norway* visit the ship looked very clean and spiffy from a recent makeover—she could rival any Hollywood star in number of facelifts, and she's only 34. Over the years, new luxury cabins and penthouses have been added, each with big windows or private balconies overlooking the sea. But because of the ship's vintage, the original cabins come in all shapes and sizes rather than the neat, identical modules you find on new ships. It's worth spending some extra time studying the deck plan and cabin specifics to be sure you're getting the sort of cabin you want.

The heart of the ship is the International Deck with its enclosed promenade most of the way around on both sides, like fashionable boulevards lined with sidewalk cafes and elegant boutiques. Two separate dining rooms, remnants of the two-class ocean liner days, are divided by the galley in a you-can't-get-here-from-there arrangement, and cabins are dispersed throughout the 10 passenger decks in random configuration.

Even from a distance (she usually lies at anchor in her ports of call) you can recognize her twin stacks and dark blue hull.

The Brochure Says

"Ever since her launch as the SS *France*, she has been hailed for her plush splendor and architectural marvels. Now, after the finishing touches of a three-year, $60 million refurbishment...she has emerged with her classic features intact: the hand-laid tile mosaics, Art Deco murals, marble statuary, teak rails, two-story Broadway theater, and the magnificent Club Internationale ballroom."

Translation

The real joy of cruising on the *Norway* for a ship buff is to recreate some of the glory and nostalgia from an ocean liner, even a liner-come-lately like the *France*. In many of the cabins, touches remain from the original; some bathrooms still have the 1960s plumbing fixtures like old-fashioned bathtubs, heated towel racks and tile mosaics. And look for the five antique slot machines on exhibit in the new marble-floored casino, probably not from the original ship but antiques nevertheless.

Cabins & Costs

Fantasy Suites: .... A

Average Price PPPD: $778 including airfare.
While we admire the original two-bedroom, two-bath grand suites on Viking Deck (Jerry Lewis always occupied one of them when he was the headline entertainer on a cruise), today's luxury-loving passengers would probably prefer one of the two new owner's suites forward on the top deck. Each has its own wrap-around terrace; a living room with leather sofa and chairs, desk, tape/CD deck, large TV, fully stocked bar, marble table, built-in cabinetry, and plenty of room for entertaining; a bedroom with queen-sized bed, big walk-in closet, marble bath with Roman tub, marble floor, separate stall shower and powder room; and concierge service.

Small Splurges: .... A

Average Price PPPD: $392 including airfare.
The junior suites on Pool Deck are marvelously light, bright rooms with three big picture windows, two lower, queen-sized or king-sized beds, sitting area with sofa and chair, dressing table with make-up lights and good mirror, mini-refrigerator, tub and shower, and concierge service.

Suitable Standards: .... C-

Average Price PPPD: From $300 to $321, including airfare.
Cabins vary widely, with the four standard outsides and one superior inside categories more or less falling into the standard cabin range. Each has a bed arrangement that sleeps two people in some fashion in lower beds, a bath with tub or shower, a chair, dresser, TV set and table. If you don't mind an inside, O 88 has a lot of room, twin beds, two dressers, two chairs and table.

Bottom Bunks: .... F

Average Price PPPD: $228 in category N, $256 in category K, including airfare.
The category N inside doubles with upper and lower berths are the bottom-of-the-line on the *Norway*, and the one we looked at recently—V 248—we could not recommend, even to the most forgiving first-timer. A tiny space with a stool, TV set, single bed and overhead bunk, with fresh carpeting and upholstery but an original bathroom with shower only and the smell of bad drains. We'd suggest spending another $190 each for the week and take a category K inside like A 023 with a double bed and upper pulldown (making it workable even for roommates who want separate beds), chair, dresser, TV set and bath with shower only.

Where She Goes

The *Norway* follows the same seven-day itinerary year-round, sailing from Miami on Saturdays and anchoring off St. Maarten, St. John, St. Thomas and Great Stirrup Cay, the line's private island in the Bahamas, for a beach day.

The Bottom Line

It's important for a potential passenger, especially an ocean liner aficionado, to make a clear mental distinction between the *Norway*, a seven-day mass-market cruise ship featuring dinner menus with fixed themes that rotate every seven days, and the *France*, an ocean liner that offered superb first-class food and service that rivaled the three-star Michelin restaurants of France on crossings in the 1960s. While the *Norway* offers extremely good seven-day Caribbean cruises for vacationers, honeymooners and first-time cruisers, you must not expect to sail in the legendary style of the French Line.

Fielding's Five

Five Lovely Locales

1. The Club Internationale looks like the kind of nightclub Nick and Nora Charles would have frequented, except perhaps for the tuxedoed mannequin seated at the player piano and those gesso gods of the sea in the side niches. Elegant green and gold silk tapestry covers the banquettes and chairs, and original light fixtures from the 1960s still adorn the walls and ceilings.

2. The Champs Elysees on starboard side and Fifth Avenue on port side are almost as grand as the originals, enclosed promenades that let you saunter past shop windows glittering with jewelry, crystal, perfumes and sequinned gowns, even a fur shop, and a sidewalk cafe where you can sit down in white wrought iron chairs for a drink.

3. The sybaritic spa compound built around the ship's indoor pool, operated by Steiner of London, a 6000-square-foot Roman spa with hydrotherapy baths, steam rooms, saunas and aquacise pool with spa treatments sold individually or part of a package, plus a 4000-square-foot health and fitness center, basketball court and jogging track.

4. The charming children's playroom called Trolland on the Norway, still has its original fairytale wall mural from the *France*; three youth counselors are always aboard, but the number swells to seven during holiday sailings and summer.

5. The Saga Theatre is a proper theatre with its comfortable row seats and balcony, just the place to watch Will Rogers ropin' and chattin' in "The Will Rogers Follies," to catch the Gerry Mulligan Quartet during the jazz festival or the Shirelles singing "Dedicated to the One I Love" during a '50s and '60s theme cruise with great rock 'n roll era names.

PREMIER CRUISE LINES

400 Challenger Road, Cape Canaveral, FL 32920
(407) 783-5061, (800) 327-7113

History . . . .

Premier Cruise Lines, founded in 1984, got some notice as a cruise line dedicated to families and as the first multi-day cruise ship sailing from Port Canaveral, but it catapulted to attention in November 1985, when it became "the Official Cruise Line of Walt Disney World," selling combination week-long land/sea vacations that allowed passengers to take a three- or four-day cruise and spend the remaining four or three days at Disney World with hotel room, rental car and admissions included in the package.

It was a great idea, first conceived around 1980 or 1981 by Bruce Nierenberg (who also later founded now-defunct American Family Cruises) and Bjornar Hermansen, when both were with Norwegian Caribbean Line (now Norwegian Cruise Line). So it was to NCL they first took the idea of basing a cruise ship in Port Canaveral to take advantage of the nearness of Disney World and tap into some of that rapidly growing leisure travel market. NCL wasn't interested, so in 1983, Nierenberg and Hermansen started up Premier with the backing of the Greyhound Corp. (later to become part of The Dial Corp) of Phoenix, Arizona.

The first ship Premier operated was the *Star/Ship Royale*, the former *Federico C* from Costa, which carried 1050 passengers when all the berths were filled, which they usually were. They bought and renovated the ship for $14 million, painted the hull bright red with orange and yellow trim, and sent it on its maiden voyage in March 1984.

In November 1985, on the heels of the Disney deal, Premier bought the *Oceanic* from Home Lines and made a major conversion that increased the ship's maximum passenger capacity from 1096 to 1800.

Premier acquired the six-year-old *Atlantic*, which became the *Star/Ship Atlantic*, after Home Lines went out of business in 1988. From a maximum of 1167 passengers, the *Atlantic* was remodeled to carry 1600. Later that same year Premier bought the 686-berth *Sun Princess* from Princess Cruises and turned it into the 950-berth *Star/Ship Majestic*, and then sold the *Royale* in January 1989 to Dolphin to become the *SeaBreeze*.

Heading into the 1990s, Premier decided to start calling itself The Big Red Boat, which was picked up instantly by TV-watching children. It also made marketing sense, because it meant instead of calling and requesting a ship by name, the passenger would take whichever Big Red Boat was handy despite the dissimilarities in the fleet.

Carnival Cruise Lines entered into negotiation to buy Premier in April 1991, then in May rescinded the offer. In June, co-founder Nierenberg resigned and sold his stock to Dial Corp. Co-founder Hermansen stayed on, trimming and streamlining company operations until his resignation in June 1992.

In March 1994, the 10-year agreement with Disney came to an end, but the line still offers Disney World vacation packages in combination with its cruises. Disney decided to start its own cruise line, called Disney Cruise Lines, with the first of two new ships scheduled to debut in January 1998. Premier went out and got itself some other 'toons from Warner Brothers' Looney Tunes—Bugs Bunny, Daffy Duck, Tweety Bird, Sylvester, the Tasmanian Devil—that Premier employees animate on board the ships.

The line operated three vessels until early 1995, when the *Majestic* was leased to CTC, a European cruise operator. At present, the *Atlantic* and *Oceanic* compose the fleet of The Big Red Boat.

Concept . . . .

While other cruise lines, particularly Sitmar, had introduced very good children's programs, nothing anywhere near the scale of Premier's family program had been seen before. Children divided into age groups have their own daily programs as full of activities as the adults', even their own shore excursions, so parents could take the kids on a cruise without having to constantly entertain them, making it a real vacation for everybody.

Signatures . . . .

Bright red hulls on both Big Red Boats.

Cartoon characters on board—currently Looney Tunes favorites such as Bugs Bunny, Elmer Fudd, Porky Pig and Tweety Bird.

Extensive children's programs that run from 9 a.m. to 10 p.m. with a staff of professionally trained counselors who divide the kids into five different age groups. At the end of the scheduled program, babysitting is available at a nominal charge. Child care for children ages 2 to 12 is offered on an around-the-clock basis.

Gimmicks . . . .

Tuck-in bedtime service for kids by one of the costumed characters ($10) or a character breakfast in a special dining room ($30 for a family of four).

Chocolate Ship cookies for kids at bedtime.

Who's the Competition. . . . .

In the short range, it's Carnival, who put its glittering new *Fantasy* into Port Canaveral on three- and four-day cruises with a Disney World package similar to the one offered by Premier. In the long haul, it's the Mouse, of course. Both lines profess to be excited about the Disney cruise ships coming into Port Canaveral in 1998 because they expect them to draw into the area many more potential passengers for everybody.

Who's Aboard. . . . .

Kids, lots and lots of kids, some 500 or so children on an average summer or holiday cruise. At the same time, the line promotes the romantic aspects of cruising to honeymooners and frequently offers singles and senior citizen specials as well.

Who Should Go. . . . .

Parents, single parents and grandparents with children. Couples and singles who enjoy being around other people's children.

Who Should Not Go . . . .

Anyone who doesn't adore children.

The Lifestyle . . . .

A lot of attention is paid to the adults on board, because the line intends to provide a vacation for the whole family, not just the children. Mom and Dad can enjoy a full day working out in the gym, taking a snorkeling tour, signing up for golf lessons, having a massage or beauty treatment at Steiners Beauty and Fitness Salon/Massage, betting on the horse races, attending the captain's champagne reception, gaming in the casino, playing family snowball bingo, hitting a late-night cabaret party before going to the gala midnight buffet at 12:30 and having some French onion soup and made-to-order omelets between 1 and 3 a.m.

Wardrobe. . . . .

The garb for these cruises is casual most of the time, although everyone in the family should bring something a little dressy for the captain's party. After dinner, unlike many lines, Premier doesn't mind passengers changing back to casual clothing for the rest of the evening on formal night.

Bill of Fare C

The dinner menu offers three appetizers, three soups, two salads and seven entrees, plus a special children's menu with familiar favorites such as cheeseburgers, chicken nuggets, hot dogs and fish fingers, along with a "health boat" selection that includes cheese pizza, beef kabob, beef and bean burrito and Spaghetti O's. Buffet breakfast and lunch is served in the cafe as well as full-service breakfast, lunch and dinner in the dining room. The Big Dipper ice cream parlor with "make-your-own-sundaes" is open throughout the afternoon. An "America the Beautiful" menu with the Looney Tunes characters strolling around the dining room is usually scheduled the last night of the cruise, with other themed dinners—French, Italian and Caribbean—also on the schedule, depending on the length of the cruise. Meals are served in the dining rooms at assigned tables during two seatings.

Showtime . . . . B

In addition to daylong activities and shore excursions, evening production shows such as "Legends in Concert" with clones of Elvis, Madonna and the Blues Brothers performing, a Carlos & Charlie's Mexico-themed party, and lots of audience participation, from costumed '50s twist parties and Country Western Jamborees to karaoke contests.

Discounts . . . .

A family reunion plan gives 10 percent off the tariff for the first two guests in each of three cabins with a minimum of 10 people and six full-fare guests. Single parents traveling with one to three children under 17 can take a category 3 through 8 cabin, pay 125 percent of the per person, double occupancy rate, and the kids pay the cheaper third, fourth and fifth guest rate for sharing the same cabin. And seniors (anyone 60 or over) and a guest traveling with them can take 10 percent off the cruise fare during the season (summer and holiday weekends) and 15 percent apiece off during the rest of the year.

Star/Ship Atlantic   ★ ★ ★

Built in 1982, the *Atlantic* is a durable vessel with high passenger density, thanks to those 452 upper berths in the cabins. A sliding plexiglass roof over the amidships terrace and pool makes the area comfortable year-round. Passenger activity is concentrated on the Pool Deck and Lounge Deck with most of the cabins and the dining room below. A group of cabins is also located forward on Lounge Deck, and the major children's play area, Pluto's Playhouse, is aft on the deck below Lounge Deck with its own kiddies' pool outside.

The Brochure Says

"While you're having fun, we provide five separate programs for kids and teens that keep them occupied every day until 10 p.m. After that, group baby-sitting is available for a nominal fee as part of our 24-hour child-care service. We'll watch the kids overnight so you can relax and dance the night away!"

Translation

You can bring the kids on a cruise and hardly ever have to see them at all—but that's not what we observe on board. On the contrary, many parents seem to want to spend more time with their kids—or the kids with their parents—on the ship and ashore, so that the children's play room is often not as busy as we'd expected. The new Voyages of Discover program (see Champagne Toast, above) acknowledges this and introduces more activities for the whole family to do together.

Cabins & Costs

NOTE:

Average per person per day prices below are for three- and four-day cruises; seven-day packages including theme park stays will be less-

expensive on a per-day basis. The prices are for two full-fare cabin occupants; third, fourth and fifth cabin occupants pay $449-$569 apiece including airfare from some cities for the three- or four-day cruise, depending on the season.

Fantasy Suites: C

Average Price PPPD: $399 including roundtrip airfare.

The largest accommodations on board the Atlantic are the category 9 apartment suites, which have a sitting room with sofa-bed and TV set and a bedroom with queen-sized bed, enough space for a family of four. While not huge, these are twice the size of the suites in the next category down, and have bathrooms with tub.

Small Splurges: C

Average Price PPPD: $329 on category 8 suites, $299 on category 6 cabins, including airfare.

All category 6 outside staterooms are almost the same size as category 8 suites, but can sleep only one child. Both categories are considerably smaller than the apartment suites. Category 8 suites have queen-sized bed or two lower beds plus third and fourth upper berths. Both have sitting area, TV sets and bathroom with tub.

Suitable Standards: C

Average Price PPPD: $293 including airfare.

Category 5 outside cabins are about the same size as the 6s and 8s but on a lower deck. A few have one upper berth for a third child, but most have two lower beds or a queen-sized bed plus two or even three additional berths, sitting area, TV and bathroom with tub. Four outside cabins are designated wheelchair accessible.

Bottom Bunks: .... D

Average Price PPPD: $213 including airfare.

The cheapest cabins are category 1 insides or outsides, 12 very tiny cabins forward on the lowest passenger decks, which means more ship motion. They have upper and lower beds and bathroom with shower only.

Where She Goes

The *Star/Ship Atlantic* sails every Thursday evening from Port Canaveral to Nassau, arriving at noon on Friday and staying past midnight so you can enjoy the local nightlife if you wish. Saturday morning you wake up anchored off Port Lucaya, a special island for beach parties, the dolphin experience, a barbecue and lots of fun and games. You sail Saturday night and arrive back in Port Canaveral early Sunday morning.

On Sunday afternoon, the ship sails at 4:30, spends Monday at sea so the whole family can explore the ship and enjoy its activities, then arrives in Nassau Tuesday morning and stays until well past midnight. On Wednesday it anchors off Port Lucaya for the same activities described above, then sails back to Port Canaveral Wednesday at 6 p.m., arriving early Thursday morning.

The Bottom Line

It's an interesting thing to see the changes Premier made in this ship to make it suitable for families with one, two or even three children when it had been a ship serving adult vacationers sailing from New York to Bermuda and from Fort Lauderdale into the Caribbean. The density was tremendously increased by the addition of third and fourth berths in most of the cabins, along with sofa bed or rollaway bed options for additional passengers where floor space would permit. There was also the necessity to create small individual areas for the various age groups of children to meet for activities, so bars were turned into teen centers, shops converted to video arcades and deck areas enclosed for children's playrooms. But the menus from Home Lines' *Atlantic* bear little resemblance to the menus from the *Star/Ship Atlantic*. There's nary a mention on the latter of essence of capon broth with quail eggs or roast pheasant with Bordeaux garnish. But let's face it, the kids—and probably their parents—wouldn't order it anyhow.

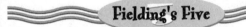

Fielding's Five

Five Family Favorites

1. The Sunrise Terrace, formerly an observation lounge, has been turned into a cafe with ice cream tables and chairs and two buffet service lines leading into it from the terrace.

2. The Galaxy Dining Room with its dome overhead serves meals at assigned tables in two seatings, with dinnertime visits from Looney Tunes characters.

3. Club Universe is a handsome room where shows are presented, along with port talks, family snowball bingo and the captain's cocktail party; don't sit behind one of the big posts, however, or you'll miss some of the show.

4. Lucky Star Casino is Mom and Dad's equivalent to Pluto's Playhouse; it has a roulette table, craps table, six blackjack tables and lots of slots.

5. The Calypso Pool is aft on the pool deck, surrounded by a natural teak deck, a lot of lounge chairs, a couple of whirlpools and a small bandstand.

Star/Ship Oceanic ★★★

A classic cruise vessel built by Italy's Fincantieri shipyard for now-defunct Home Lines in 1965, the *Oceanic* still has some charming details from the period, including the two free-form Riviera pools and the bright tile floors. The ship is clean and kept in very good shape but seems much darker in the public areas than the Atlantic. The layout is a bit different, too, with veranda suites on the topmost deck, a magrodrome sliding glass roof over the amidship pool areas, more cabins aft on the pool deck, a full deck below that of large cabins and suites, then a deck of public rooms. Below that are more cabins and the dining room. When Premier christened the ship in 1986, the godmother was Miss Minnie Mouse.

The Brochure Says

"Whether you're honeymooners, single parents, or grandparents...whether you're getting together for a family reunion or just want a vacation filled with fantasy, excitement and wonder, no other cruise offers you more than The Big Red Boat's 7-night Cruise and Orlando Theme Park Vacations."

Translation

There are two brochures from Premier, one with the theme park vacations detailed and priced and the other with the cruise itself detailed and priced. If you don't know which program interests you more, ask your travel agent or the cruise line to send you both.

Cabins & Costs

NOTE:

Average per person per day prices below are for three- and four-day cruises; seven-day packages including theme park stays will be less expensive on a per-day basis. The prices are for two full-fare cabin occupants; third, fourth and fifth cabin occupants pay $449–$569 apiece including airfare from some cities for the three-or four-day cruise, depending on the season.

Fantasy Suites: .... B+

Average Price PPPD: $399 including airfare.
Eight spacious suites with private verandas high atop the Sun Deck give a great view of the sea as well as having plenty of room for a family of four. There's a king-sized bed plus two other berths, sitting area and bathroom with tub.

Small Splurges: .... B

Average Price PPPD: $329 including airfare.
Category 8 suites on the *Oceanic* are larger than those on the *Atlantic*, and have a separate sitting area with sofa and chairs, twin or queen-sized bed with room divider and bathroom with tub. Some have room for a third passenger, some a third and fourth. Specify whether you want a double or twin beds. You may prefer the suites on Pool Deck, although slightly smaller, because many of those on Premier Deck have partially obstructed views from hanging lifeboats.

Suitable Standards: .... B

Average Price PPPD: $272 including airfare.
Most of the category 5 outside cabins have berths for third, sometimes fourth and fifth passengers, along with a choice of double or twin beds. Bathrooms have tubs and the rooms are fairly spacious and

prettily furnished in pastels. Some connecting cabins are available for family groups.

Bottom Bunks: .... *C*

Average Price PPPD: $213 including airfare.

The cheapest cabins aboard are 15 category 1 inside cabins with upper and lower berths, quite small and designated for only two passengers.

Where She Goes

The *Star/Ship Oceanic* sails Friday afternoons from Port Canaveral, arriving in Nassau late Saturday morning and staying at the dockside until past midnight. On Sunday, the ship anchors off Port Lucaya at 9 a.m. and gives you a full day ashore at the beach with lots of things to do. The ship sails at 6 p.m. and arrives back in Port Canaveral early Monday morning.

On Monday afternoons, it sails again with the midweek passengers, spending Tuesday at sea so everyone can enjoy the ship, arriving early Wednesday morning in Nassau with a whole day for shopping and sightseeing, and doesn't sail until after midnight in case you want to check out the local casinos and nightclubs. Thursday the ship spends all day at anchorage off Port Lucaya with lots of activities for both kids and grownups ashore and on the ship. It sails at 6 p.m. and arrives back in Port Canaveral Friday morning.

The Bottom Line

We like a lot about the *Oceanic*—its nice big cabins (well, some of them are!), the lovely pool deck, the cool, darkish public rooms on Lounge Deck that are a good respite from the bright Bahamian sunshine. Kids will like the big play area and supervised wading pool. Some of the former bright yellows, oranges and reds have been subdued into lavenders and burgundies on a recent refit. Now, if that maintenance man could just stay ahead of all those sticky little fingerprints everywhere and the popcorn ground into the carpeting!

Fielding's Five

Five Fun Places

1. The Riviera pools on pool deck, a pair of free-form shapes almost touching with blue tile surrounds and shady niches along the sides with tables and chairs.

2. Pluto's Playhouse, a big children's play area with a wading pool outside, bright carpeting, lots of toys and games and children's videos, an arts and crafts center, and jungle gyms.

3. Heroes and Legends, a pub and karaoke club, is a cozy little spot with Victorian decor, frosted glass and big, belly-up bar.

4. Seasport Health Center has a gym with weight room, exercycles and other machines plus a massage room.

5.   Starlight Cabaret has a 1960s nightclub look with mushroom-type lights fixed into tabletops, dance floor and bandstand.

Five Off-the-Wall Things to Do

1.   Hit the adults-only karaoke contest in the Heroes and Legends Pub.

2.   Have a tequila shooter at the Carlos & Charlie's Party in the Starlight Cabaret.

3.   Swim with the dolphins at Port Lucaya; you can have your travel agent book your appointment when you book your cruise.

4.   Get in a poker game in the Heroes and Legends Pub.

5.   Take golf lessons from the golf pro on board at poolside.

Five Good Reasons to Book This Ship

1.   To see what a 1960s ocean liner looked like.

2.   To get photographed with Bugs Bunny or have the Tasmanian Devil tuck you in bed at night.

3.   To take a cruise and stay on-site at Disney World for a family of four for around $525 a day including all meals on the ship, admissions and hotel room at Disney, rental car and roundtrip airfare to Florida.

4.   To get away on a quiet midweek vacation (when there are fewer children on board) at a 15 percent discount if one of the two of you is over 60.

5.   To enroll the kids in a professionally run children's program tailored specifically for each one's age group.

PRINCESS
CRUISES

10100 Santa Monica Boulevard, Los Angeles, CA 90067
☎ *(310) 553-1770, (800) LOVE-BOA(T)*

A new tradition aboard the newest Princess ships is to stage the captain's cocktail party in the three-story atrium lobby.

History . . . .

While the popular TV series "The Love Boat" catapulted Princess Cruises to worldwide fame, the company had been a household name on the West Coast, at least among cruise aficionados, from the 1960s.

In the winter of 1965-66, Seattle entrepreneur Stan McDonald chartered the 6000-ton *Princess Patricia* from Canadian Pacific Railway and offered cruises along the Mexican Riviera from Los Angeles. From the ship's name came the company name, Princess Cruises. The first season went so well aboard the "Princess Pat," as everyone began to call her, that McDonald soon chartered a newly-built Italian ship called the *Italia* and renamed her the *Princess*

Italia. In 1968, the *Princess Carla* (the former French Line *Flandre*), then Costa's *Carla C*, was chartered, and in 1971 the *Island Princess* (the only one of these still in the fleet).

Then London-based Peninsular and Orient Steam Navigation Company, better known as P&O (see P & O under Cruise Lines, above), the largest and oldest shipping company in the world, eyed the action and decided to come into the cruise scene with its new *Spirit of London*, which it positioned on the west coast in the winter of 1972–73 to compete with Princess. There was little competition; McDonald continued to dominate Mexican Riviera cruising, despite one travel writer's comments that aboard the Princess Pat "the standard dessert was canned peaches" and the decor "was on a par with a good, clean $7-a-night room in a venerable but respected Toronto hotel."

So in 1974, P & O acquired Princess Cruises, including its key marketing staff, and set about upgrading the fleet hardware. The *Carla* and *Italia* went back to Costa Cruises in 1974, and the *Island Princess* was purchased outright. P & O's new *Spirit of London* was added to the fleet as the *Sun Princess*, and the *Sea Venture*, sister ship to the *Island Princess*, was acquired to become the *Pacific Princess*.

Things were already going well, but destined to improve even further when TV producer Doug Cramer showed up in 1975 with a new series he wanted to film aboard a cruise ship. *Et voila!* "The Love Boat" was born.

In 1988, continuing its "if you can't beat 'em, buy 'em" strategy, P & O/Princess acquired Los Angeles-based rival Sitmar Cruises, which added three existing ships and one nearly-completed new ship, *Star Princess*, to the fleet, to bring it up to nine vessels.

Today there are still nine Love Boats cruising the seven seas, five of them from the 1988 fleet, with a 10th, the 104,000-ton giant *Grand Princess*, due to arrive in the spring of 1997 to sail the Caribbean year-round. (A prudent move, since the ship is too big to go through the Panama Canal.)

—Parent company P & O claims it invented leisure cruising in 1844 when British author William Makepeace Thackery sailed around the Mediterranean on a free ticket to publicize the service and wrote a travel book about his cruise— *From Cornhill to Grand Cairo*—under the pseudonym Michael Angelo Titmarsh.

—One of the three largest cruise lines in the world.

—Offers the largest number of world-wide destinations of any major line.

—First to introduce all outside cabins with a high proportion of private balconies (*Royal Princess*, 1984).

—First major cruise line to introduce multimedia musical shows produced in-house.

—First to install a "black box" recorder on each of its ships for additional safety data in case of an incident at sea.

—Introduced easy-to-use phone cards to make local or long distance calls from anywhere in the world with a push-button phone; the card (good for $20 worth of phone time) was originally developed as a convenience for the Princess crew (sold across the fleet, July 1995).

—TV's "The Love Boat" is seen in 93 countries and heard in more than 29 different languages. The title comes from a book written by a former cruise director named Jeraldine Saunders about her life onboard.

Concept . . . .

"It's more than a cruise, it's the Love Boat," a beaming Gavin MacLeod said on the Princess commercials.

What does that make you think of? The TV series, of course, with its glamorous, friendly crew, never too busy to intercede in someone's love affair. Luxurious staterooms and elegantly garbed passengers. Nubile nymphs in bikinis. Exotic ports, perpetual sunshine and cloudless blue skies. In other words, the perfect vacation—a cruise.

With its varied fleet of vessels, ranging from the homey, mid-sized 610-passenger *Island Princess* and *Pacific Princess* to the new 1950-passenger *Sun Princess* and the upcoming 2600-passenger *Grand Princess*, the line feels it offers "something for everyone" from "endless activity" to "total relaxation."

Signatures . . . .

The line's distinctive stack logo, the "sea witch" with the flowing hair, provides instant identification when a Princess ship is in port. Just as distinctive, but less well known, is the Princess tradition of furnishing each of its new ships with an exquisite museum-quality million dollar-plus art collections from contemporary artists such as Andy Warhol, David Hockney, Robert Motherwell, Frank Stella, Laddie John Dill, Billy Al Bengston, Richard Diebenkorn and Helen Frankenthaler.

On-board pizzerias with special ovens serve up pizzas and calzone cooked to order aboard the line's *Crown Princess*, *Sky Princess*, *Regal Princess*, *Star Princess* and *Sun Princess*.

Gimmicks . . . .

Declaring St. Valentine's Day as Love Boat National Holiday aboard all the line's vessels, with renewal of vows ceremonies in which some 4000 couples participate. The holiday also features a poetry contest and reading, romantic feature films, a Hearts card game tournament and honeymooner and singles parties.

Who's the Competition . . . .

Princess has been competing head-on with Holland America for some years, and Love Boats face some Costa competition for fans of pizza, pasta and Italian waiters.

Who's Aboard . . . .

Romantic couples of all ages who saw "The Love Boat" on TV; longtime loyals, both couples and singles, over 45; a group of younger couples who've met on board and continue to take vacation cruises together (see "Footnote" to follow); some families with children, who gravitate toward those ships that have dedicated playrooms and full-time youth counselors (*Sky Princess, Golden Princess* and *Star Princess*); people with glints of gold from head (hair coloring) to toe (gold lamé sandals or ankle bracelets), neck (gold chains) to fingertips (gold pinky rings, a gold lamé tote).

Who Should Go . . . .

Anyone who wants a very traditional cruise experience with a chance to dance and dress up; admirers of avant-garde Pompidou Center architect Renzo Piano, who designed parts of the *Crown* and *Regal Princess*; families whose teenagers like the pizzeria and the zany fountain drinks aboard the *Star, Crown* and *Regal*; young women who want to meet some Italians; anyone who loves pasta, pastries and cappuccino; fans of the Cirque du Soleil who'll adore the new avant-garde show *Mystique* on the *Crown, Regal, Sun* and *Star*. More younger passengers should be boarding, because Princess is becoming expert at giving them what they want, at least on the big new ships—a less-structured captain's cocktail party; music for listening and dancing all over the ship; lots of sundeck and water areas with swim-up bars, waterfalls, swimming pools and Jacuzzis. Families with children now that Princess is welcoming them with open arms.

Who Should Not Go . . . .

Anyone with children under 18 months of age (babies are not permitted on board); anybody who refuses to wear a tie on any occasion; anyone who would answer "Huh?" to the query, "Fourth for bridge?"

The Lifestyle . . . .

Set in the framework of traditional cruises, a day aboard a Princess ship includes a plethora of activities and entertainment, from an exercise class in the gym or a facial in the beauty salon to language lessons, pool games, bridge classes, aquacise in the ship's pool, indoor and outdoor game tournaments, bingo, golf chipping, feature films in the ship's theater or in the cabin, port lectures, shopping lectures, cooking demonstrations, galley and bridge tours, fashion shows and karaoke singing. Even kids have their own karaoke contests, along with coketail parties, coloring contests and ice cream parties.

Many evenings are relatively formal aboard, with passengers wearing their finest clothes and jewelry and Italian or British officers hosting dinner tables, but other nights, such as the traditional London Pub Night, casual wear is prescribed and beer and pub dishes are on the agenda, along with rowdy music hall songs and dances.

Wardrobe........................

Princess passengers usually have two formal nights, two or three semi-formal and two or three casual nights during a week. For formal nights, men are requested to wear tuxedos, dinner jackets or dark suits and women cocktail dresses or evening outfits. Semi-formal evenings call for men to wear jacket and tie, women to wear dresses or dressy pantsuits.

On casual evenings, men may wear open-necked sport shirts, slacks and sports outfits; women, slacks, dresses or skirts. Daytime clothing can be quite casual, but coverups over bathing suits are expected for passengers walking through the ship.

Bill of Fare..................... B+

Cuisine is Continental with an emphasis on Italian dishes. A pasta or risotto specialty is featured every day at lunch and at dinner, along with a low-fat, low-calorie selection and a vegetarian dish.

Late-night buffets aboard the Princess ships are themed, with fish and chips following London Pub Night, a pasta party, a pizza party, a champagne fountain and Crepes Suzette on French Night, and a gala buffet among the other offerings.

Meals are served in two assigned seatings, with dinners somewhere between 6-6:30 p.m. for first seating, 8–8:30 p.m. for second seating. Breakfast and lunch are also served at assigned seatings when the ships are at sea, but may be open seating when the ship is in port. Your travel agent should request your seating preference when booking. All Princess dining rooms are smoke-free.

Pizzerias that cook pizzas and calzones to order are aboard some of the line's ships (see "Signatures").

The captain's gala dinner may offer Sevruga Malossol caviar, shrimp cocktail, liver pâté Strasbourg and fresh fruit cup with Triple Sec, following by a choice of three soups, a salad, ravioli with porcini mushroom sauce, rock lobster tail, salmon en croute, pheasant breast flambé or tournedos, along with four desserts plus cheese and fruit. Wine prices aboard are generally reasonable.

Meals in the dining room and pizzeria are usually somewhat better than the buffets, but the latter are improving. The new *Sun Princess* is leading the way to better cuisine on board.

Showtime . . . . .A

Princess pioneered elaborate multimedia shows with film clips projected onto screens beside the stage and pre-recorded "click track" sweetening to swell the musical accompaniment. As other lines began using many of the same techniques, the company started updating its enter-tainment to include Nolan Miller costumes (he did the wardrobe for TV's "Dynasty"), sometimes with as many as 60 costume changes a show (nearly as many as Joan Collins made each week).

The audience gets to participate in the popular "Love Boat Legends," playing on all the line's ships, with 24 passengers selected from volunteers who audition the first day, rehearse all week and join the cruise staff and entertainers in per-forming the last night of the sailing.

Perhaps the most sensational production is *Mystique*, an innovative and elaborately costumed production with a company of 23 performers, including nine European and Asian acrobats, set under the sea in Atlantis, with inflatable scenery that literally "grows" in front of your eyes; it's remarkable. *Mystique* appears only on board the *Crown Princess*, *Regal Princess*, *Star Princess*, and *Sun Princess*.

Big Band music, a splashy new Caribbean revue, a show-biz production called *Let's Go to the Movies*, a full lecture pro-gram, trivia quizzes, "Baby Boomer" theme nights, Lon-don Pub Night and A Night at the Races fill out the fun.

On the new *Sun Princess*, big-name entertainers are sched-uled for some sailings.

Discounts . . . .

Love Boat Savers are discounts that take off from $500 to $1150 per person from the cruise-only price, but the offer is restricted to residents of the United States and Canada. The lowest fares are for the earliest bookings; discounts may decrease as the sailing date approaches. Discounts vary according to the price and season.

Frequent cruisers who belong to the Captain's Circle are mailed notices on special savings for designated sailings, including deals like two-for-one buys, 50 percent off for the second passenger in a cabin or free upgrades.

Crown Princess ★★★★★

This elegant ships while similar in size to sister ship *Star Princess*, is far from identical to her. It was built in Italy's Fincantieri yard, while *Star Princess* came out of France's Chantiers d'Atlantique.

The *Crown Princess* is unmistakable, even at a distance, because of its sloped, dolphin-like brow and strong vertical funnel. Controversial Italian architect Renzo Piano dislikes too much emphasis on the dolphin-like shape he designed—"A ship is a ship, it's not a dolphin."

The vertical funnel, a bold departure from the broad raked funnels on most of the Love Boats, he terms "a frank, clear, strong statement...and it works beautifully, by the way, to take the smoke away."

If an award were given for spacious cabins, this ship would win hands down. Cocktail lounges on board are lovely, as is a wine-and-caviar bar, a patisserie/sidewalk cafe in the lobby, a wonderful shopping arcade and a well-planned show lounge with fairly good sightlines except from the back of the main lounge.

The Brochure Says

"Her teak is from Burma, her marble from Carrera, and her fittings were forged by Italian craftsmen in shipyards over 200 years old...a masterpiece of the sea created by one of the world's most gifted architects."

Translation

Just what it says. This ship is the last word in design and decor, luxurious, graceful, stylish and very comfortable, and it whispers about its $200 million-plus price rather than shout it the way Carnival's megaliners do.

Cabins & Costs

Fantasy Suites: .... A+

Average Price PPPD: $409 plus airfare.

Top accommodations are the 14 suites, each with a double-size private veranda large enough for two lounging chairs with a small table between as well as a bigger table with two chairs, ideal for private breakfasts in the sun and sea breeze. A wide wooden doorway divides the living room with its sofa, chairs, tables and mini- refrigerator from the bedroom with its king-sized bed (which has a single mattress top rather than the two divided mattresses one usually gets when two beds are pushed together). Each room has its own TV set. A large dressing room lined with closets and enough storage space for an around-the-world cruise leads to the spacious marble bathroom with separate bathtub and stall shower. The toilet and second lavatory are adjoining, with another door that opens for the living room so it can double as a powder room when you're entertaining.

Small Splurges: ....A

Average Price PPPD: $369 plus airfare.

The category A mini-suites with private veranda are a bit smaller on both balcony and interior, but still very comfortable with bed (twins or queen-sized), sitting area with sofa and chairs, TV, mini-refrigerator, bath with tub and shower and spacious closet space.

Suitable Standards: ....A

Average Price PPPD: $235 plus airfare.

Category GG outside double cabins forward on Plaza Deck provide queen-sized beds and a convenient location, but there are only four of them. All the standards contain amenities usually found only in suites—mini-refrigerators, remote-control TV sets, guest safes and walk-in closets. Baths have showers only. Other standards offer two lower beds that can be made into a queen-sized bed.

Bottom Bunks: ....A

Average Price PPPD: $200 plus airfare for category M, $230 for category G.

Even the lowest category inside double cabin, the M category forward on Plaza Deck (only steps away from the lobby), measures 190 square feet and contains the same amenities and furnishings as the mid-range standards (see "Suitable Standards," above). The cheapest outside cabins are category G on Fiesta Deck with upper and lower berths and portholes instead of windows.

Where She Goes

In winter, the *Crown Princess* cruises the Southern Caribbean round trip from Fort Lauderdale on 10-day itineraries calling at Nassau, St. Thomas,

Guadeloupe, Barbados, Dominica, St. Maarten and the private beach at Princess Cays.

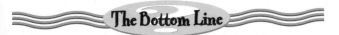

This is an exquisite ship, and generally everything runs smoothly. Newly embarking passengers are serenaded by a Filipino string trio and greeted by white-gloved stewards to escort them to their cabins. Everything you need to know is spelled out in the daily "Princess Patter" programs or advance cruise materials mailed ahead of time, making this a very good vessel for first-time cruisers. As for people who worry that there's nothing to do on a cruise, we'd like to take them on a stroll around this ship at almost any hour of the day or night, and they'd never fret again.

Super Places

1. The chic 1930s-style cocktail lounges on promenade deck, the Intermezzo, where you half-expect to see Cary (but not Hugh!) Grant at the next table.

2. The Patisserie in the three-deck atriums, the true gathering spot on the ship; you can get cappuccino and espresso all day long, accompanied by freshly baked pastries, and observe the comings and goings of fellow passengers.

3. The Presto Pizzeria on the *Crown Princess* with its Italian food-and-wine print red tablecloths, red-and-white glazed tile walls and natural teak floors, warm and inviting, serving five types of pizzas including vegetarian, plus calzones, garlic focaccio and Caesar salad, open 11 a.m. to 5 p.m., then again from 9 p.m. to 1 a.m.

Off-the-Wall Things to Do

1. Order one of the zany drinks from the boldly illustrated menu in Characters Bar, perhaps the Strip & Go Naked or Ta Kill Ya Sunrise.

2. Converse with the talking elevators, which announce each deck and caution you when you exit to watch your step.

Five Good Reasons to Book This Ship

1. To see the spectacular shows, especially *Mystique*, go to the pizzeria afterwards, talk about the performance show with other audience members, then watch the stars come in for an after-show snack.

2. To get scuba certification in the New Waves program; the course costs $370 and passengers must sign up ahead of cruise departure or at the very beginning of the cruise.

3. To attend a captain's cocktail party where you don't have to stand in line for ages to shake hands and be photographed with the captain; on these ships everyone circulates throughout the three-deck atrium, drinks in hand, and anyone who wishes to be photographed can pose on the curved staircase for the ship's photographer.

4. To spend a day at a private beach in Mayreau or Princess Cays.

5. To get more spacious cabins for the money than almost anywhere else afloat.

Five Things You Won't Find on Board

1. A gym or spa with sea views.

2. Jogging permitted before 8 a.m.

3. Locked bookcases; Princess trusts these passengers not to steal books or games.

4. The best seats for the show in the front row; third row from the back, one level up from the main seating area, is better.

5. Captain Stubing (although his alter ego, Princess spokesman Gavin MacLeod, does show up sometimes).

Star Princess ★★★★

The *Star Princess* has one of the best pool-and-sun decks at sea. It runs most of the length of the vessel and stars two large swimming pools spanned by a raised sun deck. The area is filled out by an aft buffet cafe and a forward bar and pizzeria. Overall, she heralded a "new Princess," bigger, brighter, livelier than her predecessors, with a wider appeal and more accessibility to younger passengers than any of the previous ships from either Princess or Sitmar. A little more than a year after *Star Princess* first entered service, its median passenger age was seven years lower than the line's fleetwide average.

A three-deck atrium with a stainless steel kinetic sculpture dominates the amidships area. This is the vessel that first introduced the very popular La Patisserie cafe and pastry shop in the lobby area.

The spa, beauty salon, gym and massage areas, on the other hand, were relegated to below-decks without windows rather than given a prominent and sunny spot atop the ship as on the *Sky Princess*.

The Brochure Says

"...*Star Princess* also offers some of the largest standard staterooms in the industry. Connoisseurs of fine cruising will be dazzled by this modern-day floating resort."

Translation

An apt description. It's hard to think of anything you'd get at a big Caribbean resort hotel that you can't find on the *Star Princess*, except for sand between your toes.

Cabins & Costs

Fantasy Suites: .... A

Average Price PPPD: $464 including airfare.

The 14 AA category suites are top-of-the-line, measuring 530 square feet and named for popular Mediterranean ports. Inside the sliding glass doors is an open, L-shaped room divided into sitting and sleeping areas with sofa, two chairs, coffee table, queen-sized bed, nightstands and built-in desk. There's plenty of closet and storage space, two TV sets, a dressing room with mahogany built-in dressing table and large mirror, a spacious marble bathroom divided so the tub, separate shower stall and wash basin can be closed off to let the toilet and second wash basin double as powder room. A mini-bar is stocked with complimentary beverages, and a mini-refrigerator keeps everything cold.

Small Splurges: .... B

Average Price PPPD: $407 including airfare.

The 36 category A mini-suites are 370 square feet each, with private veranda, sitting area with built-in desk and counter as well as sofa and chairs, and a large bath with tub/shower combination.

Suitable Standards: .... A

Average Price PPPD: $221–$285 including airfare.

All cabins aboard have twin beds that can be rearranged into one queen-sized bed, walk-in closet and separate dressing area, refrigerator and mini-bar, guest safe, terrycloth robes, hair dryers and color TV. Both outsides (with picture windows) and insides are the same size—180 square feet. Ten are designated wheelchair-accessible, and these measure 240 square feet with extra-wide doors and no thresholds.

Bottom Bunks: .... A

Average Price PPPD: $157 including airfare.

The cheapest cabins are M category with two lower beds, only seven of them, located forward on Plaza Deck. Furnishings are the same as "Suitable Standards."

Star Princess sails the Eastern Caribbean on a seven-day roundtrip itinerary out of Fort Lauderdale, calling in Nassau, St. Thomas, St. Maarten and the private beach at Princess Cays in winter and spring.

When a ship is this perfect for warm-weather cruising, we're puzzled as to why Princess sends it up to Alaska in the summer. But wherever it goes, it's a natural magnet for families and younger cruisers.

Fielding's Five

Five Great Places

1. The Lido Deck pools have a raised sunbathing deck between the Oasis pool, with its waterfall and in-pool bar, and the Paradise pool, which is flanked by four whirlpool spas.

2. Characters, a colorful Lido Deck bar serving up outrageous drinks, both alcoholic and non-alcoholic, including a margarita big enough for four in a goldfish bowl- sized glass with four straws.

3. Windows to the World, a circular glass-walled observation lounge above the bridge where The Dome is located on the Crown and Regal, doubles as an observation lounge and after-dark entertainment center with music. The French shipyard workers called it Le Camembert because its round shape reminded them of a cheesebox.

4. The Club House Youth Center and Off Limits Teen Center get a lot of space, making this a good ship for kids and teens.

5. The Sports Deck, with its basketball, volleyball and paddle tennis court, jogging track, state-of-the-art gymnasium and aerobics room.

Five Good Reasons to Book This Ship

1. You can spend all day on the pool deck for optimum fun in the sun.

2. It's a great place for kids, who keep busy with supervised activities from 9 a.m. to midnight, plus a kids- only wading pool.

3. Teens have their own social life on board, with special hours in the adult disco, the chance to film an episode of "Love Boat," Italian lessons, crafts, video games, talent shows and PG-13 movies nightly.

4. A museum-quality art collection of contemporary works.

5. You'll be traveling with younger passengers that get involved with a more active shore excursion and onboard sports program.

Five Things You Won't Find Aboard

1. A small intimate bar for a quiet getaway for two.

2. Fuddy-duddies.

3. An ocean view from the gym or the disco; they're on a lower deck hidden away for privacy and noise control.

4. Smoking in the dining room or show lounge.

5. The very expensive swan logo commissioned for this ship by Sitmar shortly before Princess bought the company.

☷ROYAL CARIBBEAN

1050 Caribbean Way, Miami, FL 33132
☎ *(305) 539-6000, (800) 327-6700*

The signature Viking Crown Lounge and RCCL logo.

History ....

In 1969, three Norwegian shipping companies, I.M. Skaugen, Gotaas Larsen and Anders Wilhelmsen, founded RCCL for the purpose of offering year-round seven and 14-day cruises out of Miami. Now owned by Wilhelmsen and the Hyatt Hotels' Pritzger family of Chicago, Royal Caribbean Cruises Ltd. is a publicly traded company on the New York Stock Exchange.

The spring 1996 delivery of the *Splendour of the Seas* brought the line's total to 10 vessels. Just past its 25th anniversary, RCCL is definitely one a handful of major players in the cruise industry.

—First cruise line to commission three new ships expressly for the Caribbean cruise market, *Song of Norway* (1970), *Nordic Prince* (1971) and *Sun Viking* (1972).

—First cruise line to "stretch" a ship, cutting it in half and dropping in a new midsection, then putting it back together (*Song of Norway,* 1978).

—First cruise line to commission a specially designed ship for three- and four-day cruises (*Nordic Empress,* 1990).

—First seagoing, 18-hole miniature golf course (on *Legend of the Seas,* 1995).

—First cruise line to open shoreside hospitality centers in popular ports where passengers can leave packages, make phone calls, bone up on local shopping or sightseeing, get a cold drink and use toilet facilities (1995).

Concept..............................

Consistency is the key word here. RCCL aims to provide a cruise experience to mainstream, middle-of-the-road passengers that is consistent in style, quality and pricing, with a majority of the ships following a consistent year-round schedule. Rod McLeod, head of sales and marketing, calls it "the doughnut factor" from a travel agent who once commented that what he liked best about RCCL was that all the doughnuts on all the line's ships taste exactly the same.

Signatures......................

RCCL ships are easily recognized at a distance because of the Viking Crown Lounge, a cantilevered round glass-walled bar and observation lounge high atop the ships projecting from or encircling the ship's funnel; company president Edward Stephan dreamed it up after seeing the Seattle Space Needle.

Lounges, bars and restaurants on board are named for Broadway musicals and operettas, sometimes with unintentionally funny results, as with the *Sun Viking's* Annie Get Your Gun Lounge. (That's also a musical that few of today's RCCL passengers would remember.)

Gimmicks ....

ShipShape Dollars, given out each time a passenger participates in an exercise or sports activity; with six you get egg roll. Actually, you get egg-yolk yellow T-shirts proclaiming the wearer ShipShape. Passengers compete wildly for them and proudly wear them for years afterward aboard cruise ships of competing lines.

Who's the Competition ....

RCCL competes directly with Carnival and Norwegian Cruise Line for Caribbean passengers, but it also vies pricewise with more upscale lines like Celebrity and Princess. The line's new megaliners have brought in a more glitzy sheen, with flashy gaming rooms created by a Nevada casino designer instead of a ship designer. The company has also gone head-to-head with Carnival in the mini-cruise market in south Florida, pitting its ladylike *Nordic Empress* against the neon-throbbing *Fantasy* and glow-in-the-dark *Ecstasy.* For 1997, *Sovereign of the Seas* takes the three- and four-day Bahamas run, and *Nordic Empress* moves to San Juan.

Who's Aboard.....................

All-American couples from the heartland between 40 and 60, with new clothes, new cameras and nice manners; families with fairly well-behaved children; two or three 30-something couples traveling together; born-to-shop types who find the line's newer ships with their mall-like galleries familiar and comforting; clean-cut young couples on their honeymoons; single 20-somethings on holiday sharing an inexpensive inside cabin, more often females than males.

Statistically, the median age is a relatively low 42, with a household income from $40,000 to $75,000. One-fourth are repeat passengers, half are first-time cruisers. More Europeans, Australians and Latin Americans are also gravitating to the line.

Who Should Go.....................

These are ideal ships for first-time cruisers because the staff and the signage instruct and inform without appearing to lecture, putting everyone at ease right away. Also for honeymooners, fitness freaks (except on the *Sun Viking* and *Song of Norway,* which don't have gyms), sunbathers, big families on a reunion and stressed-out couples who want some time together in a resort atmosphere. Baby Boomers and their juniors 25 to 45 years old will always be warmly welcomed: RCCL wants YOU!

Who Should Not Go ....

Dowager veterans of the world cruise.

Small ship enthusiasts.

Anyone who dislikes regimentation.

The Lifestyle ....

RCCL's ships follow a traditional cruise pattern, with specified dress codes for evening, and two meal seatings in the dining room at assigned tables for a minimum of four and a maximum of eight or ten; very few if any tables for two are available. A day-long program of games, activities and entertainment on board is supplemented by shore excursions that emphasize sightseeing, golf and watersports. In the Caribbean, private beach areas at CocaCay in the Bahamas and Labadee in Haiti are beach destinations for swimming and lunch barbecues.

Wardrobe . . . .

RCCL makes it easy for passengers by spelling out dress-code guidelines in the brochure. A normal seven-day Caribbean cruise has four casual nights where sport shirts and slacks are suggested for men, two formal nights where women wear cocktail dress or evening gowns and men wear suits and ties or tuxedos, and one or more theme nights where passengers may don '50s or country/western garb if they wish. During the daytime, comfortable casual clothing—jogging outfits, shorts or slacks, T-shirts, bathing suits and coverups—is appropriate on deck but sometimes not in the dining room.

Bill of Fare . . . . B+

Non-threatening, special-occasion food is produced by an affiliated catering company on a rotating set menu that is similar but not identical on the different ships. There's a wide variety and good range of choices, and the preparation is capable if not inspired. Dinner includes seven appetizers (four of them juices), three soups, two salads, five main dishes and six desserts (three of them ice creams). On a typical day main dishes may include crabmeat cannelloni, sole Madagascar, pork loin au jus, roast duckling and sirloin steak. In addition, a nightly vegetarian menu, a kids' menu and a ShipShape low-fat, low-calorie menu are offered.

Our very favorite from the latter seems tailored to The Ladies Who Lunch—it starts with a shrimp cocktail without sauce, then consomme, hearts of lettuce salad with carrot curls and fat-free dressing, followed by poached fish and vegetables, then rich, sugary Key Lime Pie with a whopping 12 grams of fat per slice.

Except on cruises of 10 days or longer, when cabin occupants can order from set lunch or dinner menus, 24-hour room service is limited to breakfast and cold snacks such as sandwiches, salads and fruit-and-cheese plates. Breakfast and lunch buffets are served in a self-service cafeteria with hot and cold dishes available, and early morning coffee, afternoon tea and midnight buffets fill out the legendary eight-meals-a-day format.

Captain Sealy's menu for kids includes fish sticks, peanut butter and jelly sandwiches, tuna fish, pizza, hamburgers and macaroni and cheese, plus chocolate "ship" cookies. On a recent sailing aboard the *Splendour of the Seas*, we felt the food preparation and presentation had greatly improved.

Showtime . . . . A/C

The major production shows produced by the line, complete with Broadway-style playbills and computerized light cues, are sensational on the bigger ships with their state-of-the-art technical facilities. Unfortunately, on the smaller vessels, the shows still come out of the under-inspired and overworked south Florida production companies and suffer from make-do stagecraft and poor sightlines. Passengers entertain each other at karaoke nights, masquerade parades and passenger talent shows, and pack appropriate garb for country/western night and '50s and '60s rock 'n roll night.

Discounts. . . . .

Booking six months in advance earns discounts of 10 to 20 percent off the brochure rate.

Majesty of the Seas ★★★★

RCCL concentrated on positioning the cabins forward and the public rooms aft so that passengers can make their way vertically from, say the cocktail bars to the dining room to the show lounge to the casino, and horizontally from their cabins to the public areas.

But we would still recommend that a passenger traveling from a modest B deck inside forward cabin to the sports deck area atop the ship aft take along a compass and a brown bag lunch.

The plus side of big is that the soaring sense of space makes this huge ship especially appealing to first-time cruisers accustomed to hotels and resorts. And you shouldn't get lost too often—a three-dimensional plexiglass ship directory is set in each elevator/stairwell landing to help passengers find their way around.

It's good for kids because of the way the age groups are divided into five-to-eight-year-olds, "tweens" eight to 12, and teens from 13 to 17. Teens can hang out at their own soft drink bar with its adjacent video games center and even run the special effects and light show in the teen disco.

A whole new subculture of passengers has developed around this megaship. They call themselves Trekkies (after the "Star Trek" TV series) in honor of their own journeys into space.

The Brochure Says

"Big-city dazzle with its elegant dining rooms...as tall as the Statue of Liberty...unlimited freedom to curl up with a good book, eat all the ice cream you want (and) tell the kids to ship out..."

Translation

It's a big ship but you're going to kick back and have a great time. Head up to the Viking Crown Lounge and fantasize being on eye level with Miss Liberty (only in your imagination, since this ship doesn't sail into New York). Dazzling, come-hither bright lights and a sense of action draw young and first-time cruisers who know how to have fun.

You can certainly tell the kids to ship out, with three child care programs that split age groups between 5 and 8, "tweens" 8 to 12, and teens. The last have their own club and disco called Flashes, created by a line that realizes teens are only a decade or so away from buying cruises for themselves. Attention must be paid.

Cabins & Costs

Fantasy Suites: . . . . .A

Average Price PPPD: $571 including airfare.

The Royal Suite, #1010, provides ideal digs for anyone who wants to entertain in nearly 1000 square feet indoors and out. A separate living room with private veranda, dining table with six chairs, L-shaped sofa and two chairs, wet bar stocked with liquor, soft drinks and snacks and an entertainment center with CDs and VCRs headlines the suite. In the bedroom is a king-sized bed, lovely wood dresser, a marble bathroom with double basins, Jacuzzi tub, stall shower and walk-in dressing area with large safe.

Small Splurges: . . . . B+

Average Price PPPD: $457 per person for first two passengers, $107 per person for third and fourth sharing the suite. Includes airfare.

The Family Suite, #1549, has two bedrooms and two baths, adequate sleeping, lounging and wardrobe space for a close family of five, with private veranda, sitting area, master bedroom and bath, and second bedroom with two lower beds, a pulldown berth and small bathroom with shower.

Suitable Standards: C

Average Price PPPD: $321 including airfare.

F is the predominant category of standard outside double cabins, each with its twin beds in L-shaped configuration, the ends at the L overlapping by 18 inches. In the 127 square feet, you'll find one chair (flip a coin for it), a small TV set, a tripod glass-topped table with a brass wastebasket as its base (we tried to chill champagne in it but were sternly corrected by a Bahamian stewardess), a built-in cabinet with four drawers, a closet with one full length and two half-height hanging areas plus drawers and a safe and a small tidy tile bath with shower.

Wheelchair Accessible:

Two inside category N cabins and two outside category D cabins are designated as physically-challenged accessible. They're larger than others in their price category, with good turning room for the wheelchair, and twin beds with pastel covers, along with sofa and chair. The baths have no sills, and provide grab rails by the toilet and in the shower, along with a pull-down plastic seat. Some low hanging closet racks are accessible, but the safe, located on an upper shelf, would be out of reach for someone in a wheelchair.

Bottom Bunks: .... C-

Average Price PPPD: $229 including airfare.
With the modular cabin design common to new ships, the cheapest digs often offer two lower beds and a bathroom identical to those in higher-priced categories. The bottom-dollar beds are in category Q, insides that measure only 114 square feet and are situated well forward on the lowest passenger cabin deck, but hey, they're livable unless you hit a heavy storm, which could toss you out of bed.

Where She Goes

Majesty of the Seas sails year-round, seven-day Western Caribbean round-trips from Miami (Sundays) calling at Playa del Carmen and Cozumel, Grand Cayman, Ocho Rios and, depending on the cruise, Labadee, Haiti, or Coco Cay, Bahamas, for a beach day.

The Bottom Line

The acres of astroturf and anodized bronze loungers, glittering shops and glass elevators, leather sofas, potted palms and lobby pianist make the *Majesty* look more like Marriott of the Seas to a purist.

While the cabins and interiors are as spotless as ever, the deck housekeeping is sometimes lax. A well-decked-out lady deserves better than this.

Solid mainstream ships, the *Majesty* sets out to impress from the moment a passenger boards, just as Carnival does, but it aims for a slightly more sophisticated audience. Only dedicated traditional ship buffs will find much to grouse about here.

Nordic Empress

The *Nordic Empress* actually started on the drawing board as a rather pretentiously named vessel called *Future Seas*, designed expressly for three-and four-day cruises for a now-defunct company called Admiral Cruises, an affiliate of RCCL.

Company executives define the differences on the mini-cruise vessels:

—"We try to cram a seven-day cruise into three days."

—More hectic.

—In port daily.

—More steak and lobster, fewer unfamiliar dishes on the menu.

—"Passengers want to eat and drink as much as they would in seven days." (Passengers also spend roughly the same amount of disposable income for on-board extras as they would in seven days.)

—Deck plan must be easy for the passenger to learn and find his way around in a limited time.

The Brochure Says

"A cascading waterfall. Lush tropical plants. The kind of sunlight you never get back home. Wait. This isn't an exotic port. This is your ship. The Centrum Lobby, actually."

Translation

The heart of the ship is a hotel-like lobby that connects to all the passenger decks and so helps passengers learn their way around. (It's no fun when you're on a three-day cruise and can't find your cabin for hours.) The Centrum, as it's called, is drop-dead dramatic, a great place for photographing each other. (It's also a good backdrop for a wedding, if you have romance in mind.)

Cabins & Costs

Fantasy Suites: .... A

Average Price PPPD: $623 including airfare.
The one-bedroom Royal Suite is big enough for entertaining with a wet bar, large dining or conference table, curved sofa and chairs, teak-floored veranda, walk-in closet, Jacuzzi tub, and separate marble-and-glass shower. While the price is about $100 a day more than the owner's suites, the Royal Suite incorporates space from an owner's suite and two standard cabins.

Small Splurges: .... B+

Average Price PPPD: $406 including airfare.
One of the 56 category C deluxe outside cabins with private balcony, two lower beds which can be arranged as one, a sofa, chair and coffee table, built-in dresser/desk, good reading lamp, built-in vanity table and terrycloth robes.

Suitable Standards: .... B

Average Price PPPD: $316 including airfare.
Cabins were designed with women in mind, according the ship designers, who say females comprise 60 percent of all cruise passengers. There's generous counter space in the bathroom, subdued pastel fabrics, floral watercolors and a beauty table with its own makeup lights. H and I category cabins have twin beds that convert to queen-sized, color TV, built-in dresser with stool, one chair, good storage space and small bathroom with shower only.

Bottom Bunks: C

Average Price PPPD: $233 including airfare.
Q category cabins forward on B deck are the bottom-dollar digs; expect all the standard cabin amenities in a slightly smaller space.

Where She Goes

Fridays three-day roundtrips from Miami to Nassau and CocoCay.

Mondays four-day roundtrips from Miami to Freeport, Nassau and Coco Cay.

The Bottom Line

The *Nordic Empress*, like Carnival's glittering new short-cruise megaships, is attracting a whole new set of first-time cruise passengers of all ages and ethnic backgrounds, a welcome sight in an industry that spent too many years competing for the same narrow stratum of cruise regulars.

This ship offers a gentler, quieter version of the party cruise without soft-pedaling the fun. On both three- and four-day itineraries, passengers have a full day at the beach on a private island for swimming, snorkeling, sailing and windsurfing with a calypso band and beach barbecue lunch, while competitor Carnival provides a day at sea to enjoy (read: spend money in) the ship's games, bars, shops and casinos.

The *Nordic Empress* is highly recommended for first-time cruisers of all ages, including families and three-generation groups. It's a good introduction to mainstream cruising.

Sovereign of the Seas ★★★★

Sovereign of the Seas was the largest ship ever built for cruising when it came into service in 1988. Like its newer sister ships *Monarch of the Seas* and *Majesty of the Seas*, it has a "bigger than life" theatricality and showy design that lends excitement. From the moment its mostly youngish, often first-timer passengers first board, they have the sense of arriving at a major resort. It's ideal for couples, singles and young families shopping for a Caribbean vacation that just happens to be aboard a cruise ship.

How far does the average passenger have to walk between the show lounge and the midnight buffet on a ship that is almost three football fields long? Theoretically, only a short stroll and a stairway or elevator separate the chorus girls from the cheesecake, because the ship's design concentrates the public rooms aft and the staterooms forward.

In fact, your evening could go something like this: You start at the bottom in your assigned dining room (Gigi is on A Deck and Kismet on Main Deck), then walk up one deck to the casino, to the lower level of the show lounge or the shops, then up another deck if you want to sit in the show lounge balcony or have a quiet drink in Finian's Rainbow Lounge or the champagne bar. Walk up one more deck to catch the late show in the Music Man Lounge, then up another deck to check out the disco. Finally, if you want a nightcap in the Viking Crown Lounge, catch the elevator outside the disco and ride three more decks to the top of the ship. Whew!

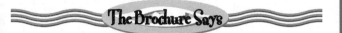

The Brochure Says

"Big. You may wonder if that's what you want in a cruise ship. Won't you get lost just trying to find your stateroom? Not with Royal Caribbean—there's always a staff member who'll point you the right way—or take you there."

Translation

None necessary.

Cabins & Costs

Fantasy Suites: .... A

Average Price PPPD: $666 including airfare.
The Royal Suite, #1010, some 1000 square feet of luxury, with private veranda, whirlpool tub, living room with wet bar, refrigerator and entertainment center—plus plenty of room for entertaining, and a big walk-in closet with generous storage space and personal safe.

Small Splurges: .... B

Average Price PPPD: $466 including airfare.
One of the eight Bridge Deck suites, with large windows, sitting area with sofa and chairs, two lower beds plus a sofa-bed for a third person, mini-refrigerator and bath with tub.

Suitable Standards: C

Average Price PPPD: $366 including airfare.
In categories F and G, you'll find twin beds in an L-configuration, small tripod brass-and-glass table, one chair, desk/dresser, bath with shower and skimpy storage space in an area approximately 120 square feet.

Bottom Bunks: C

Average Price PPPD: $233 including airfare.
The Q category inside cabins forward on B Deck are the cheapest on board, with two lower beds in parallel configuration, bath with shower, one chair and dresser.

Where She Goes

The seven-day Eastern Caribbean itinerary aboard *Sovereign of the Seas* ends in December when the ship begins three- and four-day cruises year-round from Miami to the Bahamas.

The Bottom Line

We're still not crazy about the vertical stacking that puts the cabins forward and the public areas aft. While it saves long strolls down hallways (unless your cabin is well forward) it still means a lot of stair climbing for impatient passengers who don't want to wait for the elevators.

Families with teenagers would be wiser to book one of the four newer ships—*Monarch, Majesty, Legend* or *Splendour*—because all of them have better youth facilities than *Sovereign*.

Other than that, however, you'll probably find *Sovereign of the Seas* is like your favorite resort hotel gone to sea, with everything aboard but the golf course; you'll have to book RCCL's *Legend of the Seas* or *Splendour of the Seas* for that.

ACCOMMODATIONS CHART

The following approximate daily rates, which are for two people sharing a standard double room, are all EP, in-season (December through April). Unfortunately, rates for single travelers are usually not much lower than the cost of a double room for two.

For MAP, add from $30 to $70 per person, per day.

CABLE BEACH

Establishment, Mailing Address, Telephone	Meal Plans Offered	No. Rooms	Double Room (in Season)	Credit Cards	Facilities	Other
Breezes Bahamas P.O. Box CD 13049 Nassau ☎ (809) 327-5356 (800) 859-SUPER FAX (809) 327-5155	FAP	400	$220	A, M, V, D	B, P, T, WSF, BT, DI	all-inclusive, 2-night minimum
Cable Beach Manor P.O. Box N-8333 Nassau ☎ (809) 327-7785 (800) 327-7788	EP	44	$125	A, M, V, D	B, P	studios, 1 and 2 bedrooms
Days Inn Casuarina's of Cable Beach P.O. Box N-4016 Nassau ☎ (809) 327-8153 (800) 325-2525	EP	80	$75	A, M, V, D	P	on Cable Beach, some kitchenettes complimentary continental breakfast
Forte Nassau Beach Hotel Cable Beach Nassau ☎ (809) 327-7711 (800) 225-5843 FAX (809) 327-8829	EP, BP, CP, FAP	411	$150	A, M, V, D, C, TF	P, B, BT, F, SC, S, T, PS, PDF	shops, entertainment, complimentary tennis, all-inclusive section, children's village
Nassau Marriott Resort & Crystal Palace Casino P.O. Box N-8306 Nassau ☎ (809) 327-6200 (800) 453-5301 FAX (809) 327-4346		860	$215	A. M. V. D	B, P, T, G, HC, PDF	duplex suites available room safes, 24-hour room service
Radisson Cable Beach Casino & Golf Resort P.O. Box N 4914 West Bay Street, Nassau ☎ (809) 327-6000 (800) 333-3333	EP	682	$170	A, M, V	P, PB, T, G, BT, CA, SC, S, WSF	
Sandals Royal Bahamian P.O. Box CB-13005 Nassau ☎ (809) 327-6400 (800) SANDALS FAX (809) 327-6961	EP	173	$185	A, M, V, D	B, P, T, BT	on Cable Beach, suites and villas available, complimentary transportation to casino

CABLE BEACH

Establishment, Mailing Address, Telephone	Meal Plans Offered	No. Rooms	Double Room (in Season)	Credit Cards	Facilities	Other
Wyndham Ambassador Beach Hotel P.O. Box N-3026 Nassau ☎ (809) 327-8231 FAX (809) 327-6727	EP, MAP	400	$140	A, M, D	B, P, BT, SC, WSF	health club, complimentary windsurfers, sunfish

NASSAU

Establishment, Mailing Address, Telephone	Meal Plans Offered	No. Rooms	Double Room (in Season)	Credit Cards	Facilities	Other
British Colonial Beach Resort P.O. Box N-7148 Nassau ☎ (809) 322-3301 (800) 528-1234 FAX (809) 323-8248	EP, MAP	325	$79	A, BA, B, C, D, M, V	B, P, T, BA/B, F, S, SC, MP, DI, PDF	shops, shuffleboard, ping pong, restaurants, downtown
Buena Vista Hotel P.O. Box N-564 Nassau ☎ (809) 322-2811 FAX (809) 322-5881	EP	5	$100	A, M, V, D, C		downtown, 19th-century mansion
Compass Point Gambier, Nassau ☎ (809) 327-4500 FAX (809) 327-3299 ☎ (800) OUTPOST ☎ (305) 531-8800 FAX (305) 531-5543	CP	18	$145–$300	A, M. V		studios and one-and two-bedroom cottages
Dillet's Guest House Dunmore Ave. & Strachan St. Chippingham, Nassau ☎ (809) 325-1133 FAX (809) 325-7183		7	$54	V, M		afternoon tea, senior citizen discount, continental breakfast
El Greco Hotel P.O. Box N-4187 Nassau ☎ (809) 325-1121	EP	26	$100	A, M, V, D	P	close to downtown
Grand Central Hotel P.O. Box N-4084 Nassau ☎ (809) 322-8356	EP	35	$95	A, D, M, V		
Graycliff Hotel P.O. Box N-10246 Nassau ☎ (809) 322-2796	CP	21	$165 (CP)	A, M, V, D, C, B	P	good food, old mansion

NASSAU						
Establishment, Mailing Address, Telephone	Meal Plans Offered	No. Rooms	Double Room (in Season)	Credit Cards	Facilities	Other
Nassau Harbour Club Hotel & Marina P.O. Box SS5755 Nassau ☎ (809) 393-0771 (800) 327-0787 FAX (809) 393-5393	EP	50	$80	A, M, V	P	shopping center across street, complimentary ferry to Paradise Island
Ocean Spray Hotel P.O. Box N-3035 Nassau ☎ (809) 322-8032 (800) 327-0787 FAX (809) 325-5731	EP	30	$90	A, M, V, D		
Orange Hill Beach Inn P.O. Box N-8583 Nassau ☎ (809) 327-7157 (800) 327-0787 FAX (809) 325-1097	EP	21	$90	A, M, V	P, B	kitchen facilities
The Parliament Inn P.O. Box N-4138 Nassau ☎ (809)322-2836/7 (800) 327-0787 FAX (809) 326-7196	CP	10	$70 (CP)	A, M, V, D	MP, PDF	downtown Nassau, good restaurant
Parthenon Hotel P.O. Box N-4930 Nassau ☎ (809) 322-2643	EP	18	$65	A, M, V		downtown, near beach, breakfast in room or on patio
Pilot House Hotel P.O. Box N-4941 Nassau ☎ (809) 322-8431 (800) 327-0787	EP	80	$100	A, M, V, C, D	P, BA/B, BT, F, SC	
South Ocean Golf & Beach Resort 808 Adelaide Road Nassau ☎ (809) 362-4391 (800) 228-9898 FAX (809) 362-4728	MAP, EP	250	$98	A, M, V	B, P, T, G, SC, WSF, PS	
Villas on Coral Island P.O. Box N-7797 Nassau ☎ (809) 328-1036 (800) 328-8814 FAX (809) 323-3202	CP	22	$175	A, M, V, D		each room has private pool, complimentary continental breakfast, free snorkeling, complimentary marine park, downtown transport

NASSAU

Establishment, Mailing Address, Telephone	Meal Plans Offered	No. Rooms	Double Room (in Season)	Credit Cards	Facilities	Other
Paradise Island						
Atlantis, Paradise Island P.O. Box N-4777 Nassau ☎ (809) 363-2000 (800) 321-3000 FAX (305) 893-2866	EP, MAP	1150	$145	A, M,V, D	P, T, B, SC, WSF, HC, CA, DI, PDF	aquarium and waterscape
Bay View Village P.O. Box SS-6308 Nassau ☎ (809) 363-2555 (800) 321-3000 (800) 327-0787 FAX (809) 363-2370	EP	72	$170	A, M, V	PDF	apartments, villas, laundry room, 3 pools
Comfort Suites Paradise Island P.O. Box SS 6202 Nassau ☎ (809) 363-3680 (800) 228-5150 FAX (809) 363-2588	CP	150	$120	A, M, V, D	P, PDF	use of Paradise Is. Resort & Casino beach facilities, tennis courts, health spa, family rates
Club Med Paradise Island P.O. Box N-7137 Nassau ☎ (809) 363-2640 (800) CLUBMED FAX (809) 363-3496	FAP	620 beds	call for rates	A, M, V	P, B, T	weekly rates vary according to point of origin—airfare included
Club Land'Or P.O. Box SS-6429 Nassau ☎ (809) 363-2400 (800 321-3000)	BP	72	$145	A, M, V, D		apartments and rooms, mostly time-share
Golden Palm Resort P.O. Box N-3881-1 Nassau ☎ (809) 363-3309 (809) 363-3312 (800) 832-2789 FAX (809) 363-3121	EP	16	$165	A, V, M	P	3-night min. stay
Harbour Cove—Paradise Island Fun Club P.O. Box SS 6249 Paradise Island ☎ (809) 363-2561 (800) 952-2426 FAX (809) 363-3803	FAP	250	$258	A, V, M	P, B, T	all inclusive, 3-night minimum
Holiday Inn P.O. Box 6214 Nassau ☎ (809) 363-2101 (800) HOLIDAY FAX (809) 363-2206	EP, MAP, BP, FAP	535	$110	A, M, V, D	BT, DI, PB, F, S, SC, T, PDF	rents motor scooters, children's program, refrigerators, coffee makers

NASSAU

Establishment, Mailing Address, Telephone	Meal Plans Offered	No. Rooms	Double Room (in Season)	Credit Cards	Facilities	Other
Ocean Club Golf & Tennis Resort P.O. Box N-4777 Nassau ☎ (809) 363-2501 (800) 321-3000 FAX (305) 893-2866	EP, MAP	70	$220	A, M, V, D	P, B, BT, S, SC, M/D, G, T	complimentary transportation to casino
Paradise P.O. Box SS-6259 Nassau ☎ (809) 363-3000 (800) 321-3000 FAX (305) 893-2866	EP, MAP	100	$258	M, V	B, SC, P	special sports package deals available
The Pink House P.O. Box N 1968 Nassau ☎ (809) 363-3363 (800) 363-3363 FAX (809) 393-1786	CP	4	$90	A, V, M		afternoon tea
Radisson Grand Resort Paradise Island P.O. Box SS-6307 Paradise Island ☎ (809) 363-3500 (800) 333-3333 FAX (809) 363-3193	EP, MAP	360	$210	A, M, V, D	B, P, BT, F, T, G, PS	all rooms ocean view, refrigerators in rooms, coffee makers, free transport on Paradise Island
Sunrise Beach Club & Villas P.O. Box SS-6519 Nassau ☎ (809) 363-2234 (809) 363-2250 (800) 451-6078 FAX (809) 363-2252	EP	35	$180		B, P	time-share units available, complimentary breakfast kit
Villas in Paradise P.O. Box 6379 SS Nassau ☎ (809) 363-2998 (800) 321-3000 FAX (809) 363-2703	EP	30	$135	A, M, V		some villas with private pools, 1 day free car for stays of 3 to 6 nights, 2 days free car for 7-night stays

GRAND BAHAMAS

Establishment, Mailing Address, Telephone	Meal Plans Offered	No. Rooms	Double Room (in Season)	Credit Cards	Facilities	Other
Bahamas Princess Resort & Casino P.O. Box F-207 Freeport ☎ (212) 582-8100 (800) 223-1818 (809) 352-6721	MAP, EP	960	$120	A, M, V, D	P, G, T, MP, PDF	free shuttle to beach

GRAND BAHAMAS

Establishment, Mailing Address, Telephone	Meal Plans Offered	No. Rooms	Double Room (in Season)	Credit Cards	Facilities	Other
Castaways Resort P.O. Box 2629 Freeport ☎ (809) 352-6682 (800) 327-0787	EP	138	$78	A, M, V, D	P, DI	free shuttle to beach
Clarion Atlantic Beach & Golf Resort P.O. Box F-531 Freeport ☎ (809) 373-1444 (800) 622-6770 FAX (809) 373-7481	BP	175	$135	A, BA, M, D, M, V	PDF, P, T	situated on beach, complimentary transport to golf course
Coral Beach Hotel P.O. Box F-2468 Freeport ☎ (809) 373-2468	EP	10	$85	A	B, P, F	golf privileges
Club Fortuna Beach Resort Freeport ☎ (809) 373-4000 Miami (305) 538-5467 (800) 847-4502 FAX (809) 373-5555	FAP	204	$187	major	B, P, T, BT, WSF	all-inclusive
Deep Water Cay Club P.O. Box 40039 Freeport ☎ (809) 359-4831 (407) 684-3958 FAX (407) 684-0959	FAP	11	$1195 (FAP)	none	F, PB	east end, own air strip, fishing skiff, guide and bait included in rates; minimum stay is 3 nights, closed Aug. and Sept., private airstrip, cottages
Lucayan Beach Resort & Casino P.O. Box F-336, Freeport/Lucaya ☎ (809) 373-7777 (800) 772-1227 FAX (809) 373-2826	EP, MAP	243	$155	A, M, V,T, G, BT, F	WSF, P, B,	
Port Lucaya Resort & Yacht Club Bell Channel Bay Road P.O. Box F-2452 Freeport/Lucaya ☎ (809) 373-6618 (800)LUCAYA-1 FAX (809) 373-6652	EP	160	$110	M, V, A	M/D, P	attracts cruise ship passengers, near beach, next to Port Lucaya Marketplace
Radisson Resort on Lucaya Beach P.O. Box F-2496 Freeport ☎ (809) 373-1333 (800) 333-3333 FAX (809) 373-8662	CP	500	$155	A, M, V	P, B, HC, T, BT	

GRAND BAHAMAS

Establishment, Mailing Address, Telephone	Meal Plans Offered	No. Rooms	Double Room (in Season)	Credit Cards	Facilities	Other
Running Mon Marina & Resort P.O. Box F-2663 Freeport ☎ (809) 352-6834 FAX (809) 352-6835	EP	32	$89	A, M, V	P, F	5 min. from beach
Silver Sands Sea Lodge P.O. Box F-2385 Freeport ☎ (809) 373-5700	EP, MAP	164	$105	A, M, V, D, B	B, BT, T, SC, P	apartments and suites
Xanadu Beach Resort & Marina P.O. Box F-2438 Freeport ☎ (809) 352-6782 (800) 222-3788 (804) 270-4313	EP, MAP	184	$165	A, BA, D, M, V	T, BT, P	marina on premises and villas

THE ABACOS

Establishment, Mailing Address, Telephone	Meal Plans Offered	No. Rooms	Double Room (in Season)	Credit Cards	Facilities	Other
Walkers Cay						
Walker's Cay Hotel & Marina 700 S.W. 34 St. Fort Lauderdale, FL. ☎ (809) 352-5252 (800) 432-2092 FAX (809) 352-3301	EP, MAP	62	$100	A, D	P, DI, M/ D, BT, F, S,SC, T	villas and suites
Spanish Cay						
The Inn at Spanish Cay P.O. Box 882 Coopers Town, Abaco ☎ (809) 365-0083 or (809) 365-0466 FAX (809) 365-0466	EP	12	$180-$275	M, V	T, B	
Green Turtle Cay						
Bluff House Club & Marina Green Turtle Cay ☎ (809) 365-4247 FAX (809) 365-4248	EP, MAP	25	$100	M, V	BT, SC, F	closed Sept.-Oct., all rooms have ocean views
Green Turtle Club P.O. Box 270 Green Turtle Cay ☎ (809) 365-4271 FAX (809) 365-4272	EP, MAP	30	$184	A, M, V	P, B, M/ D, BT, F, WSF, T	closed Sept.-Oct., hosts annual fishing tournament and annual regatta, units available with kitchens, boat rentals

THE ABACOS

Establishment, Mailing Address, Telephone	Meal Plans Offered	No. Rooms	Double Room (in Season)	Credit Cards	Facilities	Other
New Plymouth Club & Inn Green Turtle Cay ☎ (809) 365-4161 FAX (809) 365-4138	MAP	9	$120	none	BT, F	pets allowed
Sea Star Beach Cottages P.O. Box 282 Gilam Bay Green Turtle Cay ☎ (809) 359-6592 (800) 752-0166	EP	12	$75	none	BT, SC, F	

Great Guana Cay

Establishment, Mailing Address, Telephone	Meal Plans Offered	No. Rooms	Double Room (in Season)	Credit Cards	Facilities	Other
Guana Beach Resort & Marina P.O. Box 474, Marsh Harbour Great Guana Cay ☎ (809) 367-3590 800-BAREFOOT FAX (809) 367-3590	EP, MAP	15	$140	M, V	B, M/D, BT, S, F	7 miles of beach
Pinder's Cottages Great Guana Cay Abaco ☎ (809) 367-2207	EP	4 cottages	rates on request	none	BT, F, SC	

Elbow Cay

Establishment, Mailing Address, Telephone	Meal Plans Offered	No. Rooms	Double Room (in Season)	Credit Cards	Facilities	Other
Abaco Inn Hope Town, Abaco ☎ (809) 366-0133 (800) 468-8799 FAX (809) 366-0113	EP, MAP	12	$125	M, V	P, B, M/D, SC, F, S, WSF	complimentary bicycles, boats rented, pets allowed
Hope Town Harbour Lodge Hope Town, Abaco ☎ (809) 366-0095 (800) 626-5690	EP	21	$115	A, M, V	P, M/D, BT, SC, F, WSF	closed Sept.–mid-Oct.
Sea Spray Resort & Villas White Sound Elbow Cay, Abaco ☎ (800) 327-0787 FAX (809) 366-0065	EP	9	$170		BT, F, B,WSF	1- and 2-bedroom villas, boat rentals, complimentary use of windsurfers and sunfish, bakery on premises, catered meals available
Hope Town Hideaways Hope Town, Elbow Cay, Abaco ☎ (809) 366-0224 FAX (809) 367-2954	EP, MAP	4 villas	$160	M, V	BT	on harbor, with dock, monthly rates available
Tangelo Hotel P.O. Box 830 Coopers Town, Abaco ☎ (800) 688-4752 (809) 365-2222 FAX (809) 365-2200		12	$65	none		

THE ABACOS

Establishment, Mailing Address, Telephone	Meal Plans Offered	No. Rooms	Double Room (in Season)	Credit Cards	Facilities	Other
Club Soleil Resort Hope Town, Elbow Cay Abaco ☎ (809) 366-0003	EP	6	$115	M, V	BT, F, M/ D, P	boat rentals

Marsh Harbour

Conch Inn P.O. Box 469, Marsh Harbour ☎ (809) 367-2800 FAX (809) 367-2980	EP	9	$85	A, M, V	P, M/D, BT, SC, S	bicycles rented, good scuba operation
Great Abaco Beach Hotel P.O. Box 511 Marsh Harbour ☎ (809) 367-2158 (800) 468-4799 FAX (809) 367-2819	EP	20	$165	A, M, V	B, P, T	on waterfront, adjoins a marina, villas available, building additional rooms
Island Breezes Motel P.O. Box 20030 Marsh Harbour ☎ (809) 367-3776 FAX (809) 367-4179		8	$82	M, V		
The Lofty Fig Villas Box 437 Marsh Harbour Abaco ☎ (809) 367-2681	EP	6	$95			no pets
Pelican Beach Villas P.O. Box AB 20304 Marsh Harbour, Abaco ☎ (809) 367-3600 (800) 642-7268		5 villas	$150 dbl rm $160 per wk	A, M, V		hammocks, boat rentals

Man-O-War Cay

Schooner's Landing Resort Man-O-War Cay ☎ (809) 365-6072 FAX (809) 365-6285			$150		B, F, BT	2-bedroom units, 1-1/2 baths

ACKLINS/CROOKED ISLAND

Establishment, Mailing Address, Telephone	Meal Plans Offered	No. Rooms	Double Room (in Season)	Credit Cards	Facilities	Other
Crooked Island Beach Inn Colonel Hill ☎ (809) 336-2096	EP	11	$50	none	B, F, BT	transport provided to and from airport

ACKLINS/CROOKED ISLAND

Establishment, Mailing Address, Telephone	Meal Plans Offered	No. Rooms	Double Room (in Season)	Credit Cards	Facilities	Other
Pittstown Point Landing Bahamas Caribbean International P.O. Box 9831 Mobile, Alabama 36691 (205) 666-4482	EP, FAP	12	$100	A, M, V	B, BT, F, WSF, SC	closed Sept., Oct., bicycles rented, airstrip nearby
T & S Guest House Church Grove ☎ Church Grove	EP	10	$60	none	BP, F	

ANDROS

Establishment, Mailing Address, Telephone	Meal Plans Offered	No. Rooms	Double Room (in Season)	Credit Cards	Facilities	Other
Cargill Creek						
Andros Island Bonefish Camp Cargill Creek Andros ☎ (809) 329-5167	EP	16				
Cargill Creek Fishing Lodge Cargill Creek, Andros P.O. Box 21668 Fort Lauderdale, FL 33335 ☎ (809) 329-5129 FAX (809) 329-5046	FAP	15	$270 (FAP)	A, M	F, SC	game room, daily movies, diving
Behring Point						
Behring Point Charlie's Haven Behring Pt. Andros ☎ (809) 329-5261	EP					
Andros Town Area						
Small Hope Bay Lodge Andros Town Area P.O. Box 21667 Fort Lauderdale, FL 33335-1667 ☎ (809) 368-2014 (800) 223-6961 FAX (809) 368-2015	FAP	20 plus 3-bed-room, 3 bath villa	$300 (FAP)	A, V, M	B, BT, F, SC, WSF	complimentary bicycles, closed Sept.–Oct., Androsia works nearby
Chickcharnie Hotel Fresh Creek Andros Town ☎ (809) 368-2025	EP	8	$45	none	BT	game room, daily movies, diving

ANDROS

Establishment, Mailing Address, Telephone	Meal Plans Offered	No. Rooms	Double Room (in Season)	Credit Cards	Facilities	Other
Lighthouse Yacht Club & Marina P.O. Box Andros Town ☎ (809) 368-2305 (800) 825-5255 FAX (809) 368-2300	EP	20	$130		P, BT, M/ D, F	

Mangrove Cay

Mangrove Cay Bannister's Cottages Lisbon Creek, Mangrove Cay ☎ (809) 369-0188	EP, MAP	6	$75 (MAP)	none	BT, F, WSF	bicycles rented, shared baths, adjacent club with fish and turtle pool
Longley's Guest House Lisbon Creek Mangrove Cay ☎ (809) 325-1581	EP	5	$55	none	PB, BT, F, SC	
Moxey's Guest House Mangrove Cay ☎ (809) 329-4159	EP, FAP	6	$55	A	B, F	pool room, dancing club, some private baths

Congo Town

Emerald Palms by the Sea P.O. Box 800 Driggs Hill ☎ (809) 369-2661 (800) 325-5099 FAX (809) 369-2667	MAP	20	$100	A, M, V	P, T, BT, SC, B, F, WSF, HB	superb food and ambience

THE BERRY ISLANDS

Establishment, Mailing Address, Telephone	Meal Plans Offered	No. Rooms	Double Room (in Season)	Credit Cards	Facilities	Other
The Chub Cay Club P.O. Box 661067 Miami Springs, FL 33266 ☎ (305) 445-7830 (809) 325-1490 (800) 662-8555 FAX (809) 322-5199	EP, MAP	17	$90	A, M, V	M/D, B, F, P, T, BT	permanently docked houseboat
Great Harbour Cay Berry islands, Bahamas 3512 N. Ocean Drive Hollywood, FL 33019 ☎ (305) 921-9084 FAX (305) 921-1044 (800) 343-7256 (809) 367-8838		villas and townho uses	$90	major		private yacht club, boat rentals, 81- slip marina

BIMINI

Establishment, Mailing Address, Telephone	Meal Plans Offered	No. Rooms	Double Room (in Season)	Credit Cards	Facilities	Other
Bimini Big Game Fishing Club P.O. Box 523238 Miami, FL 33152 ☎ (809) 347-2391 (800) 327-4149 FAX (809) 347-3392	EP	50	$149	A, M, V	M/D, P, BT, F, S, SC	owned by Bacardi Rum
Bimini Blue Waters Resort P.O. Box 627 Alice Town ☎ (809) 347-2166 FAX (809) 347-2293	EP	12	$98	A, M, V	P, B, M/D, BT	water view on each side of hilltop building
Compleat Angler Hotel P.O. Box 601 Alice Town ☎ (809) 347-3122	EP	12	$85	A	SC	Hemingway memorabilia
Sea Crest Hotel P.O. Box 654 Alice Town ☎ (809) 347-2071	EP	14	$90	none		
Admiral Hotel Bailey Town ☎ (809) 347-2347	EP	27	$85	none		

CAT ISLAND

Establishment, Mailing Address, Telephone	Meal Plans Offered	No. Rooms	Double Room (in Season)	Credit Cards	Facilities	Other
Fernandez Bay Village P.O. Box 2126 Fort Lauderdale, FL 33303 ☎ (305) 792-1905 (809) 342-3043 (800) 940-1905 FAX (809) 342-3051	EP, MAP	5 cottages	$210	A	B, BT	1- to 2-person and 1- to 8-person cottages, airstrip

ELEUTHERA

Establishment, Mailing Address, Telephone	Meal Plans Offered	No. Rooms	Double Room (in Season)	Credit Cards	Facilities	Other
Harbour Island						
Coral Sands Hotel Coral Sands Harbour Island ☎ (809) 333-2350 (800) 327-0787 FAX (809) 333-2368	MAP, EP	33	$165	A, M, D, V	B, T, F, SC	3-mile beach, closed Sept.-Nov., night tennis, extensive wine cellar

ELEUTHERA

Establishment, Mailing Address, Telephone	Meal Plans Offered	No. Rooms	Double Room (in Season)	Credit Cards	Facilities	Other
Dunmore Beach Club P.O. Box 122 Harbour Island ☎ (809) 333-2200 FAX (809) 333-2429	FAP	12	$325 (FAP)	none	B, T, F, BT	closed May-July
Ocean View Club P.O. Box 134 Harbour Island ☎ (809) 333-2276	FAP	10	$125 (FAP)	M, V, C	F, SC, P, B, T, BT	
Pink Sands Harbour Island ☎ (809) 333-2030 (800) OUTPOST FAX (809) 333-2060	MAP	29	$300	A, M, V, D	B, T, F	room service available
Rock House General Delivery, Harbour Island Overseas Operator ☎ (809) 333-2053	FAP	7	$100	A, M, V	T, WSF	closed Sept.-Oct., 2-night minimum stay
Romora Bay Club P.O. Box 146 Harbour Island ☎ (809) 333-2325 (800) 327-8286 FAX (305) 427-2746	EP, MAP	38	$160	A, M, V	T, M/D, F, SC	closed Sept.–Nov., dive packages available, rooms and suites
Runaway Hill Club P.O. Box 31 Harbour Island ☎ (809) 333-2150 FAX (809) 333-2420	EP, MAP	10	$190	A, M, V	P, B	homelike atmosphere, closed day after Labor Day to mid-Oct.
Tingum Village P.O. Box 61 Harbour Island ☎ (809) 333-2161	EP, MAP, CP, BP, FAP	12	$85	A, M, V		good food and parties
Valentine's Inn & Yacht Club P.O. Box 1 Harbour Island ☎ (809) 333-2080 (809) 333-2142 Florida (305) 491-1010	EP, MAP	21	$120	M, V	P, B, M/D, WSF, BA/B	closed Sept., hot tub, scuba diving, boating, tennis, nightclub
Gregory Town						
Caridon Cottages P.O. Box 5206 Gregory Town ☎ (809) 332-2690 Ext. 230	EP, MAP	14 cottages	$30	none	T, BT, F, SC	open year-round, add $10 MAP, scooter rental
The Cove Eleuthera P.O. Box 1548 Gregory Town ☎ (809) 332-0142 (800) 552-5960 FAX (201) 835-5783	EP, MAP, FAP	28	$109	A, M, V	P, B	good snorkeling

ELEUTHERA						
Establishment, Mailing Address, Telephone	**Meal Plans Offered**	**No. Rooms**	**Double Room (in Season)**	**Credit Cards**	**Facilities**	**Other**
Oleander Gardens P.O. Box 5165 Gregory Town ☎ (809) 333-2058	EP					
Governor's Harbour						
Cigatoo Inn P.O. Box 86 Governor's Harbour ☎ (809) 332-2343 FAX (809) 332-2159	EP, MAP	28	$55	A, V, M	P, T, F, BT	refrigerators
Laughing Bird Apartments P.O. Box 76 Governor's Harbour ☎ (809) 322-2012 FAX (809) 332-2358	EP	8	$70	V, M		children under 4 free, 4-12 half price, weekly rates available, free tour of town and nearby beaches
Club Med Eleuthera P.O. Box 80 ☎ (809) 332-2270 (800) CLUBMED FAX (809) 332-2691	FAP	600 beds	call for rates	A, M, V	B, S, BT, T, G	rates vary according to point of origin—airfare included
Tuckaway Motel P.O. Box 45 Governor's Harbour ☎ (809) 332-2005 (809) 332-2013 (809) 332-2591	EP	10	$60	none		in town, fruit trees
Rainbow Inn P.O. Box 53 Governor's Harbour Hatchet Bay ☎ (809) 335-0294 (800) 327-0787 FAX (809) 335-0294	EP, MAP	10	$90	A	B, T, P	good restaurant (closed May—June and Sept.—Nov.), hotel open year-round
Scriven's Villas P.O. Box 35 Governor's Harbour ☎ (809) 322-2503	EP	4	$45	none	B, M/D, T, G, SC	
Rock Sound						
Cartwright's Ocean View Cottages Tarpum Bay ☎ (809) 334-4215	EP	5	$80	none	B	bike and moped rentals
Cotton Bay Club P.O. Box 28 Rock Sound Eleuthera ☎ (809) 334-6101 (800) 221-4542 FAX (809) 334-6082	MAP, EP	75	$260	A, M, V	P, B, F, T, G	7 miles of beach, 18-hole golf course, bike rentals
Edwina's Place P.O. Box 30 Rock Sound ☎ (809) 334-2094	EP	9	$75	none	P	closed Sept.

ELEUTHERA

Establishment, Mailing Address, Telephone	Meal Plans Offered	No. Rooms	Double Room (in Season)	Credit Cards	Facilities	Other
Ethel's Cottages P.O. Box 27 Tarpum Bay ☎ (809) 334-4233	EP	18	$70	A, B	F	
Hilton's Haven Tarpum Bay ☎ (809) 334-4281 (800) 327-0787	EP, MAP	10	$55	none	BT, F	
Ingraham's Beach Inn P.O. Box 7 Tarpum Bay ☎ (809) 334-4263 (809) 334-4285	EP	12 (apts.)	$130		B	10 percent discount for 10-day stay or longer

THE EXUMAS

Establishment, Mailing Address, Telephone	Meal Plans Offered	No. Rooms	Double Room (in Season)	Credit Cards	Facilities	Other
Happy People Marina Staniel Cay Exuma ☎ (809) 355-2008	EP	8	$90	none	B, BT, F, SC	
Peace and Plenty Beach Inn P.O. Box 29055 George Town ☎ (809) 336-2250 or (809) 336-2551 FAX (809) 336-2253	EP, MAP	16	$130	A, M, V	B, P	
Peace & Plenty Bonefish Lodge P.O. Box 29173 George Town ☎ (809) 345-5555 FAX (809) 345-5556	FAP	8	$		F, BT	fishing guides, fly-tying facilities
Club Peace and Plenty P.O. Box 55 George Town ☎ (809) 336-2551 (800) 525-2210 FAX (809) 336-2093	MAP, EP	35	$120	A, M, V	P, BT, F, SC, M/D	free bikes, free ferry to Stocking Island, no children under 6 years, club on own beach
Marshall's Guest House P.O. Box 27 George Town ☎ (809) 336-2571	EP	12	$75	M	F	
Regatta Point P.O. Box 6 George Town ☎ (809) 336-2206 (800) 327-0787 FAX (809) 336-2046	EP	5	$122	V, M	B	all units have kitchens, good view for regatta

THE EXUMAS

Establishment, Mailing Address, Telephone	Meal Plans Offered	No. Rooms	Double Room (in Season)	Credit Cards	Facilities	Other
Coconut Cove Hotel P.O. Box 29299 George Town ☎ (809) 336-2659		11	$128	V, M		freshwater pool, bath robes
Staniel Cay Yacht Club c/o Island Services 1100 Lee Wagener Blvd. #309 Fort Lauderdale, FL. 33315 ☎ (809) 355-2024 or (809) 355-2011 FAX (809) 355-2044	FAP	6	$195 (FAP)	A, M, V	BT, F, SC, WS, B	free sailboats, windsurfing for guests 3 nights and more
Two Turtles Inn P.O. Box 51 George Town ☎ (809) 336-2545 FAX (809) 336-2528	EP	12	$88	A, M, V		bicycles, some kitchens

INAGUA

Establishment, Mailing Address, Telephone	Meal Plans Offered	No. Rooms	Double Room (in Season)	Credit Cards	Facilities	Other
Ford's Inagua Inn Matthew Town Inagua ☎ 277	EP, MAP	5	$50	none	F, M/D, PDF	
Kirk & Eleanor's Walk-Inn Gregory Street Matthew Town Inagua	EP		$80			
Main House Matthew Town, Inagua ☎ 267	EP	5	$50	none		

LONG ISLAND

Establishment, Mailing Address, Telephone	Meal Plans Offered	No. Rooms	Double Room (in Season)	Credit Cards	Facilities	Other
Stella Maris Inn P.O. Box 105 Stella Maris ☎ (809) 336-2106 (305) 359-8236 (800) 426-0466 FAX (305) 359-8238	EP, MAP	50	$130	A, M, V	B, P, BT, F, SC, T, S, PDF	exceptional diving program, 3 pools, pets allowed

LONG ISLAND

Establishment, Mailing Address, Telephone	Meal Plans Offered	No. Rooms	Double Room (in Season)	Credit Cards	Facilities	Other
Thompson Bay Inn P.O. Box SM 30-123 Stella Maris ☎ Salt Pond Operator	EP	8	$60	none		some apartments, good food

SAN SALVADOR/RUM CAY

Establishment, Mailing Address, Telephone	Meal Plans Offered	No. Rooms	Double Room (in Season)	Credit Cards	Facilities	Other
Club Med Columbus Isle San Salvador ☎ (809) 331-2000 (800) CLUB MED FAX (809) 331-2222	FAP	432 beds	$150–$210	A, M, V	WSF, S, BT, T,B	virtually all-inclusive
Riding Rock Inn Resort & Marina 701 Southwest 48th St. Fort Lauderdale, FL 33315 ☎ (809) 332-2631	EP, MAP, FAP	24	$87	V	P, T, B	dive packages available, on rocky beach (sandy beach nearby)
Ocean View Villas North Victoria San Salvador Bahamas ☎ (809) 331-2694 FAX (809) 322-5080	EP	3	$55	none		
Rum Cay Club P.O. Box 22396 Ft. Lauderdale, FL 33335 ☎ (305) 467-8355 (800) 334-6869		closed inde- finitely			B, SC, F	

INDEX

Order Your Guide to Travel and Adventure

Title	Price	Title	Price
Fielding's Alaska Cruises and the Inside Passage	$18.95	Fielding's London Agenda	$14.95
Fielding's The Amazon	$16.95	Fielding's Los Angeles	$16.95
Fielding's Asia's Top Dive Sites	$19.95	Fielding's Malaysia & Singapore	$16.95
Fielding's Australia	$16.95	Fielding's Mexico	$18.95
Fielding's Bahamas	$16.95	Fielding's New Orleans Agenda	$16.95
Fielding's Baja	$18.95	Fielding's New York Agenda	$16.95
Fielding's Bermuda	$16.95	Fielding's New Zealand	$16.95
Fielding's Borneo	$18.95	Fielding's Paris Agenda	$14.95
Fielding's Budget Europe	$17.95	Fielding's Portugal	$16.95
Fielding's Caribbean	$18.95	Fielding's Paradors, Pousadas and Charming Villages	$18.95
Fielding's Caribbean Cruises	$18.95	Fielding's Rome Agenda	$14.95
Fielding's Disney World and Orlando	$18.95	Fielding's San Diego Agenda	$14.95
Fielding's Diving Indonesia	$19.95	Fielding's Southeast Asia	$18.95
Fielding's Eastern Caribbean	$17.95	Fielding's Southern Vietnam on 2 Wheels	$15.95
Fielding's England	$17.95	Fielding's Spain	$18.95
Fielding's Europe	$18.95	Fielding's Surfing Indonesia	$19.95
Fielding's European Cruises	$18.95	Fielding's Sydney Agenda	$16.95
Fielding's Far East	$18.95	Fielding's Thailand, Cambodia, Laos and Myanmar	$18.95
Fielding's France	$18.95	Fielding's Vacation Places Rated	$19.95
Fielding's Freewheelin' USA	$18.95	Fielding's Vietnam	$17.95
Fielding's Hawaii	$18.95	Fielding's Western Caribbean	$18.95
Fielding's Italy	$18.95	Fielding's The World's Most Dangerous Places	$19.95
Fielding's Kenya	$16.95	Fielding's Worldwide Cruises	$19.95
Fielding's Las Vegas Agenda	$14.95		

To place an order: call toll-free 1-800-FW-2-GUIDE
(VISA, MasterCard and American Express accepted)
or send your check or money order to:
Fielding Worldwide, Inc., 308 S. Catalina Avenue, Redondo Beach, CA 90277
http://www.fieldingtravel.com
Add $2.00 per book for shipping & handling (sorry, no COD's),
allow 2–6 weeks for delivery

Favorite People, Places & Experiences

Name

Address

Telephone

Name

Address

Telephone

Name

Address

Telephone

Name

Address

Telephone

Name

Address

Telephone

Name

Address

Telephone

Name

Address

Telephone

NEW FIELDING WEAR!

Now that you own a Fielding travel guide, you have graduated from being a tourist to full-fledged traveler! Celebrate your elevated position by proudly wearing one of these heavy-duty, all-cotton shirts, selected by our authors for their comfort and durability (and their ability to hide dirt). Choose from three styles—radical "World Tour," politically correct "Do the World Right," and elegant "All-Access."

Important Note: Fielding authors have field-tested these shirts and have found that they can be swapped for much more than their purchase price in free drinks at some of the world's hottest clubs and in-spots. They also make great gifts.

WORLD TOUR

Hit the hard road with a travel fashion statement for out times. Visit all 35 of Mr. D.P.'s favorite nasty spots (listed on the back), or just look like you're going to. This is the real McCoy, worn by mujahadeen, mercenaries, UN peacekeepers and the authors of Fielding's The World's Most Dangerous Places. Black, XL, heavy-duty 100% cotton. Made in the USA. $18.00.

DO THE WORLD RIGHT

Start your next adventure wearing Fielding's policically correct "Do the World Right" shirt, complete with freaked-out red globe and blasting white type. A shirt that tells the world that within that high-mileage, overly educated body beats the heart of a true party animal. Only for adrenline junkies, hard-core travelers and seekers of knowledge. Black, XL, heavy-duty 100% cotton. Made in the USA. $18.00.

ALL ACCESS

Strike terror into the snootiest maitre'd, make concierges cringe, or just use this elegant shirt as the ultimate party invitation. The combination of the understated red Fielding logo embroidered on a jet-black golf shirt will get you into the snobiest embassy party or jumping night spot. An elegant casual shirt for those who travel in style and comfort. Black, XL or L, 100% pre-shrunk cotton, embroidered Fielding Travel Guide logo on front. Made in the U.S.A. $29.00.

Name:

Address:

City:

State: Zip:

Telephone:
Shirt Name:
Quantity:

For each shirt add $4 shipping and handling. California residents add $1.50 sales tax. Allow 2 to 4 weeks for delivery.

Send check or money order with your order form to:

Fielding Worldwide, Inc.
308 South Catalina Ave.
Redondo Beach, CA 90277

or

order your shirts by phone,:
1-800-FW-2-GUIDE
Visa, MC, AMex accepted

International Conversions

TEMPERATURE

To convert °F to °C, subtract 32 and divide by 1.8. To convert °C to °F, multiply by 1.8 and add 32.

Fahrenheit	Centigrade	
230°	110°	
220°		
210°	100°	Water Boils
200°	90°	
190°		
180°	80°	
170°		
160°	70°	
150°		
140°	60°	
130°		
120°	50°	
110°		
100°	40°	
90°	30°	
80°		
70°	20°	
60°		
50°	10°	
40°		
30°	0°	Water Freezes
20°	-10°	
10°		
0°	-20°	
-10°		
-20°	-30°	
-30°		
-40°	-40°	

WEIGHTS & MEASURES

LENGTH

1 km	=	0.62 miles
1 mile	=	1.609 km
1 meter	=	1.2936 yards
1 meter	=	3.28 feet
1 yard	=	0.9144 meters
1 yard	=	3 feet
1 foot	=	30.48 centimeters
1 centimeter	=	0.39 inch
1 inch	=	2.54 centimeters

AREA

1 square km	=	0.3861 square miles
1 square mile	=	2.590 square km
1 hectare	=	2.47 acres
1 acre	=	0.405 hectare

VOLUME

1 cubic meter	=	1.307 cubic yards
1 cubic yard	=	0.765 cubic meter
1 cubic yard	=	27 cubic feet
1 cubic foot	=	0.028 cubic meter
1 cubic centimeter	=	0.061 cubic inch
1 cubic inch	=	16.387 cubic centimeters

CAPACITY

1 gallon	=	3.785 liters
1 quart	=	0.94635 liters
1 liter	=	1.057 quarts
1 pint	=	473 milliliters
1 fluid ounce	=	29.573 milliliters

MASS and WEIGHT

1 metric ton	=	1.102 short tons
1 metric ton	=	1000 kilograms
1 short ton	=	.90718 metric ton
1 long ton	=	1.016 metric tons
1 long ton	=	2240 pounds
1 pound	=	0.4536 kilograms
1 kilogram	=	2.2046 pounds
1 ounce	=	28.35 grams
1 gram	=	0.035 ounce
1 milligram	=	0.015 grain